SPIRIT IN THE WORLD

SPIRIT IN THE WORLD

KARL RAHNER

Translated by
William Dych, S.J.

CONTINUUM · NEW YORK

1994

The Continuum Publishing Company
370 Lexington Avenue, New York, NY 10017

Original edition: *Geist in Welt*
Kösel-Verlag, Munich, 1957

Printed in the United States of America

Library of Congress Cataloging-in-Publication Data

Rahner, Karl, 1904–1984
    [Geistes in Welt. English]
    Spirit in the world / Karl Rahner ; translated by William Dych.
      p.   cm.
    Originally published: New York: Herder and Herder, 1969.
    Includes bibliographical references.
    ISBN 0-8264-0647-5 (alk. paper)
    1. God—Knowableness. 2. Knowledge, Theory of (Religion)
  3. Thomas, Aquinas, Saint, 1225?–1274. I. Title.
    BT102.R27213   1994
    121—dc20   93-38426
                                                        CIP

Contents

Foreword, by Johannes B. Metz   xiii
Introduction, by Francis P. Fiorenza   xix
Preface to the Second German Edition   xlvii
Author's Introduction   xlix

THE TEXT OF SUMMA THEOLOGIAE I, Q. 84, A. 7   1

PART ONE
INTRODUCTORY INTERPRETATION OF
SUMMA THEOLOGIAE I, Q. 84, A. 7

   I. The Article in the Context of the *Summa
      Theologiae*   15
  II. The Title of the Article   18
 III. The *Videtur Quod Non*   22
 IV. The Formal Structure of the Corpus of the
      Article   29
  V. The First Two Sections of the Corpus   31
 VI. The First Part of the Third Section of the
      Corpus   34
 VII. The Second Part of the Third Section of the
      Corpus   38
VIII. The Third Part of the Third Section of the
      Corpus   42
 IX. The Fourth Part of the Third Section of the
      Corpus   47

X. The Fifth Part of the Third Section of the
   Corpus   49
XI. The Answers to the Objections   50

PART TWO
SPIRIT IN THE WORLD

CHAPTER ONE: THE FOUNDATION   57
  I. The Point of Departure: The Metaphysical
     Question   57
     1. The Basic Structure of the Metaphysical
        Question   57
     2. The Questionableness (*Fragwürdigkeit*) of
        the Metaphysical Question   59
     3. The "World" as the "Whence" (*Woher*) of
        the Metaphysical Question   61
 II. The Unity of Knowledge   65
III. Knowing and Known   67
     1. Being and Knowing as Original Unity in
        Being-Present-to-Self (*Beisichsein*)
        (Knowing as the Subjectivity of Being Itself) 68
     2. The Essential Indefinability of the Concept
        of Being   71

CHAPTER TWO: SENSIBILITY   78
  I. The Point of Departure for the Concept of
     Sensibility   78
 II. The Knowledge of the Sensible Other Through
     Sensibility   82
     1. Sensible Species as Self-Givenness of the
        Sensible Object   86
     2. Sensible Species as Self-Realization of the
        Sensible Object   87
     3. Sensible Species as Self-Realization of
        Sensibility   91

4. The Passivity of Sensibility   92

III. The *A Priori* Structures of Sensibility: Space   97

     1. The Mobile as the Most Universal *A Priori* of Sensibility   98

     2. The Quantitative as *A Priori* of Sensibility   101

     3. Spatiality as *A Priori* Form of the Basic Faculty of Sensibility: The Imagination   103

IV. The *A Priori* Structures of Sensibility: Time   107

     1. The Time-Forming Quality of Motion   108

     2. The Mutual Relationship of the *A Priori* Intuitions of Space and Time   112

     3. The Derivativeness of the Space-Time *A Priori*   114

CHAPTER THREE: ABSTRACTION   117

I. The Question: "The Return of the Subject to Himself"   117

II. The Indications of the Abstractive Return to Self   120

     1. The Concretizing Synthesis (*Concretio*): The Universal Concept   120

     2. The Affirmative Synthesis (*Complexio*): The Judgment and the Truth Appearing in It   123

     3. *Concretio* and *Complexio* in Thomas   126

III. The Return of the Subject to Himself, and the Agent Intellect   132

IV. The Essence of the Agent Intellect   135

     1. Agent Intellect as *A Priori* Condition of the Possibility of the Knowability of a Material Form   136

     2. Agent Intellect as Knowledge of the Confinement of Form by Matter: The Mode of the "Liberation"   138

3. Agent Intellect as "Pre-Apprehension"
   (*Vorgriff*)   142

V. *Excessus I:* Preparatory Clarifications   146
   1. The Reciprocal Limitation of Form and
      Supposite   148
   2. What Is-in-Itself (*Das Ansichsein*) as Such
      as the Form Apprehended in the
      Abstractive Pre-Apprehension   154
   3. Preliminary Clarification of the *Esse*-
      Concept in Thomas   156

VI. *Excessus II: Esse* in Thomas   163
   1. *Esse* as the In-Itself (*Ansich*) of the
      Reality Apprehended in the Judgment   163
   2. *Esse* as *A Priori* Synthesis "In Itself" (*An
      Sich*)   169
   3. *Esse* as Universal *Esse* in Formal and
      Trans-Categorical Unity   174
   4. *Esse* as Absolute *Esse*   179

VII. *Excessus III*   183
   1. The *Excessus* in Its Absolute Negative
      Infinity   183
   2. The *Excessus* to the Absolute as
      Constitutive of Human Spirituality   186

VIII. *Excessus* and Agent Intellect   187
   1. The Three Levels of Abstraction   188
   2. The Third Level of Abstraction as a
      Moment in the Judgment: Agent Intellect
      as the Exclusive Power of Forming
      Metaphysical Concepts   192

IX. The Agent Intellect as the Power of the
   Excessus to *Esse*   202
   1. The Fundamental Characterization of the
      Agent Intellect by the Abstraction of the
      First Principles   203

2. Making Possible the Abstraction of Principles by the Pre-Apprehension of Being in Its *Esse*   205

3. The Ontological Interpretation of the Light-Image (The Light as That Which Is Simultaneously "Seen" in the Object and Makes Possible *A Priori* the "Visibility" of the Object)   211

X. Abstraction as Complete Return   226

  1. The Formal Essence of the Complete Return to Self (A Form Subsisting in Itself)   227

  2. The Complete Return Specific to Man (The Return in a Conversion to the Phantasm)   230

CHAPTER FOUR: CONVERSION TO THE PHANTASM   237

  I. Defining the Question   237

 II. The Possible Intellect   241

III. The (Possible) Intellect as the Origin of Sensibility   246

  1. The Fundamental Structure of the Sensibilization (*Versinnlichung*) of the Possible Intellect   247

  2. The Necessity of the Sensibilization in Accordance with the Specific Nature of Human Spirit (The Problematic of the Body-Soul Relationship)   248

  3. The Formal Structure of the Relationship of Origin Between the Powers to Each Other and to Their Substantial Ground (Natural Emanation)   253

4. The Specific Relationship of Origin
Between Intellect and Sensibility   260

IV. The Origin of Sensibility as Conversion to the
Phantasm   264

    1. The Intrinsic Information (*Durchformung*)
of Sensibility as Conversion to the
Phantasm   266

    2. The Act of the Cogitative Sense as
Conversion to the Phantasm   268

    3. The Essence of the Reflection in the Act of
the Cogitative Sense   274

V. The Origin of Sensibility from Spirit   279

    1. Spirit as Desire (Dynamic Openness) for
Absolute Being   280

    2. The Production of Sensibility in the Desire
of the Spirit for Absolute Being   284

    3. Proof of the Formal Structure of This Line
of Thought in Thomas   286

VI. The Freedom of Spirit   290

    1. Freedom as Transcending (*Überspringen*)
Sensibility in Its Origin from Spirit   291

    2. Negation as Measure of the Freedom of
Spirit in Its Ordination to Sensibility (The
Ontological Sense of "Nothing")   297

VII. The Cogitative Sense   299

    1. The Cogitative as the "Sentient" Power of
the Conversion   300

    2. The Cogitative Sense in Its Specific
Sensibility   301

    3. The Cogitative Sense in Its Union with
Imagination in the One, Original,
Imaginative Power of the Spirit   305

VIII. Intelligible Species I: Tracing the Problematic
of the Intelligible Species Back to the More

General Problematic of the External
Determinability of an Existent   309
  1. The Connection Between the Intelligible
    Species and the Conversion   310
  2. The Reduction of the Species-Concept to
    the More General Relationship of Intellect
    and Sensibility   311
  3. The Inclusion of the Phantasm in the
    Reality of the Species   313
  4. The Differentiation of the Phantasm (as
    Material Element) from the Actuality of
    the Species (as Formal Element)   317
  5. The Concrete Actuality of the Material
    Element as Exclusive Production of the
    Formal Element (The Soul, the Only Form
    of the Body)   323
IX. Intelligible Species II: Towards the Ontology
   of Inner-Worldly, Efficient Causality   330
  1. The Question about the Species (as
    Permanent) as the Problem of Inner-
    Worldly, Efficient Causality   330
  2. The Apparent Dilemma of the Concepts
    "Action" and "Passion"   332
  3. Various Ways of an Influence Being-In the
    Patient (Received and Emanating
    Influence)   333
  4. The Nature of the Emanating Influence   339
  5. The Nature of the Medium of the Patient
    (The Concept of Matter, I)   340
  6. The Connection Between the (Merely)
    Emanating and the Received Influence
    (The Concept of Matter, II)   344
  7. Reduction of Efficient Causality to Intrinsic
    Causality   355

8. The Quidditative Identity of Emanating
   and Received Influence 358
X. Intelligible Species III: The Ontology of
   Inner-Worldly, Efficient Causality in Its
   Application to the Essence of Sensibility and
   of the Agent Intellect 366
   1. Passion (*Passio*), Intention (*Intentio*),
      Spiritual *Esse* in Thomas 366
   2. "To Receive after the Manner of an
      Intention" as the Ontological, Essential
      Definition of Sensibility 371
   3. The Results of an Ontology of External
      Influence for the Essence of Sensibility 377
   4. The Intelligible Species in Its Own Being
      Distinct from the *A Priori* Structure of
      Spirit as Such 379

PART THREE
THE POSSIBILITY OF METAPHYSICS
ON THE BASIS OF THE IMAGINATION

I. The Problem: The Unique Opening to
   Metaphysics as the Constitution of the
   Objective Openness of the World 387
II. The Possibility of Metaphysics: The
   Fundamental Act of Man as an Opening to
   Being as Such (*Excessus*) 393
III. The Limits of Metaphysics: *Esse* Disclosed in
   the Pre-Apprehension as Empty "Common
   Being" with the Transcendental Modes
   Intrinsic to It 400
IV. Man as Spirit in the World 406

Foreword

An Essay on Karl Rahner

BY JOHANNES B. METZ

Karl Rahner is today in many respects no longer a controversial and "ecclesiastically suspect" theologian; he has become "accepted." His bold theological opinions are now repeated by many—although often with thoughtless simplification and one-sidedness. However, the general acceptance of Rahner's ideas should not gloss over that astonishing emergence of Catholic theology associated today with Rahner's name. This emergence, out of the pale and often torpid world of neo-scholasticism, has occurred through a decisive confrontation between the scholastic tradition and recent transcendental and existential philosophy. It was achieved also with the help of a theological hermeneutic of biblical and theological-historical statements which were, at least in the beginning, exemplarily developed. Further, this emergence, from out of the cleft between theology and kerygma, has been given its goal in the programmatic words of Rahner, that "in fact the strictest theology, that most passionately devoted to reality alone and ever on the alert for new questions, the most scientific theology, is itself in the long run the most kerygmatic theology." Finally, this emergence has another aspect: from the professional faith of theologians to brotherly faith, and here it was aided by a theology of faith which saw faith as being ever endangered and seeking, as a *theologia viatorum* in the brotherly service of the hope of all men. Thus this emergence is one from out of the ghetto into dialogue with the socially and intellectually pluralistic world—and it ought perhaps to be said that this particular emergence took place long before the word "dialogue" became the cliché so fashionable today.

This emergence, of course, which has been here only cursorily and partially outlined, is certainly not associated only with the name of Rahner; but it is especially concentrated in his work, and quite correctly so, since Karl Rahner has been in all of the above areas more than just an interested bystander.

How, then, we may ask, did this singular and indeed unique synthesis of emergence and established acceptance come about? How was this "new theology" able so quickly to overtake a large and influential section of the general mind of the Church? If we seek a reason in Rahner himself, then beyond all rational and political explanations we must accept a trait of Rahner's theological personality—one which even the briefest portrait should not leave out, even though it may seem surprising and far-fetched. I refer to his creative affirmation of tradition, his as it were "conservatism," the constant commitment of his theological thinking to the history of the faith and of the Church.

Yet this faithfulness to tradition is by no means mere repristination, a merely invigorated repetition of historical findings; rather, it is a productive reactualization and affirmation of tradition in the present. For Rahner, the question of tradition always is a question of theology concerned both with itself and its future, so that the sought-after future mediates itself precisely through its own origin. Rahner seeks, therefore, the "ever new" never for the sake of modernity, but out of faithfulness to the incumbent historical beginning. Further, this faithfulness to historical tradition is attested not only by his vast historical knowledge, but also by that "salvaging trait" of his theological attitude in general, by his ability to integrate—reminding us of Thomas Aquinas—by which he perceives the

xiv

relevance and appeal of early words, concepts, and statements of the Church's scholastic theology and seeks to "save" them for us. It is also due to this ability that he has developed a subtle hermeneutic of the Church's official statements, thereby bringing out their total depth and breadth. Rahner progresses only so far forward as the great tradition of the Church and theology allow—often only with difficulty and protest. And he is aided in this creative affirmation of the Church's theological heritage by another of his traits, by what might be called his "Socratic attitude," his talent for asking questions, his ability for interpretation, seeing things in their truisms, waking conventional truths from their school slumber, liquefying anew once-frozen and coagulated ideas, summoning forth a statement long lost in the twilight of tradition.

Rahner mobilizes this productive affirmation of tradition by his equally sensitive and responsible theological awareness of the needs of faith in our time. I would like to emphasize here what is often not easily recognized from the style of his speaking and writing, namely, that the academic theological chair and the lecture rostrum are for him not places where he simply towers academically over his listeners; rather, they remain for him finally and always the place in which he exercises the readiness of theology to share the problems of the intellectual and social milieux, and to draw these problems into the consciousness of faith. This attitude can also explain what I prefer to call the "indirect ecumenical effect" of his theology. Rahner has written relatively little directly pertaining to interconfessional and ecumenical problems, yet he has pursued "his" theology precisely in the face of those questions which relate to the total awareness of faith today. Thereby he has brought to light much of that "Christian community" which arises when theologians of various Christian confessions face from their own viewpoint a common task and a given imperative.

Since Rahner publishes everything he teaches, there is no esoteric Rahner. He experiments with and applies his theology to a multiplicity of topics covering almost the whole field of systematic theology and also touching upon the central and special questions of pastoral and spiritual theology. This colorful variety is due not least of all to Rahner's picking up the cues for his theological reflections from the questions and appeals brought to him by Church and society. He sees this as an essential element of his "diakonia" in which he constantly mobilizes his "inner-theological" insights for a fruitful encounter with most diversified questions of a "non-theological" nature. In recent years his ever increasing number of publications has risen to such an extent that the content of his theological writings seems nearly unsurveyable in their full range, and every review of his theology seems almost inescapably to be in danger of roughly schematizing it or arbitrarily abridging it. Nevertheless, a closer look at his theology reveals a very exceptional rational consistency and inner unity, and this unity can be traced from his first large publication, *Spirit in the World,* to the seventh and presently latest volume of his *Theological Investigations.*

Spirit in the World uses a Thomistic metaphysics of knowledge explained in terms of transcendental and existential philosophy to define man as that essence of absolute transcendence towards God insofar as man in his understanding and interpretation of the world respectfully "pre-apprehends" (*vorgreift*) towards God. This thesis remains in its many variations decisive for Rahner's continuing development of theology. In 1966, for example, Rahner said in a lecture given in Chicago: "As soon as man is understood as that being which has absolute transcendence towards God (and it is surely obvious that he is such), then anthropocentricity and theocentricity in theology are not contradictories but strictly one and the same thing seen from two different aspects, and each aspect is unintelligible without the other. That theology should be anthropocentric is not opposed to its being most rigorously theocentric. But this connection is opposed to the view that man is merely one particular topic in theology among others, for example, the angels or the material world. It is contrary to the view that it is possible to speak theologically about God without at the same time saying something about man, and vice versa. Speech about God and speech about man connect not only from the point of view of content, but also from the point of view of knowledge itself."

The "anthropocentrically oriented theology" suggested in these statements characterizes Rahner's theological approach. It constitutes, as it were, the "inner form" of his theological statements, allowing him to be diverse without being arbitrary or heterogeneous. For in the end result, his theological statements always center on one thing, namely, the Word of the intractable mystery of God spoken to us in Jesus Christ as forgiveness and love, in and towards which man affirms himself, when believing, hoping, and loving he accepts the painful darkness of his existence. Rahner has developed this anthropocentrically oriented theology in reference to many individual questions and treatises—the Trinity, grace, eschatology, salvation history, and so forth. And also to Christology: "Christology is the end and beginning of anthropology, and this anthropology in its radical realization, namely, in Christology, is for all eternity theology; it is first of all that theology which God spoke in speaking his Word as our flesh in the emptiness of the ungodly and sinful; it is that theology which we pursue in faith when we do not think that we could encounter God in bypassing the man Christ and man in general."

Rahner has taken anthropologically oriented theology out of the forest of scholastic objectivism, in which dogmatic school theology was everywhere enclosed. And what theological achievement of our time can compare with this? Yet questions remain unanswered and new questions arise, and these latter must begin at as deep a level as Rahner's approach itself. For example, does not such a transcendental-existential approach (which defines man *a priori* as that being characterized by absolute transcendence towards God) concentrate the necessarily historically realized salvation of man too much on the question of whether the individual freely accepts or rejects this constitution of his being? Is there not danger that the question of salvation will be made too private and that salvation history will be conceived too worldlessly, breaking too quickly the point of the universal historical battle for man? Anthropocentrically oriented theology places the faith quite correctly in a fundamental and irreducible relationship with the free subjectivity of man. However, is the relationship of this faith to the world and history sufficiently preserved (*aufgehoben*)? This relationship to the world certainly cannot be renewed in the classical sense of a cosmology, since the faith is not in a cosmological sense worldly. But the faith is and remains (in the light of its biblical origins and its content of promise) in a social and political sense worldly. Therefore, should not the transcendental theology of person and existence be translated into a type of "political theology"? And finally, does not a radical transcendental-existential theology undervalue the importance of eschatology? Can the eschatological really be extrapolated out of the existential approach of theology? Or does not every anthropocentrically oriented theology which does not want to leave the world and history out of the sight of operative and responsible faith flow into an eschatologically oriented theology? Is the eschatological horizon broad enough to mediate (*vermitteln*) unabridged the faith and the historically emerging world? Such questions, coming out of Rahner's program, need not be solved against him, but rather can be tested and further developed in dialogue with him. For in the end Rahner's theology in all the truly great and enduring things it has given us is properly characterized by one overriding "tendency": the ever new initiation into the mystery of God's love and the service of the hope of all men.

Introduction

Karl Rahner and the Kantian Problematic

BY FRANCIS P. FIORENZA

Spirit in the World has a double significance for Karl Rahner's thought and his imposing *aggiornamento* of theology. First of all, this book represents Rahner's attempt to confront the medieval scholastic philosophy of Thomas Aquinas with the problems and questions of modern philosophy, especially as formulated by Immanuel Kant in his critical and transcendental philosophy. This confrontation is vitally important because it concerns the central problem of philosophy, namely, the nature and possibility of metaphysics, and centers on the question of the possibility of a speculative and rational theology. Karl Rahner understands this task of confrontation not as a mere apologetical defense of Thomistic ontology, but as a fruitful dialogue and receptive openness to problems and questions of Kant's philosophy. In the accomplishment of this task he has taken his guidelines from the previous work of Joseph Maréchal and Martin Heidegger and has developed an independent and original synthesis with definite differences from both Maréchal and Heidegger. In the second place, *Spirit in the World* is also important because the basic philosophical position developed here in dialogue with modern philosophy provides the unifying principle and presupposition of Rahner's whole theology. Rahner has not left the philosophical principles of this book in their formal and abstract outlines, but has developed and applied them in his many theological books and essays which can only be adequately understood when *Spirit in the World* is understood.

I. HISTORICAL SITUATION OF *SPIRIT IN THE WORLD*

A delineation of the purpose of Kant's philosophy and an understanding of the arguments of his critique of every system of rational and speculative theology helps to provide a background for a clearer insight into the problematic of *Spirit in the World*. Ten years after the publication of the *Critique of Pure Reason* in 1791, Kant wrote: "Transcendental philosophy, that is, the teaching concerning the possibility of all *a priori* knowledge, which is the Critique of Pure Reason, . . . has as its purpose the establishment of metaphysics."[1] This purpose, however, was not clearly seen by all because Kant's analyses of the structure of human knowledge resulted in a radical critique of traditional metaphysics. Thomistic and scholastic philosophers often, accusing Kant of skepticism and agnosticism, failed to realize that Kant's delineation of the limits of the use of reason had as its purpose the establishment of criteria for certain and scientific knowledge. The Neo-Kantians avoided this error, but by concentrating their studies on the *Critique of Pure Reason* and by neglecting the later attempts to establish metaphysics as a practical philosophy and as a teaching of wisdom, they understood Kant's philosophy as a mere theory of human experience or as a theoretical foundation for the natural sciences. This neglect of Kant's *Critique of Practical Reason, Critique of Judgment,* and *Opus Postumum,*[2] combined with a

---

[1] *Welches sind die wirklichen Fortschritte, die die Metaphysik seit Leibnizens und Wolfs Zeiten in Deutschland gemacht hat?*, Berlin, 1804, A 43.

[2] This continuity between this work and Kant's earlier works cannot be discussed here. Cf. V. Mathieu, *La Filosofia transcendentale e*

one-sided understanding of his *Metaphysical Foundations of Natural Science*,[3] led to the image of Kant's thought as devoid of metaphysics and enclosed within the limits of a mere formal logic. This Neo-Kantian interpretation dominated the German philosophical scene when Heidegger wrote *Kant and the Problem of Metaphysics* in order to destroy this prevailing interpretation and to demonstrate that the purpose of Kant's *Critique of Pure Reason* was to lay the foundation for metaphysics. Heidegger, however, understood this foundation in terms of his own fundamental ontology. He therefore interpreted the Kantian problematic as the radical finitude of man, and the origin of metaphysics as the comprehension of being as such. Although this interpretation does some violence to the historical meaning of Kant's *Critique of Pure Reason,* it does represent a real progress over the prevailing Neo-Kantian interpretation. Heidegger's attempt to retrieve Kant's thought from the confinement of Neo-Kantianism in Germany was paralleled by Maréchal's criticism of the completely negative attitude of neo-scholasticism towards Kant. By means of a formal comparison between Thomas and Kant, Maréchal attempted to justify a combination of the contents of the traditional Thomistic metaphysics with the transcendental method of Kant.[4]

The influence of the interpretations of Kant's philosophy by Maréchal and Heidegger form the inspiration and background of Karl Rahner's *Spirit in the World*. When Rahner was a young Jesuit student in Feldkirch and Pullach from 1924 to 1927, he did not merely follow his scholastic lectures, but spent his private time taking copious notes from Maréchal's volumes on *The Starting Point of Metaphysics*.[5] After the

l'opus postumum *di Kant,* Turin, 1958. The more general and classic work is still very useful: H. J. De Vleeschauwer, *La Déduction transcendentale dans l'oeuvre de Kant,* 3 vols., Paris, 1934–1937.

[3] Cf. Peter Plass, *Kants Theorie der Naturwissenschaften,* Göttingen, 1965.

[4] A good survey of the history, differences, and problems of the scholarship on Kant in Germany is O. Marquard, *Skeptische Methode im Blick auf Kant,* Munich, 1958.

[5] J. Donceel is preparing a translation of the important texts of this book which will be published by Herder and Herder. Father Donceel

completion of his studies in scholastic philosophy and theology he was sent, in 1934, to Freiburg to work for his doctorate in philosophy under the direction of the neo-scholastic philosopher Martin Honecker. Rahner was also able during this time to participate in the lectures and seminars of Martin Heidegger.[6] These biographical data throw light on Rahner's formative influences which led him to confront the philosophy of Thomas Aquinas with the questions and problems of Kant's philosophy as interpreted by Maréchal and Heidegger. Before discussing *Spirit in the World* and these influences in detail, we will review the nature of the Kantian problematic independently of the interpretations by Maréchal and Heidegger.

II. KANT'S CRITIQUE OF ALL RATIONAL THEOLOGY[7]

A short survey of Kant's critique of special metaphysics, that is, of rational and natural theology, easily indicates the philosophical presuppositions and the theological relevance of the Kantian problematic. Although our treatment discusses mainly the third section of the transcendental dialectic, namely, the ideal of pure reason, it should be remembered that this section presupposes the analyses of the transcendental aesthetic and analytic and of the two previous sections of the dialectic. Our treatment of Kant's critique of all rational theology is limited to (1) his critique of the transcendental ideal and (2) his critique of the conceivability of an absolute necessary being.

has performed an invaluable service by using the philosophy of Maréchal and Rahner in his college textbooks for many years. He has greatly contributed through his other publications to the reception of Maréchal and Rahner in the United States.

[6] H. Vorgrimler, *Karl Rahner, Leben, Denken, Werke*, Munich, 1963, pp. 17–43.

[7] Our general presentation follows D. Henrich, *Der ontologische Gottesbeweis*, Tübingen, 1960, pp. 137–188. Cf. the feature review of W. Janke, "Ontotheologie und Methodik," in *Philosophische Rundschau* 12 (1964), pp. 179–217, esp. 195–204.

1. The Critique of the Transcendental Ideal

Kant explains that human reason has the tendency and ability to think a totality. This ability is important because human reason can only think the individual or the limitation within the totality when it thinks the totality. In other words, the idea of limitation presupposes the totality to be limited. A similar example can illustrate this point. There are two types of predicates. One type expresses a content without limitation, for example, "goodness"; another type expresses only a specific or limited degree of some content, for example, "moderate." The second type can only be thought of in relation to the first type. The predicate of degree is only possible as a specific degree or determinate measure of some pure reality. Likewise, when a thing possesses reality in a limited measure, that is, as a finite being, then it can only be thought of as limited or as finite in relation to the idea of the totality of all reality or the most perfect being as the fullness of reality, who is the *Urbild* of all reality. Kant maintains, however, that human reason makes a grave mistake when it thinks that because a finite limited thing cannot be thought of as finite and determined without the idea of God as *omnitudo realitatis,* God must necessarily exist when finite things exist. This illusory way to God's existence confuses the real and the ideal. It does so not by deducing the existence of God from the concept of God, but by assuming the existence of God from the necessary function of the idea of God in the determination of finite beings as finite. The basis of this mistake is a twofold "natural" illusion which leads reason to presuppose first that a rule of the reasonable determination of a thing is also the real principle of a thing, and second, that a rule for the use of reason in regard to objects as they appear to us through our senses can be applied to all things including objects which transcend sense experience. Although Kant often calls this illusion natural and unavoidable, he states that reason can easily see through this illusion so that the mistake must be influenced by something else (B611–612). What is this "something else" whose "illusion" is not so easily avoided as the transcendental ideal?

2. *Critique of the Conceivability of an Absolute Necessary Being*

This "something else" is the cosmological problem of the necessary being. Kant develops this problem by demonstrating the inner unity between the cosmological problem of the fourth antinomy and the ontological arguments. Their inner unity forms the basis of rational theology and enables Kant to destroy rational theology by criticizing the inner core of the cosmological problem and the ontological arguments. Kant does so not merely by means of the logical objection, but by means of the empirical and critical objections.

According to Kant, the cosmological problem presents more difficulties than the transcendental ideal because it originates not just from our concepts of things, but from our actual experience of existing things. The conclusion that really existing contingent beings of our experience must be grounded in an unconditional necessary being appears as natural to reason as the existence of the contingent beings themselves. Kant sees the problem in the inability of cosmology of itself to decide if this absolute necessary being exists separate from the world or is the world itself. Nor can it decide what the necessary being in itself is. If reason is to conclude to the existence of a necessary being, it must arrive at an adequate idea of that being, which necessarily exists. Can reason do this? Kant's answer is no.

Kant's negative answer is the result of his critique of the conceivability of an absolute necessary being. He argues that the thought of the existence of a necessary being does not contain a specific concept of the essence of the necessary existing being. Can the thought of a necessary existing being be sufficiently specified so as to make it "thinkable" for human reason? Kant demonstrates how human reason attempts to specify the absolute necessary being by means of the transcendental ideal and the ontological arguments—an attempt which, according to Kant, was invalid and unsuccessful.

The ontological argument of Anselm based on the transcendental ideal of *omnitudo realitatis* conceives of God as the highest reality as the ground of all reality. This idea seems appropriate to specify the necessary being. Since God possesses all reality, he must necessarily exist, since existence is a reality. Kant applies the empirical objection against this usage of Anselm's ontological argument to determine and to specify the necessary being of the cosmological problem as the highest reality. He objects that existence is not a real predicate, that is, not an element belonging to a concept of a thing. Existence is not a specification of an object but only the position of an object or its relation to the subject. In other words, the concept of a thing as existent or as non-existent is the same concept. Existence does not add to or subtract from the concept of a thing because it is not a perfection of a thing but only its position, namely, whether the thing is given or not. The idea of the most perfect being does not and cannot contain (in its concept) the predicate existence, because existence is not a perfection or predicate, but only a position. This empirical objection is not to be identified with the logical objection (which Hegel falsely accuses Kant of making[8]) whose separation of concept and existence would not apply to God, but it goes further than the logical objection by indicating why existence cannot belong even to the concept of God.

This difficulty which prevents the first ontological argument from specifying the necessary being by means of the transcendental ideal was seen by philosophers before Kant who therefore attempted to develop a second ontological argument. The necessary being would be considered in this argument as *im-*

---

[8] Hegel's reduction of Kant's argumentation to the logical objection as expressed in Bering's example of the 100 taler is totally inaccurate. Kant uses Bering's example merely to indicate that existence is not an element within a concept. He is, however, quite aware of the fact that the concept of the 100 taler and the concept of God are quite different. He therefore develops the empirical and critical objections.

mensa potestas by Descartes,[9] as *causa sui* by Spinoza, and as *le véritable être* by Malebranche. These specifications of the necessary being attempt to demonstrate that the thought of a necessary being implicitly includes the thought of its existence independent of the question whether existence is a predicate or not. Kant, however, develops the implications of the empirical objection to demonstrate that human reason cannot arrive at an intelligible idea of necessary being at all. This attempt constitutes Kant's critical objection and is the core of his critique of rational theology. As he states in reflexion 6277, "The whole difficulty of transcendental theology is due to the impossibility of specifying the concept of the absolute necessity of a thing, that is, of stating the ground of its conceivability."

Kant's analysis of the modal categories[10] is the basis for this conclusion and indicates the implications of the empirical objection when developed into the critical objection. The modal categories of possibility, actuality, and necessity concern the possible, real (as actual), and necessary position (existence) of objects. They are not elements of the concept of something, but they are rather the position of a thing and its way of being given to the knowing subject.[11] Kant explains the subjective character of the modal categories in terms of his important distinction between understanding and sensitive intuition.

[9] Descartes' argument is not in the fifth Meditation but in his answer to the objections from Caterus. Descartes states that the greatest power must contain the power of its own existence, and that the idea of the greatest power leads therefore to the certitude of his existence. This argument of the first response is also treated in Number 15 of his *Principia philosophia*, Amsterdam, 1644.

[10] Cf. G. Schneeberger, *Kants Konzeption der Modalbegriffe*, Basel, 1952. He presents a complete selection of all the relevant texts. Unfortunately, his own position is closer to Wolff than to Kant, and this mars his presentation. Cf. Henrich's review in *Philosophische Rundschau* 4 (1956), pp. 118–119.

[11] Cf. Heidegger's brilliant interpretation (but for his own purposes) of Kant's modal categories: *Kants These über das Sein*, Frankfurt, 1963. Cf. also F. Kaulbach, "Die kantische Lehre von Ding und Sein in der Interpretation Heideggers," in *Kant-Studien* 55 (1964), pp. 194–220.

Whereas the sensitive intuition presents the objects as given, the understanding thinks their concepts. If this distinction between understanding and sensitive intuition did not exist, then man would be incapable of distinguishing between the possible and the real, since the root of man's ability to distinguish between the possible and the real lies not in the objective thing-in-itself, but in the knowing subject. Kant argues that if man's *understanding* formed its concepts by intuition, then it would only have as its object the actually existing object which it intuited. Man would be unable then to form concepts referring only to the possibility of a thing or to have sensitive intuitions which merely present a thing as existing to the subject but do not think its objective concept. However, it is precisely this ability of man's understanding to produce a concept of a thing irrespective of its actual existence which enables him to distinguish between actual existence and possibility.[12] The denial of this distinction between understanding and sensitive intuition, or the affirmation that the distinction between possibility and reality is not based on this distinction in the knowing subject but in the thing-in-itself, would restrict possibility to actual existence and would imply that the non-perception of a thing signifies its impossibility. The difference between possibility and actuality is not something perceived in the object-in-itself. It is based rather on man's understanding of things as possible without their having to be actual.

This subjectivization of the modal categories by which possibility, actuality, and necessity are not elements in the thing-in-itself, but the position of an object to the subject, leads to

[12] The most important Kantian text for this question is Number 76 of the *Critique of Judgment*. Schelling considers this section one of the most profound pieces of all philosophy. Heidegger's interpretation is very worthy of consideration. It is important in this discussion to remember that Kant uses the word "reality" in a different sense than we generally do. When Kant writes that reality is no more than possibility, what he means, according to his own statement in Reflexion 3706, is this: "it is here not a question of more in general, . . . but of more predicates." Cf. Kant's footnote to B 287 in his *Critique of Pure Reason*. We will explain later the meaning of possibility in relation to the problem of judgment as affirmation. Cf. Plass, *op. cit.*, pp. 44–82.

Kant's denial of the conceivability of an absolute necessary being. When the modal categories specify the relation of an object to the subject, then to define the "essence of something" only through modal categories (as identity of actuality and necessity) is to describe mere relations or positions of an object, but not to specify the subject or object-in-itself. The "thought" of such a definition through the mere combination of modal categories is impossible or unthinkable; it is a mere name or word without any conceivable content. Only something (a being) can exist or necessarily exist. To define and to constitute "something" as necessarily existing only describes its mode of being or its position, but not the being itself. It is impossible to think of modes of being without thinking of a specific being which "possesses" them. Therefore, the notion of a being whose essence is only defined through absolute necessity is totally indeterminate and unspecified. It is a mere formal and subjective notion without any content, and as such is unthinkable.[18]

3. Summary

Kant's criticism of all rational theology involves a twofold critique. First, Kant argues that any argument for God's existence based on the transcendental ideal incorrectly confuses the ideal and the real by presupposing that the reasonable determination of things is the real principle of things and that a rule for the use of understanding in regard to objects of experience applies to objects transcending experience. Second, Kant argues that human reason cannot form a concept of an absolute necessary being because necessity and existence

[18] Cf. Kant's Reflexions 6389–6395. These reflexions together with the others on rational theology in volume 18 of his collected writings (Berlin, 1928) provide an excellent complementary treatment of Kant's critique of rational theology. It is unfortunate that most of the English-language treatments of Kant's critique neglect his reflexions. The important relevant texts of Kant's composition on the progress of metaphysics, especially A 124–152, are extremely precise as to the exact nature of his critique of rational theology.

are mere positions of an object, but not elements in the things-in-themselves. "Absolute necessary being" is a mere subjective hypothesis of the mind which can in no way be adequately specified and conceived. Although this twofold critique does not imply that Kant denied the existence of God because he maintains the necessity of God as a postulate of practical reason, it appears, however, to have destroyed all theoretical knowledge of God.

This destruction of theoretical theology by Kant's philosophy was clearly seen by Hegel. He attacked Kant's denial of the conceivability of a necessary being, his subjectivization of the modal categories, and his radical distinction of being and thinking with the phrase, "God is dead." Although these words are often used today against Hegel's original intention to expound a supposedly Hegelian "atheistic" theology and philosophy, their proper historical meaning in the context of Hegel's early publication, *Faith and Knowledge,* must be understood in the light of Hegel's evaluation of Kant's philosophy.[14] As such they represent his negative judgment and critical diagnosis of the results of the subjectivization of thought in the philosophies of Kant, Jacobi, and Fichte. Hegel's whole philosophy can be considered as an attempt to overcome such an extreme formalization and subjectivization of human knowledge through the radical distinction between thinking and being. Hegel emphasizes in his critique the importance of an adequate starting point in any attempt to overcome Kant's "subjectivism." He maintains that the starting point or beginning of philosophy cannot be the purely formal thinking subject (as if the philosophical explication of this starting point would be then a subsequent bridging of subjectivity and objectivity), because from such a starting point the philosopher will never get beyond the

[14] English translation of "Glauben und Wissen," ed. G. Lasson, in *Philosophische Bibliothek* 62b, pp. 122–124. Cf. G. Rohrmoser, *Subjektivität und Verdinglichung. Theologie und Gesellschaft im Denken des jungen Hegel,* 1961. For a good counterbalance to the English-language publications with their stress on Hegel's atheism, see Q. Lauer, "Hegel on the Proofs for God's Existence," in *Kant-Studien* 55, pp. 443–465.

formal subjectivity and arrive at the absolute, if it were not already somehow contained in the starting point. Hegel proposes instead an absolute starting point which is immediate and indetermined and therefore does not contain an opposition between thinking and being. The philosopher then proceeds from his starting point *via negationis* to develop categories of thought.[15] These observations of Hegel have strongly influenced Martin Heidegger and are also implicitly considered by Karl Rahner in his dialogue with Kant.

III. MISINTERPRETATIONS AND CRITICISM OF *SPIRIT IN THE WORLD*[16]

This brief discussion of the Kantian critique of rational theology and Hegel's contrasting position illustrates the difficulty involved in a dialogue with Kant's philosophy and provides a horizon for an examination of several false interpretations and/or criticisms of *Spirit in the World*.

[15] Henrich, "Anfang und Methode der Logik," in *Hegel-Studien* I, Bonn, 1964, pp. 17–35. Cf. H. F. Fulda, "Ueber den spekulativen Anfang," in *Subjektivität und Metaphysik. Festschrift für Wolfgang Cramer*, ed. Henrich *et al.*, Frankfurt, 1966, pp. 109–127.

[16] The following secondary literature on Maréchal and his followers is worthy of note: O. Muck, *Die transzendentale Methode in der scholastischen Philosophie der Gegenwart*, Innsbruck, 1964 (*ET The Transcendental Method*, New York, 1968); H. Holz, *Transzendentalphilosophie und Metaphysik*, Mainz, 1966; R. Heinz, *Französische Kantinterpretation im 20. Jahrhundert*, Bonn, 1966. Muck gives a survey of Maréchal's thought and influences, and indicates the differences among the philosophers who follow Maréchal. His presentation consists mainly in a collection of quotations, however, and he himself is not totally convinced of the superiority of the transcendental method. Holz gives special attention to the relationship between Maréchal's ideas and Neo-Kantianism and Husserl. Heinz gives a survey of Maréchal's position and locates him within the context of the French scholarship on Kant. Since the first two books listed here give a sufficient account of the conservative Thomistic critique of Rahner and Maréchal, we will limit our treatment of this critique to that of Balthasar.

1. An inadequate interpretation often expressed in English publications reduces Rahner's argumentation to the simple statement that he and Maréchal have a dynamic viewpoint of knowledge whereas Kant's is static. This dynamic viewpoint alone corresponds to the true nature of the human intellect in its striving towards an absolute and it alone recognizes that this striving is the basis for man's knowledge of finite objects of experience as finite. This simplified interpretation proceeds often to speak of this absolute as if it were in some way objectively perceived or encountered as a transcendent Thou. A dialogic theology would then be developed without reflection on the serious problematic of the possibility of encountering God as a Thou. It cannot be too strongly emphasized that although Rahner often stresses the intellect's striving towards the absolute, his statement must be placed within the total and proper context of his whole argumentation so as to avoid a simplification which would not only ignore the heart of Kant's critical objection, namely, the inconceivability of an absolute necessary being, but would also reduce Rahner's transcendental philosophy to the obvious illusion of the transcendental ideal. A proper dialogue with Kant would have to come to terms with the problem of the conceivability of God and with the relationship between the logical and real, or regulative and constitutive use of reason.[17]

2. This Kantian problematic at the root of *Spirit in the World* provides a basis for the evaluation of criticism of Rahner's philosophy. The English translator of Rahner's first volume of *Theological Investigations* noted quite correctly that the problem of the convertibility of being and intelligibility is a fundamental theme of Rahner's book. He expressed a typical Anglo-Saxon reaction to German thought, however, by criticizing Rahner's position as "wholly unacceptable"[18] because of its

---

[17] The present Introduction does not permit a discussion of the reasons why Kantians would probably reject the position of Maréchal and Rahner.

[18] C. Ernst, "Translator's Introduction" to *Theological Investigations*, Baltimore, 1961, p. xiii, n. 1.

idealistic implications. Although the importance and implications of this criticism merit serious consideration, its full discussion would demand a treatment beyond the scope of this
short introduction. One point should be made: Kant's subjectivization of the modal categories and his radical distinction
between thinking and being led to his critique of all theoretical
and rational theology. When a theologian accepts the fundamental distinction between thinking and being as explicated by
Kant, he must either accept Kant's conclusion in regard to the
impossibility of theoretical and rational knowledge of God, or
he must demonstrate that Kant's conclusion does not necessarily
flow from his premises. This is a difficult task. German Idealism and the Maréchalian school (which despite all affinities
differs on essential points with the philosophies of Hegel and
Fichte) represent attempts to confront these Kantian conclusions by a re-examination of Kant's premises and by a specific
interpretation of the convertibility of being and intelligibility.
Therefore, before we as Anglo-Saxons living in a different
philosophical tradition label Rahner's position as idealistic or
criticize his understanding of the convertibility of being and
intelligibility, we should take into account the Kantian problematic with all its implications and consequences.

3. These considerations illustrate the degree of misunderstanding contained in the criticism raised against Rahner by
Hans Urs von Balthasar, who in the general context of his
conservative evaluations and negative criticism of contemporary
tendencies within the Church attacks not only current aspects
of the biblical, liturgical, and ecumenical movements, but also
the attempts of Karl Rahner and Johannes Metz to develop a
positive relationship to modern philosophy and the secularization
of society and its institutions.[19] Balthasar makes Rahner an

---

[19] *Glaubhaft ist nur Liebe*, Einsiedeln, 1963; *Wer ist ein Christ?*,
Einsiedeln, 1965; *Cordula oder der Ernstfall*, Einsiedeln, 1966. The
second edition of this last book contains an appendix in which Balthasar answers to those who have accused him of attacking Rahner
explicitly and unfairly. The answer is nothing but a further polemic.

explicit target of his criticism by accusing him of an anthropological and subjectivistic reduction of theology and Christianity. He popularizes and repeats thereby the critical observations of the Thomistic philosopher, Gustav Siewerth,[20] who correctly noted that the Maréchalian school is closer to Fichte than to Kant. Balthasar thus sees Rahner's theology as an un-Christian glorification of the human personality and of subjectivity, falsely concentrating on man's freedom instead of his obedience to the cross. The extent to which this severe criticism misunderstands Fichte—and thereby Rahner—cannot be discussed here.[21] What is important to note is that this criticism fails to mention the important differences between the Maréchalian school and Fichte. Maréchal explicitly rejects what he considers to be the "absolute idealism" of Fichte.[22] Balthasar in his criticism overlooks not only the importance of Maréchal's theory of objectivity with its emphasis on judgments of affirmation, but also the central purpose of Maréchal's confrontation with modern transcendental philosophy. This confrontation does not consist in a rejection of essential elements of Thomistic ontology, but rather in an awareness of modern problems and in the use of a modified transcendental method to arrive at a Thomistic ontology. An attempt is made to separate form and content, to use certain formal elements of modern philosophy in order to retain basic elements of traditional metaphysics.[28] This point will be clearly seen in the next objection.

[20] For the rejection of Siewerth's criticism as lacking a correct understanding of Maréchal, cf. Holz, *op. cit.*, pp. 130–131. Holz remarks that Siewerth accuses Maréchal of holding a position which Maréchal in fact rejects. Cf. Muck, *op. cit.*, pp. 139–143.

[21] It is interesting to note that Reinhard Lauth, editor of the new critical edition of Fichte's works, has accepted as a doctoral dissertation the work of E. Simons, *Philosophie der Offenbarung*, Stuttgart, 1966. Professor Lauth, a leader of the *Una Voce* movement which protests the use of the vernacular in the liturgy, has attacked the modern theology (implicitly, Rahner) for deceiving the German bishops. The criticism of Rahner (explicit in Simon's book) is that he is *not close enough* to Fichte. Had Balthasar consulted the Catholic Fichte scholarship, he would not have been able to criticize Rahner on this point.

[22] *Le Point de départ de la métaphysique* IV, Paris, 1947, pp. 335–455.

[28] Cf. Holz, *op. cit., pp.* 1–52.

4. A recent and often discussed criticism of Rahner's *Spirit in the World* maintains that it presupposes what Kant explicitly denies.[24] This very serious objection is the exact opposite of Balthasar's criticism. It correctly grasps the essential Thomistic content of Rahner's philosophy and accuses him of not being critical enough. Since this criticism concerns the fundamental difference between critical and non-critical philosophy, its adequate discussion lies beyond the few general introductory remarks made here.

It is true that the starting point of the Maréchalian school presupposes elements explicitly denied by Kant. This does not necessarily imply that this starting point is invalid or uncritical in relationship to the Kantian problematic, even though a Kantian would probably judge such a position from his own viewpoint as uncritical and dogmatic. Such a negative judgment would neglect the insights of Hegel concerning the beginning of philosophy and the inadequacy of a pure formal subjectivity as the proper starting point of philosophy. Such a judgment would also neglect Heidegger's insights concerning the relationship between subject and object, and his analyses showing that the asking of a question presupposes some sort of knowledge or awareness of the object sought. Any attempt to begin philosophy by a mere formal analysis of the knowing subject alone would have to come to terms with the philosophies of Hegel and Heidegger.

This criticism of Rahner's philosophy as uncritical points to the need of a closer examination of Rahner's intention and procedure in *Spirit in the World*. Although Karl Rahner attempts to confront the philosophy of Thomas Aquinas with the questions and problems of modern philosophy, he did not intend to write a critique of knowledge as a preamble and precondition to metaphysics, but a metaphysics of knowledge. He does not intend to enter into an explicit and critical discussion with modern philosophers, but merely to study the historical Thomas in the light of modern philosophy rather than in the

[24] This is the criticism of Holz, Simons, and Heinz.

perspective of his later scholastic and neo-scholastic commentators. This procedure is justified not only because it is just the beginning (and not the end) of a dialogue with Kant, but also because an adequate explanation of knowledge may be the best critique of knowledge.

IV. *SPIRIT IN THE WORLD* AND THE KANTIAN CRITIQUE

What is the relationship between Karl Rahner's philosophy and the Kantian critique? If *Spirit in the World* is primarily a metaphysics of knowledge and not a critique of knowledge, and if it presupposes in some way a knowledge of the absolute as its starting point, how is it then a true dialogue with the critical philosophy of Immanuel Kant and not just a new apologetic for that very dogmatic metaphysics rejected by Kant? How is it not merely a brilliant tactic using the arguments of the opponent to defeat him? Our introductory answer to these questions will merely indicate first, the similarity of Rahner and Kant's question, second, one basic difference between Rahner and Kant, and third, the new understanding of Thomas Aquinas provided by Rahner due to his dialogue with Kant.

1. *The Similarity of Rahner's and Kant's Questions*

Kant's analysis of human knowledge in his dissertation of 1770 led him to discover a new interpretation of the distinction between understanding and sensibility.[25] Leibniz and Wolff

[25] Cf. Henrich, "Ueber die Einheit der Subjektivität," in *Philosophische Rundschau* 3 (1955), pp. 28–69. Here the author establishes the reasons for Kant's radical separation of the two sources of human knowledge. Heidegger's interpretation to the contrary is a radical reinterpretation of Kant. The question cannot be resolved by stating that Heidegger is merely referring to the first edition of the *Critique*. Henrich's article is a brilliant analysis of the inadequacy of Heidegger on this point.

considered sensibility and understanding as faculties of one subject or substance distinguished from one another insofar as sensibility perceives the object as confused, and understanding thinks it as clear and distinct. Kant maintains, however, that sensibility and understanding are two radically distinct sources of knowledge. Whereas understanding is active and spontaneous, sensibility is passive and receptive. Both are necessary for human knowledge: the object is present as given through the sensible intuition, and is thought by the concepts of understanding. Kant developed the implications of his analysis of the sources of human knowledge to conclude that human knowledge is limited to the objects of possible experience. The spontaneity and dynamism of human reason towards an absolute unity which transcends sense experience is merely modal and logical. Since human reason cannot perceive the absolute as an object of experience, its dynamism towards an absolute cannot go beyond the modal and logical so that it is unable to form even an adequate idea of the absolute necessary being. Kant denies, therefore, the possibility of rational theology and special metaphysics.

Karl Rahner attempts a serious dialogue with Kant's critical philosophy insofar as he examines *Summa Theologiae* I, 84, 7 in the perspective of Kant's question concerning the possibility of metaphysics. The guiding question of *Spirit in the World* therefore is: How is metaphysics possible when all human knowledge is necessarily referred to sensible intuition? Rahner poses the question in Thomistic terminology as follows: How is metaphysics possible if all human knowledge occurs through a *conversio intellectus ad phantasmata?* By an analysis of this text Rahner clearly indicates that Thomas considers human knowledge as necessarily involving this *conversio intellectus ad phantasmata*. The question of the possibility of metaphysics must, therefore, be raised in the context of this Thomistic theory of knowledge, and it must be answered without neglecting the necessity of the *conversio intellectus ad phantasmata* for human knowledge. Rahner outlines an introductory and nuanced answer to this question which reveals both a revision and an assimilation of Kant's thought.

2. A Basic Difference Between Kant and Rahner

One of the difficulties in determining a central point of difference between Kant and Rahner lies in the necessity of correctly evaluating Maréchal's interpretation of Kant. Joseph Maréchal maintains that Kant incorrectly considers the activity of the human intellect in judging as a mere synthesizing of empirical data. He therefore emphasizes, against Kant, that there is a double aspect in every judgment: an absolute synthesis and an absolute affirmation. The aspect of judgment as affirmation is important because it implies that every judgment is not merely a logical synthesis or a regulative unity, but involves a direct relation to the object. The validity of every judgment with its absolute character is not merely logical but ontological, and as such anticipates the unconditional reality of God. This dynamism and orientation towards the absolute in every judgment is not just *thought* but *affirmed,* and is constitutive for the objectivity of our judgments and knowledge in general. The analysis of the orientation towards the absolute in the affirmation of every judgment is the central and critical point of Maréchal's evaluation of Kant.[26]

The major difficulty of Maréchal's interpretation is that it follows the Neo-Kantian interpretation of the nature of judgment in Kant's theory of knowledge. This interpretation of Maréchal has been propagated in the United States by Bernard Lonergan in his writing.[27] He considers Kant's theory of knowledge as perceptualistic, and accuses Kant of failing to recognize the importance of the judgment for the objectivity of knowledge, since for Lonergan the judgment relates the

[26] Rahner follows Maréchal on this point. Cf. Maréchal, *op. cit.* V, pp. 298–315.

[27] *Insight,* New York, 1957, pp. 339–342; "Metaphysics as Horizon," in *Collection,* New York, 1967, pp. 202–220.

concepts to the objects and has an unconditional character. This criticism raises two important questions. The first is: Does Kant consider knowledge primarily or solely as intuition or as judgment? When Martin Heidegger wrote *Kant and the Problem of Metaphysics* in 1929, he based his interpretation on the first edition of Kant's *Critique of Pure Reason,* considering the second edition as the result of Kant's fearful retreat from the consequences of his position. In his interpretation Heidegger maintained that knowledge is located primarily in the intuition and not in the judgment. This statement was a polemic against the Neo-Kantian treatment of all judgments as purely logical.[28] In *Die Frage nach dem Ding*[29] (a collection of Heidegger's lectures on Kant given during the winter semester of 1935–36 and published in 1962; note: Rahner completed his dissertation at Freiburg in 1936) Heidegger explicitly stated that its central section was a correction of his earlier book. Although Heidegger still emphasized the importance of intuition for human knowledge, which consists of intuition and understanding, he now explained the central importance of the judgment in Kant's theory of knowledge. He noted that Kant considered the traditional definition of judgment as a logical synthesis of subject and predicate as unsatisfactory, although not as completely false. Since it was not false but only inadequate, Kant could use the traditional definition even in the second edition. Since it was unsatisfactory, however, Kant provided a new definition of judgment in his explanation of the distinction between analytic and synthetic judgments. They differ from one another in that the analytical judgment is the basis of the objectivity of knowledge insofar as it refers the union of subject and predicate to the object as given in the concept, whereas the synthetical

---

[28] For the Neo-Kantian reply, cf. E. Cassirer, "Kant und das Problem der Metaphysik. Bemerkungen zu Martin Heideggers Kant-Interpretation," in *Kant-Studien* 36 (1931), pp. 1–26; H. Levy, "Heideggers Kantinterpretation zu Heideggers Buch 'Kant und das Problem der Metaphysik'," in *Logos* 21 (1932), pp. 1–43.

[29] Tübingen, 1962, pp. 97–189.

judgments refer to the object as outside of the concept. In other words, if the basis of the judgment is the object as a concept, then the judgment is analytical, but if the basis is the object as existing outside of the concept, then the judgment is synthetical and contributes to a factual extension of knowledge.[80] Kant's well-known sentence at the end of his *Critique of Practical Reason* is an excellent confirmation of this interpretation: "Every existential sentence . . . is a synthetical sentence because by it I go beyond the concept and state more than was thought in this concept, namely, that there is an object outside of the understanding." The problem of a correct understanding of Kant is not completely solved with this quotation because other quotations can be given to support a different interpretation of Kant. In a brilliant book on Kant's theory of the natural sciences, Peter Plass has recently formulated quite clearly the issues at hand.[81] Kant has a double understanding of objects, knowledge, and possibility. Knowledge of objects in a broad sense is knowledge of something in every representation and judgment, whereas knowledge of objects in a strict sense refers to objects of possible experience in which the judgment refers to the existence of an object outside of the concept. This explanation must be seen within the context of Kant's theory of possibility. Kant distinguishes between the

[80] *Ibid.*, pp. 128–129.
[81] *Op. cit.*, pp. 44–82. Cf. the high praise of this book by C. F. V. Weizsäcker, "Kants Theorie der Naturwissenschaft nach P. Plass," in *Kant-Studien* (1966), pp. 528f. Compare this book with R. Daval, *La Métaphysique de Kant. Perspectives sur la métaphysique de Kant d'après la théorie du schématisme*, Paris, 1951. Henrich evaluates Daval's book as the best one on Kant in many years. Cf. Henrich, "Zur theoretischen Philosophie Kants," in *Philosophische Rundschau* 1 (1953), pp. 124–149, esp. pp. 137–142. A more reserved evaluation is made by G. Pflug, "Roger Daval und seine Rezensenten," in *Kant-Studien* 48 (1956–57), pp. 86–93. Pflug locates Daval within a stream of French interpretations of Kant. The classical treatment of Kant on this subject is to be found in Klaus Reich, *Die Vollständigkeit der kantischen Urteilstafel*, Berlin, 1932. The similarities and differences among these three presentations indicate the difficulties in regard to this central point.

question as to *whether* something is possible and the question as to *how* something is possible. An answer to the latter would also be an answer to the former. This surprising statement can be understood only when we understand what Kant means by possibility and his distinction between logical and real possibility. According to Kant, the answer to the question as to *how* something is possible contains two tasks: (1) the concrete indication of the conditions of the possibility of something and (2) the proof that these conditions are fulfilled. Thus when Kant speaks of knowledge in a broad sense he is referring to the logical possibility. The reference of judgment to concepts in general occurs when he is considering the logical possibility of knowledge. When, however, he discusses synthetical judgments of fact, then he is concerned not with the logical but with the real possibility of knowledge. The real possibility of knowledge demands that the logical conditions be fulfilled, that is, that the judgment refer to the existence of the object. This synthetical judgment is necessary for the objective reality of human concepts and it alone explains fully how human knowledge is possible.

This extremely short explanation neglects the total complexity of Kant's theory of knowledge, but it suffices to lead to the second and central question: If Kant also maintained that human knowledge in a strict sense demands the judgment's affirmation of the existence of the object thought, what is the difference between the positions of Kant and Rahner?[32] The answer to this question is not immediately evident because *Spirit in the World* does not contain an explicit interpretation of Kant. It does not indicate to what extent Rahner would have avoided the misunderstanding of other students of Maréchal insofar as he would have followed the more adequate later interpretation of Heidegger. The influence of Heidegger

---

[32] Holz, *op. cit.*, pp. 42–52, quite clearly points to elements of a conception of judgment as affirmation on the part of Kant. He judges Maréchal's position as inadequate because a judgment as affirmation can have categorical necessity but not necessarily transcendental necessity.

is nevertheless important for Rahner's understanding of the objectivity of human knowledge[33] and for the clear differences between Rahner's and Maréchal's reception of Kant. Many aspects of Maréchal's position are close to Husserl and the Neo-Kantians,[34] even though Maréchal does differ from them and Kant insofar as he attempts to deduce from the universal validity of man's judgment an ontological and metaphysical significance in a strict sense. Karl Rahner, on the other hand, differs quite distinctly from Husserl and the Neo-Kantians because he has assimilated Heidegger's critique of their position.[35] Rahner does not attempt, as does Maréchal,[36] to establish the metaphysical significance of the judgment primarily as a *result* of a transcendental reduction or deduction, but applies Heidegger's insights concerning the circular structure of human knowledge. Man's question concerning being presupposes a knowledge of being and reveals the nature of man

[33] It should be noted that although both Rahner and Heidegger stress judgment as affirmation, Heidegger attempts to depart from the traditional understanding of truth expressed by the statement *veritas est adaequatio rei et intellectus,* and to develop an understanding of truth as unconcealment.

[34] Holz, *op. cit.,* gives excellent comparisons in this regard.

[35] The best presentation of Heidegger's thought, which not only gives a complete survey of this thought but also notes these differences, is O. Pöggeler, *Der Denkweg Martin Heideggers,* Pfullingen, 1963. E. Tugendhat, *Der Wahrheitbegriff bei Husserl und Heidegger,* Berlin, 1967, gives extensive treatment to the differences between Heidegger and Husserl in regard to the important question of the nature of truth. English-language publications, such as T. Langan, *The Meaning of Heidegger,* New York, 1959, unfortunately see Heidegger as an existentialist, or as purely interested in anthropological structures. Through an exhaustive presentation of Heidegger's publications, W. Richardson, in *Heidegger, Through Phenomenology to Thought,* has rejected this position. *Spirit in the World* shows how well Rahner understood the "early Heidegger" insofar as he realized that the latter's central purpose was the question of the meaning of being. Rahner's correct understanding avoids Balthasar's criticism of an "anthropological reduction."

[36] Cf. Muck, *op. cit.,* pp. 200 and 205 for the differences between Rahner and Maréchal. Note the differences between Lotz and Maréchal with regard to judgment (pp. 195–197).

as a finite being who questions about being.[37] What is the ontological possibility and ground of this questioning? It consists for Rahner in an *a priori* knowledge of being because the human intellect cannot inquire about that which is absolutely unknown and completely unknowable.[38] On the basis of these analyses he therefore clearly rejects the notion that being is unknowable and unknown (see p. 68) and affirms the primary unity and convertibility of being and knowledge. The further analysis of this unity as the possibility and basis of man's inquiry concerning being indicates the important and precise differences between Rahner and the Idealists. If a question is only possible because man is already present to the goal of his question, then why does he question? The answer to this problem is Rahner's rejection of Idealism. Man's inquiry after being indicates that man's "presence to" or "possession of" being is not absolute but finite. The very inquiry after being indicates man's "presence in being" and the finitude of his "presence" (see p. 71). Rahner completes these analyses through a description of sensibility and its importance for the knowledge of the other as other and in its dialectical unity with man's reason.

The difference with Kant is further developed in Rahner's treatment of the intellect's pre-apprehension (*Vorgriff*) within a context of his theory on the ontological significance of the judgment. These analyses form the central argument of *Spirit in the World* and constitute Rahner's explication of his starting point, namely, that the question concerning being pre-

[37] The idea that Kant is wrong to set the limits of human reason because in order to set limits one must be able to go beyond the limits, is common to Hegel's and Maréchal's critiques of Kant. Cf. the excellent comparison between Hegel, Maréchal, and Heidegger on this point by A. Chapelle, *Hegel et la religion*, Paris, 1963, pp. 187–189, n. 67.

[38] Whereas Heidegger considers transcendence to be finite, Rahner considers it to be infinite. It is questionable whether the circular structure of understanding also applies to transcendence as infinite, since it is not a question of knowing transcendence but a question of the legitimacy of the hypostasization of transcendence to an absolutely necessary transcendence.

supposes a knowledge of being. He now attempts to demonstrate that the intellect's pre-apprehension of being *(esse)* is a necessary presupposition for the objectivity of human knowledge in general. The role of this anticipation within the context of an affirmative judgment and the *conversio intellectus* insure that this objectivity of human knowledge is not merely regulative and logical, but constitutive and ontological. The metaphysical significance of this pre-apprehension of *esse* is therefore affirmed by Rahner because of its necessity for human knowledge. The difference between Rahner and Kant is thus quite evident. It can easily be ascertained in every chapter of the present book.

3. *The Significance of the Differences between Rahner and Kant*

The significance of the differences between Rahner and Kant leads to the question of the positive aspects of his dialogue with Kant. How and where does Rahner assimilate Kant's philosophy? The fruitful reception of Kant is indicated by Rahner's assumption of Kant's basic question: How is metaphysics possible if all human knowledge is necessarily referred to a sensible intuition? Rahner's answer to this question departs from the traditional scholastic and philosophical positions and offers a transcendental understanding of being. Since he is aware that all human knowledge is related to sense intuitions, he rejects those philosophical positions which maintain that a metaphysics of transcendence is possible because of a special innate idea or because of a specific and immediate intuition of a metaphysical object,[39] be it an eternal truth or an objectively conceived absolute being. He denies explicitly that the absolute is known as some object or that the human mind could form an adequate objective concept of God. Instead he

[39] Rahner is very insistent in his rejection of a metaphysical intuition. This rejection is his major correction of the Thomistic or neo-scholastic interpretations.

proposes a transcendental understanding of God, who is not known by man as an object of reality, but as the principle of human knowledge and reality. This fundamentally non-objective transcendental knowledge of God as the principle of knowledge and reality is central to Rahner's whole theology. It forms the background for his understanding of God's presence to man in grace and revelation, of the ontological and psychological unity of Christ. Rahner's discussions on the development of dogma, the anonymous Christian, the human knowledge of Christ, and on many other themes must be seen within this context.[40] This transcendental orientation of man to God is the unifying principle of Rahner's theology. It is the result of his fruitful and serious dialogue with the philosopher par excellence of modern times, Immanuel Kant. Still, it is not the end but only the beginning of a dialogue with modern philosophy.

Rahner has continued this dialogue insofar as he has used the insights of modern existential philosophy to explain this transcendental orientation to God in terms of a "supernatural existential." Man's relation to God is not an abstract or "natural" openness to God, but is the result of God's historical calling of man to himself in Christ and thereby constituting the historical nature of man. The fullness of human nature therefore culminates not extrinsically, but intrinsically in Christ. Rahner's anthropology is thus not a pure philosophical or transcendental anthropology, but is an anthropology only in relation to God's revelation in Christ.

At this point a basic difference between Rahner and other students of Maréchal becomes evident. Whereas most of Maréchal's followers have carried on their dialogue within the discipline of philosophy, Rahner has seen that a philosophical and existential theology is the only adequate horizon for a dialogue with modern philosophies and their emphasis on the dimension of history. Whereas Lonergan rejects phenomenol-

[40] For a good presentation of all of Rahner's theology, refer to D. Gelpi, *Life and Light: A Guide to the Theology of Karl Rahner,* New York, 1966.

ogy and existentialism as merely descriptive and as a purified empiricism,[41] Rahner stresses, in *Hearers of the Word* (and in all his theological writings), the ontological and theological relevance of the problems of historicity and "facticity." It is, therefore, not accidental that Rahner has not left the philosophical principles of *Spirit in the World* in their formal outlines and abstract structures, but has developed and applied them to innumerable concrete and practical problems of theology and life.

In an important, recently discovered manuscript (1965)[42] written by Kant at the end of his life, Kant explains his ideas on the concept of philosophy and reacts to some of the opinions of his students (especially Fichte). Kant emphasized that philosophy is not a scientific or mystic subject, but a teaching of practice and wisdom. Rahner's theology is the synthesis of these elements. Whereas Kant rejected the theoretical knowledge of God for a practical postulate of God, Rahner has attempted to show the relevance of a theoretical theology for pastoral theology and the practical life of the Church. This synthesis is the wisdom of Karl Rahner's theology and its source is *Spirit in the World*.

[41] Lonergan, *Insight*, p. 415. Lonergan's critique only applies to Husserl before 1913, when he conceived of philosophy in a more ontological manner. Cf. Henrich, "Ueber die Grundlagen von Husserls Kritik der philosophischen Tradition," in *Philosophische Rundschau* 6 (1958), pp. 1–26, esp. p. 2; Tugendhat, *op. cit.*, pp. 169–255. His critique of existentialism does not apply to Heidegger; it may apply to others.

[42] Cf. Henrich, "Zu Kants Begriff de Philosophie. Eine Edition und eine Fragestellung," in *Kritik und Metaphysik. Heinz Heimsoeth zum achtzigsten Geburtstag*, Berlin, 1966, pp. 40–59. Henrich has done an excellent service to Kantian scholarship by his discovery of the text and his careful edition and commentary.

Preface to the Second German Edition

THE title of this work indicates its subject matter adequately enough for the time being. The Introduction will describe the essential features of its method of investigation. References to works on Thomistic philosophy beyond those actually given did not seem appropriate since the scope of the work precluded a more thorough discussion with them, and I do not know of any works beyond those mentioned which I could have cited in complete agreement. If Pierre Rousselot and Joseph Maréchal are mentioned more than others, this should emphasize that I feel the work particularly indebted to the spirit of their interpretation of Thomas. The third part of the work remained a mere sketch of what was originally planned. What I tried to do above all else was this: to get away from so much that is called "neo-Scholasticism" and to return to Thomas himself, and by doing this to move closer to those questions which are being posed to contemporary philosophy.

The original work was finished in May, 1936, and the first edition published in 1939 by Rauch in Innsbruck. Despite all the friendly and favorable attention given it, it fell out of sight rather quickly, and perhaps somewhat undeservedly, because of the disturbances of the war. However, since it was quite soon out of print, a new edition did not seem out of place. But the second edition was not intended to be a new book: my fundamental conception has remained completely unchanged, nor do my duties allow me the time to rework the theme of the book critically as a whole or to carry it further in any fundamental way. So I merely intended to comply with the quite representative wishes for a new edition.

For this 1957 edition I am greatly indebted to my student, Dr. Johannes B. Metz, to whom I entrusted its preparation. He has gone over the text as a whole, reworking it in some instances (see Part II, Chapter 1) and expanding and supplementing it here and there by small additions to the text. He translated the Latin text upon which the work is based into German, broke most chapters down into smaller sections with subtitles, and above all, in a few sections of the text and especially in the footnotes, confronted the teaching of the book with the most important reviews of the first edition and with other works on the Thomistic metaphysics of knowledge which have appeared since 1939 and treated the thesis of this book explicitly. Hence whatever distinguishes the second from the first edition is due to Dr. Metz. Since I am in complete agreement with the results of the generous, intelligent, and penetrating work he has done on my book, it seemed superfluous to single out in particular these additions to and improvements on the text.

KARL RAHNER

Author's Introduction

THIS work intends to present one part of the Thomistic metaphysics of knowledge. If this purpose is to be understood, I must clarify in an introductory way the subject to be investigated and the way it is to be treated. Since subject and method are mutually dependent on each other, they cannot be treated separately in these introductory remarks.

By the Thomistic metaphysics of knowledge we mean the teaching of Thomas Aquinas himself. We presume the right, therefore, to try to understand him from his own writings, without appealing to his commentators and the testimony of his school, and without going into the historical origins of his doctrine.

However much this inquiry into the teaching of Thomas is a historical investigation, it is also meant to be philosophical. Our concern, then, is not with the Thomas who was conditioned by his times and dependent on Aristotle, Augustine, and the philosophy of his day. There is also such a Thomas, and we could conduct a historical investigation about him. Whether or not we are correct in doubting that such an approach could get to the really *philosophical* in Thomas, the primary concern of this historical work is not to be "history," but philosophy itself. And if what matters is to grasp the really philosophical in a philosopher, this can only be done if one joins him in looking at the matter itself. It is only then that you can understand what he means.

So our procedure here cannot be that of gathering together everything and anything that Thomas ever said, as though all were of equal weight, and organizing it according to some extrinsic principle. Such an approach cannot get back to the original philosophical event in Thomas. Rather what we must try to do is grasp his philosophy anew as it unfolds from its first and often hardly expressed starting point. Even a historical presentation of a philosophy, if it is really to get to the philosophy, cannot be merely an extrinsically organized enumeration of philosophical statements. It must relive the philosophy itself as it unfolds. But that is possible only if one takes a definite starting point and abandons himself to the dynamism of the matter itself, and in doing so, of course, constantly checks the progress of this development against the explicit statements of the philosopher whose doctrine is in question. This is all the more necessary with Thomas because he himself nowhere presents even a larger part of his philosophy in its inner development; he has not written a single sizable work embodying a systematic philosophical development. Hence the living philosophy out of which he wrote his theology was never articulated in its unity and development in any immediately and historically accessible form, but remained hidden in the silence of his thought.

If it is absolutely necessary, then, to begin with the starting point given by Thomas and to abandon one's self again and again to the dynamism of the matter itself so that the historically accessible fragments of his philosophy can really become philosophy, it is naturally inevitable that such starting points given by Thomas will be pushed further by one's own thought. So it cannot be demanded of this work that every one of its statements be verified by a citation from Thomas. The result of the method we are using no longer has the right to be called a historical presentation of Thomistic philosophy only when the progress of our own philosophizing is no longer able to verify itself by a constant appeal to lines of thought that are immediately ascertainable in Thomas.

It is only by such a method that we have a guide and a norm provided by this philosophy itself against which the historically accessible development of this metaphysics can be checked, and

1

its individual propositions weighed in their relative significance. It is only by such a method that the eternal in a philosophy can be salvaged from the irrelevance of what merely has been.

The author is aware that such a method, however necessary, inevitably has its dangers. But the reader, should his primary concern be the "historical," always has the opportunity, in fact provided by the work itself, to distinguish what Thomas explicitly said, what the precise nuances of his own explicit formulations are, and where the author under the thrust of the objective inquiry itself is seeking more or less "meta-historical" connections between the individual lines of thought which appear explicitly in Thomas. At least the author has tried honestly to keep this distinction in mind himself. Before the reader declares such connections un-Thomistic, perhaps because he is not used to them, let him ask himself if he knows of an interpretation of what appears explicitly in Thomas which provides not just a vague notion bogged down in images, but rather a really *philosophical* conception. The author adheres to the heuristic principle that when dealing with a great philosopher, which Thomas undoubtedly was, a really *philosophical* sense is to be found in his statements (which of course does not necessarily mean an objectively correct sense), and that when this attempt does not succeed, the presumption is that the interpreter has failed, not that the philosopher himself in such statements is making presuppositions which are to be explained *only* "historically" as uncritical borrowing from earlier philosophy, from medieval physics and so forth.

A work that is historical in this sense, a work which does not merely want to "narrate" what Thomas said, but tries to relive the philosophical event itself in Thomas, is naturally more dependent on what its author himself was able to understand of metaphysics than a "strictly" historical work would be. Not as though it were a question here of the author's own view, as though consciously or unconsciously he wanted to read his own opinions into Thomas. But he does not think that the danger of this is greater for him than for anyone else, because for him Thomas is not a master who forbids his students to disagree

li

with him. However, the direction of the *questions* which are posed to Thomas are given in advance by a *systematic* concern of the author, especially when these questions are trying to drive the finished propositions in Thomas back to their objective problematic.

Such an objective concern, which the author here explicitly acknowledges, is (or certainly should be) conditioned by the problematic of *today's* philosophy. If in this sense the reader gets the impression that an interpretation of St. Thomas is at work here which has its origin in modern philosophy, the author does not consider that such a criticism points to a defect, but rather to a merit of the book. And this because he would not know of any other reason for which he could be occupied with Thomas than for the sake of those questions which stimulate *his* philosophy and that of his time. Anyone who is convinced of the sway of a *philosophia perennis* at least in the great philosophers cannot reject, at least not *a priori,* the posing of modern questions in a historical work on the ground that such a procedure is not objective. The author knows that with such a method there can be question at first only of an attempt, of an attempt which at least in the new formulations, which are determined precisely by the new questions asked, departs from the traditional expression of Thomas's thought. Nevertheless, the author hopes that with this work, which is intended to be nothing more than an attempt, he will receive the favor of a judgment which shares the objective concerns of contemporary philosophy and which joins Thomas in looking first at the matter itself, and only then at the formulation which it found in Thomas.

The limited scope of this work did not permit an *explicit,* detailed confrontation of modern philosophy from Kant to Heidegger with Thomas, nor did it appeal to me to try to make the relevance of the problems treated in the book more apparent by a few timely indications of such parallels. I hope, then, that those who are familiar with more recent philosophy will take note of these points of contact themselves. For scholastic readers, who are perhaps in danger of taking exception to some

Kantian-sounding expressions in the book, let it be said here explicitly that the concern of the book is not the critique of knowledge, but the metaphysics of knowledge, and that, therefore, as opposed to Kant, there is always question of a noetic hylomorphism, to which there corresponds an *ontological* hylomorphism in the objects, in the sense of a thoroughgoing determination of knowing by being.

The present work is entitled *Spirit in the World.* By spirit I mean a power which reaches out beyond the world and knows the metaphysical. World is the name of the reality which is accessible to the immediate experience of man. How, according to Thomas, human knowing can be spirit in the world is the question which is the concern of this work. The proposition that human knowing is first of all in the world of experience and that everything metaphysical is known only in and *at* the world is expressed by Thomas in his doctrine of the *conversio* and of the intellect's being constantly turned to the phenomenon, the doctrine of the "conversion of the intellect to the phantasm." For this reason the work could have been entitled, *Conversion to the Phantasm.*

Thus the work selects a theme from the center of the Thomistic metaphysics of knowledge. From the "center" in both of the senses which this word has: the theme is taken from out of the middle of the whole metaphysics. Hence it already presupposes in a sense the first starting points out of which the Thomistic metaphysics of knowledge as a whole developed, and is thus a part of this metaphysics which comes only after many others. But it is also its center in the sense that in this theme the plurality of the Thomistic statements about the essence of human knowledge converge again into their original unity.

There follows from this at least a tentative justification of this theme, and at the same time its intrinsic difficulty. Its justification, because the theme forces one to try to grasp the whole of the Thomistic understanding of human knowing, for conversion to the phantasm is the key Thomistic term designating the unity of all man's cognitive powers in the act of knowing. Ultimately, therefore, it also designates the original unity of the one human knowing. Its difficulty, inasmuch as the theme, precisely this unity, forces one again and again to speak of something other than this unity, namely, of the plurality of the cognitive powers which are first to be united in the conversion to the phantasm. If the theme, then, in spite of its partial nature, forces us to consider the whole Thomistic metaphysics of knowledge and all its parts, nevertheless, since our theme intends to present only one section of this metaphysics, we can look to the whole only to the extent that it is absolutely necessary for clarifying questions and their attempted solutions at least to some extent.

For the reasons indicated, a completely satisfactory treatment of our question would be possible only if we made our theme the whole of Thomistic metaphysics as such. Right at the beginning, then, let us call attention to the fact that this book continually comes up against questions which it can treat only partially or even not at all. For example, the question of the Thomistic *esse*-concept is only just touched on, many problems about the essence of sensibility, about the first principles and so forth are treated but not settled. Other questions, such as that of the *species expressa,* the *verbum mentis,* the resolution of knowledge (into the first principles as well as into the *sensibilia*), the analogy of being, the unity of apperception and so forth are not mentioned at all, although they are of importance for any final understanding of the questions to be treated here.[1]

[1] For this reason, references are given in this connection to a few more recent works relevant to this Thomistic problematic beyond those cited in the text itself: C. Fabro, *La nozione metafisica di partecipazione secondo S. Tommaso d'Aquino* (Turin, 1950); J. de Finance, *Être et agir dans la philosophie de Saint Thomas* (Paris, 1945); E. Gilson, *L'être et l'essence* (Paris, 1948); J. B. Lotz, *Sein und Wert, I: Das Seiende und das Sein* (Paderborn, 1938); M. Müller, *Sein und Geist* (Tübingen, 1940); L. Oening-Hanhoff, *Ens et unum convertuntur, Beitr. z. Gesch. d. Phil. u. Theol. d. Mittelalt.* XXXVII, 3 (Münster, 1953); J. Pieper, *Wahrheit der Dinge* (München, 1947); E. Przywara, *Analogia Entis I* (München, 1932); G. Siewerth, *Der Thomismus als Identitätssystem* (Frankfurt, 1939), and *Die Apriorität der menschlichen Erkenntnis nach Thomas von Aquin: Symposion I,* pp. 89–167 (1948; also published separately), and *Thomas von Aquin: Die menschliche*

The work begins by first trying to grasp its theme as a whole. So the first section is an interpretation of an "Article" from the *Summa Theologiae,* in which Thomas himself treats the conversion to the phantasm as a whole. From this first overall view there should follow the direction our questions are to take, and in pursuing these the sense of the conversion to the phantasm should be further clarified. The second section tries to develop systematically the questions found to belong intrinsically to the problem of the conversion to the phantasm as they are treated by Thomas. From the insight thus gained into a partial question of Thomistic metaphysics, the third part tries to take a brief look at the whole of this metaphysics by asking about its possibility and its limits.

In most cases limitations of space did not permit giving the Thomistic texts to which references are made. Unfortunately, this has the unavoidable disadvantage that the reader who is working through the book carefully must now and then read through a rather lengthy text in Thomas himself to find the only sentence that the context is concerned with. By citing the numbers of the Marietti Edition (so far as they are available), or at least the pages in the Parma Edition, I tried as far as possible to minimize this disadvantage for the long texts taken from the *Commentary on Aristotle.*

Willensfreiheit (Düsseldorf, 1954); G. Söhngen, *Sein und Gegenstand* (Münster, 1930); B. Welte, *Der philosophische Glaube bei Karl Jaspers und die Möglichkeit seiner Deutung durch die thomistische Philosophie: Symposion* 2, pp. 1–190; (1949; also published separately). The author himself has published a smaller work on the concept of truth in Thomas: "A Verdade em S. Tomáso de Aquino" in *Revista Portuguesa de Filosofia* 7 (1951), pp. 353–370. English translation in *Continuum,* Vol. II, n. 1 (Spring, 1964), pp. 60–72.

SUMMA THEOLOGIAE I
QUESTION 84, ARTICLE 7

I. THE TITLE OF THE ARTICLE

Utrum intellectus possit actu intelligere per species intelligibiles quas penes se habet, non convertendo se ad phantasmata.

II. THE VIDETUR QUOD NON

AD SEPTIMUM SIC PROCEDITUR

1. Videtur quod intellectus possit actu intelligere per species intelligibiles quas penes se habet, non convertendo se ad phantasmata:

Intellectus enim fit in actu per speciem intelligibilem, qua informatur. Sed intellectum esse in actu, est ipsum intelligere.

Ergo species intelligibiles sufficiunt ad hoc quod intellectus actu intelligat, absque hoc quod ad phantasmata se convertat.

2. Praeterea, magis dependet imaginatio a sensu, quam intellectus ab imaginatione.

Sed imaginatio potest imaginari actu, absentibus sensibilibus.

I. THE TITLE OF THE ARTICLE*

Can the intellect actually know anything through the intelligible species which it possesses, without turning to the phantasms?

II. THE OBJECTIONS

1. It seems that the intellect can actually know something through the intelligible species which it possesses, without turning to the phantasms:

For the intellect comes to its actualization through the intelligible species by which it is informed. But simply by the fact that the intellect comes to its actualization, it already knows.

Therefore, the intelligible species suffice for the intellect to know something actually, and in doing so it does not have to turn to the phantasms.

2. Further, the imagination is more dependent on external sensation than the intellect on the imagination.

But the imagination can actually imagine without the sensible object being given.

* The arrangement of the text and the title are taken over from the interpretation of the Article in this work.

The translation purposely retains the Latin expression for certain concepts which could easily be misunderstood in translation. Other divergent formulations which try to preserve or to indicate the content of the philosophical expression in the translation are justified by the interpretation which follows. (For this reason, the English is based on the German translation referred to here. The term "non-worldly" [nicht-welthaft] which appears in the German, but not in the Latin original, is used in the sense explained in the Introduction. —Tr.)

3

Ergo multo magis intellectus potest intelligere actu, non convertendo se ad phantasmata.

3. Praeterea, incorporalium non sunt aliqua phantasmata; quia imaginatio tempus et continuum non transcendit.

Si ergo intellectus noster non posset aliquid intelligere in actu nisi converteretur ad phantasmata, sequeretur quod non posset intelligere incorporeum aliquid.

Quod patet esse falsum; intelligimus enim veritatem ipsam, et Deum et angelos.

III. THE SED CONTRA

Sed contra est quod Philosophus dicit, in III de Anima, quod "nihil sine phantasmate intelligit anima."

IV. THE CORPUS ARTICULI

1. The Thesis (*Respondeo Dicendum*)

Respondeo dicendum quod impossibile est intellectum nostrum, secundum praesentis vitae statum, quo passibili corpori conjungitur, aliquid intelligere in actu, nisi convertendo se ad phantasmata.

2. The Indicia of the Conversio

ET HOC DUOBUS INDICIIS APPARET

Primo quidem quia, cum intellectus sit vis quaedam non utens corporali organo, nullo modo impediretur in suo actu per laesionem alicuius corporalis organi, si non requireretur ad eius actum actus alicuius potentiae utentis organo corporali. Utuntur autem organo corporali sensus et imaginatio et aliae vires pertinentes ad partem sensitivam. Unde manifestum est, quod ad hoc quod intellectus actu intelligat, non solum accipiendo scientiam

4

Therefore, much more can the intellect actually know something without turning to the phantasms.

3. Finally, there are no phantasms of incorporeal (non-worldly) things, for the imagination does not transcend the horizon of space and time.

If, therefore, our intellect could actually know something only by turning to the phantasms, it would follow that it could not know anything incorporeal (non-worldly).

But that is obviously false, for we (also) know truth itself, as well as God and the angels.

III. THE COUNTER-OBJECTION

On the contrary, the Philosopher says (III *De Anima,* c. 7): "The soul does not know anything without a phantasm."

IV. THE SOLUTION

1. The Thesis

It is impossible for our intellect in the present state of life, in which it is united with receptive corporeality, to know anything actually without turning to the phantasms.

2. Indications of the Conversio

AND TWO INDICATIONS BRING THIS TO LIGHT

First: The intellect is an operative power which does not make use of a corporeal organ. Wherefore, it would in no way be affected in its operation by an injury to a corporeal organ, unless it required for its actualization the operation of a power which does make use of a corporeal organ. But the external senses, the imagination and the other operative powers belonging to the sensitive part of the soul make use of (such) a

5

de novo, sed etiam utendo scientia iam acquisita, requiritur actus imaginationis et ceterarum virtutum. Videmus enim quod, impedito actu virtutis imaginativae per laesionem organi, ut in phreneticis, et similiter impedito actu memorativae virtutis, ut in lethargicis, impeditur homo ab intelligendo in actu etiam ea quorum scientiam praeaccepit.

Secundo, quia hoc quilibet in seipso experiri potest, quod quando aliquis conatur aliquid intelligere, format aliqua phantasmata sibi per modum exemplorum, in quibus quasi inspiciat quod intelligere studet. Et inde est etiam quod quando aliquem volumus facere aliquid intelligere, proponimus ei exempla, ex quibus sibi phantasmata formare possit ad intelligendum.

3. The Metaphysics of the Conversio

KNOWING AND BEING

Huius autem ratio est, quia potentia cognoscitiva proportionatur cognoscibili. Unde intellectus angelici, qui est totaliter a corpore separatus, objectum proprium est substantia intelligibilis a corpore separata; et per huiusmodi intelligibilia materialia cognoscit.

HUMAN KNOWING AND HUMAN BEING

Intellectus autem humani, qui est conjunctus corpori, proprium objectum est quidditas sive natura in materia corporali existens; et per huiusmodi naturas visibilium rerum etiam in invisibilium rerum aliqualem cognitionem ascendit.

6

corporeal organ. Hence it is clear that the operation of the imagination and the other (sensible) operative powers is required for the actualization of the intellect; and this not only when there is question (in this actualization of the intellect) of acquiring new knowledge, but also when it is a question of using knowledge already acquired. For we see that when the operation of the imagination is impeded by an injury to a corporeal organ—as in the case of the insane—or the operation of the memory—as in the case of the senile—, then man cannot actually think even that which he had acquired knowledge of formerly.

Secondly: Anyone can experience this in himself, that when he tries to understand anything, he forms phantasms to serve him by way of examples, in order, as it were, to acquire in them the intuition for what he is trying to understand. It is for this reason also that when we want to help someone understand something, we propose examples to him, so that from them he can form phantasms for his thought.

3. The Metaphysics of the Conversio

KNOWING AND BEING

The reason for this is that an intrinsic homogeneity with its own proper object is characteristic of every cognitive power. Wherefore, the object of knowledge which belongs properly to the angelic intellect, which is completely separated from corporeality, is the incorporeal, intelligible substance, by means of which intelligibility it (also) knows the material world.

HUMAN KNOWING AND HUMAN BEING

However, the object which belongs properly to the intellect of man, who exists in corporeality, is the quiddity or the nature of corporeal things (things of the world). And through this nature of sensible things he also reaches out to some knowledge of non-sensible things.

7

THE BEING OF THE WORLD

De ratione autem huius naturae est, quod in aliquo individuo existat, quod non est absque materia corporali: sicut de ratione naturae lapidis est quod sit in hoc lapide; et de ratione naturae equi quod sit in hoc equo, et sic de aliis. Unde natura lapidis vel cuiuscumque materialis rei cognosci non potest complete et vere, nisi secundum quod cognoscitur ut in particulari existens.

HUMAN KNOWLEDGE OF THE BEING OF THE WORLD

Intuition

Particulare autem apprehendimus per sensum et imaginationem.

Thought

Et ideo necesse est ad hoc quod intellectus actu intelligat suum objectum proprium, quod convertat se ad phantasmata, ut speculetur naturam universalem in particulari existentem.

REPETITION OF THE WHOLE
IN A CRITICAL REVIEW OF THE OPPOSITE POSITION

Si autem proprium objectum intellectus nostri esset forma separata; vel si naturae rerum sensibilium subsisterent non in particularibus, secundum Platonicos, non oporteret quod intellectus noster semper intelligendo converteret se ad phantasmata.

V. THE ANSWERS TO THE OBJECTIONS

Ad primum ergo dicendum quod species conservatae in intellectu possibili, in eo existunt habitualiter, quando actu non intelligit, sicut supra dictum est. Unde ad hoc quod intelligamus in actu, non sufficit ipsa conservatio specierum; sed oportet

8

THE BEING OF THE WORLD

But it belongs to the essence of this nature that it exist in a material individual. Thus it is essential to the nature of a stone that it exist in this stone, essential to the nature of a horse that it exist in this horse, and so forth. Wherefore, the nature of a stone or of any material thing can also be known completely and truly only inasmuch as it is known as existing in the individual thing.

HUMAN KNOWLEDGE OF THE BEING OF THE WORLD

Intuition (*Anschauung*)

However, we apprehend the individual thing through external sensation and through the imagination.

Thought (*Denken*)

Therefore, for the actual knowledge of the object which belongs properly to it the intellect must turn to the phantasms, in order (thus) to look at the universal essence as existing in the individual thing.

REPETITION OF THE WHOLE
IN A CRITICAL REVIEW OF THE OPPOSITE POSITION

But if the object which belongs properly to our intellect were a separated, essential form, or if, as the Platonists assume, the nature of sensible things did not subsist in individual things: then our intellect would not always have to turn to the phantasms when it knows.

V. THE ANSWERS TO THE OBJECTIONS

To 1. When the possible intellect is not actually knowing, the species are (only) habitually preserved in it, as was said above.

9

quod eis utamur secundum quod convenit rebus quarum sunt species, quae sunt naturae in particularibus existentes.

Ad secundum dicendum quod etiam ipsum phantasma est similitudo rei particularis; unde non indiget imaginatio aliqua alia similitudine particularis, sicut indiget intellectus.

Ad tertium dicendum quod incorporea, quorum non sunt phantasmata, cognoscuntur a nobis per comparationem ad corpora sensibilia, quorum sunt phantasmata. Sicut veritatem intelligimus ex consideratione rei circa quam veritatem speculamur. Deum autem, ut Dionysius dicit, cognoscimus ut causam, et per excessum et per remotionem. Alias etiam incorporeas substantias, in statu praesentis vitae, cognoscere non possumus nisi per remotionem vel aliquam comparationem ad corporalia. Et ideo cum de huiusmodi aliquid intelligimus, necesse habemus converti ad phantasmata corporum, licet ipsorum non sint phantasmata.

Wherefore, the mere preservation of the species does not suffice for our actual knowledge. Rather we must use them in a way which corresponds to the things of which they are the species, that is, the natures existing in individual things.

To 2. The phantasm itself is already a likeness of the individual thing; wherefore, the imagination does not need another likeness of the individual, as is the case with the intellect.

To 3. We know the incorporeal (non-worldly), of which there are no phantasms, through a comparison with the sensible, corporeal world of which there are phantasms. Thus we know what truth is by considering the thing about which we perceive a truth. But according to Dionysius, we know God as cause both by way of eminence and by way of negation. And in our present state of life we can also know the other incorporeal (non-worldly) substances only by way of (such) a negation or by some comparison with the corporeal world. Therefore, when we want to know something of this kind (non-worldly), we must turn to the phantasms of the corporeal world, although there are no phantasms of the thing itself.

PART ONE

INTRODUCTORY INTERPRETATION
OF SUMMA THEOLOGIAE I, QUESTION 84,
ARTICLE 7

I. THE ARTICLE IN THE CONTEXT OF THE *SUMMA THEOLOGIAE*

THE Article which is to form the foundation of this work is part of a theological *Summa*, and so stands in the place assigned to it by a theological systematic. If in a philosophical systematic man is the first word, while God as the Absolute is the last word (even if the first was spoken with a view to the last), in a theological *Summa*, the absolute God in His unrelatedness to the world is the first word, and man is the last. Hence, the question about man stands in the context of questions about *created* being.[1]

The question, What is man?, refers first of all, therefore, to the essence of the "soul." Hence this question does not proceed from the multiplicity of things which man knows or presumes to know about himself back to the single ground from which this fund of knowledge about man receives sense and meaning, but rather arises at that point which is the boundary between the Absolute and man, at his essence, and this in order to re-enact the unfolding of this essence into its "powers" and "activities" from out of their ground. In this context the "soul" as the essential ground of man is considered ultimately only insofar as it is the place for a *theological* event, insofar as it can be addressed by a revelation.

The essence of man is not completely itself until he acts. Hence it is only in action that it becomes manifest what man is;

---

[1] See, for example, *Summa Theologiae* I, q. 84, Introduction: . . . *non pertinent directe ad considerationem theologi.* I, q. 75, Introduction: . . . *post considerationem creaturae spiritualis et corporalis.* I, q. 50, Introduction: *De distinctione corporalis et spiritualis creaturae.* . . . ; I, q. 45, Introduction: . . . creatio . . . ; I, q. 44: *De processione creaturarum* . . .

15

until then his essence, which was the initial object of the inquiry, does not manifest itself. Of all the "activities" of man the first part of the *Summa* speaks only of human intellectual knowing; human desire is referred to the second part of the *Summa,* and the other activities are of no immediate concern to the theologians.

The Questions which treat of human knowing are divided first of all according to an apparently extrinsic scheme: knowledge of the corporeal, knowledge of the knowing soul itself, and knowledge of the real, spiritual realities beyond the soul. But a deeper systematic reveals itself in this extrinsic scheme, and Thomas was aware of it. If for the Thomistic metaphysics of knowledge material things are the proper object of specifically human knowledge (the sense and the scope of this statement will occupy us further), then it necessarily follows that these three areas of human knowledge are not simply regions situated side by side within the realm which lies open to human knowing, all of them equally accessible. Knowledge of the knowing subject and of the Absolute are, therefore, dependent on knowledge of the essence of material things; the possibility of the former must be understood from that of the latter. Thus the Questions which treat of the "knowledge of the corporeal" assume the decisive role in determining the Thomistic conception of any human knowing at all. Questions 84 to 86 are the core of the metaphysics of knowledge in the *Summa.*

The Article we are setting out to interpret is situated within this section of three Questions about the knowledge of material things. The inner structure of these three Questions themselves and their mutual relationship are not of such transparency and intrinsic necessity that it would be worthwhile at this point to ask further about some such intrinsic necessity which perhaps is there and is the reason why the Article to be interpreted is in the precise place it actually is.[2] It is sufficient,

---

[2] Just as q. 85, a. 1 (*utrum intellectus noster intelligat res corporales et materiales per abstractionem a phantasmatibus*) is closely related in content to q. 84, a. 6 (*utrum intellectiva cognitio accipitur a rebus*

therefore, to have established rather the general context within which the question of this Article stands: it is part of the question about the human knowledge of "world"[3] as that knowledge which opens up the possibility of any and all human knowing and establishes its limits. Therefore, every partial question within these three Questions, including our Article, must necessarily take into account from the outset three things as a guide for the interpretation of its problematic: (1) it must be dealing with intellectual knowledge, because for Thomas the theologian this is the point of insertion for a theological event; (2) it must be dealing with knowledge of world as the fundamental human knowledge, and the possibility of such knowledge must be grasped; (3) in and through the knowledge of world there must open up the possibility of an access to a "beyond the world."

Thus this tentative approach towards an understanding of the Article we are to interpret is provided just by its position in the *Summa* as a whole. Actually it would now be possible to go further and pose the question of our Article just by unfolding the content that is immanent in this threefold norm. But since the text of the Article itself constantly refers back to this more general problematic, let it suffice at this point to give this general outline of the context which governs these three Questions, including the seventh Article of Question 84. It gives us the opportunity for an immediate and tentative interpretation of the Article. It nowhere intends to spare the reader the trouble of reading the Article itself.

sensibilibus), so it would also make sense to put q. 84, a. 7 after q. 85, a. 1.

[3] It must follow from the whole work that this expression is not a misleading and unjustified modernization of the Thomistic terms, *corporalia, materialia*, etc. Should anyone understand "material" and "corporeal things" in the sense of modern science by these Thomistic terms when literally translated, he would be in greater danger of misunderstanding the sense of the *cognitio corporalium* than is the case with our "knowledge of world."

17

II. THE TITLE OF THE ARTICLE

CAN the intellect actually know anything through the intelligible species which it possesses, without turning to the phantasm? This question forms the title of the seventh Article of Question 84 in the first part of the *Summa Theologiae.* Although the more exact sense of this question cannot be understood until it has been answered, nevertheless the direction which the development of thought takes in the immediately preceding Article of the same Question makes it possible for us to give a tentative explanation of its sense. The first Article of Question 84 begins with the apparently quite peripheral and inconsequential question, whether man can know corporeal things intellectually. It appears to be asking a peripheral question because it seems to presuppose that one already knows what intellectual knowing is, so that it is only dealing with the subsequent, harmless question, what one can do in particular with this intellect and its knowing now that its essence has already been established. Understood in this way it also seems to be inconsequential: however the intellect stands in relation to knowledge of the world, the answer to this question does not contain in itself any antecedent norm for deciding the question about its knowing those of its objects which do not belong to this material world. Actually, however, something else was at issue in the Articles which preceded Article 7. The meaning and the possibility of intellectual, in fact of any human knowing at all, was in question, and it is precisely this question which does not reach its decisive climax until Article 7.

In fact, in the first Article a prior option has already been decided before Thomas proceeds to raise any thematic questions: man is in possession of an "immaterial, universal, and necessary knowledge." This is the first great starting point which Thomas posits along with every great philosophy from that of the Greeks until Hegel:[1] absolute knowledge is a reality in man; it is true:

[1] For a "critical" justification of this starting point to the extent that such a justification was intended and is present in Thomas, see J. Maréchal, *Le point de départ de la metaphysique,* V: "Le Thomisme

the form of the thing known is in the intellect universally, immaterially, and immutably.

Thus the decisive point of the first Article of Question 84 is not to give as yet a metaphysical critique of knowledge, but rather of the known, and it is only supposed to open the way for posing the real question about the intrinsic possibility of a metaphysical knowledge of the world. For it is said there that the "what" of the individual thing known is in the thing and in the intellect in different ways. But this means that the knower has set himself over against the known and has already risen to a critique of the object: a definite metaphysical mode is predicated of the material object when it is said that its form, hence its being and its intelligible content, is "other" in the material being than in the intellectual knower. With that it is necessarily given that the individual material things are measured by a standard which is not intrinsic to themselves and yet does measure them, since knowing not only possesses them consciously, but distinguishes in its judgment their metaphysical mode of being from others.

But it is precisely in this way that the possibility is opened for a metaphysical critique of human knowledge, a critique which is not "theory of knowledge" but metaphysics of knowledge. Man has a necessary, universal knowledge of existing, individual things. The intrinsic possibility of such a knowledge must be grasped. The paradoxical nature of such knowledge has already been indicated in the first Article of Question 84: one way in the thing . . . another in the intellect. This distinction, expressing a known relation between object and knowledge, says that the cognitive taking possession of things is a knowledge which reaches beyond the individual things, a knowledge which

devant la philosophie critique" (Louvain, 1926), pp. 38–53. Citations which follow are always from this first edition. (Second edition: Brussels, 1949.)

When the question of the possibility and limits of metaphysics is mentioned again and again in the course of the work, it is not meant in the sense of the theory of knowledge, where it is an investigation which precedes metaphysics, but in the sense of a question which is intrinsic to metaphysics itself, in fact, coincides with it.

cannot simply be copying and having the individual material thing in consciousness, since such a passive having-in-consciousness does not contain in itself the possibility of setting the known and the knowing over against each other in their intrinsic differentiation. How is this possible, a knowledge of the individual existent which reaches beyond it, which reaching beyond is the distinguishing characteristic of intellectual knowledge?

In the subsequent Articles this question is posed more sharply. Thomas rejects on principle any possibility of deriving this knowledge, which reaches further than its immediate object and therefore is able to pass judgment on it, from another source which would supply knowledge independently of the things of the world which are to be judged.[2] The universal and necessary knowledge which judges that its first object is not universal and not necessary stems nevertheless only from the encounter of knowing with this object.

With the formulation of what follows from a consideration of Articles 2 to 6 of Question 84, we have indicated at least vaguely the essential conclusion to be drawn from them, but the problem is not yet set up in its final clarity. For such a formulation does not yet exclude the misunderstanding that for the knower to reach the metaphysical position from which he grasps and judges the world, he could indeed have contact with the world as the starting point, but in such a way that, in principle, the position thus reached could then be maintained outside of and independently of knowledge of the world. In other words, the world would be the point of departure, but not the final habitat of human metaphysics.

This is as sharply as Thomas could pose the problem, and he reaches this point in Article 7: Whether the intellect is able to know anything . . . without turning to the phantasms. Consequently, to formulate the question of the Article in the context of Question 84 as a whole we would have to say:

1. It is asking about intellectual knowing, which for Thomas is possible only in an encounter with the material world (through sensibility).

[2] *S. T.* I, q. 84, aa. 2–6.

20

2. This intellectual knowing is an immaterial, universal, and necessary knowledge, thus is already "metaphysics," which in principle transcends the object from which it took its departure.

3. It is asking whether or not this metaphysical knowledge, which transcends its point of departure, must achieve this transcendence (*Übergriff*) always and in every case in a grasp (*Zugriff*) of this material point of departure.

The intrinsic connection between the sense of this question and the tripartite outline of the problem which followed in Section 1 from a consideration of the broader context of Article 7 is obvious. The fact that the problem has been posed more sharply is also obvious. From Section 1 it followed that Questions 84 to 86 must be the core of the Thomistic metaphysics of knowledge, that the intrinsic possibility of the intellectual knowledge of world must be the foundation of any human knowledge at all. Now the paradoxical nature even of the guide to the problematic comes out more clearly: the knowledge of world is supposed to be the foundation of any human knowledge at all, and in being such it has already, as itself, transcended and judged the individual things; and yet it is supposed to be based on them, without possessing in advance and as known the standard by which it makes its judgment. The problematic between knowledge of the world and a metaphysics reaching beyond the world has pushed its way into the knowledge of the world itself. This knowledge is supposed to be based on (*convertere*) things (*phantasmata*), and yet as universal and necessary knowledge is supposed to judge these things.

This also shows that Article 7 is not an incidental question in the Thomistic metaphysics of knowledge which can be detached from the whole and answered arbitrarily. This Article recapitulates the whole paradoxical nature of this metaphysics of knowledge and poses it in its final sharpness. Thus the Article repeats in a deeper way what preceded it, and decides issues in advance which are to follow as explicit questions. That gives us the justification for interpreting this Article by itself, and also justifies our sketching the contents of the first six Articles of Question

21

84 only vaguely and insofar as they seemed of importance for an understanding of the question posed in Article 7.

III. THE *VIDETUR QUOD NON*

How the external structure of an "Article" arose historically is of no importance for our purpose.[1] In any case, our article begins with a series of three considerations which try to point the development of the question in a direction other than it is actually to take in the corpus of the Article. These are not (at least in this Article) just any "difficulties" or "objections" at all which are brought into the discussion from without, but rather this "*videtur quod non*" is supposed to focus the question and help to develop it in such a way that the question, correctly understood, can really receive an answer.

Thomas is aware of the importance of such an aporia (which is not to say that everywhere in his writings the "objections" which introduce an article are there for that reason. Often they are very superficial and irrelevant.). Working out the *question* is the first and the difficult business of the philosopher.[2] The question is first not merely because the philosophers had different opinions about the answers, but because frequently they had no questions at all.[3] Only the question opens up the realm within which the truth is even to be sought; it belongs so intrinsically to the philosophical event that on its formulation depends essentially whether the truth that is perhaps found will be recognized as such at all.[4]

---

[1] Cf. M. Grabmann, *Einführung in die Summa theologica des hl. Thomas v. Aquin* (Freiburg, 1928), pp. 64–68; F. A. Blanche, "Le vocabulaire de l'argumentation et la structure de l'article dans les ouvrages de Saint Thomas": *Rev. sciences phil. et théol.* 14 (1925), pp. 167–187.

[2] *In III Metaph.* lect. 1, n. 338–339: . . . *necesse est ut primum aggrediamur ea de quibus oportet dubitare, antequam veritas determinetur* . . . ; *In III Metaph.* lect. 3, n. 368: . . . *non est facile bene dubitare de eis* . . .

[3] *In III Metaph.* lect. 1, n. 338: . . . *quia omnino praetermiserunt de his considerare.*

[4] *In III Metaph.* lect. 1, nn. 339–340.

In order to understand the inner dynamism which seems to be at work in the way in which the objections seek a solution, recall what has been said so far: what is to be explained is the intrinsic possibility of intellectual knowledge as the place for a theological event, and therefore first of all as a universal and necessary knowledge which reaches beyond individual things and beyond the world altogether. But that seems to exclude from the outset and in two ways the thesis that knowledge of the individual things of the world is the abiding realm within which human metaphysics must permanently remain:

(a) First of all, the notion necessarily suggests itself that a universal and necessary knowledge takes place as something closed in itself and based on itself in its intrinsic possibility. If a cognitive potency and its actualization (*Vollzug*) are distinguished by such characteristics that they stand out clearly against any other (sense) knowledge, then it is just one step further to explain that the intellectual event (which is understood beforehand as a universal, necessary and immaterial knowledge), because it is in principle different, is also independent of all other knowing in its intrinsic meaning and hence in its actualization. From this it would follow that the ontological presuppositions of the *actual* realization of such knowing—Thomas calls them intelligible species—would have to be understood as that which enables intellectual knowledge to be closed in itself and to have the basis of its intrinsic possibility within itself. Then the foundation of intellectual knowledge in the sensible experience of the world, which has already been established in the sixth Article of Question 84, could logically only have the sense of an initial impulse, something presupposed, but not the sense of a basis which sustains it and makes it possible always and in every instance, a foundation on which intellectual knowledge permanently rests.[5] Then the relationship between meta-

[5] For this formulation see *In Boeth. de Trin.* q. 6, a. 2, ad 5: *Phantasma est principium nostrae cognitionis ut ex quo incipit intellectus operatio, non sicut transiens sed sicut permanens ut quoddam fundamentum intellectualis operationis, sicut principia demonstrationis oportet manere in omni processu scientiae* . . . ; in *De Anima* a. 15, corp.,

23

physical knowledge and merely sensible experience of the world would have to be thought of as just as extrinsic and loose as is the relationship in the common conception between the activity of the imagination and actual external perception.

This indicates the direction of the first two "objections." Only a few more remarks about them are necessary. It would be completely false to attribute to the concept "intelligible species" in the first objection the meaning which it can only acquire as the Thomistic metaphysics of knowledge unfolds. Hence at this point it would not further our understanding any to bring in the historical development of the *eidos-species* doctrine. It is precisely the meaning of species which is in question at this point. For obviously the meaning varies according to the option which one makes for one or the other of the alternatives with which the whole Article deals. For if we understand the concept of the intelligible species in a purely formal and tentative way as the actualization of intellectual knowledge as such,[6] obviously its material essence and its function vary depending on whether this knowledge is complete in itself or only in turning to sense experience. Since the objection presupposes the first of these alternatives and its response the second, the content of the meaning of the species-concept cannot be the same in both cases. Thus the objection becomes precisely an indication that the essence of the intelligible species is brought into the problematic by the

Thomas distinguishes two ways of starting out from the experience of the world, which starting points are presupposed but do not remain: *potentiae sensitivae necessariae*:
a) *per accidens tamquam excitantes ut Plato posuit*,
b) *disponentes tantum sicut posuit Avicenna*
and he places his own over against these two conceptions as a third possibility:
c) *ut repraesentantes animae intellectivae proprium objectum.*
In this text Thomas develops in detail the possibilities offered. For the doctrine of Avicenna on this point cf. M. Horten, *Philosophie des Islams* (München, 1924), pp. 69–71; F. Überweg-B. Geyer, *Grundriss der Geschichte der Philosophie II* (Berlin, 1928), pp. 309; Carra de Vaux, *Avicenna* (Paris, 1900), pp. 224–235.

[6] It says right in this objection: *Intellectus fit in actu per speciem intelligibilem qua informatur.* As far as the content goes, this purely formal definition comes up in Thomas again and again.

question of the Article. And thus it also becomes clear from this point of view how the whole of human knowledge is brought back into the question in this Article.[7]

Further remarks about the second objection are superfluous. It would lead us too far from the common conception of sense and imagination and their mutual relationship which is presupposed in this objection to try to penetrate further into the problematic of this relationship here. This second objection is merely intended to be an illustration of the fundamental conception of intellectual knowledge which the first objection presupposes in going counter to the direction which the final solution is to take.

(b) The second difficulty against the notion of the possibility of metaphysics within the realm of an experience of world takes its basic direction from the definition of knowledge as intuition (*Anschauung*). There lies at the basis of the Thomistic metaphysics of knowledge, as in every metaphysical doctrine of knowledge, the view that the act which is the primary foundation of all knowing is to be understood as intuition, as an immediate grasping of what is to be known in its own real and present self.[8]

---

[7] The sentence: *intellectum esse in actu est ipsum intelligere,* has nothing to do here with the principle of Thomistic metaphysics that actual knowing and the known are identical. Here it simply says: "but simply by the fact that the intellect (through the intelligible species) comes to its actualization, it already knows." For *intellectum* is the accusative of *intellectus* here, not of *intellectum* (the known).

[8] See *I Sent.* dist. 3, q. 4, a. 5, corp.: *Intelligere . . . dicit nihil aliud quam simplicem intuitum intellectus in id quod est praesens intelligibile,* Cf. A. Hufnagel, *Institution und Erkenntnis nach Thomas von Aquin* (Münster, 1932), pp. 58, 192ff., 239. Hufnagel's concept of intuition, which provides him with a guide for establishing what intuitions are taught in Thomas, is exclusively oriented towards the non-discursive at its decisive points. So naturally he can designate knowledge of the first principles and of the most universal essences as intuition, which is fundamentally the same intuition both times (despite Hufnagel, *loc. cit.*, pp. 203, 297), for what the "vision" of the most universal essences contains is just what the most universal principles express.

But that is not a concept of intuition which is in conformity with the inner movement of Thomistic metaphysics. Such a concept would have to start out from the fact that according to Thomas knowledge essen-

If there is a metaphysical knowledge, then, must there not also be a metaphysical intuition? But how can there be such an intuition in the realm of the experience of the world, since metaphysics is the grasping of what is beyond the world, the incorporeal? For if there is an intuition of metaphysical realities

tially goes out to what really exists, and that the prototype of knowing is the real identity of knowing and known being: knowing is the presence-to-self of being. Therefore, intuition in the really Thomistic sense is present only when being in its real self is apprehended through its being identical with what apprehends. The intuition of the first principles as such is an "intuition" of concepts, and Thomas is the sharpest critic of the view that in concepts as such one is already and immediately in possession of being itself without anything further. To this is added the fact that the principles themselves are based on an abstraction and are a *compositio et divisio* (because they are propositions), hence the opposite of an intuition. By the fact that they are judgments (intuitive essences, God and the angels, do not judge) the first principles are precisely the stigma of the mere rationality of our intellectual "intuitiveness," which is what we do not possess in the proper sense just for that reason. Despite Hufnagel (*loc. cit.*, p. 211, note 4; p. 241, note 4), abstraction as the formation of concepts is the opposite of the genuine Thomistic concept of intuition.

Hufnagel has replied to this critique of the Thomistic concept of intuition which he has developed or supported: "Der Intuitionsbegriff des Thomas von Aquin," *Tübg. theol. Quart.* 133 (1953), pp. 427–436. To this we would like to observe basically (anticipating what is to follow) that of course man as spirit has an intuition according to Thomas (Hufnagel, p. 434); but this intuition is precisely that of sensibility as the power of a spirit in the world, and not an independent intellective intuition which leaves the basis of the imagination. When, therefore, there is question of the relationship of abstraction and judgment to intuition (cf. Hufnagel, pp. 431ff.) by intuition (as a realizable act of knowledge) only the imagination (in the broader sense) can be understood. And in the essentially *one* human knowing (whose sensible and spiritual elements cannot be discussed in complete separation from each other [against Hufnagel, p. 429] because the one is real knowledge only in and through the other) abstraction and judgment are the intrinsic, constitutive elements for the fact that the imagination realizes itself as a power springing from the human spirit and remaining in it: as *objective* intuition of the world, in which the world as object (able to be set off and seen beyond) is already transcended in the *excessus* towards being as such (in accordance with the fundamental characteristic of Thomistic knowing; cf. Hufnagel also, pp. 430f.).

Finally, as Hufnagel himself remarks (pp. 435f.), our controversy hinges on the fundamental question of what the essence of an interpreta-

in themselves, then such knowledge and all further knowledge founded on it is independent of the experience of world, and cannot have to be based on it as on its permanent foundation.

But if it is so based, then there can be no independent metaphysical intuition, then the only intuition which apprehends its object immediately in its own self is sense intuition, imagination in the broader sense. Moreover, if it is true, as seems to be the case, that the possibility and scope of knowledge ultimately coincides with the possibility and scope of intuition, since this latter grounds and sustains the former, then intellectual knowledge would be limited essentially to the realm of the imagination; its ultimate meaning and hence its deepest roots would be the imagination, the experience of the world, and as such it would remain confined within space and time, because the imagination does not transcend space and time. All thought would be ordered as a means towards sense intuition. A human metaphysics in the Thomistic sense, which transcends everything spatial and temporal, encompasses all being absolutely, and reaches the absolute and the absolutely necessary, would be intrinsically impossible; there would be no immaterial, universal, and necessary knowledge. "Which is obviously false."

Perhaps that more or less brings to light the inner problematic that is at work in the third objection. Thomas felt the force of this apparent dilemma precisely because he did not want to evade it cheaply by opting for one alternative or the other. In fact, he felt himself abandoned by Aristotle in this question, who even for him was "the master of those who know": "Since the philosopher had said that the soul is not capable of any intellectual knowledge without turning to the phantasm, but the

tion of a philosophical text is: whether, namely, one simply relates the different descriptions of the essence of (finite) knowledge in Thomas, giving them more or less equal weight, "so that the final 'vision' of the essence must be left to the reader" (p. 435), or whether the interpreter must not be precisely that reader who achieves the "vision" which brings everything together into one, and for that reason submits in his interpretation what he was able to understand as the central conception in the Thomistic concept of knowledge: metaphysics on the basis of the imagination.

27

SPIRIT IN THE WORLD

phantasms come from the senses, he wants to show how the intellect can know something which is separated from all the senses. But there is no solution to this problem in Aristotle."⁹

Section 2 had concluded that the question in Article 7 is this: In what sense can the experience of world be the foundation for a metaphysical knowledge which reaches further than the world? The question has now been further clarified to the point that the question is now whether this intellectual knowledge is to be understood as a metaphysical knowledge closed in itself, based on itself as on its own possibility (objections 1 and 2), possessing its own content independent of sense experience (the species-question), which as such has a metaphysical intuition as its foundation (objection 3); or whether it is to be understood as a knowledge which must remain permanently on the basis of the imagination as the only foundation which makes it possible, without any metaphysical intuition by which it would be its own foundation. But if one's decision affirms the second conception of human knowledge as the only real one, then this decision must also show how metaphysics on the basis of the imagination is possible. Thus the question of the conversion to the phantasm is the question about the possibility of metaphysics based on an intuition which takes place within the horizon of space and time.

Although Thomas does not find in Aristotle any solution to the problem thus posed, yet he continues in the direction of Aristotelian metaphysics to the extent that he makes his own (*sed contra*) what is said in Aristotle's *De Anima*, Γ 7, 431, a. 17: The soul does not know anything without a phantasm.¹⁰ This

⁹ *In III De Anima*, lect. 12, nn. 781, 785. See also *De Anima* a. 6, corp. From the text taken from *In III De Anima* it could seem as though what Thomas does not find in Aristotle is only a solution for the question about the knowledge of a pure intelligence, but not for the question about the possibility of metaphysics at all. But in principle both are the same question, especially since Thomas believed that the existence of such immaterial intelligences could be known. Thus for him it is the same question with regard to all the objects of metaphysics, namely, how they can be knowable in spite of the *conversio ad phantasma*.

¹⁰ Similarly, *loc. cit.*, Γ 8, 432, a. 8 (432, a. 13–14); *De Mem. et Rem.* 431, b. 31. For historical details cf. Hufnagel, *Intuition und Erkenntnis*,

Aristotelian proposition is for Thomas not one of the views which one "also" shares, in order to assign it a quiet nook in some harmless, peaceful place where it will disturb no one (the Middle Ages loved this method elsewhere). In order to grasp this proposition in its origin and to think it out resolutely to the end, Thomas is pushed right to the depths of the Aristotelian starting point of metaphysics. It stands in the *sed contra* not merely to satisfy the requirements of an Article's form.

IV. THE FORMAL STRUCTURE
OF THE CORPUS OF THE ARTICLE

The corpus of the article is clearly divided first into three parts:

1. The decision which Thomas makes about this question: *respondeo dicendum . . .*

2. The indications: *Et hoc duobus indiciis apparet.* There are two of them. Thus this section breaks down extrinsically into two parts:

    (a) The first indication: *primo quidem . . .* [up to:] *ea quorum scientiam praeaccepit.*

    (b) The second indication: *secundo . . .* [up to:] *formare possit ad intelligendum.*

3. The third part, the metaphysics of the conversion to the phantasm: *Huius autem ratio . . .* up to the end of the corpus of the article.

To get first of all a purely formal and summary view of the movement of thought in this third part of the corpus, one has only to notice the fivefold "*autem*" which gives a simple and clear structure to the sequence of sentences. We need only take note of the words or phrases which are set off by this *autem* to understand the individual moments in the flow of thought as a whole:

1) *potentia cognoscitiva-cognoscibile:* knowing and being.

pp. 218ff.; B. A. Luyckx, *Die Erkenntnislehre Bonaventuras* (Münster, 1923), pp. 185–187.

2) *intellectus humani, qui est conjunctus corpori, proprium objectum:* human knowing and human being.

3) *ratio naturae:* the being of the world.

4) *particulare . . . apprehendimus:* human knowledge of the being of the world. —In this fourth part, where obviously the climax of the whole is first reached, let us set into further relief the following as keywords, so to speak, of the inner development of thought:

a) *imaginatio:* intuition.

b) *intellectus:* thought.

5) *si autem . . . esset . . . :* repetition of the whole in a critical review of the opposite opinion.

If we consider what this arrangement of the corpus according to purely extrinsic criteria permits us to surmise in advance about its content, one thing can be stated immediately: the movement of thought progresses just the opposite to what we could have expected from the previous considerations. In sections 2 and 3 the objections let us see the Article as the question about the possibility of metaphysics within the horizon of space and time. Judging by this arrangement, the question about the possibility of metaphysics is not raised in the corpus at all; it looks as though it is dealing only with knowledge of the world, and in fact as the only human knowledge, since the conversion to the phantasm is disclosed as the necessary presupposition of all human knowledge. In any case, it is clear from this observation that the urgent concern of Thomas was to have human knowledge as a whole founded on the basis of the imagination. How a metaphysics could still have its origin on such a basis— and he still maintains this explicitly in the corpus of the Article—that remains in the background of what is treated in the corpus of the Article. This question is not treated explicitly until the answer to the third objection. Of course, if the answer is not to be joined to the corpus extrinsically, then it must already be an intrinsic factor in determining the conception of human knowledge as an experience of the world. The intrinsic possibility of metaphysics itself must be the presupposition which is the basis for what is treated explicitly in the corpus

of the Article, for the foundation of the possibility of inner-
worldly experience as the fundamental human knowledge.

V. THE FIRST TWO SECTIONS OF THE CORPUS

If we look at the first section of the corpus of the Article
extrinsically, two statements are to be distinguished: the
thesis, and the characterization of that upon which this decision
falls. The thesis does not speak of any kind of knowing at all, of
knowing as such. It is concerned with "our intellect in the present state of life, in which it is united with receptive corporeality." The statement of the thesis does not concern man and his
being immediately, nor human knowledge as a whole, but the
intellect. Thus this latter is somehow separated and seen by
itself, as a fixed quantity defined in itself and distinguished
from others, hence as a reality about which definite statements can be made in its own right. This is all the more true—
even if we prescind from all that we know about it from the
previous sections of the *Summa*—since the intellect is obviously
seen here in contrast to the imagination, to sense, and
to the phantasms to which it is supposed to "turn." But
along with that it also seems to be just the opposite: the
intellect is a human reality (*noster*), it is "united" with
the *passibile corpus*. But this union cannot be something
which belongs to the intellect merely in addition to its
being intellect, since this characterization is clearly introduced as the reason why the intellect must turn to the phantasms in order to be able to be itself in actuality (*aliquid intelligere in actu*). One has only to notice the double combination:
"intellect—united with the passible body" and "actually
knows—by turning to the phantasms." Thus the human intellect
appears precisely not as a fixed quantity based on itself; it is
itself only in a union with what is not intellect (*corpus passibi-
le-phantasma*), and is therefore brought to a knowledge of its
essence only through an understanding of what the conversion

31

to the phantasm means. Hence this understanding cannot proceed from a hard-and-fast, univocal concept of what the human intellect is. Ultimately, both can be understood only in a single act of comprehension. Hence what appeared at first as a fixed definition of the intellect (its distinction from sense and imagination, its character as a potency for metaphysical knowledge of objects which transcend the space-time boundary of the imagination), can be considered only a tentative attempt to understand its essence. The statement of the thesis does not presuppose a metaphysical knowledge of the specific essence of the human intellect, but achieves it for the first time. Then the same thing also holds for the imagination, which can be understood in its essence only insofar as it is understood as that knowing to which human intellectuality is essentially ordered. With that we have also avoided the misunderstanding that we could know from the "pure" sensation of animals, for example, what the imagination or the phantasm are that we are speaking of here.

Just as the essence of the intellect can be understood only with that of the conversion to the phantasm in a *single* act of comprehension, so too in the same way and for the same reason the fact and the meaning of the essential unity of intellect and passible body can be defined only together with the conversion to the phantasm and in light of it. In the radical unity of intellect and imagination, the essential unity of passible body and intellect comes to light for the first time.[1] Thus the *respondeo dicendum,* which seemed at first to break down into two parts, the thesis and the apparently independent characterization of intellect and sensibility, turns out to be a single, indivisible statement expressing an essence, a statement in which Thomas ex-

---

[1] Thus the operative thought in *S.T.* I, q. 75, a. 4 is that the body belongs intrinsically to the essence of man because sensation is intrinsically corporeal. In I, q. 76, a. 1, corp. it says: *ex ipsa operatione intellectus apparet quod intellectivum principium unitur corpori ut forma,* and this is the guiding principle for the whole Article (*utrum intellectivum principium uniatur corpori ut forma*), for the argument which affirms thought of corporeal man has sense and weight only against this background. *De Anima* a. 1, corp.: *sic igitur ex operatione animae humanae modus esse ipsius cognosci potest.*

presses originally what he was able to grasp of the one human being and knowing. Thus it is shown again that the interpretation of the Article does not have to proceed from previous investigations in Thomas which are unambiguously settled and whose results must be presupposed as already established, however much, of course, these can also serve to confirm the sense of the Article, and however indispensable it is to grasp the whole of the Thomistic corpus for understanding even a short article.

If this first section of the corpus indicates once again the vast scope that is intrinsic to the question of the Article, it is also significant in another respect. To be sure, it is only as the problematic of the Article unfolds that the meaning of the "present state of life in which (the intellect) is united to receptive corporeality" can be brought out. But this characterization of the human intellect is already an option made in advance about what is to be the vantage point from which we are to come to a definition of its essence as well as to the metaphysics of that essence and its contents: the vantage point is to be the real, concrete man, his being situated in this world of space and time, hence a situation he already knows of when he gives himself to understanding it. The decision that man wants to understand himself from this standpoint has already been made in advance, consciously and deliberately decided, because as a matter of fact man sees no possibility of understanding himself from any other standpoint except that at which he has always found himself whenever he turned to himself: the world.

That also enables us to appreciate correctly the sense and function of the second section of the corpus within the whole Article. Thomas speaks here of two indications (*indicia*),[2] in which what is at issue in the Article comes to light (*apparet*). Just the word "*indicium*" can caution us against the misunderstanding that in this second section it is a question of giving the

---

[2] *Summa contra Gentiles* I, 73, says of the same thing: . . . *cuius signum est . . .*; *S.T.* I, q. 89, a. 1, corp., and *In De Mem. et Rem.* lect. 2, n. 314 the same thing is called "*experimentum*," which does not mean "experiment," since in Thomas's time one tried to reach the soul not by experiments, but through a philosophy about the *experimentum* of real human life.

"proofs" for the thesis. It is not the case that the second section proves the proposition of the first section, and that then nothing but more or less arbitrary "speculations" about the previously established fact follow in the third section. That is not the case, not because in metaphysics—and that is what is in question here —nothing at all is discovered that was not previously known, but because in metaphysics the understanding which man as such already has of himself is articulated and hence brought to itself. Metaphysics is the conceptually formulated understanding of that prior understanding which man as man *is*. And so these *indicia* simply awaken this knowledge which man has about himself and in which he already knows how he is constituted, in order to transpose it, while it remains itself, into metaphysics in the third section. Neither are these *indicia,* therefore, something like a somewhat rudimentary science of experimental psychology, for this is either a natural science, which discovers things which are not otherwise known, or a metaphysics which does not understand itself correctly, or, in the best instance, the *indicium* of a metaphysical question in the sense just indicated. Thus the *indicia* of the second section simply bid us to take our stand really and resolutely at that point which the first section pointed to: in the fact that human thought is delivered over to the powers of this earth even to the possibility of insanity (*phrenetici*) and senility (*lethargici*). The human metaphysical consideration of what man is begins at this point because in every man there is already realized what is to be understood conceptually in what follows: the human, intellective soul has its face turned towards the phantasm.[8]

VI. THE FIRST PART
OF THE THIRD SECTION OF THE CORPUS

Recall once again the purpose with which we set out to interpret the Article and its decisive sections: we are not trying to work out the questions raised by the conversion to the phantasm explicitly and in all respects, but rather to give some pre-

[8] *De Anima* a. 16, corp.

liminary indication of all that is involved in this question. So we are considering the text of the corpus only insofar as it raises the questions which are to be taken up in detail in the second part of this work. Our only concern here, then, is to assemble the questions raised by the conversion to the phantasm without being concerned with a systematic.

"Cognitive powers are proportioned to the knowable," says the first sentence of this third section, and this is obviously meant as an operative principle for answering the question of this Article in which human knowledge is to be examined. Is the sense of this proposition—prescinding completely from how penetrating it is—so intelligible to us by itself that it can fulfill this function? Perhaps the sense of the proposition can be clarified by saying first of all that a cognitive power stands invariably in a fixed relationship to its object.[1] The knowable is perhaps a word for the same thing which later on is designated proper object. Every cognitive power has an object belonging properly to itself, and this object stands in a fixed relationship to it. Thus the sentence presupposes that there are different kinds of cognitive "powers," to each of which, because of its nature and that of the object, there corresponds a definite realm of objects as the only intrinsic fulfillment possible to it. Hence there is a reciprocal and limiting *a priori* between knowing and known: the cognitive power determines *a priori* what can be its object; the object contains an antecedent law determining by what power it can be known. But saying that is far from clarifying the sense of the proposition in any decisive way. For according to what norm is this fixed relationship between cognitive power and object determined? How is this relationship to be measured? Do we not again need a standard which measures both knowing and known at once? If one would only have the sentence say in a purely formal way that the "peculiarity"

[1] The thought that in the course of the coming considerations we will have to distinguish between the object as known and the object in its "in-itself" by a distinction which applies *a priori* to all knowledge and not merely in certain instances will turn out in the course of the work to be a pseudo-problem: *being in its in-itself is being-known.* The question about the distinction between an "in-itself" and being-known by a human knowing cannot be taken up appropriately until later.

35

of the power determines *a priori* what it can apprehend, and the "peculiarity" of the object determines by what it can be apprehended, then the proposition in this formal generality is intelligible indeed, but it does not say anything. And it would be impossible to see how it could become important for what follows.

Obviously, there must be an intrinsic relationship between these two "peculiarities." The intrinsic peculiarity of the power asserts implicitly an antecedent knowability in its possible object; the intrinsic possibility of knowledge is based on the intrinsic possibility of knowability, and vice versa; and only if there is this more fundamental relationship between knowing and object can there be talk of a fixed, measurable relationship between definite cognitive powers of a specific kind and objects of a specific kind corresponding precisely to each one of them. But what is the foundation of this more fundamental relationship which gives something knowable to knowing as the intrinsic possibility of this knowing, and vice versa? The possibility of such a relationship can only be based on the fact that knowing and object are one in a more original way and do not seek a relationship to each other only subsequently to their own possibility. But what does this more original unity consist of? How is this related to the different cognitive powers and how to the different objects of knowledge? The relationship of both to their one ground is obviously the measure which determines their relationship to each other. What is this ground? The interpretation of the first sentence, which is the norm for the whole section, ends in a question.

There is also included in the first part of the third section of the corpus a sentence about the intellect of angels. Do we know anything about the intellect of angels which could be of use to us in our question about the knowledge which we ourselves are? Thomas denies, of course, that we can decide anything about the specific essence of angels.[2] And if such angels had not had a role to play in the physics of antiquity and the Middle Ages, which was also the physics of Thomas, perhaps they

[2] *De Anima* a. 16; *S.T.* I, q. 88, a. 1, a. 2; *S.C.G.* II, 46; *In III De Anima* lect. 8, n. 710: *substantiae spirituales ignotae sunt nobis.*

would not have come within the scope of his philosophizing at all. Nevertheless, sentences like the one in the present section have their philosophical significance. For in fact they are not concerned with angels—since the philosopher does not know anything about their specific essence—but they are the way in which Thomas treats the possibility of a knowledge which is based on an intellectual intuition. Thus this sentence in the first part, in a kind of preliminary attempt, is objectively the same thing as what in part five will be a repetition of the whole in a critical review of the opposite position: the "idea" of an intellectual intuition as that knowledge which is precisely what human knowledge is not, so that by holding itself up against this, human knowledge understands itself in its own essence.

To what extent is the idea of an intellectual intuition grasped by characterizing the intellect of the angel? We have seen already how for Thomas the essence of the human intellect is to be defined in light of its "being united with receptive corporeality," which is expressed again in the conversion of the intellect to the phantasm, that is, in turning to the imagination as the only and the necessary human intuition. But with that is given the concept of an angelic intellect "which is completely separated from a body," the idea of an intellect which has its intuition in itself and from itself alone, and thus is not ordered as a means to an imagination within the horizon of space and time. The single ground of knowing and object which remained obscure above, as the ground of just such an intellectual intuition, must then, according to the principle of this first part, entail an object which also transcends the horizon of space and time, stands open of itself to intellectual intuition: "intelligible substance separated from a body."

How does the idea of such an intellectual intuition help us to understand what human knowing is? This idea is obviously intended to be more than the arbitrary exercise of the negating of such an intuition, the characteristics of human intuition presupposed as already apprehended. Or is this placing of its own ontological determination over against another, thus differentiating it and establishing its limits, a more mysterious process than might be apparent at first sight? As a matter of fact, how can the human intellect thus establish itself within its own limits and at the same time give evidence of a remarkable knowledge about a possible "beyond" of these limits, which knowledge is always included in the knowledge of limits as such? How can human knowing transcend itself in this way? If it should turn out that human knowing constitutes itself as such only by transcending its own realm, then as a matter of fact forming the idea of an intellectual intuition would be an indication of the process in which the essence of human knowledge becomes manifest to itself. The possibility of the opposite position, which ascribes to man an intellectual intuition, would only show the correctness of our own position.

But these preliminary conjectures seem to have brought us into a fundamental dilemma which refutes our own position. How is human knowledge to transcend its own boundary, namely, that of the imagination which is its only intuition, without a direct view beyond the imagination, without an intellectual intuition? And if intellectual intuition means metaphysics, then this dilemma is the question about the possibility of metaphysics founded upon the imagination, the question which we have already met. It has now been defined as the question about the possibility of a transcendence of the imagination without intellectual intuition, a transcendence of such a kind that it constitutes the possibility of a human intuition on the level of the imagination, and has its intimation in the limit-idea (*Grenzidee*) of an intellectual intuition.

VII. THE SECOND PART
OF THE THIRD SECTION OF THE CORPUS

Although the sense and meaning of the first part had to remain indefinite and obscure to a large extent, the formal connection between the first and the second parts is clearly discernible. The first sentence of the first part gave a general norm for determining the proper object of a cognitive power. In the second part, human knowing and the object of human knowledge are measured against this norm, whereby this measuring and its results are set over against the limit-idea of an intellectual intuition by the introductory *autem*.

But this is where the difficulties begin also. Should the proposition that the object proportionally ordered to the human intellect is the quiddity of corporeal things be deduced from the guiding principle of the first part? Obviously not. For this formal statement, empty of any material content, does not provide a point of departure for such an insight. Or should this insight follow from this principle presupposing the union of the human intellect with the body? The clause "which is united with receptive corporeality" as the minor, together with the principle of the first part as the major, would then form an inference whose conclusion would be the second part. That might be correct from a purely formal point of view. But it was shown earlier (Section 5) that ultimately the insight into the essence of the intellect and that into the peculiarity of its activity (the conversion to the phantasm, which is only the explication of the fact that the proper object of the intellect is "corporeal" things) can be grasped only in a *single* act of comprehension. For how can a "union" between intellect and body, however it is conceived, give us an insight into the fact that the only object which the intellect can reach in an original intuition is something corporeal? But if this "union" is thought of in some quite definite way, how can one know of it without having already grasped human intellectuality's esential ordination through sensibility to being in the world? In the nature of the case, then, there is no minor which could be known independently of a knowledge of the conclusion. But where do we get this simultaneous comprehension of both at once?

We get it in that place in which the first and second sections of the corpus have already placed us in advance: the world, whose dimensions are space and time, and are such for human knowing also. We have already decided to take our stand on the basis of the imagination, but the situation has changed from what it was earlier. For this original knowledge about self, for which Thomas has already decided in advance, has in the meantime entered at once into the light and into the darkness of the problematic spoken of in the preceding section. The guiding principle in the first part was the formal and preliminary indication of the matter now at hand: the matter of determining the fixed relationship between human knowing and the human world which is its object by grasping both in their radical unity in some ground which is still unknown. The apparently so simple and self-evident parallel in the sentence of the second part: "united with a body—existing in corporeal matter" is genuinely understood only if it is seen in this way. Making them parallel does not provide the answer, but rather poses the problem of understanding the parallel as possible in the light of their common ground.

The subsequent clause in the second part also shows how much this second part provides a material content for the problematic posed in the first part, although this content is for the moment still obscure: "and through the nature of sensible things he also reaches out to some knowledge of invisible things." A model of just such an *ascensio* has already been realized in the first part in arriving at the idea of an intellectual intuition. And so the subsequent clause poses the question anew: How is such a transcendence of its own basis by the human intelligence possible without an intellectual intuition, and to what extent does it belong to the constitutive grounds of the human experience of the world, for it is only then that it can be of importance for a metaphysics of the latter.

The interpretation of this part must call attention to something further. The second part does not speak of human knowing in general, but of the human intellect, and thus sets the intellect off from man's senses and imagination. The quiddity of corporeal things (not simply the corporeal things) is ordered to the intellect as object, so that this quiddity seems to be apprehended for the first time by the intellect and not by the senses. However one might conceive this intellectual knowledge of quiddities, even if, to presuppose the most moderate position, it is only a question of apprehending some relation of order between the sensibly intuited objects, of localizing in the dimensions of space and time something sensibly intuited and apprehended as object, such an apprehension of the quiddities of corporeal things presupposes the possibility of apprehending something in consciousness as distinct from the knower, the capacity to "objectify," and an antecedent knowledge at least of space and time as such. Only thus can objectifying and localizing what is sensibly intuited be conceived as possible. But the whole thrust of the article goes to show that the imagination's intuition is the only human intuition, and without this the intellect would be blind. But does such an intuition purely as such have the possibility of objectifying and receiving the intuited as object (*Gegen-stand*)? If intuition is the immediate grasp of what is to be known in its own real, present self, can an intuition understood in this way as such and by itself alone be knowledge in any other way than by the knowing and the known being the same in every respect in an undifferentiated being-with-one-another, that is, without being set over against each other? But then, if something is to be intuited "objectively," such an intuition is possible only if it already holds before itself a field into which the intuited is projected and which is itself not intuited. Is not such intuition more than intuition? Is there not in the concept of an objective intuition a moment of transcendence beyond mere intuition and beyond what is only intuited?

And further: presupposing that man's only intuition is that of the imagination, how can that antecedent knowledge of an ordering structure be conceived as possible? This latter appeared to be the presupposition of knowledge of the quiddity of what is intuited, and this alone allows the sensibly intuited objects to be grasped as limited, as only this and only that, as only here and as only now, and thus as objects for knowing? If, in addition, the apprehension of space and time is necessary, does not this apprehension of space and time mean once again a transcendence of the mere intuition beyond itself? How is this two-fold transcendence beyond the mere intuition of the individual, which seems to be present in apprehending order and in objectifying, related to the transcendence beyond the basis of the imagination altogether which was surmised earlier? Are they ultimately the same, in however different a direction they seem at first to move? Should this be the case, then a starting point would have been found for the question, how the

SPIRIT IN THE WORLD

transcendence of the intellect beyond the imagination belongs to the constitutive elements of the human experience of the world itself. In any case, inasmuch as Thomas has the quiddity of corporeal things apprehended by the intellect, he seems to presuppose that the two-fold transcendence which alone makes this apprehension possible is precisely what the intellect has to contribute to mere sensibility as such in the constitution of the one human experience of the world.

The essence of human knowing and that of its object can only be apprehended in a single act of comprehension because they are reciprocally the ground of their intrinsic possibility and therefore ultimately spring from a single ground. Hence whichever of the two is to be apprehended, this apprehension always comprehends both of them. Not taking this into account, one can try to grasp this single whole from one or the other of its moments, or from both of them, one after the other. This double apprehension is what Thomas is undertaking here. Thus the two following parts of the third section of the corpus treat the essence of the object of human knowledge and the essence of human knowledge one after the other. In so doing, it must turn out that both times the whole is grasped.

VIII. THE THIRD PART
OF THE THIRD SECTION OF THE CORPUS

In the course of our investigation of what it means to say that the object of human knowledge is the quiddity of things of the world, the question had already arisen: What is meant by this quiddity? It obviously is to mean more than simply the thing as it is given in the intuition as such. The question about the quiddity is now posed explicitly: "but it belongs to the essence of this nature ('quiddity,' as the preceding part shows) that . . ." If one does not start out from very questionable presuppositions, which is what first raises problems for the "theory of knowledge," he will have no hesitation in starting out from the fact that fundamentally the quiddity of things of the world manifests itself in the *mode* in which it is *apprehended* as the quiddity of these things. The operative principle of the first part says just that.[1] Presupposing this, it is clear how the movement of thought progresses from the second to the third part. The second part spoke about apprehending this quiddity. Accordingly, the intrinsic essence of these quiddities must have already been disclosed in this apprehension. So it becomes obvious how, going in the opposite direction, the second sentence of the third part can speak again of a knowledge of these quiddities. Starting out from this idea, let us now schematically transpose the first sentence of the third part into the "mode of knowledge" once again. Then it would have to read something like this: "It is of the essence of the knowledge of this nature that it be known as existing in some individual, which is not without the 'knowledge' of corporeal matter. Thus it is of the essence of the knowledge of the nature of a stone that it be known as existing in this stone." By this transposition we have come up with a sentence which is identical in sense with the second sentence of this part ("Whence it is of the nature of this stone . . ."). This shows clearly that the second sentence is not a conclusion (whence . . .) from the first in the sense that something other and different follows from the first. There is question, rather, of a structural relationship which prevails in knowing and known alike.

If we now try to clarify the sense of our transposed sentence, formalizing it slightly we could translate: When we try to apprehend things of the world, we must always understand what is known (*das Gewusste*) as "known-of-something," and only in this something does the known become a thing of the world. You can relate what is known to as many "somethings" as you like. In other words, only when what is known has already been

---

[1] The *modus rei* and the *modus cognitionis* always correspond fundamentally. That the *modus rei* and the *modus cognitionis* are often distinguished in Thomas as being opposed comes from the fact that Thomas is thinking of the *modus cognitionis intellectivae humanae* as such. But the fact that he ascribes an *intelligere actu* to this *cognitio* only in the *conversio ad phantasma* is a proof that taken by itself it cannot be knowledge at all. Thus there is only the *one* knowing of the one man, and in this the *modus rei* and the *modus cognitionis* are proportional, as the operative principle of the first part stated.

43

related to this or that is it a concrete, individual thing, an object in which knowledge, still wandering and seeking its goal, comes to rest in a "this" of such a kind, in the object. As merely known, without this "whither" (*Woraufhin*) of the relation, there is no concrete "this," however complex the conception is. You can think the known as complex as you like, but there always remains the impulse to relate it to this "something," and this something always remains the empty yet necessary "whither" of knowledge. This "whither" is present in knowledge in a peculiar way, and yet is never actually known itself. Knowledge has in principle an empty "whither," never definable in itself, to which it is related. The known itself (the "essence" of the thing) is what is at this "something." The "whither" of the knowing which relates and the "whereat" (*Woran*) of the known are called Thomistically "corporeal (prime) matter." With that we have reached a tentative understanding of the third part.

Objective knowledge is not had before this reference of the known to matter. Inasmuch as this "turning to" is essential to all knowledge, all human knowledge is also a conversion to matter, and inasmuch as this matter is accessible only in the phantasm of the human imagination, all knowledge is a conversion to the phantasm. But we are already anticipating the next section. Before that, something further is in question here.

How does this reference of the known to the "whither" of the knowing, always empty in itself, and to the "whereat" of the known come about? What cognoscitive faculty does this referring? In the preceding section this objectifying seemed to be accomplished by the intellect, since pure intuition as such seemed to express an identity of knowing and the known, and so the only human intuition, that of the imagination, did not seem able to do the objectifying, to accomplish such a differentiation of the known from the knowing. On the other hand, it has now been shown that this objectifying needs a "whither" where it is to take place. Can the intellect provide for itself something which seems in principle so foreign to the intellect, since it is fundamentally indefinable? Can it hold before itself that which ever stands over against it, that on which it projects its knowledge in order to make it its object, that which always stands over aganst it because it can never be brought over into the sphere of the known?

But right at the beginning of the next part it says: "But we apprehend the particular through the senses." Does this sentence not contradict the considerations just made, according to which the intellect apprehends the concrete object in an objectification of the quiddity by referring this latter to the "whither" of the knowing, to matter? But let us first investigate the possible meanings of the sentence just cited. Does it mean: The sense as such apprehends the objective individual; or: Sensibility is one of the intrinsic, constitutive elements in the knowledge of the objective individual? If we are not to have gone off in a completely wrong direction in our earlier considerations, only the second meaning can be the one intended by Thomas. Then there remains the question, to what extent sensibility is of essential importance for the possibility of an objective knowledge of world. This much we can presume already: we have not grasped the essence of sensibility if we understand the senses as passageways through which things enter into us. According to the introductory sentence just cited, and in the light of our earlier interpretation of what has preceded, it seems that sensibility constitutes the ground, as it were, on which what is had in consciousness is placed in this process of objectification. It seems to bear in itself the "whither" of the known, which is different from the actual knowledge, while the referring of the known would then be the accomplishment of the intellect. But sensibility as intuition should express precisely the identity of what is concretely intuited in itself with the intuition in an undifferentiated being-with-itself (*Bei-sich-selbst-Sein*)! How can sensibility be both at once: the capacity to differentiate itself from another which stands over against it, and the capacity for an intuition of what is identical with itself? Hence sensibility would have to be the undivided center embracing the interiority of the knowledge as intuition, and the objectification of the intuition as knowledge. As such a center it could neither be simply with itself nor with another set over against itself. If the second (the being-with-another-set-over-against-itself) is possible only by the fact that the knower is with itself and thus can set itself over against the other and this other over against itself (although a being-with-self is also conceivable without a distinguishing-one's-self from another), then not-being-with-itself would be the essential characteristic of sensibility. But insofar as sensibility as "knowing" expresses a being-with-self, the being-with-self of sensibility would be being-with-another. Insofar as sensibility itself cannot set itself over against that which it always is as intuition, it would indeed be intuition, since it is identical with the other, but it would not be objective intuition. The objectification of that into which sensibility loses itself, which comes about through a self-liberation from sensibility and by referring the knowledge brought along in the liberation back to the "whither" given in sensibility, would then be the accomplishment of the intellect. Sensibility and intellect together would then form the one, human, objective intuition of world in space and time.

But these are all only preliminary assumptions. For have we ascertained clearly enough a criterion by which to separate intellect and sensibility in human knowledge at all? Obviously not. In fact, what forces us even to assume at all that the human experience of world, which we meet as one, proceeds from two cognitive powers? The only thing that was certain up to now was the vantage point of our enquiry, namely, the world of experience. Our considerations about the essence of the intellect and of sensibility had as their only firm point of departure just the fact that Thomas ascribes the apprehension of the quiddities of the things of our experience to the intellect, and explains sensibility as necessary for making possible the application of the knowing to the concrete thing. What distinguishes intellect and sense and what unifies them originally in this single knowing of world, this has remained obscure. Up to now, only one thing has been clarified to some extent: the one knowing of the world is a relating of the known to an undefined "whither" in which the known becomes the thing standing opposite, so that this thing itself discloses itself as the unity of an intelligibility and the "whereat" of an intelligibility.

IX. THE FOURTH PART
OF THE THIRD SECTION OF THE CORPUS

From the fundamental considerations of the first and second parts we had expected from the outset that the question about the essence of the object encountered in the experience of world would at the same time be the question about the knowledge of this object. And as a matter of fact, the problematic of the third part has already forced us to consider the question about the manner of our apprehension of the world. It is now made the explicit theme of the fourth part. This consideration must start out from the thing. A thing of the world is to be apprehended in a unity of the knowable and of matter as the "where-at" which sustains the knowable and in which it first comes to be as limited and becomes an object for us. How can such a thing be apprehended?

If we approach the text of the fourth part first of all from without, it is the division of the content which strikes us: first it speaks of sense and imagination, and then of intellect. Where do we get the right to make this division? The one human knowing of the world was given to us as the point of departure for our metaphysical explanation of human knowledge. The nature of the things of the world has been disclosed to us in a tentative way, and with that the peculiarity of human knowing also, as a referring of the known to prime matter. With that we had already reached a certain understanding of what conversion to the phantasm should mean. But the statement about the conversion goes beyond the understanding already reached when it distinguishes imagination and intellect. For this fourth part speaks of a turning of the intellect to sensibility by referring what is known universally to the concrete phantasm.

First of all one must be careful not to misunderstand from the outset this expanded statement of the fourth part about the conversion. It is not as though an intellect knew a universal quiddity first, and then afterwards turned to sensibility to further complete this knowledge. Rather, no intellectual knowledge at all comes about without its always and already being a conversion to the phantasm from the outset. The sentence: it cannot actually know without turning, etc., means to say just that. There is no actual intellectual knowledge which is not already a conversion to the phantasm. It follows just from this that in Thomas there is question essentially of *one* human knowledge whose two roots ought not to be made independent as two cognitive powers complete in themselves. It follows, moreover, that for Thomas what is known first is the concrete individual. Hence in Thomas there can only be question, not of explaining a subsequent collaboration of two independent cognitive powers, but of understanding the *one* human knowledge from this one ground in its unity and in the duality of its roots.

But where in the characteristics of human knowledge determined so far does there lie a point of departure for distinguishing in it two sources of cognitive power? It has already been said that in apprehending the quiddities of things, an anticipation (although empty) of the world in general, of space and time as a whole, and an objectification must obviously be understood simultaneously. And it seemed at the time that it was precisely for this reason that Thomas ascribed the apprehension of these quiddities to an "intellect" as opposed to the imagination. On the other hand, it followed that the empty "whither" to which the known is related must somehow be present in the knowledge itself in order that this reference of the known to the "whither" be accomplished at all. Now if this "whither" is set over against the knower himself, then knowing must set itself over against itself. It must have the world and therefore be the world itself, and it must make it into an object in that it sets itself over against it and thus over against itself. Could we say that sensibility is this being-always-and-already-in-the-world and this being-itself-world, and that intellect is the capacity to objectify world and self? Then the one, objective knowledge of world would be an intellectual differentiation of the knower and of knowing from another "whither," and the intellect would do this by referring what is known universally to a "whereat" of the known which is had in itself in sensibility. Sensibility would provide this "whither" and "whereat" since it itself would be essentially "outside itself"; but the one knower could set itself apart from this "whither" and thus make possible an objective transcendence of the known only by the fact that it is not only sensibility, but at the same time "intellect."

If we recall once again that we have already concluded to the universality of the known quiddity insofar as this quiddity can come to stand opposite in many "whithers" and "whereats," then the interpretation of the fourth part ought to have brought us to the point which was to be reached in this preparatory explanation of Article 7.

X. THE FIFTH PART
OF THE THIRD SECTION OF THE CORPUS

As far as the content goes, the sense and problematic of this last part of the corpus was touched upon already in Section 6. It deals with the limit-idea of an intuitive intellect, and by holding itself over against this, human knowing understands itself. Here, too, the idea of an intuitive intellect is understood from the viewpoint of its object. This object is designated as a separated form. Can such a thing still actually be the transcendent "object" of knowing? It would not be "in individuals," hence it would be known without being related to a "whither" of the known, and so it would no longer actually be an object to be encountered and received. Thus it could only be apprehended in a being-known which is absolutely identical with the knowing. The separated form would be an essence apprehending itself in unobjective knowledge: an intuitive intellect which possesses itself in an undifferentiated knowing. Hence the separated form would be the angelic intellect itself as we met it in Section 6. For such an intellect, the turning out of itself in the being-outside-of-itself of sensibility, a conversion to the phantasm, would be impossible. It is itself the proper object of its undifferentiated intuition.

The problematic which results from such a limit-idea of an intuitive intellect has already been touched upon in Section 6.

XI. THE ANSWERS TO THE OBJECTIONS

It was not possible in Section 3 to work out a tentative interpretation of the "*videtur quod non*" without anticipating the matter contained in the answers to these objections.

The first objection forced us into the problematic of the intellectual species. This problematic was also present in the background all through the discussions of the corpus of the Article. We spoke again and again of referring what is known through the intellect to the foreign "whither" of this known which is present in sensibility. But what is this known? It has already become clear that if the conversion to the phantasm belongs to the constitutive elements of human knowledge at all, the intelligible species cannot be understood as that which, existing by itself, fills knowledge with content. For that would make intellectual knowing a cognitive power based on itself and having its possibility completely in itself, and would exclude a conversion as the condition of its possibility. That is all the more impossible inasmuch as the phantasm obviously does not bear in itself the "whither" of the reference of the intelligible species in a completely undetermined void. Rather, this "whither" is present in sensibility as determined, not as mere prime matter, but as phantasm. But presupposing this, what else can the species contain? Can it be more than the possibility of setting the phantasm over against the knowing subject? But wherein lies the foundation of this possibility? Thus the question about the contents of the species becomes again the question about the possibility of a bringing-self-back from its abandonment in the other of sensibility by setting the knower apart from the definite other which is present in sensibility. If species expresses the possibility of setting the phantasm over against the knowing subject, then it is self-evident that the permanent possession of this possibility of itself (its habitual existence) does not yet imply any actual knowing.

From the understanding of what sensibility is which was at least presumably reached in the preceding Section, there also follows more or less the sense of the answer to the second objection. The second objection had placed the intellect in the same relationship to the imagination as this latter has to the senses; thus it had understood these three powers as coördinate, independent faculties. What distinguishes intellect and imagination followed provisionally from the question: What forced us to distinguish them at all? Objective intuition of world expressed the being-given-away of knowing to the other (sensibility) and at the same time setting the knower apart from the other which is itself (intellect). Since the other is an individual, there is need of a reference (conversion) to the individual whenever the knowing itself is not this individual. But if sensibility is of itself being-given-away to the other, no conversion is necessary because sensibility is the other individual. Imagination and sense (we still do not have any criterion for distinguishing them) as sensibility bear in themselves the "individual likeness." But that is not true of the intellect, which is in fact the "recollection" of the knower *over against* the other, and only through this can this other appear as objective. Therefore, it needs a conversion to reach the individual other. The only thing that remains obscure in this answer to the second objection is what this "likeness" in sensibility means.

The third objection dealt with the possibility of metaphysics on the basis of the imagination, on which basis the conversion to the phantasm places human knowing. Thus insofar as both questions (the possibility of metaphysics within the realm of the imagination and establishing thought in this realm through the conversion) coincide objectively, a final clarification of this answer to the third objection can be reached only in the course of the explanation of the conversion itself. There can only be question here, then, of clarifying the problematic of such a metaphysics once again by means of this answer. Granted this confinement within the realm of the imagination, how is an object to be reached which itself does not also belong to this realm? Obviously, it cannot be a question of reaching such objects subsequently; that would be tantamount to leaving the

51

basis of imagination and would implicitly endow man again with an intellectual intuition. Therefore, such metaphysical apprehension must belong to the *a priori* conditions of man's being situated on the basis of the imagination itself.

In the answer to the third objection, Thomas characterizes the mode of metaphysical apprehension by three words: *excessus, comparatio, remotio* (excess, comparison, removal). Undoubtedly, there exists between these three acts of metaphysics an intrinsic connection by which one is made possible by the other, and obviously all three acts are held to be necessary for reaching a metaphysical object for the first time. If the comparison and removal did not also belong to the constitutive acts of the first metaphysical knowledge, then the field of the imagination would have been left from the outset. Both of these acts express of themselves a conversion to the phantasm, hence they must intrinsically characterize the *excessus* which is fundamental to metaphysics if this latter is not to be confused with an intellectual intuition. But how is a *remotio* possible, that is, a denial, negation, and removal of determinations which are valid only in the realm of the imagination? Obviously, the *comparatio,* the comparison between a sensible and a metaphysical object, is supposed to make the discovery of the difference between them possible, which then is to lead to an explicit differentiation of the two, a *remotio.* For merely leaving off the determinations of the sensible objects cannot as such and by itself give us a metaphysical object. But if the *remotio* presupposes the *comparatio,* how then is the *remotio* still a constitutive act for metaphysics at all? The *comparatio* seems to have already reached the metaphysical object immediately and in advance. Only in such a case does a comparison between the metaphysical and the sensible object seem possible at all. But how does this transitory encounter with the metaphysical object from the basis of the imagination take place? Obviously, through what Thomas calls here the *excessus.*

But what is this transcendent reaching beyond the field of the imagination, which is supposed to be the fundamental act of metaphysical knowledge, and in which an object outside of the

52

dimensions of space and time is to be grasped for the first time? Does not the idea of such an *excessus* bring us again to intellectual intuition? How is it to be thought of otherwise? How can it be understood in such a way that it encompasses the *comparatio* and *remotio* in itself as moments of its own essence in the one fundamental act of metaphysics? We have already concluded that these three acts cannot be independent acts connected in series one after the other only subsequently to their own essential being. The only thing clear at the moment is that, on the one hand, the *comparatio* and *remotio* presuppose such an *excessus* as the condition of their possibility, and on the other hand, that they could not be counted among the fundamental acts of metaphysical knowledge if this *excessus* were an intuition of the metaphysical object in its own immediate self. For then a *comparatio* and *remotio* would be an act entirely subsequent, since the metaphysical object would have been reached already by an immediate intuition into itself, intrinsically independent of the imagination and the conversion to the phantasm. Thus the question about the possibility of metaphysics on the basis of the imagination is the question about the sense of this non-intuitive *excessus* as the condition of the human imagination, of the human experience of the world.

We have already met the question of the *excessus* in the problematic of the whole of Article 7 quite often, but under different names: as a transcending comprehension of the world as a whole, as a conscious transcendence towards another, as *ascensio,* as the possibility of the limit-idea of an intuitive intellect.

There is one thing further to be noted in this third answer. It shows that we would not go beyond the scope of the Thomistic problematic by considering the *excessus* not as something which comes subsequently to the experience of world, but as the very condition of the possibility of the experience of world. In the objection and the answer to it, along with really metaphysical objects of knowledge (God, angels), truth also appears as belonging to the very thing whose possibility on the basis of the imagination is being investigated, and which is supposed to be

SPIRIT IN THE WORLD

made possible through the *excessus*. The *excessus* to metaphysics, which takes place in a conversion to the phantasm, is considered to be a condition of the truth of the knowledge of world. Thus the truth of the human experience of world is, as it were, the mid-point between experience of world and metaphysics, insofar as it is on the one hand related to the world possessed in sensibility and so always consists in a consideration of the thing through a conversion to the phantasm, and yet on the other hand it contains a being-set-apart from knowledge and thing, and only in this does the knowledge become truth and the thing become object. In this being-set-apart, truth appears over against the world and thus is possible only in an *excessus* beyond the world which is possessed in sensibility. Therefore, it already belongs in the realm of metaphysics. Thus the *excessus* which makes it possible is the condition of the true experience of world.

That brings to a close the tentative and exploratory interpretation of Article 7 of Question 84. Its point was only to ascertain the scope of the problematic of the conversion in a kind of preliminary exercise which used as its guide the Article which treats the conversion explicitly, and in this way to avoid either going beyond its scope, or underestimating the breadth of the question. Since that was the only purpose of this first part, a systematic summary of what has been gained so far from the interpretation of the text should not be necessary. The second part will have to give this systematic in its own way. For the same reason, the second part will not have to refer back to the first explicitly.

PART TWO
SPIRIT IN THE WORLD

CHAPTER ONE

THE FOUNDATION

I. THE POINT OF DEPARTURE: THE METAPHYSICAL QUESTION

1. The Basic Structure of the Metaphysical Question

MAN questions. This is something final and irreducible. For in human existence the question is that *fact* which *absolutely* refuses to be replaced by another fact, to be reduced back to another fact and thus to be unmasked once again as being itself derivative and provisional. For every placing-in-question of the question is itself again asking a question, and thereby a new instance of the question itself. So the question is first of all the only "must," the only necessity, the only thing beyond question to which questioning man is bound, the only circle in which his questioning is caught, the only apriority to which it is subject. Man questions necessarily.

But this necessity can only be grounded in the fact that being is accessible to man at all only as something questionable [*Fragbarkeit*], that he himself *is* insofar as *he asks about being,* that he himself exists as a question about being. For not just any question can ground the necessity of questioning as such: man could turn away from this or that question and thus free himself from the impelling need to question; he could sometimes get away from such a question completely. However, the question about being in its totality is the only question from which he cannot turn away, which he *must* ask if he wants *to be* at all, because only in this question is being in its totality (and so his own also) given to him, and this only as something questionable. For this reason the proposition stating the necessity of questioning in human existence includes in itself its own *ontological* proposition which says: man exists as the question about being. In order to be himself he necessarily asks about being in its totality. This question is the "must" which he himself *is* and in which being as that which is questioned presents and offers itself, and at the same time, as that which necessarily remains in question, withdraws itself. In the being of the question, which man is (so that he needs to question) being as that which is questioned both reveals itself and at the same time conceals itself in its own questionableness [*Fragwürdigkeit*].

Now from out of this situation which is peculiar to him and which constitutes his being, man asks about individual existents, he asks about many and even all of them. However, the metaphysical question is not any question at all about any object at all within the implicitly presupposed horizon of the question about being itself. The metaphysical question is rather the surmounting of this naïveté. It is the reflexive articulation of that question which pervades the ground of human existence itself, the question about being. For in fact, to put it first of all quite formally, the metaphysical question is that question which in a final and radical sharpening of man's questioning turns upon itself as such and thereby turns upon the presuppositions which are operative in itself; it is the question turned consciously upon itself, the *transcendental* question, which does not merely place something asked about in question, but the one questioning and his question itself, and thereby absolutely everything. But then it is precisely the thematization, the explicit, conceptually formulated repetition of the question which man necessarily exists as: the question about being in its totality. The metaphysical question as transcendental question is this pervasive question about being itself raised to conceptual form. In actually asking the metaphysical question man becomes aware of what he is in the ground of his essence: he who must ask about being.

2. The Questionableness (Fragwürdigkeit) of the Metaphysical Question

But this brings out the questionableness of the metaphysical question. Every question has a point of departure, and so, too, the metaphysical question. But what is to be its point of departure? Where is it to find the unquestionable ground on which to establish itself and on which the answer it seeks can be firmly based? For the metaphysical question does not concern this or that, but everything at once, being in its totality as something questionable. And this question about being in its totality is precisely that which cannot be so thought and so posed as though it were setting out to ask from a point "next to" or "outside" or "beyond" itself, which point itself would be given in unquestioned possession. Being in its totality can only be questioned as that which again constitutes in its turn every question about it (for the question certainly is not nothing). The being that is questioned is at once the being of the question and of the one questioning. But where can such a question begin, since it has no point from which it could take its departure? How can it find an answer at all, since there is no unquestioned basis available upon which it could establish the answer? Or has Thomas perhaps not posed the metaphysical question so sharply, did he as a metaphysician not venture to ask it this way? But he did. According to Thomas, metaphysics treats being in general; the "universal doubt about truth" belongs to metaphysics as necessarily as the "universal consideration of truth."[1]

So the metaphysical question can take a point of departure for its questioning, and so the content of its answer also, only from itself, from the compelling necessity to ask about being in its totality. This need to question is the only point of departure for the metaphysical question that has its foundation in itself. It

---

[1] *In III Metaph.* lect. 1, n. 343.

starts out from this point not in such a way that it leaves the starting point behind after the first step, never again to look back. Rather the metaphysical question probes into this very need to question: *simul universalem dubitationem prosequitur.*[2] According to Thomas, it is precisely the characteristic of the metaphysical question and thus of metaphysics itself that it must defend its own principles: *disputat contra negantem sua principia.*[3] It maintains its own basis only in this controversy. The question itself is the terrain on which it settles. Only there does it find that firm ground which is the primary basis of all human science. There alone is the absolute beginning of metaphysics. Metaphysics takes the "whence and whither" [*Woher und Wohin*] of its asking about being in its totality precisely from this very asking as that original, prevasive "must" which questioning man himself is. From out of this "must" all actual asking and questioning is stimulated and thus made possible.

But insofar as in metaphysics the question about being as a transcendental question consciously turns upon itself, looks at and questions itself, it reveals itself as a *knowledge* of man about his own questioning essence: he is already with being in its totality (*beim Sein im ganzen*); otherwise, how could he ask about it? In his first question (which always takes place with the question about being as its ground) he is already *quodammodo omnia* (in a certain way everything),[4] and still he is not yet that, he is still nothing, "*tabula rasa, materia prima in ordine intellectus*" (a clean slate, prime matter in the order of intellect),[5] for precisely what he does is *ask* what he means when he asks about being in its totality.

But this brings out the paradoxical nature of this first

---

[2] *Loc. cit.* The exact *ontological* sense of the question developed here is to be noted; then one cannot play off *S.T.* I, q. 5, a. 2, corp., against the Thomistic text quoted here, as B. Labebrink does in *Hegels dialektische Ontologie und die thomistische Analektik* (Köln, 1955), p. 470, n. 1.

[3] *S.T.* I, q. 1, a. 8, corp. See *In Post. Anal.* I, lect. 20 (Parma 120); lect. 21 (Parma 122).

[4] *S.C.G.* III, 112, and frequently elsewhere.

[5] Such expressions occur frequently in Thomas, e.g., *De Ver.* q. 10, a. 8, corp.

starting point of all metaphysical enquiry. It cannot be said in one word where this question begins. It takes its departure from nothing, insofar as it already comprehends the whole in order to start out on its way; in order to be the one who asks about being in its totality, man is already at the goal when he begins, since he must already know of being in its totality if he asks about it; and at the same time he confesses by his question that he himself is not the goal, but a finite man. This gives the starting point of metaphysics a peculiar duality and a unity at once: the starting point is questioning man, who as such is already with being in its totality. This starting point of metaphysics is also its limit, because this starting point is a question, and no answer reaches out beyond the horizon which the question has already set as a limit beforehand. "The later investigation of truth is nothing other than the solution of prior doubts."[6]

3. The "World" as the "Whence" (Woher) of the Metaphysical Question

How can we clarify the starting point of metaphysics in its unity and duality? We have already met the unity in duality of this starting point in another form in the introductory Section. In an initial decision, Article 7 of Question 84 established as a basis the knowledge of the fact, which knowledge is already and always presupposed, that man always finds himself already in the world when he ponders who and what he is. And the Article gave us as a guide to its own investigation the knowledge of a fixed relationship between knowing and known insofar as both spring from a single ground. So the question is: How can these two things posited in Article 7 be reached from the description of the starting point of human metaphysics given so far; how can it be shown that the two of them, mutually clarifying and justifying each other, are objectively identical?

When man ventures to ask about everything, he starts out from "nothing." And yet this "nothing" cannot be an empty void which man fills arbitrarily according to his own whims, and

---

[6] *In III Metaph.* lect. 1, n. 339.

from which he could wander in any direction he liked. For he is summoned to ask about being in its totality. So this "nothing" itself must have imposed upon him the task of reaching out after being as such. Just this much shows already that this "nothing" at the beginning of the questioning which man is, is not a vague, empty void, the place for arbitrary wandering, but rather the unambiguous need to be able and to have to encounter being in its totality in his questioning. But this does not yet describe unambiguously the whence of this being-already-and-always-with-being-in-its-totality (*Je-schon-beim-Sein-im-Ganzen-Sein*). Man would not stand questioning, and hence as finite, before and in being as such if in his questioning he could comprehend being in its totality however he liked and according to his own choice, from any point of this being at all. If he could determine by his own choice this "nothing" which is the "whence" of his questioning, he would already be with being in its totality in such a way that he would have mastered it and would not have to question any more. What, then, is the existent with which man always and necessarily already is, and at which point he is called into the presence of being in its totality? It is the things of the world, he himself with his corporeality and with all that belongs to the realm and to the environment of this corporeal life.

We are not asking here how being in its totality is related to this "world" as the whence of his asking about being. Only this much is certain: man is in the presence of being in its totality insofar as he finds himself in the world. The "present state of life, in which he is united with receptive corporeality" is the only "state" that Thomas knows anything about in which man who asks about being exists. His man dwells on earth, and it is not given to him to exchange this dwelling place for a heavenly one at his own discretion. Even Thomas's theology is not a flight from the earth, but the hearing of the word of God within the narrow confines of this world and within the flitting brevity of an earthly hour. It remains on the basis of the imagination, for even the revelation still takes place "through likenesses taken from sensible things."[7] And even if man wanted to flee this world as the place of all his questioning—by mysticism or sui-

---

[7] *In Boeth. De Trin.* q. 6, a. 3, corp.

cide or any other way—and could thus reach some other place for an understanding of being, he would still have begun on this earth. But this shows that for Thomas there is only *one* knowing, in which man is himself: a knowing being-with-the-world [*ein wissendes Bei-der-Welt-Sein*]. Only here is man called into the presence of being in its totality. It is here that he carries on the business of his metaphysics.[8]

In this knowledge of the world man has already and always comprehended being in its totality when he asks about it. Hence a relationship between being and knowing is already understood simultaneously in the most general question of metaphysics. How can we clarify this? The operative principle of the first part of the third section of the corpus in Article 7 of Question 84 posed the same question to us. If we notice further that in our considerations so far we have always spoken of *the* knowledge of world, and that consequently we always considered and had to consider this as *one* knowledge, there follow two questions:

1. The question about the unity of man's knowledge of the world. Because the material content of this question coincides with the question of the whole book, our only concern at first will be to acquire some directions of a methodological kind for continuing the whole investigation, and this by a formal consideration of this one knowledge of the world as the starting point for asking about being.

2. The question about the relationship of knowing and being in general, the anticipatory (*vorgreifenden*) understanding of which makes the question about being in its totality possible.

But before this the point that gave rise to these two questions requires some further attention itself. The one starting

---

[8] See for example *S.T.* I, q. 86, a. 2, corp. How decisively Thomas maintains this single starting point is shown, for example, in *S.C.G.* II, 60, where from the fact that we acquire our knowledge from the senses it is deduced that the intellect does not have and could not have a further and separate source of knowledge for itself: *quia natura non abundat superfluis;* otherwise the intellect would have a double knowledge: *unam per modum substantiarum separatarum* (an intellectual intuition), *aliam a sensibus acceptam (scientiam); quorum altera superflueret.*

point of metaphysics appeared to involve a peculiar paradox. Now this paradox also betrays itself in Thomas's formulation of the problem of the conversion to the phantasm: whether the intellect can actually know anything . . . without turning to the phantasms. When so posed the question has already reached the dimensions of a question about the intrinsic *possibility* of such knowing. If we come upon this knowing "from without," in its actualization (*Vollzug*), in the actual realization of its possibility, we always find it to be already with the phantasm, to be already and invariably located at a definite here and now, to be already and invariably with the "likeness of the individual thing which is here and now."[9] On the other hand, according to the formulation of the problem, this knowing in the here and now of world is found to reach the here and now only by a conversion. Thus it can have turned to this here and now only from being in its totality, for every here and now is supposed to be reached by this conversion. And yet such knowing can in its questioning comprehend being in its totality, from which it must come, only in the here and now, only in this present state of life, because all asking as an actual knowing already presupposes the conversion to the here and now as a condition of its possibility. So the paradox of the starting point of human metaphysics in its unity and duality shows up in the formulation of the problem of the conversion to the phantasm: with the here and now of the world and with being in its totality.

But does not the question about the conversion contain the answer in itself from the outset? For precisely what is being asked in this question is whether anything—and so everything —can be known only by the knower's being with a here and now of some existent in the world. Then is not what we designated as the starting point still in question precisely in the problem of the conversion?

Now it could be said that it is not the conversion as question, but only as answer, that contains in itself this paradoxical duality of the starting point of metaphysics, that it is only the answer which decides that knowing is possible only when it has

[9] In *De Mem. et Rem.* lect. 2, n. 314; See *S.T.* I, q. 85, a. 5, ad 2, etc.

encountered a definite point of the world, which encounter is in itself a coming from the breadth of being in its totality. Before this answer, what is still open is precisely whether knowledge of this or that individual in the world is possible only by coming from absolute being, and whether knowledge of being in its totality is possible only by an encounter in the here and now of the world. In this conception, however, the question about the conversion itself would not be a metaphysical question at all, but would be identical with establishing the place where the question of human metaphysics begins. As a matter of fact, maintaining the necessity of a conversion to the phantasm is, as a proposition, identical with establishing the place from which we ask metaphysically about being in its totality, and so the proposition as such is already established when the problem of the conversion first begins. For as a metaphysical question, this problem asks about the intrinsic possibility of such a conversion, about all that is already said implicitly in the statement of the proposition. And what is noteworthy in the development of the intrinsic possibility of the conversion to the phantasm is this: it is concerned not so much with the arrival at the here and now of the world, but with this coming from being in its totality. But then the conversion is asking about the possibility of metaphysics itself. Thus, this question shows itself to be metaphysical in its origin.

II. THE UNITY OF KNOWLEDGE

The problem of the conversion to the phantasm is for Thomas a question of grasping human knowing as *one* insofar as all knowledge is placed upon the one basis of the imagination. If the unity of this human knowledge is to be grasped in its possibility, then this unity is already presupposed insofar as man in the world is the only man that Thomas knows, and for him it is only a question of understanding the possibility of this man who always finds himself already knowing in the world. What matters, then, is to gather in advance from the concept of this already presupposed unity indications to help in the investigation of its intrinsic possibility, which possibility is what is asked about in the conversion to the phantasm.

What is united in this unity of knowledge? Knowledge of an existent in the world in its here and now and knowledge of being in its totality. If we say that sensibility is being with a thing in the here and now of the world, and that intellect is the knowledge of being in its totality, we can also say that it is a question of understanding the intrinsic possibility of the unity of sensibility and intellect, the fact of which unity forms the point of departure for all our considerations. More precisely, it is a question here of gathering formal indications to help in arriving at this understanding, which indications are already grasped simultaneously with the unity of knowing which has already been affirmed.

If we use the word *animality* instead of sensibility, and *rationality* instead of intellect, then our question is about the unity of the rational and animal. Thomas treats this question formally in *In VII Metaph*. lect. 12.[1] The question there is how genus (animal) and difference (rational) in the definition (rational animal) are one. They ought not to be thought of as two things which are grounded in themselves as their own possibility and come together only subsequently; in fact, they should not be considered as two "parts" of man in the first place. The genus already contains within itself the difference, just as that which is indeterminate, but which must be determined if it is to be at all, already contains its determination potentially.[2]

Thus the genus cannot be apprehended as something immediately possible without its difference being simultaneously understood. And vice versa, the same holds for the difference. This says that what is united in the unity of human knowledge can in every case be understood only within the totality of this knowledge. Our being with the here and now of the individual things of the world through sensibility is of such a nature that as such and in its concrete possibility it is already and always being with being in its totality through intellect, and vice versa.

[1] N. 1537ff.
[2] See *De Anima* a. 11, ad 19: *ipsa anima sensibilis in homine est rationalis, in brutis vero irrationalis.*

66

But from this it follows that neither sensibility nor thought as such can be met with in the concrete by itself; where they are found they are always already one.[3] And this is true not in the sense that one could be reduced to or deduced from the other, but in the sense that each one is itself and different from the other only in its unity with the other. Thomas is so aware of this relationship that he explicitly emphasizes that we ought not to think that sensibility, which belongs also to man, is found in animals in its "pure" state. It is found in animals not as "pure," not "as such," but determined in a particular way as animal sensibility, as lion sensibility, and so on.

But there follows from this an indication of the only way of speaking which is adequate for such a situation: statements about sensibility which apprehend its essence completely cannot be made unless they already express the essence of thought simultaneously. And since, nevertheless, statements about sensibility and thought must be made one after the other, each further statement affects and modifies the sense of the previous statements. And all of them have their ultimate meaning only in the totality.

III. KNOWING AND KNOWN

When man becomes a metaphysician, he finds himself, by the fact that he is with individual existents here and now, already and always with being in its totality. If, then, this being-in-the-world is to be understood, it is important to clarify what that antecedent comprehension (*vorgängige Umgreifen*) of being in its totality involves.

If man, in order to come to a knowledge of an existent here and now, is already and always with being in its totality, then in the necessity by which he dwells with the individual existent in his knowledge, he affirms the questionability (*Fragbarkeit*) of being in its totality. Hence he has already come upon a fundamental determination of being as such: being is being-able-to-be-known (*Sein ist Erkanntseinkönnen*). But in this

---

[3] See also on this point *In VII Metaph.* lect. 9, n. 1462ff.

determination two others are again contained: (1) an original unity of being and knowing, and (2) an essential indefinability of what being expresses.

1. Being and Knowing as Original Unity in Being-Present-to-Self (Beisichsein) (Knowing as the Subjectivity of Being Itself)

Being is questionability. Now one cannot ask about being in its totality without affirming the fundamental knowability, in fact a certain *a priori* knownness of being as such. What is absolutely unknowable cannot be asked about, in fact what is absolutely unknown cannot be asked about. Every question is evoked by an antecedent summons from what is questioned, which as conscious (although not *reflexively* known, or although not even knowable reflexively) and as known (although not *explicitly* known, or although not even knowable explicitly) is present in the question itself. Thus in view of the reality of the question about being, the concept of a being unknowable in principle, in fact of a being even only factually (totally) unknown, is rejected as a contradiction. "For whatever can be can be known."[1]

But this fundamental relationship between being and knowing can be grasped in its possibility only if it is not added as a relationship established subsequent to being and to a cognitive power, as a subsequent relationship which would only be accidental to both of them, but especially to being. "For the intelligible and the intellect must be proportional (however, not only that, but also:) they must be of a single origin, since the intellect and the intelligible in act are one" (because otherwise the factual unity of being and knowing in actual knowing could not be made intelligible in its possibility).[2]

Thus being and knowing exist in an original unity. Knowing does not come upon its object by chance. Thomas explicitly rejects the common conception of knowing as a coming upon

[1] *S.C.G.* II, 98.
[2] *In Metaph. Proem.*

something.[3] Knowing does not come about "through a contact
of the intellect with the intelligible thing," but being and knowing are the same: "the intellect and the known and the knowing
are the same." Knowing is the being-present-to-self of being,
and this being-present-to-self is the being of the existent (*Er-
kennen ist Beisichsein des Seins, und dieses Beisichsein ist das
Sein des Seinden*). Therefore the beingness (*Seiendheit*), the
intensity of being (*Seinsmächtigkeit*) of the being of an existent is determined for Thomas by the *reditio super seipsum*, the
intensity of being is determined by the degree of possibility of
being able to be present to itself.[4] Knowing is thus essentially
"subjectivity," not a "being dispersed to many," in which dispersion to objects one could, in a metaphysical misunderstanding, see the "objectivity" of knowledge.[5] Being is the one ground
which lets knowing and being-known spring out of itself as its
own characteristics, and thus grounds the intrinsic possibility of
an antecedent, essential, intrinsic relation of both of them to
each other. Knowing is the subjectivity of being itself. Being
itself is the original, *unifying* unity of being and knowing in
their *unification* in being-known. In this latter the two of them
are not brought together accidentally, purely factually and extrinsically, but are actualized in their original relatedness to
each other. The transcendental intelligibility of being cannot be
conceived in any other way: "for a plurality is not unified of itself."

If being able to know and knowability are thus intrinsic characteristics of being itself, then an actual, individual knowing cannot be definitively conceived in its metaphysical essence if it is
understood merely as the relationship of a knower to an object
different from him, as intentionality. The fundamental and first
point of departure for a metaphysically correct understanding
of what knowledge is must rather be seen in the fact that being
is of itself knowing and being known, that being is being-pres-

[3] *S.C.G.* II, 98, towards the end; *De Ver.* q. 8, a. 7, ad 2.
[4] *De Ver.* q. 1, a. 9, corp.; q. 10, a. 9, corp.; *S.C.G.* IV, 11.
[5] *Opusc.* 28, c. 1; cf. P. Rousselot, *L'intellectualisme de Saint Thomas*
(Paris, 1924), p. 5, n. 3. It is always this second edition that is cited
in what follows (Third edition: Paris, 1946).

ent-to-self (*Beisichsein*). *Intellectus in actu perfectio est intellectum in actu*[6]: the complete, ontological actualization of the intellect is the actually known, an essential proposition which can also be reversed: the actually known, in order to be itself, must be the ontological actualization of the intellect itself. In such formulations "intellect" stands for any knowledge at all. In such a statement Thomas reaches quite explicitly the ontological understanding of metaphysics which is quite current today (as opposed to a purely ontic mode of consideration). Knowing is understood as the subjectivity of being itself, as the being-present-to-self of being. Being itself is already the original, unifying unity of being and knowing, is onto-logical; and every actual unity of being and knowing in the actualization of knowledge is only raising to a higher power that transcendental synthesis which being is "in itself."

It would be a complete misunderstanding to want to understand the identity of knowing and known which is expressed in these and similar formulations[7] in the sense that the known as such must be known precisely by a knower as such, and that the knower as such must have a known. *Perfectio* expresses rather an ontological actuality of the intellect as a being. "The intellect and what is known are the same."[8] "The known is a perfection of the knower."[9] Therefore, one would run the risk of missing the metaphysical sense of this principle of the Thomistic metaphysics of knowledge if he were prematurely to attribute any arbitrary sense he happens to hit upon to the likeness, the species, by which Thomas sees this identity between knowing and known produced in many cases, if he were to get any vague, common notion at all of an "intentional representation," which is present in the intellect and produces this union between knowing and known. Rather the principle that being is being-present-to-self and that thus the known is always the being of the knower must be taken seriously, and then it must follow from this what species means.

[6] *S.C.G.* II, 99.
[7] *S.T.* I, q. 14, a. 2, corp.; q. 55, a. 1, ad 2; q. 85, a. 2, ad 1; q. 87, a. 1, ad 3, etc.
[8] *S.T.* I, q. 87, a. 1., ad 3.
[9] *S.C.G.* II, 98.

Only by taking this principle literally can we reach an understanding of what "matter" means, of how Thomas arrives at the proposition: in immaterial beings, the intellect and what is known are the same,[10] only then does it become clear what "subsisting in itself" means, and so forth. It is only in the light of this proposition that we can gain access to the metaphysical concept of sensibility that is present in Thomas, only then can we understand that the knowability of a being varies according to what it is.[11]

And vice versa: if we succeed in making all of these fundamental intuitions of Thomistic metaphysics intelligible in the light of this principle of the Thomistic metaphysics of knowledge, then that furnishes us with the clearest proof that we have interpreted this first principle of the metaphysics of knowledge correctly. Since the process of proving this goes on repeatedly in one way or another throughout the course of the whole work, there is no need at this point to go further into the proof that the interpretation of this principle that was only indicated here is what Thomas himself meant.

2. The Essential Indefinability of the Concept of Being

In showing itself to be the antecedent and original unity of knowing and known, this being shows itself to be essentially indefinable. This description of being followed from what we called its questionability. This questionability (*Fragbarkeit*) is such that it remains questionable (*fraglich*), that is, it is a questionability that is not always and totally eliminated when it receives an answer. This questionability shows that being is being-present-to-self. But it seems contradictory to say that being is being-present-to-self and that being always remains questionable. Why must being be asked about if being is already and always being-present-to-self? The one who must ask is being because in asking about being he is already with being, and yet he is not it

[10] *De Spir. Creat.* a. 1, sed contra, n. 8; a. 8, ad 14; *S.T.* I, q. 87, a. 1, ad 3, etc. Cf. Hufnagel, *Intuition und Erkenntnis* . . ., p. 70.
[11] *In VIII Metaph.* lect. 2, n. 1304: *secundum enim quod aliquid est ens, secundum hoc est cognoscibile.*

because he is not yet with being in its totality in such a way that this being-with-being is a questionless possession of being in its totality. Thus the being that must ask is non-being, is deficient in its innermost ground of being. The intensity of its being is finite, and therefore it must ask, therefore it is not absolutely present-to-itself. But then the concept of being itself proves to be variable in its content. It is not a univocally definable quantity from which something unambiguous can be drawn about its content, about knowing as the presence-to-self of being. The material insight that was reached at first, namely, that being is being-present-to-self, has been transposed into a formal scheme, namely, that the intensity of knowledge is parallel to the intensity of being, that an existent is present-to-itself insofar as it is being, and that, vice versa, the degree of this "subjectivity" is the measure of an existent's intensity of being. This consideration at the same time distinguishes our metaphysical approach towards an understanding of the *a priori* unity of being and knowing from a possible idealistic misunderstanding.

As clear as Thomas is about the material insight, that being is the being-present-to-itself of an existent, in general he still prefers to formulate this fundamental idea of his metaphysics of knowledge formally, since that brings out at the same time the indefinability of the concept of being itself. "The relationship of things to being and to truth is the same."[12] "Since everything is knowable insofar as it is in act . . ."[13] and so on. The distinction of the levels of knowledge according to the degree of immateriality is, as will be shown, just another expression of the same principle. According to what was said earlier, the degree of potency for being can never be the point of departure for determining the degree of being-present-to-self (as the degree of potency for knowledge and of knowability at once) in the sense that this would be deduced as a conclusion from the potency for being already materially determined antecedently. In the statement about the relationship between the potency for being and being-present-to-self there is question of an essential determination in which the subject of the proposi-

[12] *S.T.* I–II, q. 3, a. 7, corp.
[13] *In II Metaph.* lect. 1, n. 280.

tion (although in a formal way) says the same thing as the predicate: the "insofar as it is in act" is absolutely identical with the "so far is it knowable." Expressed Thomistically: "truth" is a transcendental determination of "being."

From this there follows a tentative understanding of various concepts which are of fundamental importance for understanding the Thomistic metaphysics of knowledge: the concept of "knowability" and the relation of knowledge and knowability to "matter."

Knowability itself (*cognoscibilitas, cognoscibile*) is not a univocal, hard-and-fast concept. If being means being-present-to-self, and if there are existents of different intensities of being, then there are different degrees of being-present-to-self. But the fundamental meaning of knowability is to-be-able-to-be-present-to-self. Therefore, there are different degrees of knowability itself. Knowability does not mean the indifferent being-there (*Dastehen*) of an essence in itself with the indifferent possibility of being known by another (and so under certain circumstances by itself also), should this other succeed in apprehending this essence by means of its cognitive faculty structured in a corresponding way. In such a conception there would be no intrinsic degrees of knowability as such, but rather knowability would merely be the extrinsic relation of an essence to a knower that was suited to it. In this conception it would make no sense to contrast some things as actually knowable with others as only potentially knowable.[14] The knowability of an existent is not first of all the possibility of being known by others (this other might sometimes accidentally and in fact be this existent itself), but is originally being-able-to-be-present-to-self (and only then derivatively also a "being-able-to-be-with-others"), and this being-able-to-be-present-to-self as an intrinsic determination of the essence of being itself varies with being's intensity of being.

[14] E.g., *S.C.G.* II, 98: *substantiae separatae sunt secundum suam naturam ut actu existentes in esse intelligibili.* II, 91: there are *secundum naturam suam intelligibilia* and *quae non sunt secundum se intelligibilia.* Without this insight the whole Thomistic doctrine of abstraction is utterly unintelligible.

Now if the being-able-to-be-present-to-self of being is an essentially indeterminate and variable quantity, and if according to experience (this is brought in here for the sake of simplicity in the development) there is a being that does not know in any way, hence is in no way present-to-itself, then the being of this existent itself cannot be present-to-itself, it cannot belong to it- self, it must be the being of "another." This "other" must on the one hand be real, but on the other hand it cannot have being in itself and of itself. This empty, in itself indeterminate "wherein" (*Worin*) of the being of an existent, in which being is in a such a way that it is not for itself but for that, and so is not "present- to-itself," is called Thomistically prime matter. It is now self- evident that knowing and knowability as presence-to-self and being-able-to-be-present-to-self are in a fixed relationship to the relation of being to matter. The intensity of being can now be formally determined from the relationship of being to matter, and then be transposed materially into knowledge and know- ability.

Thus it becomes intelligible how for Thomas an essence which has no intrinsic relatedness to matter is by this very fact already actually present-to-itself: it is knowing and actually knowable. Therefore, this actually knowable by no means expresses in the first instance a relation to another knowing, but is a determination of the essence of being in itself: it has no intrinsic relatedness to matter. If it were in and at matter, the being of an existent would disperse itself. By the fact that it is without matter, it is therefore present-to-itself, knowing and known by itself. What is only potentially knowable is such not because accidentally and as a matter of fact it is not known by anyone, but because its being is the being of the empty "other" of matter in such a way that it in no way belongs to itself, it is not present-to-itself, and in this mode of existence it cannot in principle be present-to-itself, it remains and must remain essentially potentially knowable.

This also gives us the genuine and original concept of the "proper object" of a knower, although Thomas usually uses it in its application to definite levels of knowledge, and because of this the real point of origin of the concept is hidden to a superficial consideration. If being is primarily presence-to-self, then the real and original object of a knowing being is that with which it originally is: itself. And from this it is self-evident that the intensity of being of the knower and that of what is originally known stand in a fixed relationship of equality.

Thus for the Thomistic metaphysics of knowledge the problem does not lie in bridging the gap between knowing and object by a "bridge" of some kind: such a "gap" is merely a pseudoproblem. Rather the problem is how the known, which is identical with the knower, can stand over against the knower as other, and how there can be a knowledge which receives another as such. It is not a question of "bridging" a gap, but of understanding how the gap is possible at all. If being is being-present-to-self, then in such a concept of knowledge it is perhaps easy to see further how a being could know another in its being-present-to-itself insofar as it apprehends itself as the creative ground of this other. In this case the other is not the "proper object" at all. But given such an approach to the essence of knowing, the question becomes more difficult how in such an approach a receptive knowing can be shown to be possible, in fact how there could be a non-knowing being at all.[15]

For the Thomistic metaphysics of knowledge it is only from the concept of being as being-present-to-self and of knowing as the presence-to-self of being, as the subjectivity of being itself,

---

[15] C. Nink (*Ontologie*, Freiburg, 1952, p. 115 with note 112) takes exception to the understanding of being as being-present-to-self developed here (whereby knowing is the essential subjectivity of being itself), saying that being-present-to-self is "not the essence of an existent, of its being and its action," but *follows* "from its being and action." However, for the *onto-logical* concept of the being of an existent, knowing, subjectivity, hence being-present-to-self is precisely not something subsequent, a consequence (although this follows with "logical necessity"). For then being itself in its "real in-itself" would once again be set off from knowing, and hence—to formulate it in the terms that have become current in this problematic—would ultimately be developed as a merely *ontic* concept from which knowing, subjectivity "follows."

If Nink wants to understand that being-present-to-self follows from the being of the existent itself *really* as well as logically (as his conception of the "logically necessary consequence" suggests), then we would have

that a metaphysical insight is to be had into the possibility of a receptive knowing of another. In this problem it is never a question of understanding how another could be known as the secondary object of a knower which is itself the object known first. For in this case there is no question of receptive knowing at all, since such a knower is present-to-itself from the outset and does not come to itself from the other, but through its own self-possession it simultaneously apprehends others besides.[16] Hence in the problem of the possibility of receptive knowing it is a

to ask how this following really and logically can be distinguished from our understanding of being as being-present-to-self. Ultimately what can "*really* and logically" mean that is *objectively* relevant other than that being *as itself* (in its "in-itself," in its "physical nature") is precisely "logic," but that means knowing and being known?

In other words, the distinction between being and being-present-to-self can only designate that onto-logical and in this sense "*real*" distinction, that difference that obtains *in being itself* and (however this is understood) does not come to it or follow from it. This distinction (whatever you might call it) ultimately does not set being (as what is in its own self in "pure facticity") off from being-present-to-self, but rather realizes once again in this *distinguishing*—since and insofar as this is to have ontological and not merely "purely logical" significance—that irreducible ontological synthesis (of being and logic) which being "in itself" is and which cannot be further resolved even "purely logically," because then logic (which of course even as logic necessarily "is" something) would eliminate itself and hence there could no longer be question of even a formal, "purely logical" distinction. There is shown clearly here the ever present and insurmountable *ontological circle of all logic*, which can never be "pure formal logic" at all (as opposed to "being-in-its-own-self"). Basically this holds also for the rejection of our understanding of being as being-present-to-self in B. Labebrink (*op. cit.*, pp. 213, and 459, note 77). With regard to Labebrink's opinion that we "narrow" being down to being-present-to-self, our interpretation of the concept of matter in Thomas (cf. below, Ch. 4, Sections 5 and 6) should be consulted especially.

[16] At this point we do not yet have to go into the question whether such a non-receptive knowing of another could also be conceived in a way other than by the fact that the knowing is creative, is *intuitus originarius*. Thomas ascribes to the angels a knowledge of material things which obviously cannot be creative in the strict sense. But since for Thomas receptive knowledge of the other is essentially sentient, he conceives the knowledge of the angels as a participation in the creative knowledge of God, as a *scientia quasi activa*. But we will have to refer briefly to this matter later.

question of a knowing whose proper object is something other than itself.

Insofar as the decision we met with earlier about how man is to understand himself says precisely that he invariably finds himself already with the other of the world, hence that the other as such is his proper object, that his being-present-to-self is thus a being-with-the-other, and that he wants to understand himself in all his potentialities from this basis, then the problem of receptive knowing is identical with the question about man, and it will turn out to be the question about the conversion to the phantasm.

Just from what has been said so far it follows that the possibility of such knowing will have to be found by determining the intensity of being which is disclosed in such knowing. This is what decides *a priori* what its proper object is; this is what decides the question: what must the existent be with in order to be present-to-itself?

Insofar as man is *one* existent and thus represents a definite intensity of being, he also possesses *one* knowing, and every question about his knowing is in its first beginning and its final solution the question about this *one* knowing. Therefore, different cognitive faculties must be shown to be such by making it intelligible why and how they flow from this one being of this definite intensity of being.

If we call this being-present-to-self as being-with-another sensibility, and being-present-to-self as being-placed-over-against-another thought, then correspondingly the questions which are to be treated in what follows are:

1. The one knowing as sensibility: *praesentia mundi* (the presence of world) (Chapter 2).
2. The one knowing as thought: *oppositio mundi* (the opposition of world) (Chapter 3).
3. The one knowing in its unity itself: *conversio ad phantasma* (conversion to the phantasm) (Chapter 4).

CHAPTER TWO

SENSIBILITY

I. THE POINT OF DEPARTURE FOR THE CONCEPT OF SENSIBILITY

IF we start out from the fundamental premise of the Thomistic metaphysics of knowledge that knowledge is the being-present-to-itself of an existent of a definite intensity of being, which presence-to-self is just the material expression of the intensity of being itself, it follows necessarily that the knower of such an intensity of being and the known are identical.

Presupposing this, however, how can there be a knowledge of another as such in which this other is the proper object of the knowledge, that is, in which there is no knowledge antecedent to the other in which the other is known through the object of this knowledge, which object is identical with the knowing? That is the problem posed to us by the question about the essence of sensibility. This problem seems to be insoluble given the fundamental premise about the essence of knowing which we just mentioned. For if something is present-to-itself in knowledge by the fact that it possesses a definite intensity of being, and if presence-to-self and a definite intensity of being are the same, then one's own intensity of being, one's own "subjectivity" seems essentially and necessarily to be the first object known, the proper object. A subsequent inference to a cause producing an intensification of being, whereby the knower would reach that intensity of being which expresses presence-to-self, could not change anything in this relationship. The cause so inferred would neither be the proper object known first, which is the foundation of any knowledge at all, nor would it be intuited, that is, apprehended immediately in its own self. In this case the knowing would remain in its fundamental act an intuition of its own intensity of being, and would not be a receptive intuition of another, of something objective in its own self. The increased intensity of being through which the knower comes to himself gives the knower only himself, and even if this intensification as such (which is always that of the being of the knower) should give evidence of its being produced by another and be apprehended as produced by another, the knower would perhaps know of that other doing the producing, but he would not be with the other as something intuited. An inference from a subjective affect to what causes the affect does not ground the genuine possibility of intuiting the other, does not make the knowledge transcendent in its origin.

How must a knower be understood ontologically, if, in spite of the metaphysical premise that knowledge is the presence-to-itself of an existent of a definite intensity of being, nevertheless there is to be an intuitive knowledge of another as the proper object? If according to the fundamental premise of the Thomistic metaphysics of knowledge only that which the knower itself is is known as proper object, and if, nevertheless, there is to be a knowledge in which this known as proper object is the other, then both of these can be understood as simultaneously possible only by the fact that *the knower itself is the being of the other*. The being of what intuits receptively must be the being of another as such. Antecedent to any apprehension of a definite other, the knower of itself must have already and always entered into otherness. For so long as being, which says being-present-to-itself, remains within itself, possesses itself in its own ground and possesses its determinations as its own, there is no possibility from the start that it and with it the intensification of being, wherever it comes from, be originally present-to-itself in any other way than as being present-to-itself in the same indifferentiation in which it exists in itself

79

ontologically. Only if a being is ontologically separated from itself by the fact that it is not the being of itself, but the being of what is absolutely "other," can it have the possibility of possessing a foreign ontological actuality as its own in such a way that everything that is its own is by that very fact another's because the being of the knower in question is not being for itself, but being for and to another.

This absolutely other, to which a being must be given away from the outset if it is to be able to have a receptive intuition of a definite other at all, must on the one hand be a real principle of the knower, but on the other hand cannot itself have being of itself and in itself. For as being it would itself fall under the law that being means being-present-to-self. That being of the knower which would belong to another which exists of itself would then be conscious precisely as the being of that which is in itself present to itself, in other words, another *as such* could not be had in consciousness in this way. *That real non-being, as the being in which a being is separated from itself, is called Thomistically prime matter.* Thus receptive knowledge is essentially conceivable only as the being of something material; it is sensibility.

But that seems to lead us into a fundamental contradiction. For earlier we saw prime matter precisely as the reason why there could be an existent which is not a knower, although being in itself means being-present-to-self; we saw it as that which gives an existent the possibility of being without retaining the meaning of being, namely, being-present-to-self. Accordingly, at the moment in which an existent is conceived of as being so deficient that its being is no longer the being of itself, but the being of a real and empty potency different from itself, this existent seems to be utterly unable to be present to itself in any way any more, and so any possibility of knowledge is eliminated. Thus intuition of another as proper object seems to presuppose an intensity of being of such a kind that this being is not its own, but that of matter; and intuition as knowledge seems to demand a potency for being which excludes materiality.

Now if, however, there is such a thing as sensibility, that is, the receptive intuition of another as such, it is clear from the paradoxical nature of such an intuition just indicated that the essence of sensibility can be apprehended only by defining it dialectically from two sides. That holds for the determination of the intensity of being of a sentient knower as well as for the peculiarity of the presence-to-self that belongs to sense knowledge.

If knowing is the being-present-to-itself of being, but knowing the other as proper object means essentially and ontologically being-away-from-self-with-the-other (*Weg-von-sich-beim-andern-Sein*), then the being of the sentient knower can only be understood as the mid-point[1] poised between a real abandonment to the other of matter and an intrinsic independence of being over against matter, so that the sensible act is in undivided unity material (*actus materiae*) and, as material, the act of the assertion of being (of form) over against matter (*actus contra materiam*).

Likewise the conscious being-present-to-itself of the sentient knower can only be defined negatively from two sides. It is neither a presence-to-self (a *redire in seipsum*) which could possess itself as set over against the other, nor can it be being-with-the-other in such a way that it would have lost itself utterly in this other with the elimination of any consciousness. The being of the sentient knower is present-to-itself, but this being is precisely the undivided mid-point poised between a total abandonment to the other and an intrinsic independence over against this other. In the light of this metaphysical concept of sensibility it is easy to see that the question whether sensibility as such perceives only its own "affections" or the "outside world" does not make any sense. It does neither the one nor the other because the interiority of sensibility as the act of mat-

---

[1] See *De Ver.* q. 1, a. 11, corp.: sense is *quodommodo medius inter intellectum et res*, wherein *res* is what absolutely does not know, while intellect is characterized precisely by the fact that an "*in seipsum reflecti*" belongs to it (*S.C.G.* IV, 11; *S.T.* I, q. 87, a. 3, ad 3) of which the "*in se subsistentem esse*" is only the ontological formulation (*S.T.* I, q. 14, a. 2, ad 1; *I Sent.* dist. 17, q. 1, a. 5, ad 3), which again is the same as "*non super aliud delatum esse* (*I Sent., loc. cit.*).

ter is precisely its exteriority, and vice versa, and every separation between the two requires an act which would not be material. It is clear that sensibility as such cannot be observed in us at all by introspection and experimental tests, prescinding completely from the fact that an observation which wants to discover one thing among others always presupposes a notion of what it is looking for already. An appeal to experience, which can always bring into view only the whole of the one human experience, thought included, is therefore irrelevant with regard to this concept of sensibility.

What has been said so far was only supposed to show that a knowledge which as such is receptive, that is, which has the other as its proper object, is necessarily material, and hence means sensibility. We will have a further opportunity later to give a more exact proof that this thesis is Thomistic. In the meantime it might suffice for this purpose to have shown that this thesis follows necessarily from the fundamental Thomistic presupposition that knowing is the being-present-to-self of the knower himself. Therefore, if there is to be any knowledge at all of another as the fundamental and first knowledge, if the world is to be the first and only intuition of man, then human intuition must be sensible, the being of the one intuiting must be the being of the other, of matter. In any case we have reached at least a tentative understanding of what it should mean when Thomas says that sensibility is material.[2]

II. THE KNOWLEDGE OF THE
SENSIBLE OTHER THROUGH SENSIBILITY

In the preceding Section it did not yet become clear how the materiality of the receptive knower is related to the individual, sensibly perceivable object which is supposed to manifest itself. Indeed it was said that that knower which has the other as the proper object of its intuition must from the outset, according to the principle of the identity of knowing and what is known first, have entered into otherness (*Andersheit*), into matter in

[2] *S.T.* I, q. 12, a. 4, ad 3; q. 75, a. 3; q. 85, a. 1, corp.

order that such an intuition of another as such could be possible at all. But this does not yet make intelligible how this otherness is related to the individual, other object, and how therefore the knowledge of the individual, other object becomes more intelligible with the statement, receptive knowledge is necessarily material.

Even an only partially satisfactory answer to this question is not possible at this point for several reasons. First, because then the Thomistic concept of matter would have to be treated extensively here, which the scope of this work makes impossible. Then the problematic of efficient and transient causality in Thomas would already have to be treated at this point. But if this is to be really worked out in such a way as would be adequate for the solution of the problem in question here, going back to what is usually said explicitly in Thomas about the concept of efficient causality would not suffice. It is only by tracing efficient causality back to material and formal causality that we would have the means for understanding the problem of the influence of the sensible object upon sensibility in such a way that Thomas's statements about sensibility become really and intrinsically intelligible. But the very process of tracing this back can be shown clearly enough to be Thomistic only if it is shown by the example of the origin of the faculties from the substantial ground of an existent that the self-realization of an existent is a genuine Thomistic concept, and that without this concept the idea of the agent intellect as the pure spontaneity of thought is untenable. But because tracing this back does involve these presuppositions (origin of the faculties, agent intellect) which must be treated explicitly in their own place in this work, it is not advisable that we anticipate these themes now as the presuppositions of a consideration offered here in its own right. When these questions are treated explicitly in their own place, we will have a further opportunity to come back to the problematic in question here, although in a broader context. Here it can only be a question of giving those helps towards the clarification of the question at hand which can be given here at this point.

We must first recall once again that the fundamental under-

standing of the Thomistic metaphysics of knowledge has to start
out from the fact that knowing is being-present-to-self, the re-
flectedness (*Reflektiertheit*) of a being of a definite intensity of
being upon itself. Therefore, the real essence of knowing cannot be understood ultimately as an act produced by the knower
which merely leaps out, as it were, to the "in-itself" (*Ansich*)
of an object, tries to grasp it, or would have it in itself in a
"merely mental existence," in an "intentional mode of being,"
whereby "intentional" means first and foremost that it is not given
in knowing in its real self. All such notions contradict the fundamental Thomistic statement that knowing in the original sense
is not *actio* (production of an apprehending act), but *actus,* that
is, actuality which is present to itself.[1] According to Thomas,
the ontological unity of knowing and object is not produced by
the knowledge (as an "intentional" apprehension), but logically
precedes it; it is not the result, but the cause of the knowledge
(as consciousness in the proper sense).[2] Of course there are
objects of knowledge which are not identical with the knowing
in their own reality, but those are by this very fact not the proper
object of the knowing in question (of a man, of an angel, of God,
and so forth), but are known only insofar as the being, which is
present-to-itself, of what is the knowing subject and object at once
contains in itself a reference to them ontologically. Expressed
species, mental word, mental concept, and so forth are the Thomistic expressions for that ontological determination of the cognitive faculty which by its presence brings it about that the
knower knows it, and by its conscious, ontological reference
also brings the object, which in its own self is not present in the
knowing, to consciousness for the knower. Therefore, neither is
such an object intuited. And vice versa: when an object is
intuited, that is, when it is present in the knower in its own real
being, there is no expressed species, thus neither in the beatific

[1] Cf. Maréchal, *op. cit.* pp. 60ff.; *De Ver.* q. 8, a. 6, corp., especially
towards the end of the first section; *S.T.* I, q. 18, a. 3, ad 1; q. 14,
a. 2, ad 2; q. 56, a. 1, corp.
[2] *S.T.* I, q. 54, a. 1, ad 3; *De Ver.* q. 1, a. 1, corp.

SENSIBILITY

vision of God nor in sense intuition.[3] The species without qualification is to be distinguished from this expressed species. What
species without qualification (also intelligible species, sensible
species) means will have to occupy us often. In general only
this much can be said here, that it is the ontological ground of
the fact that a definite cognitive faculty apprehends a definite object of knowledge. Every further interpretation of the
species-concept in the sense of an intentional representation and
so forth is false or is to be designated at this point at least as
premature.

Therefore, it would be completely false to want to conclude
too hastily from the use of the species-concept to clarify sensibility in Thomas that Thomas represents a "critical realism,"[4]
according to which a "subjective" influence of the external object
is felt and from that, through inference or some other way, the
external object is apprehended. Thomas is a "naïve" realist if
one wants to call his metaphysical realism that.[5] One has only
to understand this naïve realism in its fundamental metaphysical
presuppositions, and then he appears much more critical than
any critical realism.

If the meaning of Thomas's "naïve" realism is to be understood, then three statements must be understood in their
intrinsic compatibility:

1. In external sense preception there is an (impressed) species; but this as such is not what is perceived.[6]

2. External perception forms no expressed species,[7] so that
the object is apprehended in its immediate, real self.[8]

[3] *Quodl.* 5, a. 9, ad 2.
[4] Cf. J. Geyser, "Wie erklärt Thomas von Aquin unsere Wahrnehmung
von der Aussenwelt?", *Phil. Jahrb.* 12 (1899), pp. 130ff.
[5] *S.T.* I, q. 85, a. 2, ad 2.
[6] *De Spir. Creat.* a. 9, ad 6; *In III De Anima* lect. 8, n. 718.
[7] *Quodl.,* 5, a. 9, ad 2. See also *loc. cit.,* corp., and S.T. I, q. 85,
a. 2, ad 3. The expression *species expressa* (*impressa*) does not occur
literally in Thomas; he calls it the *verbum cordis,* etc. But since it is
clearly the same thing, and since *"verbum"* cannot aptly be applied to
sensibility, we express the content here in the later scholastic
terminology.
[8] *S.T.* I, q. 85, a. 2, ad 2.

85

3. An object can be apprehended immediately in its own self, that is, be intuited, only if it is in its own actuality an actuality of the knowing itself.

These statements are first of all of a very different origin and also seem to be contradictory. The first part of the first statement proceeds from the "naïve" view that the sense objects "affect" sensibility, must register themselves. The second part of the first statement and the second statement are expressions of "naïve realism." The third statement is essentially of a metaphysical origin which has already been indicated in the preceding Chapter. These three statements seem to be contradictory: the third seems to cancel out the second directly. The second does not seem to fit with the first, for an immediate apprehension of the external object in its own self seems either to make a species, which always seems to express something like a representation of the object within knowledge, superfluous, or at least to reduce it to a mere stimulus upon which the actual perception then follows afterwards. But this last assumption again contradicts the passivity of sensibility as it is taught by Thomas.[9] In any case, from these apparent contradictions this much is clear, that the sense which the concepts involved in these statements have in a given instance can be established in their more exact meaning only by taking all the statements into account together. If we let these statements mutually clarify one another in their respective meanings, the following insights result:

1. Sensible Species as Self-Givenness of the Sensible Object

If there is no expressed species in sense perception, then the thing must be apprehended in it in its own self. This statement is to be taken in its literal sense, not only in the sense in which ultimately all knowledge which "intends" an object goes out to the self of this object, to its "in-itself" (Ansich). Thomas maintains this in this sense of every "direct" knowledge, even where

[9] S.T. I, q. 79, a. 3, ad 1, etc.

he assumes an expressed species.[10] Hence, if there is no expressed species in external sensation, and yet the thing itself is to be intuited, then the (received) sensible species, through which the sense object and sensibility are identical (the sensible in act is the sense in act),[11] can only be something in the thing itself. Hence the thing in its own self must project into the medium of sensibility. The sensible species is an actuality of the thing itself. This proposition follows unambiguously from the denial of an expressed species, presupposing the proposition: "the sensible in act is the sense in act." That such a view ought not to be considered to lie necessarily outside Thomistic thought follows just from the fact that according to Thomas the ontological presence of God as the Absolute Being suffices in knowledge for the vision of God (presupposing the light of glory), so that the absolute being of God Himself is the impressed intelligible species for its immediate apprehension. In external perception the species is an actuality (determination) of the thing itself. In this general formulation we are in complete agreement with the results of Siewerth's work.[12] Where we part from him in the more exact interpretation of this thesis will become clear in a moment.

2. Sensible Species as Self-Realization of the Sensible Object

If, however, it is to make some sense that when Thomas speaks of the sensible species he obviously understands it somehow as an "effect" (*Wirkung*) of the external object and as its "representation" (*Stellvertretung*),[13] and if, nevertheless, the species is to be something in the thing itself, then obviously it cannot be

---

[10] *S.T.* I, q. 85, a. 2, together with *Quodl.* 5, a. 9.

[11] *S.T.* I, q. 14, a. 2, corp. See *In III De Anima* lect. 13, 787f.; *S.C.G.* I, 46: *per speciem sensibilem sensus est actu sentiens.*

[12] G. Siewerth, *Die Metaphysik der Erkenntnis nach Thomas von Aquin,* I: "Die sinnliche Erkenntnis" (München and Berlin, 1933), *passim.*

[13] One could consult the texts with which Siewerth tries to make his thesis compatible (p. 60ff.), or, e.g., *Quodl.* 8, a. 3, corp.

understood as a static determination which always belongs to the thing, but as a determination which the thing produces as its own in that and insofar as it remains in the medium of sensibility. The species is a determination of the object itself in such a way that the object has it as its own property insofar as it produces it in the medium of sensibility as its own, as making it manifest as its "self-realization" (*Selbstvollzug*). Therefore, on the one hand, the species brings the object in its own self to givenness, yet on the other hand it can be understood as its "representative effect." If the object must produce itself anew as determined in such and such a way in the medium of sensibility, this does not say that this determination according to its intrinsic quiddity could not belong to it independently of its self-realization in the medium of sensibility, especially since Thomas ascribes to any body at all in its efficient operation an extension of its formal being (which it nevertheless already possesses in itself independently of this extension) in the medium of air,[14] so that the likeness of color as intentional being is already present in the air through the operation of the body.[15] But that the ontological actuality which the object brings as its own into the medium of sensibility (in which medium it comes to self-reflectedness, to consciousness) is not simply and absolutely that which already belonged to it before it became identical with the sensibility but means a new self-actualization of the object through which the object has an influence upon sensibility, this is shown just by the fact that Thomas denies that a cognitive faculty can be determined by an object in its formal being as such and as already possessed from the outset, at least in all cases where this object is not the absolute and pure being of God Himself.

Thomas's thesis,[16] the intrinsic grounding of which we do not have to go into here, excludes Siewerth's thesis in the sense (and only in this sense!) that the species is that being of the object

---

[14] *De Pot.* q. 5, a. 8, corp.

[15] *S.T.* I, q. 67, a. 3, corp.

[16] *S.C.G.* II, 98; *De Ver.* q. 8, a. 7; *S.T.* I, q. 56, a. 2, obj. 3 and ad 3. See also *S.C.G.* III, 51 along with the commentary of Franz von Silvestris on this text.

itself which it already and always possessed. But if, nevertheless, the species is to be the self-giving of the object in sensibility, then it can be an "effect" of the object on sensibility only in such a way that this effect is the new *self*-realization of the object in the medium of sensibility. As we said before, we cannot show until later that this thesis, inferred here from Thomistic presuppositions, is also immediately Thomistic.

We are now in a position to understand correctly, at least in a tentative way, some Thomistic concepts which play a role in his metaphysical explanation of sensibility. Thomas says that sense knowledge involves a change in the spiritual *esse*,[17] that the sensible species has a spiritual *esse*, an intentional *esse*, that it is an "intention."[18] Just from what has been said it follows that one would misunderstand these terms if one wanted to think that the intentional spiritual *esse* is to be understood as opposed to a natural *esse* in the sense of today's "intentional," "ideal" being, and as being-in as opposed to "real" being. That such a conception misses the Thomistic sense from the outset follows simply from the fact that Thomas knows an intentional *esse*, an intention, where there is no question of knowledge at all. Thus light and colors are in the air spiritually in an intentional *esse*;[19] the power of a principal agent is in the instrument "intentionally."[20] Yet in such cases the intentional *esse* is obviously a real physical being. Consequently, the spiritual *esse* of the species expresses a real *esse*, it is "spiritual" neither in the sense of modern "intentionality" nor of immateriality in the proper sense, because of course sentient knowing must be essentially material.[21]

[17] *S.T.* I, q. 78, a. 3 corp., etc.
[18] *S.T.* I–II, q. 22, a. 2, ad 3; I, q. 78, a. 3, corp., etc. Further texts later.
[19] *S.T.* I, q. 67, a. 3 corp.; *De Ver.* q. 27, a. 4, etc. Further texts later.
[20] *De Ver.* q. 27, a. 4, ad 4; *De Pot.* q. 3, a. 7, ad 7; q. 3, a. 11, ad 14.
[21] In this sense Thomas can say in general: *oportet quod sensus corporaliter et materialiter recipiat similitudinem rei quae sentiter* (*In II De Anima* lect. 12, n. 377). Notice that he says "*materialiter*," not "*naturaliter*." What *esse naturalis* means is to come up in a moment.

89

Here, spiritual *esse* is rather that real physical being which reflects upon itself, is present to itself as the act of matter, which through its definite intensity of being, despite its alienation from self as the being of matter, is as such present to itself. Why and in what sense Thomas can ascribe an intentional *esse* to light and colors will be shown later. The correspondence of the mode of being of light and colors with that of the species consists in the fact that they are both intrinsically (in being, not only in becoming) dependent on the object producing them, although for completely different reasons. In any case, the point of comparison can only be a property which belongs to both of them as real being. Therefore, natural *esse*, as opposed to intentional *esse*, is not simply to be rendered "real being," but is that inferior physical being which is not present to itself in self-reflection. If, then, Thomas distinguishes the individual senses[22] according to whether there is only a spiritual change or in addition a natural change also in the sentient knower, this says that in some senses the "influence" (in the sense already indicated) is totally reflected upon itself (or at least perdures only as such), while in other senses there is also an influence whose existence does not depend on whether or not it is also "present to itself" and which therefore can also be ascertained by another perceiver as a natural quality of the sense organ as a physical body. Thus, for example, the dampness or the warmth of an organ, which contact with a definite object brings about, is in itself merely a natural quality of the organ whose being does not depend on whether it is conscious or not.

Further, it can now be made clear what it means to say that sentient knowing is "receiving a species without matter."[23] Again this does not mean first of all that there is question merely of an "intentional" being of the "form" in sensibility. There is nothing further to be said on that point. But neither does this expression

22 *S.T.* I, q. 78, a. 3, corp.; *In II De Anima* lect. 14, n. 418; *In I Metaph.* lect. 1, n. 6; *S.T.* I–II, q. 22, a. 2, ad 3.
23 *In III De Anima* lect. 2, n. 590; *In III De Anima* lect. 24, nn. 553–554.

mean that the species in its real, physical being is independent of matter. If as such a being it were intrinsically independent of matter (in which case the same would have to hold for the substance in which it is), then together with this latter it would be a "thing subsisting in itself," which completely contradicts the materiality of sensibility, especially since the species also is explicitly designated as being in matter (*cum appenditiis materiae*, with the conditions of matter).[24] The species is "without matter" first because, as will be shown, the influence of the object on sensibility is an expression of its form, not of its matter, although the object always operates as a whole, and then secondly, because the being-present-to-itself of the species is essentially an expression of the opposition of this being over against matter, *actus contra materiam*, however much this opposition also remains an inhering in matter in an indivisible unity.

3. Sensible Species as Self-Realization of Sensibility

By the fact that the sentient cognitive faculty is the being of matter, its being has entered into otherness from the outset and thus of itself has opened up the possibility that a being coming to appearance in it might manifest itself as other. For only if the being which becomes conscious in and through its increase in being (which increase is produced from without) is of itself in otherness can the increase in its intensity of being, which as such is consciousness (the sensible species), appear as other than the knower. Otherwise it would be apprehended precisely as the being of the existent which exists in itself and so undifferentiated from it. Of course, to understand this situation it must be noted that the being which is the act of matter possesses by this very fact the other as identical with itself and thus does *not set itself over against* the other, whereby the other first becomes "other" in the strict sense. It is not sensibility that accomplishes this, but rather this is the first distinctive mark of thought, that being which, as the act of matter, nevertheless remains free of it. But we have still to treat of that. Now in order that the sentient knower apprehend the other in the sense in which that is pos-

[24] *S.T.* I, q. 79, a. 3, corp.; *I Sent.* dist. 8, q. 5, a. 2, corp., etc.

SPIRIT IN THE WORLD

sible to sensibility at all, not only in the sense of a universal
otherness, but in its definite quality as a definite object other
than itself, two things are necessary: on the one hand, the
species, which is the actuality of the object itself, must be produced by the sentient knower himself, because otherwise it
would not possess the intensity of being which implies self-
reflection; and, on the other hand, the species must be the self-
realization of the sensible object itself, because otherwise this
would not be intuited in its own self. How they can both be
compatible will be shown later. It is already evident at this point
that this must follow from a general theory of efficient causality
as such, because otherwise the essential passivity of sensibility
would be destroyed.

If we look back at the three propositions enumerated earlier,
it follows that the (impressed) species is at once the self-realization of sensibility in the otherness of matter and the self-realization of the sensible object. Insofar as it is the self-realization of
sensibility, it is conscious; insofar as it is the actuality of the
object itself in the otherness of matter, the other object is intuited as other in its own self and so there is no place for an
expressed species. But that brings us to the problem of efficient
causality which cannot be treated explicitly until later.

4. The Passivity of Sensibility

Let us now expand the considerations made so far about sense
knowledge in general in a few further directions. If sensibility
is to be intuition of the other as such, then, presupposing the
proposition about the identity of knowing and the known, it is
self-evident that sensibility must be "passive."[25] For if upon
reception of an influence from without the act of perception
would objectively follow only subsequently to the determination
produced by the object, and follow as a spontaneous reaction
to the determination from without, then what is perceived would
be precisely the ontological actuality produced by such a reaction, hence it would be its own reality, not that of the other.
Consequently, the determination produced by the object is not

[25] S.T. I, q. 79, a. 3, ad 1; S.C.G. II, 57; De Ver. q. 26, a. 3, ad 4.

to be understood as a preparatory stimulus, upon the reception of which sensibility would produce its act and in it its "intentional" object, but rather this determination, that is, the species, which is the actuality of the object itself, is itself in its formal being brought to consciousness in sensibility as a passive faculty. Thus the passive determinateness of sensibility comes to exist within the interior of the sense act itself. Correspondingly, Thomas also rejects the concept of an agent sense.[26]

From this it can also be understood why and in what sense the objects of external perception are actually sensible in such a way that there is nothing potentially sensible.[27] This is just another formulation of the proposition that there is no agent sense, for an agent intellect is required precisely because the first objects of human thought are only potentially intelligible in themselves. If the sense objects themselves are actually sensible (and insofar as they are), then that means that they must be sensibly conscious in their own selves, because otherwise, like what is potentially intelligible, they would have to be elevated by a special spontaneous power from the state of being potentially sensible, which is all they would have "in themselves," to being actually sensible, which new state would then never belong to them in themselves any more than material things ever become actually intelligible in themselves.

Now sense objects, however, are evidently not always and already of themselves actually sensible in such a way that they would also be in themselves actually sentient, which you would have to expect at first on the basis of the proposition: the sense in act is the sensible in act, because, on the basis of the general proposition about the identity of knowing and the actually known, what is actually knowable is by that very fact also actually knowing. If, nevertheless, the sense object as such (as "outside the soul")[28] is to be actually sensible, then, maintaining the basic insight of the Thomistic metaphysics of knowledge just mentioned, that can only be understood in such a way that

[26] *De Spir. Creat.* a. 9, corp.; *De Anima* a. 4, ad 5; *S.T.* I, q. 79, a. 3, ad 1.

[27] *S.T.* I, q. 79, a. 3, ad 1; q. 84, a. 4, obj. 2 and ad 2; *De Spir. Creat.* a. 9, corp.

[28] *S.T.* I, q. 79, a. 3, ad 1.

the sensible object, insofar as it is outside the soul, projects into sensibility (wherefore sensibility itself must be "outside itself") and in this medium (and only in it) acquires through its own operation that intensity of being which implies consciousness. Thus it can be in itself actually sensible, although it can be that only in the medium of sensibility, so that in this and not in itself it is actually sentient.

But if the sensible object's self-realization, which is conscious and through which this object itself is actually sensible, is possible only in the medium of sensibility, because otherwise it would have to be actually sentient in itself, then that also makes it clear that this being-in (*Insein*) of the self-realization of the sensible object in the medium of "passive" sensibility cannot be understood in the sense of a mere local presence or in the sense that it is borne by a sensibility which stands in an absolutely passive relationship to it. In such a view it would not be conceivable how the self-realization of the sensible object would have that intensity of being which would make it actually sensible, because it could obviously produce this ontological actuality for itself only if it also became thereby actually sentient itself. The intensity of being which makes the self-realization of the sensible object in the medium of sensibility actually sensible must be bestowed upon it by sensibility itself. But this bestowal (because there is no agent sense) cannot be understood as an act which follows after this self-realization of the sensible object. So once again we are brought to the thesis that the self-realization of the sensible object must be identical with the self-realization of sensibility (with the "passive" reception of the species). Insofar as this one actuality is the active self-realization of the sensible object, this is actually sensible in its own *self* and therefore intuited; insofar as this actuality of the object is produced by sensibility itself, it is *actually* sensible and therefore conscious for sensibility. But this presupposes that in general the passive reception of a determination by the one receiving intrinsically includes, as such a reception, a production of this determination by the one receiving. As we said before, that this conception of passivity is Thomistic is not to be shown until later.

But already at this point an essential characteristic of sensibility can be gathered from what has been said. If the intensity of being of the sensible species, which constitutes its consciousness, is grounded in sensibility itself, and in fact in such a way that it bestows this upon the species by the "passive" reception of the latter, then sensibility at this level of being must already and always be complete (*vollendet*) and hence is already and always of itself, as the act of matter of such an intensity of being, possession of world (*Welthabe*). In the final analysis, therefore, the sensible object does not penetrate into the interior of sensibility, but sensibility as the act of matter has already moved out into the exterior of the world, and as act over against matter is always of such an intensity of being that what enters into its medium is by that fact already reflected upon itself, is already conscious, and only means a formal delimitation of that possession of the world which sensibility already and always is through its being. It is in this way that we are to understand that according to Thomas sensibility on its level already has "through generation" that degree of being which on the level of intellect is reached only through the habitual knowledge of a knower who has already learned,[29] and that sensibility, although it is determined by the sensible object ("although [the sensible] determines [the sense] itself") has the greater intensity of being (is "more noble").[30] Only if we understand sensibility as the already complete possession of the world in the exteriority of matter can we understand the strange reason Thomas gives as to why sensibility does not need an agent sense: the sensible is found in act outside the soul, and therefore (!) there is no need to posit an agent sense.[31] Sensibility must of itself already be "outside the soul," so to speak, and yet as such it must have that intensity of being which implies consciousness, and then it needs no special power in order to bring into such "interiority" what is outside sensibility, outside the soul.

If sensibility is thus of itself already and always complete possession of the world (although in an *empty* anticipation [*An-*

[29] *In II De Anima* lect. 12, n. 374. Cf. Siewerth, *op. cit.*, pp. 91–95.
[30] *In III De Anima* lect. 3, n. 612.
[31] *S.T.* I, q. 79, a. 3, ad 1.

tizipation] of possible objects, so that it is "in potency" for the formal delimitation of its already opened breadth by an object which determines it),[32] then its ontological structure gives prior indication of the structure of the possible objects which can come to appearance in it. These *a priori* structures of sensibility as the structures of its possible objects are to be investigated in the following sections.

By explaining the sensible species as the sensible object's own new self-realization (but not as its already and always possessed static being), we do not think that the thesis that the being of the sensible object comes to exist in the medium of sensibility itself contradicts those Thomistic texts in which the species appears as different from the object, as a likeness.[33] To see this, one only has to notice that "species" does not simply mean intentional representation, and that a being can also be a likeness of something by the fact that, as the self-realization of an object become conscious, it represents and reveals this in its inner essence. Thomas says of sense knowledge at one point: "it is not to be understood as though the agent (the sensible) produces in the patient (the sense) a species that is numerically identical with the one it has in itself; rather, it generates one like it."[34] Here we can observe what Thomas has to say of the species and of the likeness in its original genesis, as it were: the sensible object already and always has a species (it has it in itself), it is its quidditative essence itself in its accidental impress. But it cannot come to reflection in sensibility simply through this species (it does not produce a species numerically identical) because it is a finite object, and this is possible only for the absolute *esse* of God. Therefore, the sensible needs a new self-realization of this species (it generates), which generation as the self-realization of the sensible on the one hand brings this

---

[32] See *In III De Anima* lect. 3, n. 612: *est enim (sensibile) secundum quid nobilius (quam sensus), scilicet inquantum est actu dulce vel album, ad quod est sensus proprius in potentia.* Moreover, it will have to be shown later that this "potentiality" in a certain respect is precisely the expression of the greater intensity of being of the sense in relation to the sensible, and thus does not express an ontological inferiority, as is otherwise the case with the potential in relation to the actual.

[33] Cf. the texts in Siewerth, *op. cit.*, p. 67ff.

[34] *Quodl.* 8, a. 3, corp.

to exist in sensibility in its own self, and on the other hand brings it about that the newly produced species is "like" the already and always possessed species and thus is a likeness of the object itself. The only presupposition in this interpretation is that a transient influence upon another as patient is also and essentially always a self-realization of the agent in the medium of the patient.[35] If this is the case, which is to be shown later, then texts about the species as likeness and so forth can no longer offer any fundamental difficulties against our explanation of sensibility. Hence a more detailed interpretation of such texts appears superfluous.

III. THE *A PRIORI* STRUCTURES OF SENSIBILITY: SPACE

Knowing is being-present-to-self (*Beisichsein*), the reflected-ness-upon-itself (*Insichreflektiertheit*) of being itself. Knowing will know something to the extent in which it *is* this something. From this it follows that it is established *a priori* in the being of a knower what it can know, because its being is the *a priori* norm for what it can become. The ontological structure of a knowing essence is the *a priori* norm of its possible objects. The structure of an existent of a definite intensity of being can be transposed into the structure of its presence-to-self, in fact it is already and always this, and thus is also the structure of its proper object, and hence also the *a priori* condition for all else that is to be known by it. That is all the more true since knowledge is a result of the ontological unity of object and cognitive faculty, but this becoming-one has the *a priori* norm of its possibility in the being of the cognitive faculty as the existent which unites the object with itself. Since the *a priori* of knowledge is grounded in the structure of being, and since an onto-

[35] This presupposition is to be further developed at great length below (cf. Ch. 4, Section 9) and shown to be a maxim of Thomas. It is decisive for understanding the specific "immediacy" of the sensible thing reached in the species. (See J. de Fries, *Scholastik* 15 (1940), p. 407.)

logical union of knowing and known must also and necessarily respect the intrinsic ontological structure of the known, the *a priori* of knowledge does not conceal the nature of possible objects, but has already and always *revealed* it.

1. The Mobile as the Most Universal A Priori of Sensibility

What are the *a priori* structures of sensibility? Sensibility is just as much the act of matter as it is act over against matter, so that every attempt to understand it without this essential dimension is fundamentally erroneous. Accordingly, sensibility is the presence-to-itself of a being (form) as form of matter. We saw matter as the empty, in itself indeterminate (but being in potency for all forms) whither (*Woraufhin*) of our knowing and the whereat (*Woran*) of the known, of the form.[1] Vice versa, of course, the "forms" meant here can be defined only through their essential reference to such a whither and whereat. Matter as necessarily indeterminate in itself is not intrinsically ordered to a definite form. Therefore it always keeps the existent determined by the form in potency for non-being and for change; it is the ground of "motion."[2] All "motion," in which something becomes something from something, presupposes a similar indeterminate ground in which it takes place.[3] If sensibility is the act of matter, then as such it is essentially the being-given-over (*Hineingegebensein*) of being into the ground of its potency and its change, into the ground of the unlimited "nothing" which matter is.[4] Its *a priori* norm

---

[1] Thomas knows this way of acquiring the "concept" of matter explicitly, the *"via praedicationis."* See *In VII Metaph.* lect. 2, n. 1287. It is only the matter reached in this way that discloses itself to us here as the ground of motion. Whether and how the concept of matter could also be reached from motion alone (*per viam naturalis philosophiae*) does not have to occupy us here.

[2] *In II Metaph.* lect. 4, n. 328.

[3] We are establishing the concept of "motion" here in the way in which Thomas defines it over against other similar concepts, e.g., *S.C.G.* II, 17 and 19; *De Ver.* q. 26, a. 1, corp. (*passio proprie dicta*).

[4] *In II Metaph.* lect. 4, n. 328: *Ipsa materia habet rationem infiniti et ipsi infinito, quod est materia, convenit ipsum nihil.*

is therefore "motion" as a characteristic of the existent which, since it is in the infinite "nothing," is always intrinsically inclined towards another existent.[5] An existent is the possible object of sensibility insofar as it is subject to motion as its fundamental ontological state, because sensibility itself is subject to motion.

If, on the other hand, sensibility, in strict unity with the fact that it is the act of matter, nevertheless is also the act of form over against matter, then together with the fact that it is understood as motion it must also comprise the strongest assertion of form over against motion which is possible in matter. Motion as

[5] If here and there in Thomas sensibility does not appear to be *motus* in the proper sense, a *motus imperfecti*, but *actus perfecti* (*I Sent.* dist. 37, q. 4, a. 1, ad 1; *IV Sent.* dist. 17, q. 1, a. 5, sol. 3, ad 1; *S.T.* I, q. 18, a. 1, corp.; I–II, q. 31, a. 2, ad 1; II–II, q. 179, a. 1, ad 3; *De Ver.* q. 8, a. 14, ad 12; *De Pot.* q. 10, a. 1, corp.; *In VI Phys.* lect. 8 (Parma 431b, below); *In III De Anima* lect. 12, n. 766), that only means that the being-present-to-itself of the form as such, whenever the form is given in sensibility in the corresponding degree of being, no longer has the character of a new becoming with respect to this givenness, but is its formal effect, which ultimately only confirms our understanding of it. See *In III De Anima* lect. 12, n. 766: . . . *est actus perfecti, est enim operatio sensus iam facti in actu per speciem suam.* It has already been shown that this *operatio* ought not to be understood as a new coming to be after the *fieri in actu per speciem* (which *fieri* itself is as such an *actus imperfectus*). The consciousness of the form in the medium of sensibility as such is *actus perfecti,* but this does not deny that the ontological process by which this form extends into sensibility is a becoming in the proper sense, a *passio* in the proper sense. See *S.C.G.* II, 57: *sensus est igitur virtus passiva ipsius organi.* *S.T.* I, q. 85, a 2, ad 3: . . . *duplex operatio: una secundum solam immutationem et sic perficitur operatio sensus per hoc quod immutatur a sensibili.* Similarly, I, q. 27, a. 5, corp.; *Quodl.* 5, a. 9, ad 2: *cognitio sensus exterioris perficitur per solam immutationem sensus a sensibili . . . non format . . . sibi aliquam formam sensibilem.* See also *In VII Phys.* lect. 4 (Parma 455), where *sensus* and *intellectus* are explicitly distinguished with regard to their *pati,* their *motus* (*passio et alteratio magis proprie dicitur in sensu quam in intellectu*), while in the texts which seem to deny a *motus proprie dictus* to *sentire* they always appear together. *In VII Phys.* lect. 6 (Parma 460), it says in addition: *alteratio . . . est in tota parte animae sensitivae* (but the *alteratio* belongs to *motus* in the proper sense), and this *alteratio* is excluded from the intellect. *Comp. Theol.* (ch. 128) teaches in the same way that sensibility is intrinsically moved.

the actuality (presence) of the already real possible as such,[6] that is, that real letting-self-slip-away (*Sichentgleitenlassen*) of one way of being determined by reaching out towards a new way, within the scope of which one already and always stands because he is in potency for it, such motion is, therefore, on the one hand that wherein sensibility itself is further exercised, insofar as motion is the indication of materiality, and sensibility is the act of matter, and, on the other hand, is that against which sensibility asserts itself, insofar as it is an act over against matter. Since matter as empty indeterminateness and indifference can of itself contain no antecedent norm for determining the direction of its motion, two things follow: on the one hand, sensibility as the act of matter is the "illogical" being-impelled-further through sense impressions which displace and follow one another without any evident connection; and, on the other hand, sensibility as the highest act of form over against matter is already as such (not first through thought) the beginning of a synthesis of what is (spatially and temporally) only scattered and indifferently juxtaposed one after the other, and this goes beyond the synthesis of a merely corporeal form-matter-thing.

Thus the unity of material things itself (one as the principle of number) has an intrinsic gradation; it is greater in the sentient knower in spite of its materiality than in the merely corporeal. The peculiarity of this unity of the sentient knower, which also gives greater unity to its known than it has of itself, is perhaps the most original indication of the *a priori* of sensibility. For only in this way would the peculiarity of sensibility be distinguished not merely from the spiritual and immaterial, but also from what is below the sensible, the merely corporeal. However, this characterization of the peculiarity of sensibility is not worked out explicitly enough in Thomas. He is satisfied essentially with the dialectical, two-fold assertion that sensibility is material, and that it is "receiving a form without matter" in the sense already explained. But the intrinsic peculiarity of sensibility within material being is only very vaguely indicated by

[6] In III Phys. lect. 2–3 (Parma 295ff.). See the reference given above to *motus* (*passio*) *proprie dictus*.

the "without matter." Insofar as the development of this work requires more that sensibility be distinguished from the peculiarity of the spiritual and intellectual, this deficiency in Thomas is not very considerable for our question.

If sensibility is to be distinguished from the intellectual, then it is to be considered as a material power. But according to what was just said, that means that it is to be understood as mobile. The *a priori* norm for its possible objects must lie in its ontological constitution. But what is mobile has space and time as its most explicit characteristics.[7] Therefore, space and time will be the *a priori* forms of pure sensibility. With this proposition we do not intend to deny that in the course of the Thomistic problematic as such the question could be raised whether the *a priori* of sensibility could not be understood still more fundamentally. Just the fact that in the search for the *a priori* structure of sensibility we first came upon matter and the mobile points in this direction. But since Thomas himself characterizes the imagination as being limited in space and time right in the classical article about the conversion to the phantasm, it is sufficient for our purpose if sensibility is seen as being *a priori* spatial and temporal.

2. *The Quantitative as* A Priori *of Sensibility*

We saw the known (the form, the idea)[8] as the universal, the unattached which, indifferent in itself towards any definite "that," can come to exist as a thing any number of times in the whereat (*Woran*) of matter and is multiplied only in such whereats. As form *prior to* being referred to a whither (*Woraufhin*) and whereat, the known distinguishes itself from other forms by being qualitatively determined and thus is "one" in and through its differentiation from others. Thomas calls this unity transcendental unity and distinguishes it strictly from numerical unity, i.e., one as the principle of number, the one among many of the same, which is one precisely by the fact that it is not distin-

---

[7] For the relationship of *motus* to space and time, see *I Sent.* dist. 8, q. 3, a. 3, corp.; *In VIII Phys.* lect. 1 (Parma 293b).
[8] *S.T.* I, q. 15, a. 1, corp.

101

guished from the others by a qualitative difference.[9] A form as
such cannot be enumerated with others because without this
reference it cannot be thought of as multiplied, since in its multiplicity it would be thought of as concretized in a whereat (subject) as a thing (as subsistent).[10] The known, the form as same
and multiplied in many, becomes able to be enumerated only
in matter. But that means: an ontological actuality becomes
"quantitative" through matter, becomes an individual among
many like it, a one in the genus of quantity, one as the principle
of number.[11] This brings us to the concept of the quantitative:
the juxtaposition (*Nebeneinander*) of the same. But this being-
quantitative is not only, and not primarily, a relationship of
several separate things juxtaposed, but with matter itself is
already intrinsic to the individual thing in its own right: it is
quantitative in the spatial sense. The ontological actuality of its
form, its transcendental unity, is intrinsically extended in a
plurality of the same, in divisibility: *Quantitas se tenet ex parte
materiae.*[12]

Sensibility is the act of matter. Therefore, the *a priori* norm
for its possible objects is determined in the light of its being
quantitative. It is the faculty for apprehending the multiple
same and the spatial as such[13]: ". . . it does not transcend the
continuum."[14] What is to become its object must be subject to
and be able to be subject to the ontological spatiality of sensibility,
hence must be spatial itself. This *a priori* spatiality of sensibility

[9] *In III Metaph.* lect 12, n. 501; *In V Metaph.* lect. 8, n. 875; lect.
10, n. 901; *In X Metaph.* lect. 3, n. 1981; lect. 8, n. 2093, etc.

[10] See *S.C.G.* I, 30; *De Spir. Creat.* a. 8, corp.: *forma . . . si ponatur
abstracta vel secundum esse vel secundum intellectum, non remanet
nisi una in specie una; S.C.G.* IV, 65: *non possunt apprehendi multae
albedines nisi secundum quod sunt in diversis subjects.* Cf. also
Rousselot, op cit., pp. 83ff.

[11]*De Pot.* q. 9, a 7, corp.

[12] *S.T.* III, q. 2, corp.; I, q. 3, a. 2, sed contra.

[13] Notice that in such formulations it is always a question of the
proper object. It is not in question here whether and how a cognitive
faculty of another ontological structure can know the quantitative and
the multiple, in the way of course of its own and different proper
object.

[14] *S.T.* I, q. 84, a. 7, obj. 3; *De Pot.* q. 3, a. 19, corp.; q. 10, a. 1,
corp.

is, along with the empty, potential infinity of matter as such, potentially infinite.[15] Insofar as sensibility is already and always complete possession of world, it is therefore already pure intuition of space as such, prior to any individual determination by a definite sensible[16]; in the empty infinity of this pure intuition it receives the limited spatiality of the individual sensible thing as limiting. This of course in no way says that sensibility as such could make space as such the "object" of its intuition. Reflection upon the formal, *a priori* principle of knowing is possible, as will be shown later, only on a basis of a pre-apprehension (*Vorgriff*) which surpasses the finite scope of this *a priori*. Insofar as this spatiality follows from the nature of sensibility as such, it pervades as an *a priori* every individual sense as being a mere variation of sensibility as such. The quantitative is therefore a "common sensible."[17]

3. Spatiality as A Priori Form of the Basic Faculty of Sensibility: The Imagination

The quantitative (spatial) is the *a priori* of sensibility as such, because sensibility itself is quantitative, and therefore the pure intuition of every sense is quantitative, although with the variation which corresponds to the nature of each sense. Now the individual senses do not stand indifferently one beside the other, and this not merely because from the standpoint from which we came upon sensibility we have no reason at all to distinguish senses according to the external position of the sense organs (which distinction itself is possible only with the help of the external senses); nor merely because there is a single subject of sensibility which possesses and is the one world in those dimensions which we subsequently divide among the individual senses. Rather the reason is that being-quantitative proved to be a characteristic of sensibility as such if sensibility is to be

[15] *S.T.* I, q. 7, a. 3, corp.; ad 2 and ad 3; a. 4, corp. towards the end, and ad 1. Cf. Maréchal, *op. cit.*, pp. 119–21.
[16] Cf. Maréchal, *op. cit.*, pp. 118f.
[17] *S.T.* I, q. 78, a. 3, ad 2; *In II De Anima* lect. 13, n. 393ff.; *In III De Anima* lect, 1, n. 576ff.; *De Sensu et Sensatio* lect. 2, n. 29.

an immediate possession of the other as such. But this is to
come upon sensibility at a point which still lies prior to a possible unfolding into several different sense faculties. Thomas
calls this "point" the common sense. We must not misunderstand this concept by understanding it extrinsically as the concept of a faculty which subsequently gathers together the per-
ceptions of the individual senses so that they are all known of
one subject. This function of the common sense is only an
indication of the fact that the individual external senses
spring from it and remain in it as their creative ground. The
common sense is the "common root and principle of the external
senses," the "fountain and root of all senses . . . from which
proceeds the power to sense in all the organs."[18] The *phantasia*
(imagination) and the memory also spring from this common
sense as the one source and supporting ground of sensibility as
such; it is their root.[19] They belong so intimately to it that they
almost appear as "passions," intrinsic properties of its own essence,[20] and are called individual potencies only in a diminished
sense. Thomas calls the common sense the "root of the imagination and memory,"[21] and the "root" keeps what springs from it
so very much with itself that the act of the latter is always and
beforehand the act of the common sense also ("they presuppose the act of the common sense").[22] In this work, there can
be no question of going into the more precise relationship between the common sense, the imagination, and the memory. In
any case, they belong so intimately together that we might place
them over against the external senses as a single sense-totality
from which these latter first originate and in which they come

[18] *S.T.* I, q. 78, a. 4, ad 1; q. 1, a. 3, ad 2; *In III De Anima* lect.
3, nn. 602, 609.
[19] *In De Mem. et Rem.* lect. 2, nn. 319, 322; *S.T.* I, q. 78, a. 4,
obj. 3 and ad 3. The *aestimativa* as opposed and in relation to the other
internal senses does not have to be considered here, nor do the small
variations in the conception of the memory between *S.T.* I, q. 78, a. 4,
corp. and *In De Mem. et Rem.* lect. 2. In the former it belongs more
clearly to the *aestimativa*, in the latter to the *phantasia*.
[20] *In De Mem. et Rem., loc. cit.,* n. 319.
[21] *Ibid.,* n. 322.
[22] *Ibid.*

to exist as in their permanent ground.[23] We might call this one totality of internal sensibility the internal sense (although Thomas usually speaks of the internal senses), or still more simply imagination. For as has already been shown, the imagination at least approaches the common sense very closely because they have the same formal object.[24] Moreover, we then have the means to characterize the common sense in what is peculiar to it, without having to define it by going backwards from the external senses which have their origin in it. Finally, the imagination always appears in Thomas as the faculty which is necessary for the intellect and immediately borders on it,[25] which is also shown in the fact that the phantasm necessary for all knowledge, which is superior in the order of objects than the sensible thing and borders immediately on the actually intelligible,[26] is the act of the imagination.[27] But then for Thomas, with his conception of the relationship between the higher and lower potencies of one subject, it is self-evident that the external senses must have their abiding origin in the imagination.[28] That gives a right to call internal sensibility simply "imagination."

Thus the imagination in Thomas is not merely the faculty for

[23] The *sensus communis* is *"nobilior"* and therefore it is the root which supports the external senses: see *In III De Anima* lect. 3, nn. 602 and 612, in the light of *S.T.* I, q. 77, a. 4 and a. 7: the more perfect faculty lets the less perfect spring from it and holds it in its ground as its subject. Now the *imaginatio* and *memoria* belong so closely to the *sensus communis* that they must participate in its relationship to the external senses. For this metaphysical relationship of cognitive powers in general, see Siewerth, *op. cit.*, pp. 22ff. That the *imaginativa* (and hence the other internal senses) must be included with the *sensus communis* with regard to this relationship of origin also follows from the fact that it is *altior potentia quam sensus externus* (*S.T.* III, q. 30, a. 3, ad 2). It is also shown there that the quantitative is assigned to the *imaginatio* as its formal object as it is elsewhere to the *sensus communis: De Ver.* q. 15, a. 2, corp. *In De Caelo et Mundo* II, lect. 13 (Parma 111b) says: *Imaginatio una est virtus omnium sensibilium quae tamen sensus participat per diversas virtutes.* In *S.C.G.* I, 65 the *imaginatio* is explicitly placed over against the external senses with which it has an *ordinatio* as *virtus unica superior*.

[24] See *Der Ver.* q. 15, a. 2, corp.

[25] *S.T.* I, q. 55, a. 2, ad 2.

[26] *S.C.G.* II, 96.

[27] *I Sent.* dist. 3, q. 4, a. 3, corp.

[28] *S.T.* I, q. 77, a. 4 and a. 7.

gathering sense impressions into a whole, but the supporting ground of the possibility of these impressions, insofar as it lets the external senses flow from itself "through a certain natural emanation" (*resultatio*).[29] It is only because of this that as imagination and memory it can gather together the external impressions into one and preserve them. What Thomas says of the common sense holds for what we are thus calling imagination: it is the fountain and root of all the senses. Therefore, what could be affirmed as the *a priori* form of sensibility as such can now be asserted of its root, the imagination: the *a priori* form of the imagination as the basic faculty of sensibility as such is the spatiality of the multiple same, which is such because it is materially quantitative. Therefore, as an already complete actuality, the imagination is pure intuition of unlimited spatiality.

Thomas calls this unlimited spatiality as the pure intuition of the imagination "insignate, intelligible matter," although this expression just by its formulation indicates that Thomas is speaking of this *a priori* of pure intuition in connection with intellectual abstraction and is considering it in this respect.[30] Space as the pure intuition of the imagination appeared as the empty and unlimited "wherein" of the multiple same, as the "continuum"

[29] See *S.T.* I, q. 77, a. 7, ad 1.

[30] To clarify this sentence, we mention by way of anticipation that the first level of abstraction consists objectively in a universalizing objectification of what is sensibly given and intuited. Just from that it is clear that with this abstraction there does not enter in any increase in the material determinations of what was already given sensibly in the undifferentiated center of subject and object. But then the same holds also for the following two degrees of abstraction: objectively, they are nothing other than the separative setting in relief of the two elements of what was already given objectively in the first abstraction: the pure intuition of space and time (second degree of abstraction) and the *a priori* of the intellect (the transcendentals) (third degree of abstraction), both of which were already given simultaneously with the first level of abstraction in the objectification of the *a posteriori* sense data as the necessary conditions of the possibility of such an objectification. Therefore, as far as content goes, the intelligible matter must have already been given if the first level of abstraction is not to bring an increase in the content of the determinations. For these three levels of abstraction, see *In Boeth. De Trin.* q. 5, a. 3

which the imagination does not transcend. But this is precisely the Thomistic concept of intelligible matter also: "intelligible matter which is the continuum itself."[31] Thus intelligible matter is also explicitly placed in relation to the imagination.[32] Intelligible matter is the object of mathematics, which is ordered in a special way to the imagination.[33]

This has clarified at least one step in our approach to the question: What is it, then, that the intellect turns to in the conversion to the phantasm? The phantasm is the act of the imagination as the source of sensibility, whose *a priori* form is space as the characteristic of the quantitative plurality of the same. It is to the act of such an imagination that the conversion of the intellect takes place.

IV. THE *A PRIORI* STRUCTURES OF SENSIBILITY: TIME

The *a priori* form of sensibility was shown to be that of mobile being. But for Thomas, the mobile is an existent which has the totality of the realization of its potentialities as well as each individual one still ahead of it as "future,"[1] and is in motion towards it. Such an existent is temporal. It cannot be our intention here to develop the Thomistic concept of time in detail. We can only give a few indications, which as such must always remain unsatisfactory.

[31] *In VII Metaph.* lect. 11, n. 1508; 1533.

[32] *In VII Metaph.* lect. 10, nn. 1494–95. For the fact that intelligible matter is the object of mathematics, see *loc. cit.*

[33] See *In Boeth. De Trin.* q. 6, a. 1, *ad secundum quaestionem,* corp. and ad 4: *imaginationi subjacent . . . ; modus mathematicae . . . ab imaginatione;* likewise, *loc. cit.,* a. 2, corp.: Mathematics as *"deduci ab imaginationem."*

[1] *IV Sent.* dist. 17, q. 1, a. 5, sol. 3, ad 1: *semper expectat aliquid in futurum ad perfectionem suae speciei . . . ; De Ver.* q. 8, a. 14, ad 12: *. . . Quae expectat aliquid in futurum ad hoc quod eius species compleatur.* Only that is temporal.

1. The Time-Forming Quality of Motion

First of all for Thomas time essentially has something to do with motion, it is intrinsic to every motion: *aliquid motus.*[2] In contrast to this, the division of the parts of a motion into a numbered succession by a comparison with a first motion of an astronomical kind is something subsequent, although Thomas includes measuring in the definition of time. This comparative measuring is something subsequent because it comes about through the intellect[3] and thus is not properly motion at all. Hence it does not enter into a consideration of the material element of time as opposed to the formal element of dividing and numbering, nor into a consideration of the intrinsic temporality of motion. Therefore, the question about the measure of this measuring and numbering (about the motion of the heavens) is irrelevant to us here. Thomas himself also knows a time intrinsic to every motion, and so he knows many times: " a measure which is in the measured (that is, in what is mobile) as an accident in its subject, and this is multiplied as the measured is multiplied."[4]

Now, to what extent does motion form time, and what concept of time do we thus acquire if it is thus formed by motion as its intrinsic determination? We can pose the question about the formation of time by motion in this way because the "accident" of time is obviously meant as a *"per se* accident," but such accidents, as will be shown later, are formed according to Thomas by the subject itself. Motion is not a succession of states which constitute it by being placed one after the other. Motion is not formed out of such states, but is itself what first forms them. Hence, it is not composed of past, present, and future, but lets these come to be for the first time. Thomas explicitly denies that a succession of states, each of which is based on itself and is in no need of something to come in order to be itself, is a motion. Such a succession would not be a motion in

[2] *In IV Phys.* lect. 17 (Parma 362a).
[3] *I Sent.* dist. 19, q. 5, a. 1, corp.; *II Sent.* dist. 12, q. 1, a. 5, ad 2, etc.
[4] *II Sent.* dist. 2, q. 1, a. 2, ad 1.

the proper sense "because it is not from potency to act, but from act to act."[5] Only that changing being is in motion in the proper sense which has a definite quiddity only insofar as it is on the way to something which it not yet is: "It is always awaiting something in the future for the perfection of its species"[6]; "an action . . . which is awaiting something in the future so that its species be completed."[7] Hence, there is motion and time only when there is a stretching-ahead-of-self (*Sichvorstrecken*) towards something in such a way that this stretching-ahead-of-self primarily grounds the momentary "state."

Thomas calls this stretching-ahead-of-self an "ordination to a further act," whereby he emphasizes that this ordination is more than merely existing in potency for this further act (*existere in potentia ad ipsum*), which is only the presupposition of this ordination and the point of departure for the motion. What is moved has this stretching-ahead-of-self only insofar as it is moving out of its own potency ("insofar as it is compared to something less perfect: a relation to an anterior potency").[8] This stretching-ahead-of-self is a "tending into act,"[9] a proceeding further into act" as a moment in the motion, which is different from the potency and the incomplete act (each momentary state of what is moved).[10] Only that is in motion which is in each momentary state through the fact that it is tending from an earlier state to one that is to come. Only that is in time whose every momentary state tends to change into another in accordance with its own intrinsic meaning, and only through this is it itself: "those things are said to be in time of themselves for which succession or something pertaining to succession is of their essence."[11] And this is true to the point that the "repose" of what is mobile does not mean an intrinsic being-elevated-

---

[5] *I Sent.* dist. 37, q. 4, a. 1, corp.
[6] *IV Sent.* dist. 17, q. 1, a. 5, sol. 3, ad. 1.
[7] *De Ver.* q. 8, a. 14, ad 12.
[8] *In III Phys.* lect. 2 (Parma 295–96).
[9] *In VIII Phys.* lect. 10 (Parma 500a).
[10] I *Sent.* dist. 19, q. 2, a. 1, corp.
[11] *S.T.* I–II, q. 31, a. 2, corp.

above change, but a destruction of its own essence: "repose is not the negation of motion, but its privation."[12] Only such a change, in which each moment, in order to be itself, has a reference to another before and after it, is a continual motion, and as such forms time. This continuity which forms time is precisely not a succession of "nows succeeding one another"; such "time" would not be the time of what is mobile, human time.[13] The continuity of motion, which forms time through this continuity, is so far from being a static succession of moments (*nunc*), that in principle no "points" of time at all can be indicated which are immediately one after the other,[14] and that the proposition is true: "Every part of motion is motion."[15] Every moment of motion contains the whole of motion in itself because it comes from the earlier state which is a striving towards the state that is to come.

This becomes still clearer if we consider that what is mobile has an end,[16] a whither (*Woraufhin*) of its motion (which, of course, does not necessarily have to be a point at the end of the motion, but in material things as such is the totality of the motion, since the potential infinity of matter as a whole can never be converted into actuality all at once). Now Thomas sees explicitly that, in motion, one state does not pass into another in a movement towards this other, but in a reaching out towards the final end of the motion: "The inception of something is always ordered to its consummation."[17] The end is prior in intention[18]: the end is the beginning of motion. "The end has the nature of a cause."[19] "That . . . which is for the end . . . is willed for the sake of the end,"[20] in which it is to be noted that, according to Thomas, every being has only *one*

<hr/>

[12] *In IV Phys.* lect. 20 (Parma 370).
[13] See, for example, *S.T.* I, q. 53, a. 3, corp.; q. 61, a. 2, ad 2; q. 63, a. 6, ad 4; I-II, q. 113, a. 7, ad 5; *De Ver.* q. 8, a. 4, ad 15; *I Sent.* dist. 8, q. 3, a. 3, ad 3; dist. 37, q. 4, a. 3, corp.; *De Instantibus* c. 1; c. 4.
[14] *In IV Phys.* lect. 8 (Parma 430); *De Instantibus* c. 1.
[15] *I Sent.* dist. 37, q. 4, a. 1, ad 3.
[16] *III Sent.* dist. 27, q. 1, a. 4, ad 11.
[17] *S.T.* I-II, q. 1, a. 6, corp.
[18] *S.T.* I-II, q. 1, a. 3, ad 2; a. 1, ad 1.
[19] *S.T.* I-II, q. 1, a. 1, ad 1.
[20] *S.T.* I-II, q. 8, a. 3, corp.

SENSIBILITY

motion to *one* end.[21] Therefore, the motion takes hold of each
of its moments only insofar as it is from and towards its end. The
present of the motion (its momentary state) is thus a vindication
of its past in reaching-out-towards the future, and only in this
reaching-out-of-the-past-into-the-future does the present maintain itself. "In those things which act for an end (and everything acts for an end!) all things intermediate between the first
agent and the last end are ends with respect to what precedes,
and active principles with respect to what follows."[22] The beginning contains the end in itself and itself in it. "The act is in
the potency itself in a certain way."[23]

Hence, the motion of what is mobile forms time. But something material is necessarily mobile, as has already been shown.
And sensibility has already been shown to be the motion of
something imperfect, that is, a motion in the proper sense. Thus,
from the outset, it forms time by its very essence. What is to be
its object falls under the law of time because it must become
one with it ontologically; it is object only insofar as, along with
sensibility, it itself extends into time, thus forming time. Its
duration can be grasped sensibly in its own self as the delimitation of the potential unlimitedness of the *a priori*, time-forming
movedness of sensibility. Thomas emphasizes again and again
the connection between the temporality and the sensibility of
our knowledge.[24] The succession of thoughts and images as a
movement of the soul enables us to apprehend and experience
time: "We experience motion and time simultaneously."[25] Just
as space showed itself to be an *a priori* law of the imagination,
so also is time. "Magnitude, motion, and time, insofar as they

21 See *S.T.* I-II, q. 1, a. 5.
22 *S.C.G.* III, 2.
23 *S.T.* I–II, q. 27, a. 3, corp.
24 *S.T.* I, q. 85, a. 5, ad 2; q. 107, a. 4, corp.; I-II, q. 53, a. 3, ad 3;
q. 113, a. 7, ad 5; III, q. 75, a. 7, corp. (*prolatio verbi est sub motu
caeli*); *I Sent.* dist. 8, q. 2, a. 3, corp.; dist. 38, q. 1, a. 3, ad 3; *IV
Sent.* dist. 17, q. 2, a. 1, sol. 1, ad 1; *Periherm.* I, lect. 2 (Parma 3):
De Mem. et Rem. lect. 2, n. 319f.; *S.C.G.* I, 102; II, 96, towards the
end; *De Instantibus* c. 1.
25 *In IV Phys.* lect. 17 (Parma 362a). According to the context, it is
a question of time in the proper sense and motion in the proper sense.
Quite similar is *De Instantibus* c. 1.

are in the phantasm, are apprehended and known by the common sense."[26] Along with the potential infinity of the imagination as the act of matter, time as its *a priori* intuition is also infinite in the same sense, insofar as it has no intrinsic limit from the empty indeterminateness of matter, so that essentially the imagination always stands open to a further whither of its motion.[27]

2. The Mutual Relationship of the A Priori Intuitions of Space and Time

How are the *a priori* intuitions of space and time related to each other? A few things have already been said about this insofar as space and time were understood as characteristics of what is material. Even in Thomas's phraseology, space and time appear together repeatedly (time and the continuum; time and place; here and now).[28] They belong closely together insofar as, according to Thomas, they stem from materiality and its being quantitative. Now, quite frequently it certainly seems as though Thomas wants to deduce temporality from spatiality. He sees the continuity of motion, which first forms time in the proper sense, grounded in spatial relationships.[29] But it is to be noted that in such expressions Thomas has in mind the concept of time as the external measure of motion by the motion of the heavens, which does not come into consideration for our question about

[26] *In De Mem. et Rem.* lect. 2, n. 319.
[27] *S.C.G.* II, 38 (*infinitum . . . in successione*); *S.T.* I, q. 7, a. 3, ad 4. Thomas knows a *tempus imaginarium* as the extension of time beyond real motion which forms time (*De Pot.* q. 3, a. 1, ad 10), as *quasi subjectum eorum quae in tempore aguntur,* which extends beyond real time and the really temporal (*loc. cit.,* a. 2, corp.), and in fact as unlimited time (*loc. cit.,* a. 17, ad 20). Such an imagination of unlimited time is possible only if the imagination itself has no limit in its dimension. Similarly, *II Sent.* dist. 1, q. 1, a. 5, ad 7; ad 13, etc.
[28] *S.T.* I, q. 16, a. 7, ad 2; q. 75, a. 6, corp.; q. 84, a. 7, obj. 3; I-II, q. 113, a. 7, ad 5; *In De Mem. et Rem.* lect. 2, n. 314; *De Instantibus* c. 1; *In IV Phys.* lect. 17 (Parma 362b); *De Pot.* q. 9, a. 7, corp.; *II Sent.* dist. 3, q. 1, a. 2, corp.; dist. 23, q. 2, a. 1, ad 3; *S.C.G.* I, 102; III, 84.
[29] *I Sent.* dist. 8, q. 3, a. 3, corp. and ad 4; *Quodl.* 9, a. 9, corp.; *In V Metaph.* lect. 15, n. 985.

the relationship between the spatiality and the intrinsic temporality of something mobile. As a matter of fact, Thomas also knows an intrinsic temporality in the proper sense in "movements" which are not spatial, an intrinsic temporality of sensibility which as such is not external, local motion.[30] To this is added the fact that the temporality of the material (and thus of sensibility) intrinsically determines not merely its activity, but also the very being which is antecedent to the activity as its ground.[31] Its *esse* is the *esse* of something corruptible, it is intrinsically perishable, for its ontological actuality is always inclined towards the indifference of empty matter and thus convertible into nothing[32] because in its narrowness it can never completely fill the unlimited breadth of matter.[33] Thus it is the tendency of form towards matter (its being-in matter, its union), it is already and always tendency, inclination towards more than what it actualizes and fills, towards the further potency of matter, and it thereby forms motion, which forms time. In any case, all of this shows that, for Thomas, time belongs to the constitution of the pure intuition of sensibility at least as essentially as space does.

[30] For the three kinds of motion of which only one is spatial motion, see *In V Phys.* lect. 4 (Parma 388f.). Nothing alters Thomas's conception as a consequence of the fact that local motion is the prior, external condition of the other kinds of motion. This priority ought not to be understood as though local motion constituted the other kinds intrinsically. Thomas explicitly denies that of *alteratio* (*In VIII Phys.* lect. 14, Parma 511–12). But from this it follows that there is a time-forming motion which intrinsically is not local motion. All the rest (local motion as presupposition, as the "more perfect" and so on) is then inconclusive speculation which has nothing to do with our question.

Thomas knows an intrinsic time which is not the time of a local motion, the time of the *motus animae*, of sensibility (*In IV Phys.* lect. 17, Parma 362b; *De Instantibus* c. 1), and the time of every other motion which is not local motion: *I Sent.* dist. 37, q. 4, a. 3, corp.: *oportet cuilibet motui . . . adesse successionem . . . et ita tempus*, which principle is then applied explicitly to the *motus augmenti et diminutionis* and the *motus alterationis* with the conclusion: *et tunc tempus per se ipsum* (hence intrinsically) *motum mensurat.*

[31] *S.T.* I, q. 10, a. 5, corp.

[32] For this expression, see *S.T.* I, q. 75, a. 6, ad 2.

[33] *II Sent.* dist. 7, q. 1, a. 1, corp. The *potentia materiae* is the intrinsic *principium corruptionis: S.T.* I, q. 50, a. 5, ad 3.

3. *The Derivativeness of the Space-Time* A Priori

Does this describe the *a priori* structure of sensibility for the Thomistic metaphysics of knowledge adequately? In itself it does not. Time and space in themselves define only the *a priori* of the imagination (of the common sense) in a somewhat adequate fashion. Insofar as sensibility as such emanates from the root of the imagination, its *a priori* law prevails throughout the whole of sensibility. But this latter is not thereby apprehended in its *a priori* structure as yet. Thomas determines what is the *a priori* form of sensibility, or of one of its powers, in connection with the question about the formal object of a sense faculty. For formal object (*ratio formalis*) means nothing other than that respect, antecedent to the factual apprehension of the individual thing, under which such a thing can be the object of this faculty at all, a respect which is *a priori* grounded in the nature of the faculty in question.[84] Thus the formal object is the principle of the synthesis of the factually given individual objects, the cause of the union of these objects in the one knowledge by one power. But the principle of synthesis is always prior to what is to be unified, and must in itself be one.[85] So the cognitive power must contain this principle of synthesis in itself; it is determined by the essence of the synthesis[86]; the scope of this

---

[84] *S.T.* I, q. 1, a. 3, corp.; q. 59, a. 4, corp.; II-II, q. 59, a. 2, ad 1; *S.C.G.* I, 76; *S.T.* I, q. 1, a. 7, corp.: *proprie autem illud assignatur objectum alicuius potentiae vel habitus, sub cuius ratione omnia referuntur ad potentiam vel habitum, sicut homo et lapis referuntur ad visum inquantum sunt colorata. Unde coloratum est objectum proprium visus.* See *III Sent.* dist. 27, q. 2, a. 4, sol. 1, corp. and ad 3.

[85] *S.T.* I, q. 65, a. 1, corp.: *si enim diversa in aliquo uniantur, necesse est huius unionis causam esse aliquam, non enim diversa secundum se uniuntur.* The principle is used here in Thomas in another context, but as a principle, that is, according to Thomas it holds universally. *S.T.* I, q. 3, a. 7, corp.: *quae enim secundum se diversa sunt, non conveniunt in aliquod unum nisi per aliquam causam adunantem ipsa.* Similarly, *S.C.G.* I, 18; *In VII Metaph.* lect. 13, nn. 1588–89.

[86] See *S.T.* I, q. 14, a. 12, corp.: *secundum modum formae quae est principium cognitionis.* In this sentence there is question first of all of the species considered ontologically, but as such it is dependent on the essence of the knower. *In II Metaph.* lect. 5, n. 332: *requiritur autem ad quamlibet cognitionem determinato proportio cognoscentis ad cognoscibile. Et ideo secundum diversitatem naturarum et habituum accidit diversitas circa cognitionem.*

114

synthesizing faculty expresses itself in the breadth of the formal object. Now, according to Thomas, the formal object of sensibility is not adequately determined just by space and time. For Thomas knows a formal object of the individual senses which is narrower and more determined than that of the common sense, of the imagination.[37] Therefore a complete comprehension of the *a priori* forms of sensibility would have to go into these formal objects.

However—and this at the same time gives the reason why that is not required here—these *a priori* forms are not of the same importance for characterizing sensibility as such as are space and time. For they do not touch sensibility immediately in its one common root for all sense faculties as such, in the imagination. In fact, this latter lets the individual senses emanate from itself and is thus itself fully determined in its essence only by what proceeds from it as from a fountain and root, just as it also, as phantasy in the usual sense, brings back into itself what it lets emanate. And to that extent one can correctly say that sensibility could be more correctly defined Thomistically as the *a priori* possession of world as such (in the whole *a priori* of sensibility of a qualitative kind also) than as *a priori* being in space and time.[38] Nevertheless, the essence of sensibility is to be determined in the first instance in the light of that from which it comes itself, from matter. As the form of matter, it is first of all determined by quantity in the metaphysical self-constitution of a natural thing into that which it is, and only then by qualitative determinations.[39] Space and time are rooted in quantity as the expression of matter[40] (as opposed to the qualitative as the expression of form). Therefore, as common sensibles, these characterize the imagination in a

---

[37] *S.T.* I, q. 78, a. 3.
[38] Cf. Siewerth, *op. cit.*, p. 104.
[39] *S.T. I*, q. 3, a. 2, sed contra: I–II, q. 52, a. 1, corp.; III, q. 77, a. 2, corp.; *IV Sent.* dist. 12, q. 1, a. 1, sol. 3, corp.; *S.C.G.* IV, 63; *In Boeth. De Trin.* q. 5, a. 3, corp.
[40] *In IV Sent., loc. cit.* Quantity is an expression of matter in its empty, diffusive indeterminateness. Insofar as matter is the subject of form, the "wherein" in which alone the qualitative can come to exist, quantity is also the first in the order of the development of a substantial essence into its "accidental" properties.

more primary and original way and thus also sensibility as such.

What are the results of our consideration of sensibility so far for the purpose for which it was undertaken? In the metaphysical question man asks about being in its totality, whatever this being might mean. But in this question he is located at a definite place whose boundary he does not over-step and which contains in itself an indication of how the question is to be posed, and by that very fact of how it is to be answered also. He asks as one who is already and always in the world. He is already and always in the world through sensibility. It was important to understand sensibility as well as possible as the basis of his metaphysical enquiry. Sensibility was shown to be the possession of another because it is the act of matter, because it is the ontological actuality whose essence is consciousness in such a way that it is thereby the actuality of the empty, indetermined limitlessness of matter. Hence sensibility is already and always in time and space, since it forms time and space itself. The other, which sensibility as possession of the world already and always has and is, is temporal and spatial. That is all that is given to it in its own self, all that it can intuit. "The imagination does not transcend time and the continuum."

CHAPTER THREE

ABSTRACTION

I. THE QUESTION:
"THE RETURN OF THE SUBJECT TO HIMSELF"

WHEN man begins to ask about being in its totality, he finds himself already and invariably away from himself, situated in the world, in the other through sensibility. Sensibility means the givenness of being (which is being-present-to-self) over to the other, to matter. So the sensible is always situated at that undivided mid-point between self-possession through a separative setting-self over against every other (*Sichabsetzen*), and a total abandonment (*Verlorenheit*) to the other which would completely conceal the existent from itself. But man asks about being in its totality, he places it in question comprehensively and in its totality (and thereby himself), and by doing this he places himself as the one asking in sharp relief against all the rest, from world and from himself as being already and always in the world through sensibility. Thus he "objectifies" the other and his abandonment to it that is already realized in sensibility. He returns from "outside," where he already and always was. The other, which he himself was in sensibility, which he received and which was conscious to him in such a way that as sentient knower he could not separate himself from it, since sensibility as such only receives the other in that it becomes it:

117

this other now places itself at a distance from the knower, it becomes object (*Gegen-stand*).

It is not until then that man stands in the world as man, not until then that he is on that ground on which he found himself situated for his metaphysical enquiry and on which in his initial option he had already decided to remain in the pursuit of his metaphysics. In principle, our consideration of what we called sensibility did not permit us to grasp this ground completely. For it was shown that precisely if sensibility is to be the first and original reception of the other, of the world, if it is to be receptive intuition, it made this possible only by the fact that it became an ontological abandonment to the other, an act of matter. Therefore, it cannot let the other stand over against it at a distance as object because it is not "subjective" enough itself, it is too "objective," it is always and essentially actuality of the other.

The capacity of the one human knowledge to place the other, which is given in sensibility, away from itself and in question, to judge it, to objectify it and thereby to make the knower a subject for the first time, that is, one who is present to himself (*bei sich selber*) and not to the other (*beim andern*), one who knowingly exists in himself, this we call thought (*Denken*), intellect. For Thomas, this possibility of the complete return to the self is metaphysically the most decisive characteristic of intellect as opposed to sensibility.[1] It is first through thought that the undifferentiated unity of sensibility and sensible object which is had in sensibility, of subject and object, really becomes the subject who in his self-possessed existence (*Insichselberständigkeit*) has a world over against himself; it is first through thought that human experience of an objective world becomes possible. So our question now is about the one human knowing as thought: *oppositio mundi* (opposition to world).

If the one human knowledge of the world is of such a nature, then the grasping of its possibility must take place in two phases: in sensibility as such, man has already and always lost himself in the world (or would have, if his knowledge could ever be sensi-

[1] S.C.G. IV, 11.

bility alone). He acquires his position as man in a self-liberating return from his abandonment in the subject-object unity of sensibility. And yet he possesses himself as one who has really become a subject only in that he places himself over against himself and turns again to this world. These two "phases" are of course not to be thought of as coming one after the other; they mutually condition each other and in their original unity form the one human knowledge. In the Thomistic metaphysics of knowledge this liberation of the subject from sensibility's abandonment to the other of the world is treated under the heading "abstraction"; turning to the world, which has thus become objective, is called the conversion to the phantasm.

From a merely literal understanding of the two terms, it follows that, if our analysis of sensibility is correct in the light of Thomistic metaphysics, then the conversion to the phantasm as a process of human knowledge can make sense only if a turning from the phantasm precedes it, for sensibility already and always expressed a being with the phantasm, with the world. How can a conversion to the phantasm as a process *of thought* be necessary, unless an abstraction preceded it? And vice versa: such abstraction obviously presupposes that the subject reaches itself as consciously possessed only in such a coming from the world, for otherwise abstraction could not be considered a fundamental process in being-present-to-self through thought. But then, just this also means that such abstraction, such a return to self, cannot have the sense of a complete liberation from the sentient possession of the world. For otherwise, it would not be intelligible at all why the return of the subject to himself takes its start at this possession of the world. But then the conversion to the phantasm is an intrinsic characteristic of abstraction itself insofar as it is only an indication of the fact that abstraction is always a coming from world and can only exist as a continual coming from world.[2] A considera-

---

[2] *Ibid.: primum suae cognitionis initium ab extrinseco sumit . . . ; procedit ab aliquo exteriori. . . .* It is to be noted there that this starting point is at the same time an abiding foundation: *non est intelligere sine phantasmate (ibid.)*, hence a *principium ex quo incipit . . . non sicut transiens sed sicut permanens (In Boeth. de Trin.* q. 6, a. 2, ad 5).

tion of these two "phases" will have to take note of this intrinsic unity of abstraction and conversion, although it must treat them one after the other. This also makes it clear that the conversion cannot be treated without knowing what abstraction is. The two chapters about the one human knowing as thought are divided under these two headings.

II. THE INDICATIONS OF THE ABSTRACTIVE RETURN TO SELF

Before the attempt can be made to grasp the intrinsic *possibility* of that return of the knower to himself which puts him at a distance from the world, the return must be understood to some extent in its *actual* characteristics. This possession of world through thought gives three indications of its nature which mutually complement and clarify one another: the universal concept, the judgment, and the truth of the judgment.

1. *The Concretizing Synthesis* (Concretio): *The Universal Concept*

When abstraction is spoken of in the Thomistic metaphysics of knowledge, what is meant in the first place is the formation of a universal concept. If, then, abstraction is supposed to accomplish the differentiation of subject and object, the first indication of what this is must be given in the universal concept. A universal concept is a known intelligibility that exists in many and can be predicated of many. Our question here is not in the first place how the formation of such a concept takes place in detail, where it gets its definite content, or how it is intrinsically constituted. Our only concern first of all is its formal essence. In the universal concept a being (form, substantial or accidental essence) as such is apprehended of many possible existents (subjects). It would no longer be a universal concept if its content could be completely separated from its reference to possible subjects which could be determined by it. However "abstract" from possible subjects it might be conceived, the reference to possible subjects belongs to it essentially. Just when the known content of the universal concept is supposed to be thought of by itself by attempting to put its relation to a subject in parentheses (for example, "color" as such, independent of a possible colored thing), the universal concept is made into an individual thing which is itself again a synthesis of a universal and a subject. It becomes a thing which one can bring to consciousness in its meaning only by distinguishing a universal (that which makes color color: coloredness) and a subject (that which becomes "color" through coloredness).

It is important for an understanding of the whole conversion to make this characteristic structure of our thought clear. Conversion is precisely the reference of the universal to a "this." If according to Thomas there is supposed to be no knowledge without a conversion, one could object against this thesis that at least the conception of the universal concept and the universal, essential judgment, neither of which are related to a concrete "this," excludes such a conversion. But, as a matter of fact, all of these universalities too must always be thought of in a conversion. We apprehend the universal itself as object of our thought precisely when it is conceived *as* universal, once again in a concretizing conversion of the second order, so to speak, as an object which again is itself intrinsically structured as a known real object. Our known intelligibilities are similarly formed in all cases, and they are universal or concrete only by the fact that they are either related immediately and as such to the concrete thing given in sensibility, or only mediately. The singular concept always already contains in itself a universal ("this thing of this kind"), and the universal as such is still related to a "this" ("the kind of this thing"), or is itself conceived as a "this of this kind." The Thomistic theses that intellectually there are only universal concepts, and that the universal concept is known only in a conversion to the phantasm, are the two descriptions of this one structure of any and all of our knowledge, and they must be kept together.

If the non-concrete as such is made an object of thought, then by this very fact it functions as a concrete, for then one thinks something about it, and this "it" is related to the "something" as a concrete to its universal (to the form). An "it" alone, without a "something" about it, cannot be conceived in thought at all. "It" can be sensibly intuited. But then it is not given objectively through sensibility alone. One can deny in a *judgment* that the "it" is in itself different from a "something" (in an attempt to conceive the form subsisting in itself). But then the question arises, and still remains to be solved, whether after this negation through *judgment* an object of thought still remains at all. Every conception in thought, whether universal, singular, or individual, is knowing something about something. So that what was at first shown to be a characteristic of the universal concept turns out to be not merely a characteristic of the universal concept as such, but an expression of the essential mode of our human knowing all together: something is always known about something. As a matter of fact, it is here that the return of the subject to himself becomes manifest.

Every objective knowledge is always and in every case the reference of a universal to a "this." Hence the "this" appears as the reference point standing over against the knowing to which the knower refers what is (universally) known by him. But then the subject with the content of his knowledge (the universal concept) already stands to some extent at a distance from the "this" to which he refers the content of the knowledge. This content of knowledge is universal precisely because it stands on the side of the knowing subject in its opposition to the "this" and therefore can be related to any number of "this's." Or, to put it vice versa: precisely by the fact that the subject disengages the content of the universal concept from the undifferentiation of subject and object in sensibility (which does not at all have to mean a diminution of its content, because of course in this disengagement only a completely empty "this" has to remain behind), the subject attains to itself for the first time in its opposition over against the "this," it turns back to itself and thus for the first time has an object (*Gegen-stand*) to which it can refer the known which is brought along in its return to itself and thus has become universal. The return of the knowing subject to himself and the liberation of a universal from its "subjects" is one and the same process. Thus the universal concept is actually the first indication of the opposition between subject and object which first makes possible an objective experience. *Accordingly, abstraction as acquisition of the universal concept is the realization of this return* (reflexio) *of the subject to himself.*

2. The Affirmative Synthesis (Complexio): The Judgment and the Truth Appearing in It

Actually, this already gives us the point of departure for apprehending the second indication of the return to the self, the point of departure for understanding the judgment. We saw the universal concept essentially as the "what" of a possible something, as a known intelligibility able to be synthesized with a possible subject. But this means that the universal concept, which Thomas usually calls the simple apprehension, is distinguished from the judgment, in which it is the predicate, not as a part from the whole, into which the concepts (subject, predicate) are pieced together only subsequently to their own intrinsic constitution, but as a possible from an actually realized synthesis of subject and predicate. For the reference to a possible subject already belongs to the universal concept as such. But at the same time, this means that the proposition is *prior to* the universal concept, since the realized synthesis is prior to the possible. It is from the realized synthesis that the nature of the possible synthesis will have to be discovered more precisely, and in so doing, we will also be able to eliminate the obscurity which has existed in our statements so far about the reference of a universal to a possible subject standing over against it.

Usually the subject of a proposition is not a "this" which is completely indetermined in itself. It is already by itself the synthesis of an empty "this" with a universal, known intelligibility. The same holds, and in fact necessarily, for the predicate of the proposition. The universal concept of a predicate must already be concretized before it is ascribed to the subject; it must already be thought of as related to a possible subject. Then the judgment identifies the subject (the "this") of the subject of the proposition with that of the predicate. Thus subject and predicate are already and always of themselves a *concretum* (of the first or second order), that is, a universal in its being-in a "this" (anyone at all). In Thomistic terminology this synthesis is called *concretio*. We might translate *concretio* as concretizing synthesis. We can now formulate what was said of the universal concept as follows: every universal concept is apprehended with and in a concretion that is necessarily conceived simultaneously, and every individual is conceived objectively in a concretion which already contains in itself a universal differentiated from the "this."

Now usually the judgment is understood as the synthesis of the two concepts of subject and predicate. This understanding can be justified so long as one is aware of the intrinsic structure of the concept itself, which in each instance is a concretizing synthesis itself. Presupposing this, how is the synthesis of the two concepts of a proposition to be understood more precisely? Obviously in this way, that the universal contained in both concepts is synthesized with the same supposite. In the judgmental synthesis, therefore, it is not at all a question of the synthesis of two quiddities of the same order with each other, but of the reference (*Hinbeziehung*) of two quiddities to the same "this." In this process the subject in its concretizing synthesis, which is presupposed, not accomplished, has only the function of determining and indicating that definite supposite to which the universal of the predicate is to be related. While the predicate as such, in its concretizing synthesis which we just considered, was the possible synthesis of a universal with any "this" at all, now the subject determines unambiguously what "this" is meant. The synthesis of the universal contained in the predicate with this definite "this" is now realized in the judgment. The concretizing synthesis as possible (since it is a synthesis with any "this" at all) is converted into one actually realized, insofar as it is no longer any "this" at all that is held before the concretizing synthesis that is given with the concept of the predicate, but that supposite already determined by the subject of the proposition. It is to this that it has to be related, and in the judgment is also factually related. Thomas calls this synthesis *"complexio," "affirmatio,"* which we want to render as affirmative synthesis.

Looked at correctly, objective knowledge is not reached until the affirmative synthesis, or expressed in another way: *a concretizing synthesis occurs in real thought only as an affirmative synthesis.* Objective knowledge is given only when a knower relates a universal, known intelligibility to a supposite existing in itself. First of all, it needs no further explanation that the judgment attains to a supposite existing in itself (*ad rem*), since for the time being we can leave aside the question precisely what this "in-itself" (*Ansich*) is. Therefore, we only want to say that the judgment does not consist in relating and connecting the known, universal quiddities as such which stand on the side of the knowing subject, but in referring these to the "something" standing over against the knowing subject, which is designated by the quiddity of the subject of the proposition, and of which the quiddity of the predicate is affirmed. Even if an attempt is made to conceive a universal concept by itself, it succeeds only in an affirmative synthesis, in a judgment. For if such a concept is thought "alone," then this thinking thinks something about it, as was said before. In this process it is itself conceived as something already objectified, as something existing in itself which thought holds before itself as something standing opposite, and to which as object (*res*) the knower relates a known intelligibility. Hence the universal concept is already and always conceived as independent from thought as knowing, as existing in itself and so as definite, and thus not merely a synthesizing, but an affirmative synthesis takes place.

Therefore, there is no knowing by human consciousness at

125

all except in an affirmative synthesis, and this judgment is not connecting concepts, as though these were the fundamental elements of thought and the role of judgment were only to connect them subsequently, but it is referring knowing to an in-itself (*Ansich*), and in this reference concepts are present as moments possible only in the judgment. Concepts occur either in a judgment about things, or as objects of a judgment about concepts. This also says that the opposition between subject and object, which takes place in the abstractive return of the subject to himself, which return forms universal concepts, is as a matter of fact the affirmative synthesis.

Finally, there has already followed from this the third indication of the complete return of the subject to himself, namely, truth. It is not that the concretizing synthesis as such is true or false, but that its successful or unsuccessful reference to the thing itself in the affirmative synthesis is true or false. Accordingly, insofar as truth means a relation of knowing to a reality existing in itself, and insofar as the return takes place in this affirmative synthesis, this also says that truth creates this opposition between subject and object for the first time, and that this opposition is not possible at all without truth.

3. Concretio *and* Complexio *in Thomas*

So far we have omitted going into Thomistic texts lest the course of the development be interrupted by a tedious textual interpretation of Thomas's statements about this question. The omission is to be made up for now by giving a brief proof that the development we have given corresponds to the Thomistic conception.

1. The concept of *concretio* in Thomas.[1] Actually this concept was present in the background throughout the whole of our development of the essence of sensibility according to Thomas. Sensibility is always an already accomplished concretion, and therefore it cannot itself apprehend the occurrence. For sensibility is the being-present-to-itself of an

[1] Cf. on this point Maréchal, *op. cit.*, pp. 202ff.

ontological actuality (form) in its abandonment to the other of matter, insofar as it is the form of a material supposite; hence it cannot bring to givenness a separative reference of the form to the supposite. Thus sensibility knows "materially and concretely,"[2] and is therefore only knowledge of the individual. "Vision can in no way know in abstraction that which it knows in concretion."[3] Insofar as the return of the subject to itself, which separates subject and object, the abstraction, always begins at the undifferentiated being-with-the-other of sensibility, man cannot completely free the knowledge abstracted and taken along in the return from its relation to the sensibly given in which it was already and always concretized. Thus, thought is an "apprehending . . . the concrete in abstraction"[4] as *one* action. Man can achieve his abstract knowledge, if it is to become objective, only in a concretizing synthesis, in a "supposite," in a "subject." "Whatever our intellect designates as subsisting it designates in a concretion."[5] The designation of something objective, in which the knowing is to come into possession of the object as such, is "designating in a concretion," that is, it is the designation of a composite insofar as it is the synthesis of a *"quo aliquid est,"* of a "form," an *"aliquid, quod inest,"* and a "supposite," an *"aliquid quod subjicitur,"* a "subject."[6] Therefore, it is true that "What is designated concretely is designated as existing in itself, as a man or as a white thing . . . what is designated abstractly is designated after the manner of a form."[7] Therefore, a real thing (*res subsistens*) in itself can also be designated only by a concrete term (God, not divinity; animal, not sensibility, and so on).[8] Thus "animal" is the designation for concretized sensibility: "Animal is derived from sentient nature

[2] *S.T.* I, q. 86, a. 1, ad 4.
[3] *S.T.* I, q. 12, a. 4, ad 3.
[4] *Ibid.*
[5] *S.C.G.* I, 30. For the application, see e.g. *De Pot.* q. 7, a. 2, ad 7.
[6] *S.T.* I, q. 13, a. 1, ad 2 and 3; a. 12, ad 2.
[7] *I Sent.* dist. 33, q. 1, a. 2, corp.
[8] *S.T.* I, q. 32, a. 2, corp.; see *In VII Metaph.* lect. 2, n. 1289: *concretiva sive denominativa praedicatio.*

127

by way of concretion."[9] From what we said earlier about sensibility it follows necessarily that the already accomplished concretion belongs to material things, including sensibility, as an ontological predicate, and that the concretion as a *process* is a characteristic of our thought, but its necessity for our thought is derived from sensibility.[10]

2. The concept of *complexio* in Thomas. Among known intelligibilities Thomas distinguishes between incomplex (indivisible) and complex. The incomplex are, for example, house, army, man, the content of a definition, and so on.[11] Just from this alone it becomes clear that the concrete things that we were just talking about belong to the incomplex, hence that the concretizing and the affirmative synthesis are not the same. The complex is an *enuntiabile*,[12] a judgment. Man always knows "according to a certain synthesis."[13] This synthesis (*complexio*) takes place "through affirmation or negation," in a judgmental affirmation or negation. Why a judgment and its affirmation must be understood as a synthesis, and in fact, as one which does not coincide with the concretion, also becomes clear in Thomas: the complex comes about through a "comparison of the incomplex (hence of the already concretized universal!) to the thing," through a synthesis of the concretized universal with the definite "in-itself of the object."[14] Insofar as the defi-

[9] *S.T.* I, q. 3, a. 5, corp.
[10] *S.T.* I, q. 12, a. 4, ad 3.
[11] *In III De Anima* lect. 11, n. 746; n. 761-2; *Periherm.* lib. 1, lect. 3 (Parma 5); *III Sent.* dist. 23, q. 2, a. 2, sol. 1, corp. Above, *homo* was an example of a *concretum: I Sent.* dist. 33, q. 1, a. 2, corp. It follows necessarily from the examples (definition, etc.) that the simplicity and indivisibility of an *incomplexum* should not be understood as the uniqueness of a conceptual note. The "unity" excludes only the affirmative synthesis, but not a complex concretizing synthesis of many conceptual notes on a common supposite.
[12] *S.T.* II–II, q. 1, a. 2, corp.
[13] *Ibid.*
[14] *S.C.G.* I, 59: *complexum in quo designatur comparatio incomplexi ad rem. In VI Metaph.* lect. 4, n. 1223ff. (the whole *lectio*); *S.T.* I, q. 16, a. 2, corp.: In the judgment *aliquam formam significatam per praedicatum . . . applicat (intellectus) alicui rei significatae per subjectum.* Notice that it does not say: *"applicat subjecto,"* "relates to the

nition as a mere synthesis of conceptual notes as such does not
yet contain any affirmative reference to a thing in itself, any
"comparison or application to the thing," it is still incomplex
unless it implicitly contains the judgment of the objective compatibility of its notes, or the judgmental reference of the definition to a thing in itself as something really defined by it.[15]
So it is self-evident that truth in the proper sense, that is, as
known conformity with the thing itself, can be given only in the
complex, but not in the incomplex.[16]

From what has been said so far, it follows that for Thomas
the meaning of the judgment is not exhausted by saying that it is
a synthesis of two concepts,[17] but that the really constitutive
moment of the judgment is the reference of the concretizing synthesis of subject and predicate to the thing itself, the affirmative
synthesis. Through this, truth first becomes a characteristic of the
intellectual process.[18] Truth is only present when the known is
related to the "in-itself" (*Ansich*), to the *esse* of the thing,[19] when
there is given an "application to the thing."[20]

To what extent the universal concept with its concretizing
synthesis, the judgment as affirmative synthesis, and truth, are
also for Thomas himself indications of the complete return,
which as a fundamental process of thought first makes the
other, which was received in sensibility as undifferentiated from
itself, the object of experience, that must follow from what is to
be said about the intrinsic possibility of this return according to
Thomas. But precisely from what has been said it follows that
the question about the possibility of the return coincides ob-

concept of the subject," but: relates the content of the predicate to the
thing (*res*) designated by the concept of the subject. The "whither" of
the proposition's affirmation is not the concept of the subject, but the
thing in itself, the *res*.
[15] *In VI Metaph.* lect. 4, n. 1237; *S.C.G.* I, 59; *S.T.* I, q. 17, a. 3, corp.;
I Sent. dist. 19, q. 5, a. 1, ad 7; *De Ver.* q. 1, a. 3, corp.
[16] *S.T.* I, q. 16, a. 2, corp., and the texts in the previous note.
[17] For the fact that the concretion is also found in the judgment, see
S.T. I, q. 85, a. 5, ad 3.
[18] Cf. the previous note; *Periherm.* lib. 1, lect. 3 (Parma 5–6).
[19] *I Sent.* dist. 19, q. 5, a. 1, corp. and ad 7; a. 3, corp.
[20] See for this expression, *S.C.G.* II, 96 at the end; I, 59.

jectively with the question: What are the *a priori* conditions of the possibility of the affirmative synthesis? For synthesis this offers for the first time an object which stands over against the subject and of which this latter can affirm its knowledge. Truth is only another name for the same thing. "The essence of truth is first found where the intellect first begins to have something proper to itself which the thing outside the soul does not have."[21] In sensibility, knowledge has nothing by itself alone because it is identical with the thing. It is only in thought that it returns to itself with its knowledge in a separation from the "thing outside the soul," and thereby can relate its knowledge to the thing and be conscious of the success of this reference, can make a true judgment. What was said at the beginning of this section about the reference of the universal acquired in the abstraction to a "this" has been clarified in our consideration of the judgment to the extent that in this process the decisive thing for the differentiation of subject and object is not the concretizing synthesis as such and by itself, but the affirmative synthesis.

This judgmental reference of the knowledge to an "in-itself," as to that which does not owe its being to the psychic occurrence of this knowledge as such, is essential to the judgment, the synthesis (*complexio*). This does not say that knowing *as such* necessarily attains to a being which, being different from the thinking, is apprehended only by such a reference which intends and applies a liberated content of knowledge. Such an opposition does not belong to the essence of knowing as such. On the contrary: knowing as such is to be understood first of all as a being's being-present-to-self. But precisely from this it follows that the known is apprehended as it is in itself. The apprehension of an "in-itself" is therefore conceivable without setting apart in opposition the knowing subject and the object, without a judgment as affirmative synthesis.[22]

But *human* knowing is first of all being-with-the-world (*Bei-der-Welt-Sein*), a being-with-another in sensibility, and there-

21 *De Ver.* q. 1, a. 3, corp.
22 Therefore God, for example, does not judge: *S.T.* I, q. 14, a. 14; q. 85, a. 5, corp.; *S.C.G.* I, 58–59, etc.

fore knowledge of this other in its in-itself (*Ansich*) as proper object is only possible by setting the other opposite and referring the knowledge to this other which is set opposite and exists in itself. Therefore this other appears as normative in respect to such knowing, as the measure of the knowledge,[23] as something which can be met or missed in this reference, so that the possibility of missing its intention, the possibility of error is always essential to such judgmental knowing. In the stationary self-possession of an in-itself in the identity of being as a being-present-to-self, that is not possible. Hence in such an ideal case, in intuition in the Thomistic sense, there can be no question of judgment or of error, no more than of being measured by the object (as proper object) in the strict sense, because of course the knowing is from the outset and ultimately remains identical with the object, since the thing in its in-itself comes to givenness for itself. Therefore, intuition in Thomas is always true.[24] But human knowledge, which is not pure sensibility, possesses the other in thought strictly as such as that which is not identical, and reaches it therefore only in a reference of the knowledge to the "in-itself," *ad rem*. It is only in the synthesis (*complexio*) as the characteristically human way of knowing that the in-itself of the thing as such can be reached by man.

Such a reference (*Hinbeziehung*) is essential to human knowing. Insofar as thought necessarily thinks objectively, there is no thought without the affirmation of an in-itself. Man always thinks something of another something and thus always supposes something which is in itself (*Ansichseiendes*). Even if he doubts or denies that he reaches this in-itself in his knowledge, that his thinking is true of something which is in itself, he supposes such an in-itself. For doubt or denial of such an in-itself constitutes one anew: the "that such a thing is not to be reached," the "that we are able to decide nothing about such a possibility," all of

---

[23] *S.T.* I, q. 21, a. 2, corp.; *S.C.G.* II, 12; *De Ver.* q. 1, a. 2, corp.; a. 8, corp.; *De Pot.* q. 7, a. 10, ad 5, etc.

[24] Thus there can be no error in sense intuition as such: *S.T.* I, q. 17, a. 2; *De Ver.* q. 1, a. 10 (this article is of greater metaphysical clarity and sharpness than the one in the *Summa*); nor in intellectual intuition (of the angels): *S.T.* I, q. 58, a. 5, etc.

this supposes something which is thought of independently of the actual process of this thinking, hence as in itself.[25]

We will have to examine in more detail what this in-itself [*Ansich*] is which the affirmative synthesis reaches.

III. THE RETURN OF THE SUBJECT TO HIMSELF, AND THE AGENT INTELLECT

Let us clarify once again the point which our considerations have now reached. The one human knowledge is objective reception (*Hinnahme*) of the other, of the world. In order to

[25] See *S.T.* I, q. 2, a. 1, ad 3 and obj. 3: *veritatem (in communi) esse est per se notum; quia qui negat veritatem esse, concedit veritatem non esse; si enim veritas non est, verum est veritatem non esse.* (For the fact that Thomas admits the correctness of the argument in this objection, see *loc. cit.* ad 3 and *I Sent.* dist. 3, q. 1, a. 2, corp.: *veritatem autem esse est per se notum.*) The proof of this proposition, "*veritatem esse est per se notum,*" should not be taken as a pure reduction to absurdity which only tries to prove a contradiction between the concepts; "*verum est*" and "*veritatem non esse.*" Such a proof would be inconclusive, for no contradiction can be shown in the mere concept "*veritatem non esse*" as such. For if there were no truths, then at least this would be "true," not in the sense of the "true" as it is understood in the assumption mentioned, but in the sense that there are no truths of this kind any more than there are falsities, that this "*verum*" of the assumption is not the contrary but the contradictory of the opposite assumption (namely, that there are truths). The whole proof is rather a kind of transcendental deduction of the fact that *actual* thought (*qui negat . . . concedit*) includes essentially a reference to an in-itself ("that there are no truths"). It is not a question of proving a contradiction between the concepts thought of, but between the implicit and the explicit of the actually realized thought: the elimination of an in-itself explicitly realized in thought implicitly establishes one again. Thomas himself says with perfect clarity that he does not see a simple contradiction between the concepts as such in *I Sent.* dist. 19, q. 5, a. 3, ad 3: *Et si objicitur: "veritas non est, ergo veritatem esse est falsum, quantum ad illud tempus in quo non erat veritas creata," dico quod non sequitur: quia quando non est veritas, nec etiam falsitas est.* Hence according to Thomas, if there is absolutely no truth, neither is it false that there is truth, which, in the purely logical understanding of the above proof of the in-itself, would be the presupposition of its validity. We will have to come back to this question. On this point and for further Thomistic texts, cf. Maréchal, *op. cit.,* pp. 42ff.

grasp the possibility of an intuitive reception of the other as such on the basis of the presupposition of the identity of knowing and being, sensibility as the act of matter was introduced. As such it does give the other, but not as something objective about which something true can be affirmed in a judgment. The capacity to objectify by placing knowing and known over against each other we called thought, in whose characteristics as a universal, judgmental, and true knowledge we found the indications of this placing the known in opposition and objectifying it, and for the return of the knower to himself.

How are we to grasp the possibility of this abstractive return? From what was said about sensibility it follows first of all negatively as our first and self-evident conclusion that sensibility as such cannot accomplish this return, the being-present-to-oneself over against another.

The intellect is present to itself over against another in thought, and as such it can relate a universal to a supposite, make a judgment, and grasp the truth of a judgment. It is present to itself as placed over against another. Both of these taken together describe the essence of human knowledge: man is present to himself as himself, since in relating the universal, known intelligibility to something and in judging about something he differentiates himself from this something. But it is only *in* this differentiation over against another that he is present to himself in knowing self-possession. To want to deny that he is present to himself only in this way would mean leaving the basis upon which our questioning must permanently remain, the initial decision that man always finds himself as already being with the world. Hence his being-present-to-himself is grounded in a standing-over-against world, although it is not only presence-to-self as being-with-the-other, that is, it is not only sensibility.

In the formulation, "present to self over against another," there is already contained a clue for understanding more precisely what human thought is. Presence-to-self (*Beisichsein*) as being-present-to-oneself (*Beisichselbersein*) and being-present-to-oneself as being-placed-over-against-another (*Gegen-anderes-*

133

gestellt-Sein) constitute in this duality the one fundamental constitution of the human intellect, and this is expressed in the Thomistic concepts of the agent intellect and the possible intellect, although each of these two terms expresses the whole fundamental constitution in different respects.

For if being-present-to-itself were possible to human thought without being placed over against another, then the first-known (the proper object) would be the being of the knower himself.[1] Then there would be no possibility of an agent intellect, insofar as this means precisely the capacity to differentiate what is known universally from another existent, and by doing this to make possible for the first time an objectifying reference, by the knower, of the knowing to what is meant. There would also really be no place for a possible intellect either, that is, for a capacity to receive knowledge about another as given by this other. For in this presupposition the intellect would already and always have the possibility of being-present-to-itself through itself alone; therefore, it would already be present to itself in advance and would have already and always known itself, without being dependent on another manifesting itself to it and thus giving it the possibility to be present to itself in setting itself over against this other. If, vice versa, the knowledge were presence-to-self, not as placed over against another, but only as being with the other, then such knowledge would merely be sensibility, which of its essence excludes being-present-to-*oneself;* a liberation of being (knowing) from that about which something is known would be impossible. There would only remain the capacity for the passive reception of another in an ontological abandonment to the other.

From these tentative formulations of what agent intellect and possible intellect mean Thomistically, it is already clear that the agent intellect is the moment that preëminently characterizes the intellect. For the possible intellect can only be defined

---

[1] For this consideration, see *S.T.* I, q. 54, a. 4, corp.: the intellectual intuition of the angels is a being-present-to-oneself, without there being thereby any question of a being-placed-over-against-another.

as a power receptive of the other, and because it must wait upon an encounter with the other, it is in itself empty (possible). But that is a definition which formally applies to sensibility also. But if it is so understood of the possible intellect that the reception of the being of what is known happens in such a way that it is differentiated from this and referred to the known as to another, then the intellectuality of the receptive power is defined precisely by that which is the function of the agent intellect.

What was indicated briefly here was merely supposed to be a consideration of the question: Under what Thomistic heading do we have to look for that with which we are dealing at this stage of the work, namely, the possibility of the complete return? Actually, what Thomas says about the agent intellect is his answer to this question. In accomplishing its function the agent intellect sets the knower over against what exists in itself (*das Ansichseiende*) by the abstraction of being from the existent.

IV. THE ESSENCE OF THE AGENT INTELLECT

However indubitably the point of departure from which we have reached the concept of the agent intellect lies within the field of the Thomistic problematic, yet its further development is not to be left in the first place to the inner dynamism of this point of departure itself. Rather we will begin first of all with what Thomas said explicitly about the agent intellect so that we may keep all the more certainly within the limits of his philosophizing.

How does Thomas introduce the concept of the agent intellect? The form (the knowable as such) in material things is the form of matter. As such it is necessarily individuated and therefore, concludes Thomas, not "actually intelligible." First we must explain this conclusion. We saw earlier that for Thomas the knowability of a being varies intrinsically with the degree of its intensity of being *(Seinmächtigkeit)*. Now "actually intel-

135

ligible" is not simply to be made equivalent to "actually knowable" in the broader sense. For in sensibility we met something actually sensible which as such also falls under the generic actually knowable. Therefore, if Thomas denies an actual intelligibility of the form insofar as it is the act of matter, he must be understanding by this a knowability of a higher order.

1. Agent Intellect as A Priori Condition of the Possibility of the Knowability of a Material Form

Knowability in general is the being of a thing insofar as it stands open of itself to some knowledge, insofar as, of itself, it can come to exist within the region of the identity of being and knowing. Intelligibility is the knowability of an existent with respect to thought as such, the indications of which we considered in Section II above. Form as the act of matter is not able to stand open to this thought, to become manifest in thought through identity with it. For in order to do this, it would have to be universal (to bring in the first fundamental indication of thought), and that is precisely what the form cannot be, insofar as, being antecedent to knowledge, it is already concretized in a definite supposite by its matter. Hence, if sensibility and its objects are to be the only source of human knowledge, something actually intelligible cannot simply be received passively from sensibility, and so it can owe its origin only to a spontaneous activity of thought itself, over against what is given sensibly, that is, to the agent intellect. Thus the agent intellect is introduced again and again in Thomas as the *a priori* condition, inherent in thought itself, of the possibility of something actually intelligible, which actual intelligible as such is not found in sensibility, and according to the evidence of experience does not come to man from elsewhere, especially since what is constituted as actually intelligible refers of itself back to sensibility.

Here are a few references to individual texts in Thomas for this. An actually intelligible is known when something is apprehended "as one in many and about many"[1]; "universals . . .

---

[1] *De Anima* a. 4, corp.

are actually intelligible."[2] "In those things in which individuation comes about through this signate matter, the individuals are not actually intelligible."[3] Hence sensibility does not reach anything actually intelligible; it is the abandonment to the many "this's" of matter as such.[4] This being the case, human universal knowing needs a faculty, the "agent intellect which makes the species received from sensible things intelligible."[5] "But Aristotle maintained that they (the forms existing universally in themselves) subsist only in sensible things (hence always in an already realized concreton) which are not actually intelligible (precisely because of this concretion). Therefore he considered it necessary to posit some power which would make what was potentially intelligible actually intelligible by abstracting the species of things from matter and from individuating conditions. This power is called the agent intellect."[6]

We must insert a digression here. Thomas came to the concept of the agent intellect from that of actual intelligibility as universality. As Thomas is aware, that is to see intelligibility from the specifically human level of being and from human thought. But there are levels of being with their corresponding knowability which are actually intelligible, without for that reason being universals, and without, therefore, universality always having to be the mark of all thought and of every actual intelligibility. But for a metaphysics of human knowledge, being-present-to-oneself is defined as not-being-the-act-of-matter, and insofar as human thought is only possible in being set over against another, hence by the possession of a material form over against its supposite, the universal is the mark of actual intelligibility. Levels of being which in themselves have no ordination to the empty "this" of matter in which they would

[2] De Spir. Creat. a. 9, corp.
[3] S.C.G. II, 75.
[4] S.T. I, q. 12, a. 4, corp. and ad 3; q. 85, a. 1, corp.; S.C.G. I, 65; In V Metaph. lect. 13, n. 947.
[5] S.C.G. II, 96
[6] De Spir. Creat. a. 9, corp. See S.T. I, q. 54, a. 4, corp.; q. 79, a. 3; De Anima a. 4; De Spir. Creat. a. 10, corp. at the beginning; In III De Anima lect. 10, n. 731; S.C.G. II, 59; II, 77.

be multiplied (separated forms) are in themselves actually intelligible without for that reason having to be universals.[7] They have a formal individuality which grounds a "specific" difference from other forms. But they cannot be multiplied as the same, precisely because that includes an ordination to the empty indeterminateness of matter. But insofar as forms are concretized in matter, they are with another, and therefore as such they cannot also be present to themselves, neither as knower nor, therefore, as known.

2. Agent Intellect as Knowledge of the Confinement of Form by Matter: The Mode of the "Liberation"

Lest the wording of the text in which Thomas describes the function of the intellect be misunderstood, we must never lose sight of the way in which Thomas arrives at the concept of the intellect. When it is said that the agent intellect liberates an intelligible species, impresses it on the possible intellect, and so on, such images are to be explained in the light of the metaphysical formulation: to make what is potentially intelligible actually intelligible, and not vice versa. Our consideration arrived at this formulation directly from a question in which thought comes upon the agent intellect as a metaphysical presupposition which can never be observed as such, since thought has always abstracted when it begins to reflect upon itself. The figurative expressions in which the activity of the agent intellect is described should not mislead us to the assumption that the sensible form as such in its qualitative content is brought to another "level." For if we keep in mind the proper formulation of abstraction, there still remains the question, What is it supposed to mean when it is said that the form becomes actually intelligible insofar as it becomes universal, and vice versa. Certainly it can be said first of all that it comes about by the form being "liberated" (abgelöst) from the matter in which and by which it is individuated. Thomas expresses himself this way

---

[7] See S.C.G. II, 75; De Anima a. 17, ad 5; a. 2, ad 5 and 6; a. 3, ad 17; S.T. I, q. 86, a 1, ad 3.

again and again, and we have frequently followed him in this way of speaking in one form or another. Thus this formulation is justified as a provisional formula which briefly sums up the results of the question.

But now, since abstraction is our explicit theme, the question is how this liberation (*Loslösung*) of the material form from matter, by which its referability to many "this's" is known, is to be understood, and how it can be grasped in its possibility. For if we wanted to retain what is figurative in this mode of expression and to assume that there is question of an actual liberation (whether of a real or intentional kind is not relevant here) of the form from matter, then abstraction would become intrinsically contradictory. For the form of a material thing as being and as known is intrinsically and essentially related to a "this."[8] How, then, is it to be "detachable" either as being or as known? Now we have not overlooked what has gone before, and so have found therein a hint in the fact that we said it is liberated in such a way that it retains its ordination to a possible "this" and can be thought of as real only in a concretion. The statement is correct, but it is not to the point in the question that concerns us now, for it presupposes the liberation of the form as already accomplished and only points out how the origin of the form from the concrete can and must remain explicit, but it does not make the liberation itself intelligible in its possibility.

For the question is precisely, to what extent knowing can know in the form its reference to other "this's" as to that in which it is sensibly and intuitively apprehended. Nothing of the kind is to be seen in its intuited content. A "comparison" with others that are similar already presupposes an antecedent abstraction, since a comparison as such is nothing but the reference of a form as something belonging to several supposites in the same way. In any case, the comparison of two forms with each other to establish their sameness is subsequent to the distinction between the form and the concrete "this," since two "this's," as such cannot be compared with each other. Or, to formulate

[8] *De Ver* q. 8, a. 6, ad 5: *constat enim quod formae naturales numquam intelliguntur sine materia, cum materia in earum definitione cadat.*

139

the problem another way, how do other possible "this's" present themselves before knowing in such a way that they appear as possible subjects of a form seen in a definite concrete thing? Their form and their supposite would already have to be differentiated from each other, hence the abstraction would have to be presupposed as having already taken place. Or, the same thing seen from the viewpoint of the form, how can it be seen in the form that it is only accidentally the form of precisely this sensibly possessed "this," in which alone, as a matter of fact, it is a form "in concretion"? Or still more simply: How can the form and the "this," being and an existent, be differentiated from each other at all, since they are always given in sensibility only as one, since being always occurs and can occur only as an existent?

In any case, this can be said first of all: The factual accomplishment of this liberation is grounded in the antecedent, although not independent, knowledge of the contingency of the sensible concretion, which is always already accomplished antecedent to sense knowledge and in which alone the sense possesses being.[9] Such contingency, of course, is not a sensibly intuited datum, is not one thing among other things in the form, but is the mode of being of the form itself, its limitedness in matter ("contraction," "confinement"), which of its essence is hidden from sensibility. Therefore the form must be known as limited by the "this" whose form it is; only then can it be known that it is "broader" in itself and so able to be related to other "this's," and then for the first time can it appear as ontologically different from matter, from its supposite, and as universal in itself. Hence the intellectual element in abstractive thought is the knowledge of the confinement of form by matter and only that; a qualitative content of the sensible itself is not transferred to the level of the intellect.

Just from this it follows that abstraction cannot be thought of, in a naïve interpretation of the figurative formulations in

[9] *De Ver.* q. 25, a. 1, corp.: *sensus est apprehendere hoc coloratum,* but not the color itself.

Thomas, as a production in the intellect of an intellectual "double" of what is sensibly given in intuition, as an "image" (*Bild*) which the intellect looks at as sensibility looks at its objects. It cannot be thought of that way because then a conversion to the phantasm would be superfluous and senseless from the outset. Prescinding from its intrinsic impossibility (what, for example, would an intellectual color be?), such an image by itself and as such would be just as concrete as its sensible model and therefore could not be universal in itself at all except through its reference to the many of which it is the image; but it is precisely the possibility of this reference which is to be made intelligible. "Intelligible species" as such (that is, insofar as the term does not include what is sensibly intuited), in spite of the Platonic origin of the terminology, does not have the character of an image in Thomas. Only the sensibly intuited has the character of an image.

A short digression on this point.[10] It is only in this conception that it becomes intelligible why Thomas can speak again and again of "seeing the intelligible species *in* the phantasms,"[11] of seeing everything which it sees "*in* the phantasms."[12] Thomas draws this conclusion himself: "For the agent intellect does not make something actually intelligible as though the intelligible flowed from it into the possible intellect (hence the agent intellect does not produce a double of the phantasm in the possible intellect, and in fact this conception is erroneous for the reason already cited), for then we would not need phantasms and the senses for understanding; (a conversion to the phantasm would not be necessary, and Thomas illustrates the correct conception by a comparison which puts our interpretation beyond doubt:) just as in a certain way light makes colors actual, not as though it had them with itself, but insofar as in a certain way it gives

[10] For what follows, cf. Maréchal, *op. cit.,* pp. 148ff.

[11] *S.T.* II–II, q. 180, a. 5, ad 2.

[12] *In Boeth. de Trin.* q. 6, a. 2, ad 5; similarly, *In de Mem. et Rem.* lect. 2, n. 316 (*in phantasmatibus inspicere*); *S.T.* I, q. 86, a. 1, corp. (*in phantasmatibus intelligere species intelligibiles*); III, q. 11, a. 2, ad 1 (*a phantasmatibus et in phantasmatibus apprehendere species intelligibiles*).

them visibility."[18] For the rest, this conception of the intelligible species must be further corroborated from our understanding of abstraction, an understanding which is to be further developed. Of course it is not to be denied by these considerations that the Thomistic way of speaking loses in clarity because of the use of the *eidos* concept for understanding abstraction.

This reveals the function of the agent intellect to us more clearly. It is not the power to imprint on the possible intellect a spiritual image of what has been sensibly intuited. It is precisely in this way that the intelligible species cannot be understood. The agent intellect is rather the capacity to know the sensibly intuited as limited, *as* a realized concretion, and only to that extent does it "universalize" the form possessed sensibly, only to that extent does it liberate the form from its material concretion.

3. Agent Intellect as "Pre-apprehension" ("Vorgriff")

We must therefore ask how the agent intellect is to be understood so that it can know the form as limited, confined, and thus as of itself embracing further possibilities in itself, as bordering upon a broader field of possibilities. Obviously this is possible only if, antecedent to and in addition to apprehending the individual form, it comprehends of itself the whole field of these possibilities and thus, in the sensibly concretized form, experiences the concreteness as limitation of these possibilities, whereby it knows the form itself as able to be multiplied in this field. This transcending apprehension of further possibilities, through which the form possessed in a concretion in sensibility is apprehended as limited and so is abstracted, we call "pre-apprehension" ("*Vorgriff*"). Although this term is not to be found literally in Thomas, yet its content is contained in what Thomas calls "*excessus*" (excess), using a similar image.[14]

---

[13] *Comp. Theol.* c. 88.

[14] For the concept of the *excessus*, see *S.T.* I, q. 84, a. 7, ad 3: the *excessus* is necessary for apprehending the objects of metaphysics in spite of the fact that sensibility is the abiding ground of our knowledge.

So our task will be to determine the breadth of the horizon comprehended *a priori,* which horizon, apprehended as such in the pre-apprehension, offers the possibility of experiencing the forms of sensibility as limited, of differentiating them from the ground of their limitedness, the sensible "this," and thus of creating for knowing the possibility of a complete return.

Concretely, our question will read: Is this horizon that of the imagination of infinite space and time, or is it broader, in principle unlimited in every dimension, the horizon of being absolutely, which thus discloses itself as transcending space and time?

From the above definition, the nature of this pre-apprehension can be further clarified immediately in one respect: pre-apprehension as such does not attain to an object. By its very essence, it is one of the conditions of the possibility of an objective knowledge. Every represented (*vorgestellte*) object of human knowledge (that is, of a knowledge in the form of a knowing of something about something, which form is verified in every judgment) is able to be apprehended itself only in a pre-apprehension. If the pre-apprehension itself attained to an object of the kind that a judgment presents to knowledge, then this pre-apprehension itself would again be conditioned by another pre-apprehension. On the other hand, the essence and the breadth of the pre-apprehension can only be determined by establishing that to which it attains. From this it follows that:

1. This "whither" (*Worauf*) of the pre-apprehension as such is not a humanly conceivable object, for the reason already given.

2. This "whither" must be designated after the manner of a human object. For when a condition of the possibility of objective knowledge is thematically made the object of a reflexive knowledge, this can only be done by this reflective knowledge

Thomas refers to *De Divinis Nominibus* of the pseudo-Areopagite. But Thomas's commentary on this work (c. 1, lect. 3, Parma XV, 271ff.) does not offer anything for our question about the meaning of the *excessus*-concept. In *In Boeth. de Trin.* q. 6, a. 2, corp. the *excessus* and the *remotio* appear as conditions for reaching the object of metaphysics. See also *ibid.,* a. 3, corp., towards the end.

itself subjecting itself to all the conditions of human knowledge. But among them belongs the concretion of the known "what" with a something of which this "what" is affirmed in a conversion to the phantasm. In other words, the whither of the pre-apprehension, if it is to be spoken of explicitly, must be conceived (designated) as an object, although not meant (affirmed) as such.[15]

3. Although the "whither" of the pre-apprehension as such is not an object, yet it can disclose objects beyond the one for whose apprehension the pre-apprehension occurred in a definite act. This disclosure is not meant as a presentation of the object in its own self (otherwise the pre-apprehension as such would attain to an object), but it comes about in that the pre-apprehension implicitly and simultaneously affirms (*implicite mitbejaht*) the real possibility of these other objects within the scope of its "whither." In its actual realization (*realen Vollzug*) (as action, whose "whither" must be really possible) the pre-apprehension establishes what can come to exist within the breadth of the pre-apprehension according to its essence. Otherwise the pre-apprehension would attain to a "more" which would be nothing. The knowledge of privative unlimitedness, to use some Thomistic terminology which is to be explained in a moment, would be the condition of the knowledge of the negative. But as a matter of fact it is just the opposite according to Thomas.

4. Insofar as the pre-apprehension is only *one* of the conditions of human knowledge, which is the knowledge we know about, we know philosophically of no human knowledge in which the pre-apprehension does not go beyond what is "grasped" (*Griff*), beyond the objective, concretizing knowl-

---

[15] Following Thomistic terminology, we can call such an "object" an object of the second order as opposed to the objects which are conceived in their real self (*intentio prima*). For the content of this distinction, see *I Sent.* dist. 2, q. 1, a. 3, corp., at the beginning; *De Pot.* q. 7, a. 9, corp.; a. 6, corp. For the terms themselves (*prima-secunda*): *I Sent.* dist. 23, q. 1, a. 3, corp.; dist. 26, q. 1, a. 1, ad 3; *III Sent.* dist. 6, q. 1, a. 1, sol. 1, corp.

edge. Thus human knowledge, about which alone we know anything philosophically, always falls short essentially of its complete fulfillment, which fulfillment is designated by the breadth of its pre-apprehension. Nevertheless, this pre-apprehension towards this ideal with all that it simultaneously affirms as really possible is not an inconsequential supplementation, but the condition of the possibility of any objective knowledge at all.

5. The pre-apprehension can be explained more precisely in the fact that it is the movement of the spirit towards the whole of its possible objects, for it is only in this way that the limitation of the individual known can be experienced. This totality, precisely as the "whither" of the pre-apprehension, cannot be the subsequent sum, but only the original unity of the possible objects. Now what was said of the pre-apprehension seems at first to contain a contradiction. As such it cannot by itself attain to an object, that is, to that which man can represent (*sich vorstellen*) in his knowledge. Yet, on the other hand, the pre-apprehension cannot reach out into "nothing" (which we still have to discuss), nor can it perhaps reach out to another object in such a way that along with this object it would not be conscious at all. Prescinding from everything else, that is already excluded by what the pre-apprehension is supposed to accomplish. So the "whither" of the pre-apprehension can reveal itself only in the consciousness of the pre-apprehension itself as such, although the pre-apprehension can only be made thematic in the assertion of a "whither." But that means nothing other than that the pre-apprehension (and its "whither") is known insofar as knowledge, in the apprehension of its individual object, always experiences itself as already and always moving out beyond it, insofar as it knows the object in the horizon of its possible objects in such a way that the pre-apprehension reveals itself in the movement out towards the totality of the objects. Thus the pre-apprehension has a being which makes it apprehendable, without it needing an object beyond that object for the objectifying of which it takes place, without the totality of the possible objects in their own selves having to be apprehended by the pre-apprehension.

145

V. *EXCESSUS I:*
PREPARATORY CLARIFICATIONS

The intellect abstracts the forms given in concretion in sensibility insofar as it knows their limitation produced by the already realized synthesis of sensibility, and it does this by the fact that in apprehending them, it comprehends the breadth of their possibilities in a pre-apprehension. There follows for us the task of determining the scope of the *a priori* pre-apprehension of the agent intellect. It is this as known, that is, as implicitly and simultaneously apprehended (*miterfasst*) in every apprehension of a form, which also indicates the absolute scope of the possible intellect.

It could seem at first as though the breadth of the intellectual pre-apprehension as the condition of abstraction would be as great as that of sensibility's pure intuition of space and time as such. Thus the pre-apprehension would be related to the total range of sensibility's possible intuition and thereby would disclose the limitedness of the intuition of the individual. The *a priori* of the intellect would be as extensive as that of sensibility. That seems to suggest itself just by reason of the fact that we meet the intellect and its function only as a condition of the possibility of apprehending objectively what is sensibly given. Of course, this presumption is not meant in the sense that sensibility, by the pure intuition of space and time as such, would be capable all by itself of apprehending the limitation of what is sensibly given. Space and time are expressions of the empty indeterminateness of matter, of its "nothing." This matter, and with it space and time, comes to being and knowledge in sensibility as the act of matter precisely insofar as it is limited to a definite "this," to a here and now.[1] Thus in the individual act of sensibility the pure intuition is indeed operative in the apprehension of the individual, but precisely not as known distinctly (*abgehoben*), or otherwise the empty possibility would already have to be knowable as such, and not only in-

[1] *De Ver.* q. 25, a. 1, corp.

sofar as it comes to exist in the actuality of the form. To put it another way, the sense, the imagination, has a formal object, but the sense itself never knows the formal object as such, but only insofar as, antecedent to the knowledge itself, the formal object is already limited by its own actuality in an ontological concretion as the presupposition of the sense knowledge. The sense does not know space and time, but, just as it is confined in the here and now by its own actuality, so too by itself it possesses only the here and now, but not insofar as the here is a point of space as such, nor insofar as the now is coming out of the past and reaching ahead to the future. Moreover, a more exact insight into the untenability of the assumption just mentioned follows from the second assumption to be treated directly.

It could be assumed that the *a priori* scope of thought as a non-sentient faculty is the scope of space and time, that is, *the horizon of sense intuition as such.* Thought would apprehend this horizon and in this pre-apprehension would experience the sensible form as limited and thus would abstract. Thomistically expressed, this thesis would read: The formal object of the agent intellect is mobile, material being, being as the principle of number, the being of the plurality of the same, of the quantitative, of the existent in space and time, the quiddities of material things. Insofar as the agent intellect itself would not be a sense faculty, it would not itself be subject to the limitation of matter, hence it could apprehend its potential scope as such, experience the limitedness of the form on this basis, and thus the universality which belongs to the form in itself. Does this assumption explain the possibility of abstracting and objectifying the sense data of the world and the complete return?

Before this question can be treated directly, three preliminary questions must be clarified:

1. The more exact relationship of form and supposite in their reciprocal limitation and limitedness must be discussed, for our formulations about them so far seemed to oscillate insofar as a limiting function was affirmed of form *and* matter;

2. We must ask what precisely is to be abstracted as "form";

3. From the clarification of the second question there must

147

follow a tentative definition of what is to be understood Thomistically by "*esse*," that which is reached by the intellectual preapprehension which makes abstraction possible.

1. The Reciprocal Limitation of Form and Supposite

The form as the content of the predicate in a proposition, as that which is known of something and is referred to this something in a concretizing and affirmative synthesis, has always appeared in our investigations thus far as the universal, the unlimited in itself (at least relatively), insofar as it appeared able to be related to many possible somethings ("this's"). The form in itself is the unlimited, that which is limited by the supposite to which it is referred insofar as, as form unlimited in itself, it becomes precisely this "this." On the other hand, *form* appears to be what limits, and *matter* what is unlimited in itself, insofar as this latter in its empty potentiality can be the supposite of many forms, and through this definite form it comes to be something of precisely this kind, whereby it cannot be something else. For example, redness in itself can be the redness of many "this's"; it becomes limited, the redness of precisely this red thing, and vice versa: this "this" could be red or blue, and through redness it becomes precisely red and not blue.

Before we go further into the unlimitedness of both form and matter, we must refer to a limitedness which is already proper to form and to matter taken by themselves. Form has a qualitative limitation of itself, for example redness and not greenness. At this point in the progress of our considerations, we can clarify to what extent such qualitative determinateness can be compared, and only thus be able to be known as limitedness at all, only if we have gained the insight that everything qualitative, everything that is in the dimension of essence, has an intrinsic ordination to the one *esse*, and if essence is seen as potency for this. Matter is already limited in itself insofar as it can be supposite only for such ontological actualities whose intrinsic essence is not of itself repugnant to concretization in matter. That there can be such an immaterial being (separated form) is at first presupposed here and must be proved later. Matter is already further limited in itself insofar as the empty "this" in itself is always already individuated, and precisely for this reason can contain no ontological actuality, must be "nothing," since otherwise the opposition between an ontological actuality universal in itself and an individual "this" in which the former is limited would begin anew.[2]

It is to be noted in this connection how we came upon the "concept" of matter: matter of itself is the individual (and to that extent definite), empty (that is, distinct from knowable and so universal ontological actuality, and therefore indeterminate) "this" as the bearer of a form, of an ontological actuality.[3] Therefore no common concept can be formed of such "this's" *per se*. Matter in itself has no "form," which alone can ground a universal concept; it is "one" only "through the removal of all distinguishing forms."[4] Therefore, a genuine con-

---

[2] *II Sent.* dist. 12, q. 1, a. 4, corp.: *oportet esse absque forma, quia omne subjectum quod habet formam* (that is, everything of which something can be known) *divisibile est in formam* (the known: *omnis cognitio est per formam, loc. cit.*) *et subjectum formae* (that to which the knowledge goes).

[3] Therefore it is true of matter as the real nothing of finite things: *secundum se neque esse habet neque cognoscibilis est* (*S.T.* I, q. 15, a. 3, ad 3), so much so that even in God it does not have an idea which would be different from that of the totality and of form (*ibid*). Therefore it can be grasped by us only as that to which something known is related: *secundum analogiam tantum* (*II Sent.* dist. 12, q. l, a. 4, corp.; see *II Sent.* dist. 17, q. 1, ad 4). In *S.T.* I, q. 87, a. 1, corp. it says: *non cognoscit materiam primam nisi secundum proportionem ad formam,* and *In VII Metaph.* lect. 2, n. 1296: *(materia) secundum essentiam suam non habet unde cognoscatur, cum cognitionis principium sit forma. Cognoscitur autem per quandam similitudinem proportionis . . . materia prima est scibilis secundum analogiam. In VIII Metaph.* lect 1, n. 1687: *materia non potest inteligi sine intellectu formae, cum non apprehendatur nisi ut ens in potentia ad formam.*

We cannot go into the question here how God knows prime matter. As the origin of being in its totality, hence of prime matter also (to the extent that an origin can and must be affirmed of it), He knows it otherwise than does the finite intellect, which can never encounter anything but a being that has already originated. See *De Ver.* q. 3, a. 5; *S.T.* I, q. 15, a. 3, ad 3; q. 57, a. 2, corp.; *S.C.G.* I, 65; 71.

[4] *S.T.* I, q. 16, a. 7, ad 2; *De Ver.* q. 1, a. 5, ad 15; *I Sent.* dist. 2, q. 1, a. 1, ad 3.

149

cept of individuality cannot be formed of what is individuated by matter; in individuality as such there is precisely no *"communitas rei."*[5] That we must nevertheless speak of the "one" matter as the *selfsame* in many things is ultimately explained only from the whole of what we are dealing with in this work: we can designate anything at all only "in concretion," and so even in the ultimate "this" we distinguish again between individuality as such and the many ultimate "this's" themselves, and thus form from this "universal" individuality a universal "this,"[6] the "one" matter which is apparently definable.[7] To what extent matter as a whole (logically prior to being informed by forms) as "matter with unlimited dimensions" is nevertheless also "one," without having the unity of the universal concept or the unity of the individual one, that can be treated appropriately in another connection.

Thomas brings out clearly the limitedness which matter has in itself: "prime matter even in its potentiality (in the infinity which has already been mentioned) is not absolutely infinite, but only relatively; for its potentiality is extended only to natural forms."[8] Similarly in many other places.[9] And likewise with the intrinsic limitedness of forms in themselves: they have an intrinsic infinity but this is always (except in the *esse* of God) only "relative."[10] Every essential nature is limited to the scope of its specific notes,[11] so that there is something limited through form, something "contracted" that is such through the limited nature.[12] Therefore, there is "a more and less according to the grade of the different forms,"[13] "virtual quantity"

[5] *S.T.* I, q. 30, a. 4, corp. and ad 1–3; *I Sent.* dist. 25, q. 1, a. 3, ad 4.
[6] *S.T.* I, q. 30, a. 4, corp.: *individuum vagum.*
[7] Thomas is aware that this is impossible in itself: *Quodl. 9,* a. 6, ad 3.
[8] *S.T.* I, q. 7, a. 2, ad 3.
[9] *De Anima* a. 9, corp.; *II Sent.* dist. 30, q. 2, a. 1, corp.
[10] *S.T.* III, q. 10, a. 3, ad 3; cf. ad 2.
[11] *Ibid.,* ad 2: *omnium essentia . . . limitata sub ratione unius speciei;* similarly *Quodl. 3,* a 3, corp.; *I Sent.* dist. 43, q. 1, a. 1, corp.
[12] *S.T.* I, q. 7, a. 2, corp.: *finitum secundum formam . . . ; contractum ad terminatam naturam.*
[13] *De Spir. Creat.* a. 8, ad 8.

of varying quantity.[14] The ultimate reason for this limitation is to be sought in the fact that essence is to be conceived as potency (which implies limitation in itself) with respect to *esse*, whose finiteness, as the limitation by essence of what is infinite in itself, makes possible the comparison between the scope of the various essential natures.[15] We will have to come back to this later.

We now continue the consideration of the intrinsic infinity of matter and form. But this infinity differs fundamentally in the two of them. Thomas himself brings this difference out clearly from the essence of the two infinities: "Therefore, we must consider that something is said to be infinite from the fact that it is not limited. But in a certain way, matter is limited by form, and form by matter: matter by form insofar as before it receives form (of course it is not a question of temporal priority),[16] matter is in potency for many forms, but when it receives one, it is limited by it. On the other hand, form is limited by matter insofar as a form considered in itself is common to many, but by the fact that it is received in matter, it becomes specifically the form of this thing. However, matter is perfected by the form by which it is limited, and so a relative infinity is attributed to matter; it is of the nature of an imperfection, for it is as matter without any form. But form is not perfected by matter; rather[17] the form's fullness is contracted by matter. Wherefore infinity, insofar as it is had on the part of form not determined by matter, is of the nature of a perfection."[18]

---

[14] *De Ver.* q. 29, a. 3, corp. That is the intrinsic limitation of being from form, which is to be distinguished from *quantitas dimensiva*. Thomas also calls this *quantitas virtualis spiritualis magnitudo: S.C.G.* I, 43; see also *S.C.G.* III, 54; *De Ver.* q. 2, a. 2, ad 5; a. 9, ad 7, etc.

[15] For this see, for the time being, *De Pot.* q. 1, a. 2, corp.; *De Ver.* q. 20, a. 4, ad 1 (*esse finitum*); q. 29, a. 3, corp.

[16] *S.T.* I, q. 66, a. 1.

[17] It is to be noted here exactly in what the distinction consists, because it is not present in every respect. Insofar as the form also can come to be as real actuality only in concretion, in this respect a "*perfici*" *in materia* (although not *through* it in the proper sense) can be affirmed.

[18] *S.T.* I, q. 7, a. 1, corp. Similarly, *I Sent.* dist. 43, q. 1, a. 1, corp.

Thomas calls the infinity of matter a privative, material (*secundum materiam*) infinity, that of form a negative, formal (*secundum formam*) infinity.[19] The infinity of matter is *privative* insofar as it expresses the empty, unlimited potentiality of matter, and this latter is thus thought of as deprived of form[20] (which potentiality it also retains when determined by form),[21] whereby a perfection (actuality, form) is denied of matter towards which it is intrinsically ordered. Thomas calls the infinity of the form in itself *negative* insofar as an intrinsic limitedness is denied of it. Thomas always uses the term "negative," as opposed to privative, where there is question of a "lack" which does not make the thing imperfect beyond what is "normal."[22] The other two terms (material and formal) are self-explanatory.

Of importance for our purpose in this distinction in the nature of the infinity of matter and form is the way in which these infinities can be the object of *knowledge*. For from this difference there also follows a radical difference in the knowledge of them. Thomas's statements on the matter are based on the proposition, "all knowledge is through form or act." All knowledge attains to an ontological actuality as the ground that makes it possible. Knowing always finds itself already with a formed actuality, and thus apprehends itself as made possible by this and as essentially turned towards this.[23] Its known and

[19] For the term: *S.T.* III, q. 10, a. 3, ad 1; *I Sent.* dist. 3, q. 1, a. 1, ad 4; *S.C.G.* I, 43; *De Ver.* q. 2, a. 2, ad 5; a. 9, ad 7; *De Pot.* q. 1, a. 2, corp. For "*secundum formam-secundum materiam*": *S.T.* I, q. 7, a. 1, corp.; q. 25, a. 2, ad 1; q. 86, a. 2, ad 1; *Quodl.* 3, a. 3, corp., etc.
[20] See the previous note.
[21] *S.T.* I, q. 66, a. 2, corp.; *II Sent.* dist. 12, q. 1, a. 1, corp.
[22] See, for example, *S.T.* I, q. 12, a. 4, ad 2; *II Sent.* dist. 43, q. 1, a. 6, corp., etc.
[23] *S.T.* I, q. 87, a. 1, corp.: *Aliquid . . . sub cognitione cadit, prout actu est. Et hoc quidem manifeste apparet in rebus sensibilibus: non enim visus percipit coloratum in potentia, sed solum coloratum in actu.* This "*apparet*" is to be understood in the sense that we gave the "*indicium, experimentum, apparet*" in Section Five of Part One: as an indication of how man always comes upon his knowledge, as a directive to take his knowledge as it is: turned towards reality before possibility.

only knowable is thus actuality. From this fundamental self-understanding which knowing has of itself, it then necessarily follows for Thomas that the privative infinity, which matter is in its empty potentiality, not only can be known only *at* the actuality in which it is apprehended, but also only *through* this actuality: "but such (privative) infinity is unknown by its very nature, because it is matter with the privation of form[24] . . . because a form is known of itself, but matter without form is unknown."[25]

Thomas stresses this principle again and again. In contrast to the negative infinity of form as ontological actuality, the privative infinity of matter as the merely possible, as the nothing, in which form is contained and through which it is limited, is the object of knowledge not of itself, but only through the form: "An infinity which is had on the part of matter not perfected by form is unknown of itself, for all knowledge is through form. But an infinity which is had on the part of form not limited by matter is of itself preëminently known."[26] That privative infinity is known from negative infinity has already been sufficiently verified by the texts cited earlier about the knowledge of matter by analogy with form. If we formulate these results once again in a somewhat different way so that their significance for our theme will be brought out more clearly, then we can say: the potential infinity of the limiting principle of an existent (privative infinity) can be known only through the positive infinity of a formal actuality (at a negative infinity). Matter is not known in an apprehension apprehending it immediately, but as opposition, as limitation of the form as universal. Accordingly, knowledge of it already presupposes abstraction of the form; it is not really known in the abstraction of the form, but in the conversion of the form to that from which it was abstracted, to the sensibly given and already concretized form.

Therefore the knowledge of matter as such is for Thomas not

---

[24] *S.T.* III, q. 10, a. 3, ad 1. See *S.C.G.* III, 54.

[25] *S.T.* I, q. 86, a. 2, ad 1.

[26] *S.T.* I, q. 12, a. 1, ad 2, See *Quodl.* 3, a. 3, corp.; *I Sent.* dist. 3, q. 1, a. 1, ad 4; *IV Sent.* dist. 49, q. 2, a. 1, ad 12; *De Ver.* q. 2, a. 2, ad 5.

153

really a condition of the possibility of the knowledge of the universal (negatively infinite) form, but vice-versa. This relationship between the knowability of privative and negative infinity of course holds not merely for matter and form in the strictest and most proper sense, but anywhere at all where a potential and a formal infinity are found,[27] since this relationship resulted from the essence of knowledge as a capacity directed to formal actuality. It is always true that man knows the finiteness and limitedness of a concrete, ontological determination (of an existent) insofar as it is held in the broader "nothing" of its potentiality; but this broader nothing itself is known only insofar as it itself is held against the infinity of the formal actuality as such (of being), whatever this might be: essence or *esse*. In the pre-apprehension of this all knowledge is grounded.

2. *What Is-in-Itself* (Das Ansichsein) *as Such as the Form Apprehended in the Abstractive Pre-Apprehension*

We are asking about the scope of the pre-apprehension which first makes abstraction possible, that is, the knowledge of the limitation of form by the concretion and the synthesis (*complexio*) which are always given sensibly as already realized. To be able to determine this scope we must first bring out more clearly what it is that is "liberated" by this pre-apprehension that reveals limit. What "form" is it whose limitation is to be apprehended by the pre-apprehension? First of all, it is obvi-

27 Wherefore the general formulation in Thomas: *S.T.* I, q. 12, a. 1, corp.: *unumquodque . . . cognoscibile secundum quod est in actu;* I, q. 14, a. 3, corp.: *. . . cognoscibile secundum modum sui actus. Non enim cognoscitur aliquid secundum quod in potentia est, sed secundum quod est in actu;* I, q. 84, a. 2, corp.: *nec ipsa potentia cognoscitur nisi per actum.* Similarly I, q. 87, a. 1, corp.; a. 2, corp.; a. 3, corp.; *De Ver.* q. 2, a. 4, ad 7; q. 13, a. 3, corp. etc. Thus also the *"privatio"* is known through the positive: *S.T.* I, q. 14, a. 10, corp. and ad 4; *I Sent.* dist. 36, q. 1, a. 2, corp. and ad 4; *Quodl.* 11, a. 2; *In IX Metaph.* lect. 10, n. 1894: *ex actu cognoscitur potentia.* Here there is also a further reason for this relationship: *quia intellectus actus est.* In knowledge the knower experiences himself as increasing actuality. Therefore in the light of the original identity of knowledge and object, the same must hold of the object also.

ously a question of a liberation from that subject which is given in sensibility as something real and concrete. For it is of this that something is first affirmed. It is over against this that the knower who knows objectively first sets himself. But this is to say that what is "form," in other words, predicate in the affirmative and not merely concretizing synthesis, is what is first and fundamentally liberated. Thus there is question of the abstraction which is, as it were, the negative phase of the affirmative synthesis. The "concrete" which arises through a merely concretizing synthesis as such, or more correctly, would arise if it could take place by itself, is not yet an object (*Gegen-stand*), as has already been shown. Hence the form of such a synthesis in itself can in no way reveal what was liberated in the decisive abstraction (which is always the negative phase of a synthesis) as an abstraction from a genuine, unique "this" that was given in sensibility as real.

Now what is the form in the affirmative synthesis which as such was also that of the fundamental abstraction? If we go back to what was said about the essence of the affirmative synthesis, we must say first of all that what was meant in the affirmative synthesis was *what-is-in-itself* (*das Ansichsein*), what is absolutely in the sense that the content of the affirmation (the form in the usual sense as a qualitative content of knowledge) attains to the thing (*ad rem*) in such a way that what was meant in the judgment (the form of the predicate) already belongs of itself to the thing designated by the subject of the proposition, that is, it belongs to it independently of the realization of the affirmative synthesis, and so an already realized synthesis (*complexio*) is always given prior to the affirmation of the judgment. Consequently, the judgment "through affirmation" only recognizes that synthesis antecedent to itself as existing, and does this by realizing it anew (*im Nachvollzug*).[28] What is given antecedent to thought and yet really given to human knowing is this already realized synthesis (*complexio*) in sensibility.

[28] *In IX Metaph.* lect. 11, n. 1914: *est verum, si componitur in re quod intellectus componit.*

We can therefore say that what the abstractive pre-apprehension attains to as unlimited is what was affirmed as limited in the synthesis (*complexio*), the objective in-itself (*Ansich*) of the known. Hence what-is-in-itself as such (*das Ansichsein überhaupt*) is apprehended in the pre-apprehension.

But what is this in-itself that is apprehended in formal universality in the pre-apprehension and, in the synthesis of the judgment, is applied to what is designated by the subject of the proposition? Thomas answers: the *esse*. A preliminary clarification of the *esse* concept in Thomas is necessary before we present the Thomistic proof for this proposition.

3. Preliminary Clarification of the Esse-Concept in Thomas

The only point of this Section is to have reached by the end of it an understanding of *esse* first of all as the expression of the content of what is meant by the in-itself, and this by simply giving what Thomas says from the viewpoint of this in-itself. What this *esse* is in its own self in Thomas is then to be presented more precisely and systematically in the following Section, but of course even then only in a tentative way, since it is neither intended nor possible to write a Thomistic ontology as a whole here.

Lest we lose the connection of what follows with the whole investigation, we will once again sum up the latter in two propositions:

(a) If human knowledge has its first object, that upon which all others are based, in the other of the world possessed in its own self in sensibility, then it can know *esse* as the real and only being-in-itself (*Ansichsein*) only insofar as it is given to it in sensibility in its concrete, limited self. Thus, when we ask what *esse* is, we must always refer also to the "*ens*" (being) which is had in its own self in sensibility, and without this sensibly given being, absolutely no knowledge of what *esse* should mean is possible. But even with this explicitly emphasized, the question still arises as to how this being can be known as real by thought, that is, *objectively,* something which sensibility cannot accomplish. Abstraction is necessary for that. And so the following investigation moves at first exclusively in the direction of the abstraction of *esse* and the understanding of *esse* insofar as this is revealed precisely in abstraction.

(b) If human knowledge is an objective knowing of this other in differentiation from the knowing subject, then it can know this *esse* as the being-in-itself (*Ansichsein*) of the definite other objectively only insofar as this *esse,* given in sensibility as limited, is apprehended as unlimited in itself in a pre-apprehension attaining to *esse* as such.

Now what is this *esse?* If it is understood first of all purely by way of definition as identical with the in-itself (*Ansich*), we can say tentatively: there is a knowledge of *esse* where a synthesis, able to be encountered as always and already realized, is given antecedent to the affirmative synthesis realized in thought. That is only another description of what was understood heretofore by the in-itself intended in the judgment. But now *esse* always means to-be-actual (*Wirklichsein*), to-be-real (*Realsein*) in a sense in which this word is always somehow understood. But why can *esse,* as the synthesis which is able to be encountered as already realized antecedent to the affirmative synthesis, be identified with *esse* as to-be-real? In its common conception, what is in-itself (*Ansichsein*) seems to occur in two fundamentally different kinds which are independent of each other: "ideal" being-in-itself as the essential validity of propositions in themselves and so on of (Thomistically expressed) "eternal truths," that is, truths of timeless validity; and as real existence (*reales Existieren*) (whatever this word might mean more precisely). Both kinds seem to present an "in-itself" which is always already realized antecedent to the affirmative synthesis to be accomplished intellectually and to which this latter is related, and are thus an "in-itself," but they seem to be intrinsically and fundamentally distinct and independent of each other.

Thomas does not know these two different kinds which stand side by side and with equal validity. For him, *esse* as "to-be-real" (*Wirklichsein*) *is* the only fundamental in-itself, and anything is an in-itself only insofar as and to the extent that it expresses "to-be-real." Thus for him the judgment, which attains to an in-itself (*applicatio ad rem*), attains to *esse*,[29] which in Thomas always expresses to-be-real. *Esse* is therefore not one of the ways in which an already realized synthesis is given antecedent to the synthesis to be accomplished by affirmation, but is itself the only in-itself.

To prove that this is really Thomas's understanding we begin with a text which is related to the same line of thought[30] which was the Thomistic "transcendental deduction" of the fact that the affirmative synthesis always attains to an in-itself. We are referring to Part I of the *Summa*, Question 16, Article 7, objection 4 and response 4. In this article Thomas poses the question, "whether created truth [by which simple propositions of a finite content are to be understood, for example, mathematical, ethical, metaphysical propositions[31]] is eternal," which question he decides in the negative. Thomas knows only one truth as the characteristic of a realized judgment. The truth of propositions is nothing but the truth of the intellect attaining to the in-itself of real being: "the truth of propositions is nothing other than the truth of the intellect."[32] The intellect attains to the being of things, not to a truth of propositions, so much so that even things themselves are "true" only consequent upon and analogous to the truth of thought constituted in the intellect by

---

[29] *In I Sent.* dist. 19, q. 5, a. 1, corp. and ad 7; *De Ver.* q. 1, a. 5, ad 19; *In Boeth. de Trin.* q. 5, a. 3, corp.: *secunda operatio (intellectus) respicit ipsum esse rei; S.T.* I, q. 14, a. 14, ad 2: *compositio enuntiabilis significat aliquod esse rei; In II Metaph.* lect. 2, n. 298: *esse rei est causa verae existimationis quam mens habet de re.* For this reason the *esse* of the copula in a proposition is also grounded in the esse of the thing: *fundatur in esse rei quod est actus essentiae (I Sent.* dist. 33, q. 1, a. 1, ad 1).

[30] *S.T.* I, q. 2, a. 1, obj. 3 and ad 3; similarly *De Ver.* q. 1, a. 5, obj. 2, 3, 5, 18 etc.; *I Sent.* dist. 19, q. 5, a. 3, obj. 3 and 4 and the corresponding responses.

[31] *S.T.* I, q. 16, a. 7, obj. 1: *ratio circuli; duo et tria esse quinque;* similarly, *De Ver.* q. 1, a. 5, obj. 8; *I Sent.* dist. 19, q. 5, a. 3, obj. 7: *omne totum est maius sua parte; De Ver.* q. 1, a. 4, obj. 3 and ad 3 applies it in the same sense to the existence of moral principles (*rectitudo*).

[32] *S.T.* I, q. 16, a. 7, corp.

an actually realized judgment.[33] Thus thought attains to being, not to propositions valid in themselves. Therefore there are eternally valid truths only presupposing an eternally existing intellect and thus an eternally and really existing object, and in fact through this presupposition, and thus as a property of this existing thought, so that taken strictly there are not many eternal truths, but only one. Thus it is shown that the idea of eternal truths, of ideal validities has no place in Thomas's metaphysics of knowledge. The only in-itself that he knows is real being.[34]

Thomas now proposes to himself the difficulty which sounds exactly like his "transcendental deduction" of the ordination of human knowing to an in-itself: "If truth began when previously it was not [which can be supposed as possible, if true propositions are conceivable only as the function of an existing intellect], it was true that there was no truth, and it was true with some truth; and so truth was before it began." Thomas absolutely denies this conclusion (that is, it was true that there was no truth): it was not true that there was such truth (namely, "that there was no truth").[35] According to Thomas, because it is *not* "true that . . . ," it is of course not therefore "false, that . . . ,"[36] but from the merely logical supposition: there was no truth, it follows logically, prescinding from an intellect which thinks this proposition, only that the proposition, "There is no truth," would be neither true nor false, but would not be at all; in other words, that one could not speak of any kind of an existence or non-existence of this proposition at all, of an ideal or real kind. Thus Thomas can maintain his proposition, that the created truths are not eternal. Our concern first of all is not

[33] *De Ver.* q. 1, a. 2; *S.T.* I, q. 16, a. 7, corp.
[34] Cf. for this St. v. Dunin-Borkowski, "Die 'ewigen Wahrheiten' im System des heiligen Thomas von Aquin," *Stimmen der Zeit* 108 (1925), pp. 31–34.
[35] *S.T.* I, q. 16, a. 7, ad 4: "*Si veritas incepit cum ante non esset, verum erat veritatem non esse, et utique aliqua veritate verum erat, et sic veritas erat antequam inceperet.*" And Thomas's answer: "*non erat verum veritatem talem esse.*"
[36] *I Sent.* dist. 19, q. 5, a. 3, ad 3.

to justify the presupposition because of which Thomas denies
that there are such eternal truths outside the eternal intellect of
God and its object, which is identical with Himself. There is
question here only of showing from the line of thought just
developed that Thomas knows of no in-itself as absolute validity, etc., independent of the real *esse* of an intellect and its object,
and this precisely in the consideration which led him to an
in-itself which is necessarily pre-supposed for human knowing.[87]

Therefore, to-be-in-itself (*Ansichsein*) and *esse* as to-be-real
[*Wirklichsein*] coincide for Thomas. Objective knowing attains
to real being in principle. From that it follows, to anticipate a
conclusion which is to be developed more thoroughly in a moment, that "essences" can be the in-itself of an objective knowledge only in an ordination to *esse*. "Essence" is never in Thomas
a "pattern" that dwells in an ideal in-itself, indifferent of itself
to real being, but is only the potency for *esse,* and can be conceived objectively in its own self only as such. Thomas knows
essences only as the limiting potency of *esse,*[88] as the real
ground and expression of the fact that *esse* in the individual
"this" is not given in its unlimited fullness. Beyond that they
are nothing.[89] Therefore, further determinations are not added

---

[87] Be it noted only in passing that the ultimate reason why Thomas
rejects Anselm's ontological proof for the existence of God also lies
in this conception. (*S.T.* I, q. 2, a. 1; *I Sent.* dist 3, q. 1, a. 2, *S.C.G.* I,
10–11; *De Ver.* q. 10, a. 12): a judgment cannot be apprehended as
ideally valid except insofar as one already knows thereby that he has
apprehended *esse* in it. Therefore the premises of the Anselmian proof
cannot be apprehended as valid in themselves (objectively) and then
afterwards existence be discovered in their affirmation, which existence
would then be known subsequently as objectively real.

[88] *De Pot.* q. 5, a. 4, ad 3: *Esse est actus essentiae. S.C.G.* II, 53 gives
the reason why essence is to be understood as potency to *esse* as its act:
*In quocumque enim inveniuntur aliqua duo, quorum unum est comple-
mentum alterius, proportio est sicut proportio potentiae ad actum . . .
Ipsum igitur esse comparatur ad omnes substantias creatas sicut actus
earum . . . Comparatur substantia omnis creata ad suum esse sicut
potentia ad actum. De Pot.* q. 7, a. 2, ad 9: *Esse* is the *actus essentiae*
and *inter omnia perfectissimum,* for: *actus semper perfectior potentia.*

[89] *De Pot.* q. 3, a. 5, ad 2: *Ex hoc ipso quod quidditati esse tribuitur,
non solum esse, sed ipsa quidditas creari dicitur, quia, antequam esse
habeat, nihil est nisi forte in intellectu creantis, ubi non est creatura,*

to *esse* in the sense that it would be perfected by them, brought from empty indeterminateness to a full, determined content. Such determinations are either simultaneously given with *esse* as such (simple perfections), "since nothing is outside it except non-being,"[40] or they are only confining limits of the fullness which *esse* would have in itself, for "that which is most formal of all is *esse* itself"[41]; *esse* is determining, fulfilling, not determinable and fulfillable. Therefore, it cannot really be determined by another, as though it were in itself an empty, material indeterminateness which would become more through the determinations. Form, species, and so on, limit *esse* only as every potency limits its act. "The *esse* of man is limited to the species of man because it is received in the nature of the human species, and the same is true of the *esse* of a horse and for any

sed creatrix essentia (that is, even before the creative mind of God, the quiddity is not an object through some kind of an ideal being which would belong to the quiddity in itself; rather it is an object only in the sense that the divine intellect apprehends its own creative, existing essence). As a consequence of this, Thomas denies that the possibility in God to create something presupposes a real possibility of being created: *S.T.* I, q. 9, a. 2, corp.; *De Ver.* q. 2, a. 10, ad 2. Therefore according to Thomas, the definition of a concept goes beyond a merely verbal explanation only when it is related to a real thing (*res*): *nec enim super talem rationem* (that is, *ratio significans idem quod nomen*) *addit aliquid definito, nisi quia significat essentiam alicuius rei* (that is, insofar as the quiddity, the known, is apprehended as the essence of an actually or possibly existing object; this is the way "*res*" must be understood in this context; as a merely "intentional object" of a meaning, as a mere content of meaning, this *res* could not be distinguished from the "*talis ratio*" because this latter would also be a "*res*" in this sense), *unde si non sit aliqua res, cuius essentiam definitio significet, nihil differt definitio a ratione exponente significationem alicuius nominis: Post. Anal.* lib. II, lect. 6 (Parma 193a). It is clear that for Thomas the known (the thought content of a word) is not yet necessarily an essence; it is not an essence until the known is known as the what of a thing, wherein thing, although indeed it apprehends the existent from the side of quiddity, nevertheless expresses an essential ordination to *esse*. Cf. also J. de Tonquédec, *La critique de la connaissance* (Paris, 1929), pp. 322ff. and A. Forest, *La structure métaphysique du concret selon Saint Thomas d'Aquin* (Paris, 1931), pp. 151–154.

[40] *De Pot.* q. 7, a. 2, ad 9.
[41] *S.T.* I, q. 7, a. 1, corp.

161

other creature . . . it is limited to some mode of the perfection of being."[42]

But that requires a radical revision of the common concept of *esse*. *Esse* is no longer mere being-at-hand (*Vorhandensein*), the indifferent ground, as it were, upon which identical and undifferentiated ground the different essences must stand, if in addition to their real ideal being they also wish to be really. *Esse* is not a "genus,"[43] but appears rather as intrinsically variable, not as statically definable, but oscillating, as it were, between nothing and infinity. The essences are only the expression of the limitation of this *esse*, which is limitless in itself, to a definite degree of the intensity of being in this or that definite "being." Thus the essences no longer stand unrelated one after the other, but are all related to the one *esse*. And *esse* is not the emptiest, but the fullest concept. The "ideal" necessity of the coherence of two conceptual contents, the "ideal" necessity to make an affirmative synthesis between two concepts, is then self-explanatory: the one *esse* of the intensity of being which the one essential concept indicates has in itself and of itself the notes which the other concept expresses. And it is the same with an "ideal," "logical" impossibility: the one, unified *esse* is the reason why two conceptual contents are mutually exclusive in the dimension of essence.

The preceding was only supposed to serve as an indication that Thomas identifies the in-itself to which the affirmative synthesis attains, and which as a whole the preapprehension apprehends in abstraction, with what he calls *esse*. This *esse*-concept is now to be developed at least to such an extent that the nature of the pre-apprehension which attains to *esse* can be brought out more clearly. In the course of this, it will be unavoidable that much of what has been said so far will be treated anew.

---

[42] *De Pot.* q. 1, a. 2, corp. Similarly, *S.T.* I, q. 7, a. 2, corp. towards the end.

[43] *De Pot.* q. 7, a. 3, corp.: *Nihil ponitur in genere secundum esse suum, sed ratione quidditatis suae quia esse uniuscuiusque est ei proprium et distinctum ab esse cuiuslibet alterius rei.*

VI. *EXCESSUS II: ESSE* IN THOMAS[1]

The conclusion of the preceding section sought first of all only to show that for Thomas the absolute scope of the in-itself intended in the judgment coincides with the scope of *esse*. We must now expand this statement by asking what are the reasons in Thomas for this identification.

1. Esse *as the In-Itself* (Ansich) *of the Reality Apprehended in the Judgment*

We should not expect a long discussion of this question in Thomas. To him his view seems self-evident; whether correctly or incorrectly is a question which has little immediate concern for a historical work. His viewpoint is self-evident to him because he finds himself situated in the world from the outset and it is to this that knowledge attains. But the world is real. So for him the problem, what in-itself belongs to the objects of knowledge, never came up at all in such a way that it became questionable whether knowledge could attain to objects which would have a "validity" other than the "validity" of this real world as such. That the object of knowledge, upon which all

---

[1] For the whole Section, cf. F. M. Sladeczek, "Die verschiedenen Bedeutungen des Seins nach dem heiligen Thomas von Aquin," in *Scholastik* 5 (1930), pp. 192–209; 523–550. A. Marc, *L'idée de l'être chez Saint Thomas et dans la scolastique postérieure* (Paris, 1933; Archive de Philosophie X, 1, 1–144). See in addition the works of de Finance, Gilson, Lotz, Müller, Przywara, Siewerth, and Söhngen mentioned in the first note of the Introduction. The concept of being is developed only briefly here and from the viewpoint of our purpose, the metaphysics of knowledge. Such an abbreviation is not without its dangers in the discussion of the concept of being, for it opens out into the whole of its problematic in every aspect under which it is discussed. So a certain amount of obscurity was unavoidable here. The function of the *actus essendi* for example, but above all the thorough-going analogy of the concept of being (which cannot be thought of as the result of a subsequent "comparison" of concepts univocal in themselves: *S.T.* I, q. 13, a. 5, ad 1) are not brought into the discussion. For the latter problematic, cf. the author's *Hörer des Wortes* (Munich, 1941; ET *Hearers of the Word*, New York and London, 1968), pp. 58ff.

other knowledge which perhaps is still possible is based as on its sustaining ground, was the forms of sensible things, is for him a presupposition.[2] From the outset, truths and validities are for him always true and valid of the real world. Thus, in referring to knowledge, Thomas always had in mind really human knowledge, that with which man finds himself in the real world. The thought that knowledge could be defined as the apprehension of validities, of a pure order of essences, is for him, therefore, fundamentally untenable. Thus, from the outset, even the knowledge of quiddities and their necessary relations to one another is for him knowledge of the relationships of existing things; to put in parentheses an ultimate reference in a quiddity to the real actuality would be for him equivalent to eliminating the quiddity itself.

And it is only on the basis of this presupposition that it is still a question for Thomas whether we apprehend truths and validities of this kind in an in-itself which perhaps still belongs to them when they are separated from the real world (as "separated, subsisting forms"), or only in their real being in the things of the world. And in this question, too, the decision falls without hesitation in favor of the second assumption. This is so not merely because this assumption avoids the insoluble problem how these validities existing "in themselves," that is, separated from the real world ("subsistent forms"), are still able to be the intrinsic law of the real world ("the separated species of these corporeal things"),[3] and why we should be able to know the world only via an in-itself of that kind,[4] but also because Thomas does not see why in the first assumption man, who is himself through his knowing, finds himself real in the real

2 See *S.T.* I, q. 84, a. 4, corp.; q. 85, a. 1, corp.; q. 87, a. 2, ad 2; q. 88, a. 3, corp.; *De Ver.* q. 10, a. 6.

3 See *S.T.* I, q. 84, a. 1, corp.

4 *S.T.* I, q. 84, a. 1, corp.; . . . *scientias et definitiones . . . non referri ad ista corpora sensibilia, sed ad illa immaterialia et separata, ut sic anima non intelligat ista corporalia, sed intelligat horum cor-poralium species separatas.* Thomas develops this problematic of the *corporalium species separatae* extensively in connection with Aristotle in his commentary on the *Metaphysics*.

164

world at all.[5] So for Thomas, knowledge appears from the outset as attaining to the things of the real world, and he sees no
reason to extend the in-itself of the real world of objects by an
ideal in-itself which is in principle independent of this world.
That, however, the objects of possible knowledge existing in
themselves do not coincide simply and absolutely with the in-
itself of the spatial and temporal world follows for Thomas not
from the fact that human knowing attains to an ideal in-itself as
to a realm of objects coordinate to the real world and apprehended with equal primacy, but only from the fact that the
affirmation of a real and yet not worldly in-itself belongs to the
conditions of the possibility of knowing the real, worldly in-itself.
   Thus in Thomas the judgment as affirmative synthesis always
attains to an in-itself, and this is always *esse*. A difficulty against
this seems to follow from texts in Thomas himself. According
to him there are judgments (which as such have their objective
in-itself) which attain to a non-*esse,* so that an *esse* "in the
thing" does not always correspond to the *esse* of the proposition's copula.[6] But first of all we must say that even in these

[5] *S.T.* I, q. 84, a. 4, corp.: *sed secundum hanc positionem sufficiens
ratio assignari non posset, quare anima nostra corpori uniretur.* See also
the continuation of the sentence cited.
   [6] See *In V Metaph.* lect. 9, n. 896; *De Ente et Essentia* c. 1; *III Sent.*
dist. 6, q. 2, a. 2, corp. and ad 5; *Quodl.* 9, a. 3, corp.: *respondeo
dicendum quod esse dupliciter dicitur ut patet per Philosophum . . .:
uno modo secundum quod est copula verbalis significans compositionem
cuiuslibet enuntiationis quam anima facit; unde hoc esse non est aliquid
in rerum natura, sed tantum in actu animae componentis et dividentis;
et sic esse attribuitur omni ei, de quo potest propositio formari, sive sit
ens, sive privatio entis; dicimus enim caecitatem esse. Alio modo esse
dicitur actus entis, inquantum est ens, id est quo denominatur aliquid
ens actu in rerum natura.* The following development should show that
according to Thomas the division of *ens* made here is not meant to
constitute two equal realms of objects. Even when the *ens* of the
judgment (the copula) seems to reach beyond real being, this *ens* remains grounded in real being. The same thing holds then of the texts
which in a somewhat different and formal way distinguish three realms
of objects in judgmental affirmations, as do *I Sent.* dist. 2, q. 1, a. 3,
corp.; dist. 19, q. 5, a. 1, corp.; dist. 30, q. 1, a. 3, corp. etc. For
further texts, see Sladeczek, *op. cit.,* pp. 206f., notes 65–68.

texts Thomas does not ascribe an ideal in-itself to the objects intended in such judgments, but an "*Esse* in the act of the soul."[7] Further, the cases that Thomas is thinking of here are always "privation,"[8] "negation and the like."[9] However much the possibility of a negation in thought opens the way to a metaphysical problematic, such objects of a judgment which "are-in-themselves" but do not really exist are not an instance belying the fact that every judgment that attains to an in-itself has a real in-itself as its foundation. For Thomas is aware, although he does not bring it out explicitly in the places cited, that such an objective unreality is the limitation and privation of a real being, and thus its in-itself is still necessarily grounded upon the in-itself of an *esse*.[10] The fact that Thomas always refers only to such examples (privation, negation) in the case of an unreal object of judgment that is in itself shows precisely, then, that he knows of absolutely no objects of judgment that are not essentially grounded in *esse*: "The fourth genus [of what can be *ens* (being) in some sense, that is, an object of knowledge] is that which is the most perfect, namely, that which has an *esse* in nature without any admixture of privation and has a solid and firm *esse* as though existing in itself, such as substances are. And all the others are related to this as to the first and principal genus. For qualities and quantities are said to exist insofar as they exist in a substance; modes and generations insofar as they tend towards a substance or to something mentioned before; privations

---

[7] See *Quodl.* 9, a. 3, corp. and ad 4.

[8] *De Ente et Essentia* c. 1 (*privationes et negationes*); *Quodl.* 9, a. 3, corp. (*privatio entis*).

[9] *In V Metaph.* lect. 9, n. 896.

[10] *Affirmatio et negatio reducuntur ad idem genus* (*S.T.* I–II, q. 71, a. 6, ad 1), and indeed in such a way that the *negatio . . . constituitur tamen in specie per reductionem ad aliquam affirmationem quam sequitur* (*S.T.* I–II, q. 72, a. 6, ad 3). *Semper enim in rebus negatio fundatur super aliqua affirmatione, quae est quodammodo causa eius* (*ibid.*, corp.). This affirmation must be at least *intellecta* or *imaginata: De Malo* q. 2, a. 1, ad 9. See also *I Sent.* dist. 35, q. 1, ad 2. Why negation is always grounded in the apprehension of something positive for Thomas was explained in the preceding section.

and negations insofar as they remove one of the three mentioned before."[11] Accordingly, Thomas does not know any other objects of knowledge except such as are related to *esse* in some mediate or immediate way. There are no objects which are able to be objects of knowledge and which are absolutely and in every respect independent of *esse*.

Thomas himself proposes the objection: Yet there are objects of knowledge (*verum*) which are not related to real being (*ens*),[12] for even non-ens (non-real-being) can be the object of knowledge.[13] He answers that the non-real-being has of itself no possibility of being the object of knowledge.[14]

But how can it nevertheless, as is the case, be the object of knowledge? Thomas answers that such an object is known "insofar as the intellect makes it knowable . . . insofar as non-being is a certain being of reason, that is, apprehended by the reason."[15] At first the answer does not seem to clarify the question very much. For it is precisely the being of reason which should not designate a realm of objects which would be independent of real being (*ens*), since object (*verum*) and real being (*ens*) are to be shown to be identical, and obviously a mental existence should be ascribed to the being of reason even less than should an existence constituting it in the first place.

[11] *In IV Metaph.* lect. 1, n. 543.

[12] *S.T.* I, q. 16, a. 3: *utrum verum et ens convertuntur.* If the article is not to be asking about a tautology from the outset, that is, if from the outset *ens* is not to mean the same thing as *verum* in its purely verbal definition, *ens* can only mean a real being. Then to answer the question of the article in the affirmative means not merely that every real being can be an object of knowledge, but also vice versa (*converti*) that only what is a real being in some way, and to the extent that it is such (*inquantum habet de esse, ibid.,* corp.) can be an object of knowledge.

[13] *Ibid.,* obj. 2.

[14] *Ibid.,* ad 2: *non ens non habet in se unde cognoscatur. S.T.* I, q. 16, a. 5, ad 3: *non habent in seipsis veritatem. S.T.* I, q. 16, a. 7, ad 4: *non ens non habet ex se ut sit verum, sed solummodo ex intellectu apprehendente ipsum.*

[15] *S.T.* I, q. 16, a. 3, ad 2; a. 7, ad 4: *ex intellectu apprehendente illud;* a. 5, ad 3: *sed solum in apprehensione intellectus.*

When it is not a question of the proper object of an intuition, the act of apprehension, not its object, has mental existence.[16] So, to explain the answer correctly, we must begin with the fact that it cannot contradict what Thomas said first, namely, that such a non-real-being (*non-ens*) has of itself no possibility of being an object (*verum*), cannot of itself manifest itself. The "making it knowable," the "*esse* in the act of the soul" of rational being can therefore only mean that the intellect can conceive of an unreal object insofar as it negates the reality of an object, consequently apprehends the *esse* of a possible real object, so that this (negating) apprehension of a real object is the abiding presupposition for objectifying an unreal object.

Thomas says this explicitly: "the falsity . . . of a principle is only known through the privation of truth, as blindness through the privation of sight."[17] In the texts cited above blindness was always the example for an unreal object of knowledge. Hence an unreal object is apprehended only as the negation of a real existent, its apprehension is therefore always based on the apprehension of a real being. That is easy to see in the example of blindness, for the privation is related as a form, as it were, to a real subject by an affirmative synthesis.[18] Hence this example can give the impression that it does not prove the point that is at issue here: that *every* being of reason, every conceivable object of knowledge that does not really exist, for example, the objects of pure mathematics, essentially includes an apprehension and an affirmation of real being. Yet Thomas considers the example of blindness in such a way that it is supposed to be an example for every unreal object, for he counts even the objects of mathematics, for example, among the objects which have their ultimate, abiding ground (a remote foundation) in the apprehen-

---

[16] Otherwise, Thomistically expressed, the *species expressa* would be the object of knowledge, which is incorrect according to Thomas: *S.T.* I, q. 85, a. 2. In any case, there are also "*entia rationis*" for Thomas which are a *res quae intelligitur*, not an *intentio intellecta*, that is, are the thing meant, not the meaning known of the thing. For these concepts, see *S.C.G.* IV, 11.

[17] *De Ver.* q. 3, a. 4, ad 4.

[18] *II Sent.* dist. 37, q. 1, a. 2, ad 3.

sion of what really exists, and must be understood as a negation of the same, so that their objectification is always simultaneously also an affirmation of their ultimate sustaining ground, *esse*.[19]

Hence we can say in summary: Every judgment attains to *esse* mediately or immediately (even in the case of beings of reason), or, expressed first more precisely and more cautiously, attains to what really exists, to *ens*. Where that is not the case, there is no true judgment at all.[20]

2. Esse *as* A Priori *Synthesis "In Itself" (An Sich)*

We have come to a point which makes it necessary to repeat once again something which has already been developed, and to advance this earlier development explicitly up to the point we have now reached. Objective knowledge was shown to be possible only by the knowledge of the intrinsic limitedness of the object with which the judgment is concerned. For the objectifying judgment is the reference of a universal (the predicate) to a definite individual which is indicated by the subject of the proposition. This intrinsic limitedness of the definite individual, in which the universal affirmed of it is found to be limited, was

[19] *I Sent.* dist. 2, q. 1, a. 3, corp.: . . . *remotum fundamentum est res ipsa . . . sicut est abstractio mathematicorum et huiusmodi.* See also *In Boeth. de Trin.* q. 5, a. 3, where the connection of mathematics with the other sciences is developed in a way that shows that Thomas knows no intrinsic independence of this realm of objects from the knowledge of the real. The same thing follows from his doctrine of the three degrees of abstraction, of which the second liberates the object of mathematics; and from his doctrine connected with this, that mathematics does not abstract from the *materia intelligibilis.* See also *S.T.* I–II, q. 8, a. 1, ad 3; *illud quod non est ens in rerum natura, accipitur ut ens in ratione* (the *in ratione* is to be taken with *accipere:* "is understood [conceived] in thought as '*ens*' [real being]"). *De Natura Generis* c. 1: *Cum nihil sciri possit nisi secundum quod est actu . . . unde nec oppositum eius intelligere potest intellectus, non ens scilicet, nisi fingendo ipsum ens aliquo modo; quod cum intellectus apprehendere nititur, efficitur ens rationis.*

[20] Thus the chimera, which has neither a *fundamentum in re* (which means real being) *proximum* nor a *fundamentum remotum,* is a *conceptio falsa,* and as such gives no object at all which would really be *an* object: *I Sent.* dist. 2, q. 1, a. 3, corp.

SPIRIT IN THE WORLD

shown to be knowable only in a pre-apprehension reaching beyond the limited, to more than what the limited is. This "more" has appeared so far as the negative (formal) infinity of "form" in itself. But "form" has been understood so far predominantly as essence (*essentia*) or as the essential characteristic of an object, as the "what" of an affirmation about something. Not only were the examples of the universal, the unlimited, always taken from this order of quiddities, but also the abstraction of the universal as such appears in Thomas chiefly as the liberation precisely of a quiddity.

Now, on the other hand, we have concluded that the judgment as affirmative synthesis attains to an in-itself which ultimately is always *esse*. Certainly it has already been shown along with this that essences are apprehended as potencies for and limitations of *esse*. But it has not yet become clear enough that *esse* itself, as unlimited in itself, is apprehended in an abstractive pre-apprehension, and not merely essence alone (the form as essence). When this is shown, the connection between this abstraction and that of the form as essence will follow necessarily: the abstraction of *esse* is the condition of the possibility of the abstraction of form.[21] For the in-itself is always grounded in an *esse*. Hence insofar as, on the one hand, a form can only be objectified in a reference of this quiddity to an in-itself, and, on the other hand, this in-itself is *esse* and must be known as such, a knowledge of *esse* is a condition of the possibility of objectifying the form as quiddity. But without such objectifying, the abstraction of the form as such is inconceivable, since the latter is only the negative phase of the former. For the form can be "liberated" from the real concrete thing in which, at least at first, it must be given, without thereby becoming a determination of the liberating subject itself, only if it can be related to an in-itself. A return of the knowing subject to himself with his knowledge

---

[21] In this metaphysical sense, *ens* is "the first" *quod cadit in apprehensione* (*S.T.* I–II, q. 94, a. 2, corp.)—as an *a priori* condition of possibility, as the horizon of every (taking place in intellectual apprehension) conceptual abstraction of the quidditative form. (See J. de Vries, *op. cit.*, p. 408.)

without the possibility of relating this knowledge to another in-itself would as a matter of fact not be a return, since it does not express the possibility of the separation of the knowing subject from his knowing (the form, the idea). But with that we are anticipating later discussions. There is question at first only of showing that *esse* itself must be "abstracted" in a pre-apprehension, from which it follows that the pre-apprehension, as the activity of thought that makes an abstraction possible, *at least also* encounters *esse*.

The pre-apprehension of *esse* must be able to be apprehended in a way similar to the way that the pre-apprehension of the form as in itself negatively unlimited appeared: the form as content of the predicate of the proposition appeared, with re-spect to the concrete thing to which the judgment relates it, as broader in itself, as universal, since it is able to be affirmed of many possible concrete things. Now, this is also the case with *esse*. To-be-in-itself (*Ansichsein*) as *esse* can be affirmed of many in-dividuals. In the individual judgment, an *esse* is ascribed to (or at least implicitly affirmed of) the object of the judgment designated by the subject, which does not necessarily belong precisely to this object alone, but is in itself broader, universal and unlimited. This is shown in the apprehension of the *esse* of many of the same thing: such an *esse* is itself one and many. This unity of *esse* appears most clearly in the fact that there belongs to one *ens* as a single real thing different determinations (as its parts, its essential or accidental properties) which make up a single reality in that they appear united in the one *esse* of this real thing. For if each of these determinations were real through its own reality, then there would be just as many real things as there are determinations, and not a single real thing; but it is to be a determination of this latter as a single thing which alone constitutes the essence of these determinations.

Thus Thomas says, for example:[22] "*esse* belongs properly to that which has *esse* and is subsistent in its *esse*. But forms and other things like them are not called beings as though they

22 *S.T.* I, q. 45, a. 4, corp.

themselves exist (as though they had their own in-itself of themselves), but because something exists through them."[23] But from this it follows necessarily that the one *esse* which bestows reality upon the essence and its accidents must have the intrinsic freedom and infinity to bestow reality as much upon one quiddity as upon another. But this means that in every essential judgment (e.g. the tree is green) a universal *esse* is also simultaneously affirmed which, as one, is able to include in itself the quiddity of the subject and that of the predicate (being tree and being green), and to that extent is one and universal (that is, is the being of many determinations). Thomas also develops the same ideas as here in the case of the substantial parts (essential principles) of a single real thing.[24] Thomas himself emphasizes the relation of the one *esse* of a real thing to the plurality of its determinations, and through this one *esse* these quiddities really become determinations of a single real thing:[25] "It is impossible for something which is one to have two substantial *esse*'s, because one is grounded in being [unity follows real being; where there are two grounds of real being, two *esse*'s, there are also two things]; wherefore, if there are many *esse*'s according to which something is called being without qualification, it is impossible that it be called one. But there is nothing against the *esse* of one subsistent thing being in relation to many [that is, that one *esse* be the ground for the reality of many determinations],[26] as the *esse* of Peter is one, but is related to the various principles which constitute Peter."[27]

---

[23] See *S.T.* I, q. 5, a. 1, ad 1; q. 39, a. 3, corp.: *accidentia . . . esse habent in subjecto. In VIII Metaph.* lect. 4, n. 1352: *accidentia vero non habent esse nisi per hoc quod insunt subjecto.*

[24] *S.T.* I, q. 90, a. 2, corp.; q. 45, a. 4, corp.

[25] *III Sent.* dist. 6, q. 2, a. 2, corp.

[26] See *ibid.*, ad 1.

[27] Similarly, *Comp. Theol.* c. 212 etc. See also *S.T.* III, q. 17, a. 2, corp., where only *one esse* is ascribed at least to the substantial parts of the essence together with the integrating parts of a thing, while here the *esse* of the accidents is separated as a second *esse* from that of the substance. Then in *S.C.G.* IV, II and *S.T.* III, q. 77, a. 3, ad 2 it becomes clear that Thomas indeed ascribes their own *esse* to the accidents, but one that remains intrinsically dependent on the *esse* of the substance. Even

The one reality, the one *esse* of the one real thing is thus the reality of different determinations, and therefore universal in itself as something capable of being the reality of different quiddities by its intrinsic nature. And it is as such a universal that the *esse* in every judgment, even in the essential judgment, is apprehended. The affirmative synthesis attains to the one *esse* insofar as the quiddities of the subject and of the predicate have their unity in it as one. This statement is ultimately only another expression of what was said earlier: the affirmative synthesis attains to something which is always already realized *"in rerum natura,"* to a synthesis "in itself." But this in-itself is precisely *esse.* Insofar as an existent has *esse,* the plurality of its determinations is unified into a synthesis which is always already realized and given prior to the affirmative synthesis, that is, into a really existing essence. And insofar as *esse* is apprehended in the judgment as something of many quiddities, it is essentially apprehended as universal.

in this conception of the relationship of a thing to its accidental determinations, it remains true that the one *esse* of the one thing is the unity of the thing with its accidental determinations. See also *S.T.* I–II, q. 4, a. 5, ad 2: *idem est esse formae et materiae et hoc idem est esse compositi.* Similarly, *II Sent.* dist. 1, q. 2, a. 4, ad 2. We would also have to compare the texts where Thomas infers the uniqueness of the essential form from the essential unity and the one *esse: S.T.* I, q. 76, a. 3, corp.; a. 4, corp.; q. 77, a. 2, ad 3 etc. Cf. also for this whole question R. Jolivet, *La notion de la substance* (Paris, 1929), pp. 57–60.

We still have to go into a difficulty in one of the texts in Thomas. According to *De Ver.* q. 21, a. 5, ad 8, the essence is already one in itself, and not first through *esse.* But it is to be noted that according to Thomas, as has already been shown, the ordination of the essence to its *esse* is so essential that without this it is nothing at all. Thus the essence can be understood as already one in itself (of course in this ordination to *esse* which belongs to it *as* essence) without its becoming one only through its actual existence on the basis of a real *esse.* But this does not deny the point that is at issue here: that the essential determinations of a quiddity are *one* essence through the one *esse* insofar as this one, universal (in a sense still to be explained) *esse* organically unifies these many essential determinations in its "universal" unity. So here too the conception ultimately remains: *omne autem compositum habet esse secundum quod (esse) ea, ex quibus componitur, uniuntur: De Pot.* q. 7, a. 1, corp. For the relationship of *esse* and essence see: M. Müller, *Existenzphilosophie im geistigen Leben der Gegenwart* (Heidelberg, 1949), Excursus I.

3. Esse *as Universal* Esse *in Formal and Trans-Categorical Unity*

To keep this from being misunderstood, we must define more precisely in two respects what has been said about the universality of *esse*. It is to be understood as a formal and as a trans-categorical unity.

Esse has a formal (negative) infinity. The affirmative synthesis attains to an in-itself that is being (*ens*). But, expressed in another way, this means that the concretizing synthesis of the subject and predicate of the proposition as concepts becomes something objective existing in itself by the affirmation of *esse*. But *esse* has been shown to be universal itself in the judgment, to be the ground of the reality of many (all) possible quiddities. The way we speak of *esse* as the full ground of all the determinations of an existent does not go essentially beyond Thomas. For he speaks of *esse* himself as what is "innermost" in every existent.[28] The concrete essence of something which exists in itself, expressed in the concretizing synthesis as such, is thus the expression of the extent to which, in a definite existent, *esse,* the ground of reality for an existent, can let such an existent really exist. This brings out already the peculiarity of the "universality" of *esse*. The universality of a material, essential form consists in the fact that it can be repeated in many material subjects (as form of prime matter) as the same form: universality as the repeatability (*Wiederholbarkeit*) of the same. The universality of *esse* also appears as repeatability, insofar as many of the same can really be, insofar as many concrete instances of the same quiddity are apprehended as existing. This universality of *esse* is only another expression for the universality of form insofar as this is conceived as the quiddity of many existing things.

But the universality of *esse* manifests itself in still another way

[28] *S.T.* I, q. 8, a. 1, corp.: *esse est magis intimum cuilibet et quod profundius omnibus inest.* Similarly, q. 105, a. 5, corp. towards the end. *II Sent.* dist. 1, q. 1, a. 4, corp.: *esse est magis intimum cuilibet rei quam ea per quae esse determinatur. De Anima* a. 9, corp.: *esse est illud quod immediatius et intimius convenit rebus.*

174

which is proper to itself: it is the one realizing ground of many essential determinations. Hence it is universal as the unified fullness which releases out of itself the essential determinations of an existent as those of a single thing and holds them together in itself. For *esse* was called precisely that being-in-itself (*Ansichsein*) in which the determinations affirmed in the judgment are one. But this means that *esse* does not mean the empty indifference of a mere existence which prescinds completely from what exists by it. Therefore, *esse* is not something which, after the manner of a potency bereft of determination, is filled and determined by determinations which are added to it. For these determinations are real and so determine precisely through *esse*. So *esse* is "formal,"[29] not indeed in the sense that it is itself a form, a quiddity in the proper sense, which Thomas explicitly denies.[30] For *esse* is precisely that which brings the quiddity (form) to reality. But *esse* is formal in the sense that it is that which is affirmed of something, that it is thus what determines this something, although in another way than is the case with the form in respect to its subject, since it is not one determination among many, but the one ground of all real determinations.

Further, *esse* is the "most formal and most simple": "nothing is more formal or more simple than *esse*."[31] Again not in the sense of empty indeterminateness, for then, of course, *esse* would be identical with matter; it would not be the "most formal," but the most material. So far is it from being this, that in the text cited, Thomas deduces precisely from this that pure *esse*, if it exists as such, can receive no further determinations at all. The simplicity of *esse* is to be understood accordingly. It is not, to use a word to be explained in a moment, the simplicity of the concept "something," bereft of all determinations

---

[29] *S.T.* I, q. 4, a. 1, ad 3; q. 7, a. 1, corp.; q. 8, a. 1, corp.; *S.C.G.* I, 23; *De Pot.* q. 7, a. 2, ad 9.

[30] *S.C.G.* II, 54. That is also shown in the fact that Thomas distinguishes clearly between *actus* (*esse*) and *potentia* (*forma, essentia*) even in immaterial essences: *S.T.* I, q. 50, a. 2, ad 3; *S.C.G.* II, 52–54. For more details, cf. Sladeczek, *op. cit.*, pp. 200f.

[31] *S.C.G.* I, 23; *S.T.* I, q. 7, a. 1, corp: *maxime formale omnium.*

175

but remaining nevertheless in the categorical order, but the simplicity of that which receives no determinations "from without" because everything possible is already included in it as in its one ground.[82]

The empty, indetermined something, *ens commune* (common being) as Thomas calls it, should not be confused with *esse* in Thomas. Rather, *ens commune* is already a something which comes to be through a concretizing synthesis of *esse* with a quiddity emptied of all more precise determination, with an entity (as a material form). The word "entity," denoting the emptiest quiddity, could be translated as any-quiddity.[83] By this concretion *esse* is already limited in the sharpest way conceivable, so that determinations can be added to *ens commune,* indeed not properly "from without" (because of course all of them are also being), but nevertheless in such a way that *ens commune* becomes thereby richer and fuller.[34] Thus it is understood why among all concrete things the merely existing (*aliquid, ens commune*) is the most imperfect, the emptiest, and yet *esse* itself is more perfect than anything else that can be thought of as liberated from concretion: "although what lives is more noble than what exists, nevertheless, to exist is more noble than to live."[35] But on the other hand, even *ens commune,* precisely in its emptiness, indicates the fullness of *esse:* its indetermined quiddity is only the representative symbol for all possible determined quiddities and thus gives expression to the fact that precisely this *esse,* which is the in-itself even in *ens commune,* can bear all these possible quiddities in itself as the ground which bestows reality upon them, and can produce them from itself.

Thus, *esse* is the most formal in the sense that it expresses

---

[82] See *S.T.* I, q. 3, a. 7, corp.: *quinto* . . .

[83] For the term *"entitas,"* see *S.T.* I, q. 16, a. 6, corp. towards the end; q. 48, a. 2, ad 2, where it becomes clear that *entitas* is the collective name, as it were, for the quiddities which are divided up into the categories: *entitatem rei, prout dividitur per decem praedicamenta.*

[34] See *I Sent.* dist. 8, q. 4, a. 1, ad 1.

[35] *De Pot.* q. 7, a. 2, ad 9; *De Ver.* q. 22, a. 6, ad 1; *S.T.* I, q. 4, a. 2, ad 3; I–II, q. 2, a. 5, ad 2; *De Divinis Nominibus* c. 5, lect. 1 (Parma XV, 348); *I Sent.* dist. 17, q. 1, a. 2, ad 3.

not just any fullness at all, but absolute fullness in unity, which of course we can think of only by enumerating many existing determinations and negating their difference. For *esse* appeared as the inner ground which holds together in its unity the determinations of an existent as its own, and lets them separate out as different from each other in such a way that they always still remain those of a single existent in its in-itself and can be related to this in-itself. So the *esse* of an individual being appears first of all at least as the intrinsic, sustaining ground of all the determinations which can possibly belong to the existent in question. But it is also in itself the fullness of all possible determinations absolutely. For in every judgment it is the same to-be-in-itself (*Ansichsein*) that is pre-apprehended. Insofar as all possible quidditative determinations are real through *esse* as to-be-real (*Wirklichsein*) in the usual sense, in every judgment the same *esse* is pre-apprehended, in every judgment a knowledge of the same *esse* is simultaneously known. But this *esse* manifested itself as the act of quidditative determinations not merely in the sense that they are real through it in some sense or other, but in the sense that *esse* is the unified ground of the determinations which produces them from itself as its own, holds them together in itself, and has already anticipated them in itself.

But it follows from this that *esse* in itself must be the absolute ground of all possible determinations: it is in itself "of all things the most perfect,"[36] fuller than anything else that can be thought of as reality with a particular determination.[37] It is in itself "the actuality of every form,"[38] "the actuality of every thing,"[39] the unified, generative ground of every conceivable quidditative determination.[40] Therefore, it possesses with respect to every

---

[36] *De Pot.* q. 7, a. 2, ad 9; *S.T.* I, q. 4, a. 1, ad 3.
[37] *Ibid.: esse est nobilius quam vivere,* etc.
[38] *S.T.* I, q. 3, a. 4, corp.
[39] *S.T.* I, q. 5, a. 1, corp.; *See De Spir. Creat.* a. 8, ad 3.
[40] *Esse* is the fullness of all determinations: *omnium autem perfectiones pertinent ad perfectionem essendi; secundum hoc enim aliqua perfecta sunt, quod aliquo modo esse habent: S.T.* I, q. 4, a. 2, corp. *Esse inter omnes alias divinae bonitatis participationes, sicut vivere et*

such determination the character of what determines, of an "agent," not that of a passive receiver. Its infinity is not that of the empty, passively receptive potency, but that of the already and always possessed fullness of all conceivable determinations. "Therefore, *esse* itself must be compared to essence . . . as act to potency."[41] Thus, as the fullness of all determinations, *esse* cannot be act in such a way that it is simultaneously related as potency to any further determination at all: "*Esse* itself is the ultimate act which can be participated in by everything; it participates in nothing itself."[42] Thus, the infinity of *esse* is of a formal (negative) kind.

From this it also follows that the universality of *esse* in itself is of a trans-categorical kind.[43] For it is the one ground of all categorical determinations.

What has been said about *esse* cannot be understood as though the *esse* in itself just described were present as such in its whole fullness in the individual object of our judgments as the ground of its being. For then the fullness of all determinations would have to belong to each of these objects, and that necessarily. Moreover, *esse* as such would then no longer be the "whither" of the *pre*-apprehension, but an object of the first order for knowledge, for the concept. Rather, the judgment which ascribes certain quidditative determinations to something which exists in itself, to the exclusion of other possible determinations, is implicitly and precisely a judgment that *esse* does not belong in all its fullness to this thing which exists in itself. But this also means that the real objects of our judgments are

---

intelligere et huiusmodi (that is, all the possible determinations of an existent), *primum est et quasi principium aliorum, praehabens in se omnia praedicta secundum quendam modum unita: I Sent.* dist. 8, q. 1, a. 1, corp. *Ipsum esse in se praehabet omnia bono subsequentia: S.T.* I–II, q. 2, a. 5, ad 2.

[41] *S.T.* I, q. 3, a. 4, corp. See also the texts already cited in the previous paragraph.

[42] *De Anima* a. 6, ad 2.

[43] See *Post. Anal.* lib. 11, lect. 6 (Parma 192): *esse* is not a genus. Likewise, *II Sent.* dist. 11, q. 1, a. 2, ad 2; *IV Sent.* dist. 12, q. 1, sol. 1, ad 2; *De Pot.* q. 7, a. 3, corp.; *esse* is not a species: *IV Sent.* dist. 12, q. 1, a. 2, sol. 3, corp.

not distinguished perhaps merely by their quidditative determinations, but precisely by their *esse* as the ground of these latter.[44] Thus, every judgment is precisely a critique of the object, an evaluation of the measure of *esse* which belongs to what is judged. In the essential judgment, the thing-which-exists-in-itself which is meant in the subject of the proposition is limited by the quiddity of the predicate which, as form, already expresses limit in itself; it is partially deprived of the fullness which *esse* expresses in itself. Therefore, the objects of possible judgments are distinguished in their *esse* as such:[45] *esse* can be affirmed of them only analogously insofar as the determinations in each of them are related in the same way to the ground of their reality, that is, to the *esse* proper to each, and insofar as the *esse* of each of these objects as limited by its essence must be understood as a partial realization of *esse* in itself.

Hence we can say in summary: In every judgment, and thus in every abstraction, a universal *esse* is simultaneously grasped in a pre-apprehension. Therefore, what has been said about the complete return, abstraction, and the pre-apprehension, is to be referred accordingly to *esse*.

4. Esse *as Absolute* Esse

Now what is this *esse*? It has been shown to be the "whither" (*Worauf*) of the pre-apprehension which is the condition of the possibility of abstraction, and hence of the complete return which makes possible an objective human knowledge. From what was said earlier, it follows that the "whither" of the pre-apprehension as such is not an object (of the first order). Thus *esse* is first of all just the expression of the scope of the pre-apprehension itself, an object of the second order. Neither is it, therefore, the object of a metaphysical "intuition." For, on the one hand, it has been shown to be just the "whither" of the

[44] To this extent Thomas can say: *esse uniuscuiusque est ei proprium et distinctum ab esse cuiuslibet rei: De Pot.* q. 7, a. 3, corp.

[45] *IV Sent.* dist. 12, q. 1, a. 2, sol. 3, corp.: *Unaquaeque res habet proprium esse suae speciei.*

pre-apprehension, that which describes its scope, and is given only in the consciousness of the pre-apprehension itself; on the other hand, in the finite real—only the real can be intuited—it is not given at all as such, and in absolute *esse,* in which it is realized as such, it cannot be intuited objectively (for a reason to be explained in a moment) in the mode of human knowledge, which alone is the object of philosophical consideration.

But in this "whither" of the pre-apprehension, to add this here by way of anticipation (presupposing thereby the results of the next Section), an object does manifest itself in a way indicated earlier: the Absolute Being, God. This Absolute Being is not apprehended as a represented (*Vorgestellter*) object. For the *esse* apprehended in the pre-apprehension, as only implicitly and simultaneously apprehended (*miterfasst*) in the pre-apprehension,[46] was known implicitly and simultaneously (*mitgewusst*) as able to be limited by quidditative determinations and as already limited, since the pre-apprehension (*Vorgriff*), if it is not to be a "grasp" (*Griff*), can only be realized in a simultaneous conversion to a definite form limiting *esse* and in the conversion to the phantasm. The fullness of being which *esse* expresses is therefore never given objectively. If *esse* is made objective in reflection in order to be known (*gewusst*) itself (not merely implicitly and simultaneously known [*mitgewusst*] in the pre-apprehension), then that can only be done insofar as it is itself concretized again by a form. This is either a definite form, and then it limits *esse* to the fullness of a definite degree of being, or it represents every form, it is the form of *ens commune* (any-quiddity), and then its *esse* is indeed not limited to any definite degree of ontological actuality, but for that reason is completely reduced to the empty void of *ens commune.* Hence, insofar as this *esse* simultaneously apprehended in the pre-

---

[46] To this extent, Thomas can say: *intellectus noster hoc modo intelligit esse, quo modo invenitur in rebus inferibus a quibus scientiam capit, in quibus esse non est subsistens sed inhaerens. Ratio autem invenit quod aliquod esse subsistens sit: De Pot.* q. 7, a. 2, ad 7. Moreover, in such and similar formulations it is to be noted that the question involved is what being is the object of the objective apprehension, not what being is the object of the pre-apprehension as such.

apprehension is able to be limited, it shows itself to be non-absolute, since an absolute necessarily excludes the possibility of a limitation. This *esse* apprehended in the pre-apprehension is therefore in itself *esse* "*commune*" ("common" *esse*), although this must not be equated with *ens commune*.

But in this pre-apprehension as the necessary and always already realized condition of knowledge (even in a doubt, an in-itself, and thus *esse* is affirmed) the existence of an Absolute Being is also affirmed simultaneously (*mitbejaht*). For any possible object which can come to exist in the breadth of the pre-apprehension is simultaneously affirmed. An Absolute Being would completely fill up the breadth of this pre-apprehension. Hence it is simultaneously affirmed as real (since it cannot be grasped as merely possible). In this sense, but only in this sense, it can be said: the pre-apprehension attains to God. Not as though it attains to the Absolute Being immediately in order to represent (*vorstellen*) it objectively in its own self, but because the reality of God as that of absolute *esse* is implicitly affirmed simultaneously by the breadth of the pre-apprehension, by *esse commune*. In this respect, grasping absolute *esse* would also completely fill up the breadth of the pre-apprehension. But, on the other hand, insofar as in human knowledge, which alone is accessible to philosophy, the pre-apprehension is always broader than the grasp of an object itself because of the conversion to the phantasm, nothing can be decided philosophically about the possibility of an immediate apprehension of absolute *esse* as an object of the first order.

This is in no sense an "*a priori*" proof of God's existence. For the pre-apprehension and its "whither" can be proven and affirmed as present and necessary for all knowledge only in the *a posteriori* apprehension of a real existent and as the necessary condition of the latter. The proofs of God's existence in Thomas[47] are only the application of this situation in his metaphysics of knowledge to his ontology of the real: the real and limited existent that is affirmed requires as its condition the reality

[47] *S.T.* I, q. 2, a. 3; *S.C.G.* I, 13.

181

of an unlimitable, absolute *esse*. Instead of this we have simply said: the *affirmation* of the real limitation of an existent has as its condition the pre-apprehension of *esse*, which implicitly and simultaneously affirms an absolute *esse*.

To avoid a possible misunderstanding, we will add right away a further general remark about this "implicit and simultaneous affirmation of the absolute" (*Mitbejahung des Absoluten*) which takes place in every judgment. As does every metaphysical *a priori*, this "implicit and simultaneous affirmation" expresses (as the word itself indicates) a certain *conscious givenness* (*Bewusstseinsgegebenheit*) of what is affirmed.[48] But it is to be noted right away that there are essentially different kinds of such "consciousness" (*Bewusstheit*). So in this "*a priori* consciousness of the Absolute" (in this "transcendental experience (*Empirie*) of the Absolute") there is absolutely no question of an "objective-thematic knownness" (*Gewusstheit*), but of an "unobjective-unthematic consciousness" (*Bewusstheit*) which of itself, in its pure apriority, cannot be raised to the level of reflexive knowledge at all. Hence a thematic knowledge of God, a reflexive articulation and categorical formulation of this *a priori* knowledge of the Absolute, hence a "proof of God's existence" in the proper sense, does not become superfluous at all, but is first made possible and also (as intrinsically necessary to such "knowing") is demanded by the peculiar nature of this *a priori* knowledge. On the other hand, God can never be a pure *a posteriori* if man is ever to know anything at all about Him. An absolute *a posteriori*, and in this sense absolutely "unknown," something "coming from without" in every respect, is not knowable at all to a human subject according to Thomistic principles. For knowing is essentially the self-present (*beisichseiende*) actuality of the subject itself. But this can never be accomplished exclusively by the known object. For how, then, would the known as such be itself a mode of the presence-to-self of the knower, a mode in which the knower is present, transparent

---

[48] Cf. J. de Vries, *op. cit.*, pp. 408f. For the different modes of such conscious givenness, see for example the author's *Schriften zur Theologie* III (Einsiedeln, 1956), p. 130, note 1.

(*gelichtet*) to himself? According to Thomas, it is rather this that is true: an object which is known by a subject can, as known by the subject, never bring about by itself *alone* that actuality of the subject in which it is known, because this actuality of the knowing always expresses also the self-presence (*Selbstgegenwart*), the being-present-to-itself (*Beisichsein*) of the subject. Every knowledge of another by man is a mode of his self-knowledge, of his "subjectivity"; the two are not merely extrinsically synchronized, but intrinsic moments of the one human knowing. Now this holds also for man's knowledge of God. And his transcendental-*a priori* "knowledge" (*Wissen*) of the Absolute, which is the condition of the possibility of an articulated, objective knowledge of the Absolute, is only the application in the metaphysics of knowledge of the "*anima* (which as itself is of course always subjectivity, "knowing") *quodammodo omnia*" ("the soul is in a certain way everything").

Let us go back now and summarize by way of transition to the next Section: objective knowledge was shown to be made possible only by a pre-apprehension. At the beginning of Section V we asked about the scope of this pre-apprehension. This question has now been answered: *esse* in the sense explained designates the scope of the pre-apprehension. This result is now to be clarified still further in a few directions.

VII. *EXCESSUS III*

1. *The Excessus in Its Absolute Negative Infinity*

The pre-apprehension attains to *esse* as the unified, full ground of all possible real determinations, to which *esse* there belongs a negative infinity. This has already been shown. But there still remains in this definition of *esse* a further question which we must now go into explicitly. In the formal treatment of the concept of negative infinity it was shown that the negative infinity of form does not at all exclude an ultimate intrinsic

183

limitedness of form in itself, that such an infinity in its formal concept expresses only a "relative infinity." So the question is whether, according to Thomas, *esse* as "what is formal in everything" can also express in its negative infinity an ultimate intrinsic finiteness. Thomas answers this question in the negative. The negative infinity of the *esse* of the pre-apprehension is meant absolutely; but again, not in the sense that the *esse* of the pre-apprehension could not be made finite in the objects for whose apprehension the pre-apprehension takes place. Rather, it is meant in the sense that the *esse* of the pre-apprehension does not come of itself to a limit intrinsically, that is to say, it is not the full ontological ground of all possible determinations merely insofar as it indeed contains all of these in itself, but all of these together would be a finite possibility with an intrinsically finite *esse*.

We already prepared the way for the proof of this absolute negative infinity which belongs to the pre-apprehension when we clarified the relationship which exists between the knowability of a privative and of a negative infinity.

The "whither" of the pre-apprehension is "more" than what is to be apprehended because it is supposed to reveal the limitation of the latter. The "whither" does not of itself have a privative infinity with respect to what is to be apprehended. For otherwise the pre-apprehension would attain to "nothing," to the mere possibility of what is to be apprehended as actuality. But the possibility is known from the actuality, and not vice versa. Further, it has already been shown that the pre-apprehension attains to *esse* as "what is formal in everything," hence to a negative infinity, and in fact to that which stands in potency to no further determination.

This "whither" of the first and fundamental pre-apprehension of human objective knowledge cannot be intrinsically finite, so that its negative infinity would be merely "relative." Otherwise two possibilities would be conceivable: either the pre-apprehension reveals this ultimate finiteness of being, or this finiteness remains hidden to it.

If the pre-apprehension itself were to reveal the intrinsic

finiteness of being, that would be possible only by the fact that it pre-apprehended "nothing." But it affirms the "whither" of its pre-apprehension as being, as really "more" than that which it knows as finite, and it knows the privative infinity, which in this assumption would be a "nothing," from a negative infinity. Therefore, this assumption shows itself to be intrinsically untenable. Not indeed in such a way that a direct, logical contradiction between the two concepts "*esse*" and "finite" was shown, which attempt would fall into the paralogism of the Anselmian proof for the existence of God (an infinite *esse* would be seen from our concepts to be in itself intrinsically uncontradictory), but rather that the contrary assumption, that *esse* is intrinsically finite, goes against the implicit supposition of the assumption itself, which expresses a pre-apprehension of *esse* and not of nothing.

This also shows that the second assumption is impossible, namely, that the intrinsic finiteness of its "whither" could remain hidden to the pre-apprehension. For the preceding consideration has shown that the pre-apprehension reveals *esse* as absolutely unlimited in itself. Against this assumption there is a further point to be made: in this assumption how could the finiteness of *esse* come up even only subsequently as a possible philosophical problematic? The conditions of the possibility of such a problematic would have to be shown where *esse* itself becomes manifest, that is, in the pre-apprehension itself. But this leads us back into the first assumption.

In the second assumption it is said that the intrinsically finite "whither" of the pre-apprehension reveals the greater finiteness of the object of the first order of knowledge, without the knowledge of the finiteness of the "whither" being itself the condition of the possibility for the knowledge of the first finite object itself. Now in this case, this "whither" would either be being in its totality, or a limited region of being in its totality. In the first case it is not intelligible how there could be a pre-apprehension of being in its totality without it manifesting itself as finite, since the supposition is that it is finite even in its totality, and without it being comprehended in its totality by the fact that the pre-apprehension goes beyond the totality to nothing. In the

185

second case the "whither" of the pre-apprehension would ultimately be an existent itself (a something in which being [*Sein*] as such is limited by a being-thus [*Sosein*]). But the pre-apprehension as such cannot attain to an object which is of the same kind as that whose knowledge it is supposed to make possible.

2. The Excessus *to the Absolute as Constitutive of Human Spirituality*

Consequently, the pre-apprehension attains to an *esse* which is of an absolute negative infinity. With that we have discovered in the pre-apprehension as a fundamental act of human knowing its decisive characteristic: human knowledge as pre-apprehending is ordered to what is absolutely infinite, and for that reason man is spirit. He always has this infinite only in the pre-apprehension, and for that reason he is finite spirit. Man is spirit because he finds himself situated before being in its totality which is infinite. He is finite because he has this infinite only in the absolutely unlimited breadth of his pre-apprehension. Therefore he is not absolute *esse* himself, and in his concretizing thought he can never represent (*vorstellen*) and objectify it because in such thought it cannot be represented and objectified in its totality, since *esse* in itself has no form distinct from itself which completely preserves the fullness of *esse* and which could be distinguished from it, and thus could be affirmed of it in a concretizing and affirmative synthesis without limiting it. So man knows of infinity only insofar as he experiences himself surpassing all of his knowledge in the pre-apprehension and as open to being in its totality. Man is "*quodammodo omnia*" ("in a certain way everything"). What this *quodammodo* expresses has now been shown: he is everything "*in excessu,*" in the pre-apprehension. He knows of absolute *esse* in that he experiences his movement towards *esse*. Therefore he is spirit. In the fact that he knows of absolute *esse only in this way* he experiences his finiteness.

That gives us Thomas's answer to the problematic which

was raised at the beginning of Section V: the *excessus* attains not to material, quantitative being, to being in space and time, to intrinsically finite being, but to the essentially unlimited *esse*. We will have to show explicitly later that and in what sense this shows that metaphysics is possible.

In the pre-apprehension of *esse* the being of the individual object is shown to be limited. It is here that the abstraction of form is also to be grasped in its possibility. It was indicated briefly above wherein this connection lies.[1] This question is to be taken up again when the relationship between *excessus* and the complete return is treated explicitly later.

This last part of our presentation of the Thomistic metaphysics of knowledge, at least looked at extrinsically, was able to be guided more by the dynamism of the matter itself. So there still remains the task of showing that this development is given in Thomas himself. The following sections are to serve this purpose.

VIII. *EXCESSUS* AND AGENT INTELLECT

The pre-apprehension of *esse* in itself has shown itself in an objective development of Thomistic presuppositions to be the decisive process of abstraction. The power of abstraction is called in Thomas the agent intellect. We had developed this concept up to now in a more formal way and only to a point which still lies prior to the insight into the pre-apprehension of *esse*. For the agent intellect has appeared so far as the power of liberating (*Ablösung*) a quiddity from its concretion in sensibility. Now it has been shown[1] that this takes place only in an abstractive liberation of *esse* from the concrete existent in the pre-apprehension. But for the historical purpose of this work there still remains the question whether Thomas himself also understood the agent intellect explicitly as the power of ab-

[1] In Section VI, 2 of this Chapter.
[1] Pp. 169ff.

stracting *esse*. This question must now be answered. It is to be expected that the answer will also further clarify the objective problematic which was present in Thomas.

The agent intellect is the power of abstraction, of grasping the universal from the concrete of sensibility. Now Thomas knows three kinds of abstraction. The consideration of these three levels of abstraction and their mutual relationship should bring to light whether by the term, "agent intellect," Thomas was thinking of a concept which includes in itself what we called the abstractive pre-apprehension of *esse*.

1. The Three Levels of Abstraction

If we prescind for the moment from the sequence of the three levels of abstraction, which will have to be treated explicitly in its own problematic, Thomas enumerates three degrees of abstraction:

1. The abstraction of a universal essence from the concrete "this" (the *materia signata*—signate matter) in which it is given in sensibility;

2. The abstraction of the quantitative (*materia intelligibilis* —intelligible matter) from the qualitative which still includes in itself the universal essence apprehended in the first level;

3. The abstraction of transcendental determinations which belong to an existent absolutely, and not only to that existent whose being is concretized in matter.[2]

These three degrees must first of all be explained briefly one by one. The first abstraction is "from sensible, individual matter."[3] Actually the whole chapter about sensibility spoke again

---

[2] The most important texts to be considered for the three degrees of abstraction (some of them treat the question under the heading of the division of the sciences) are: *In Boeth. de Trin.* q. 5, a. 1; a. 3; a. 4; q. 6, a. 1; a. 2; *S.T.* I, q. 85, a. 1, ad 2. Besides these, the texts treating the individual kinds of abstraction must be taken into account, and these are to be mentioned later. Cf. also Maréchal, *op. cit.*, pp. 165–201.

[3] *S.T.* I, q. 85, a. 1, ad 2.

and again of this abstraction. A quiddity is apprehended which can be real in many "this's." It is the abstraction of what is the same in many. To this it must only be noted further that in this abstraction there is no question of a knowledge of the intrinsic metaphysical essence of a material thing. Indeed Thomas's way of speaking often sounds as though the metaphysical essence of a thing were already known through the abstraction from the conditions of matter.[4] But Thomas is aware that as a matter of fact such a knowledge is not an affair of the fundamental, simple abstraction at the beginning of the whole knowledge process, but is its goal that is never completely reached.[5]

The abstraction from sensible, individual matter (if we prescind from the second and third levels implied in it) accomplishes nothing but the knowledge that the quiddities given immediately and sensibly (which are not the metaphysical essence of the thing) can be real in many "this's," and that these quiddities always are and remain "universal," however complex they might be conceived,[6] unless they are related to the concrete "this" which is had in sensibility, to the "individual, sensible matter." The quiddity which is abstracted in this first level is what is given immediately and sensibly (for example, this sensibly intuited round, red thing becomes *a* round, red thing). This is known as universal. This degree of abstraction cannot and will not accomplish more. Therefore it is self-evident that such abstraction is always already accomplished when there is question of thought, since it is already presupposed even in the first and most simple judgment (e.g., "there is a red thing"), and objective knowledge is not possible without a judgment. Pre-

[4] See the references to Thomas in Hufnagel, *Intuition and Erkenntnis*, pp. 209f.

[5] Cf. the texts in *ibid.*, pp. 206–7. We depart from Hufnagel in the more precise interpretation of the texts.

[6] *I Sent.* dist. 36, q. 1, a. 1, corp.: *quocumque modo universalia aggregentur, numquam ex eis fiet singulare, nisi per hoc quod individuantur per materiam.* Likewise *II Sent.* dist. 3, q. 3, a. 3, corp.; *In VII Metaph.* lect. 15, n. 1626; *De Anima* a. 20, corp.; *De Ver.* q. 2, a. 5, corp.; *S.T.* I, q. 14, a. 11, corp.

SPIRIT IN THE WORLD

cisely insofar as in this abstraction nothing at all of the quidditative determinations of the apprehended objects offered by
sensibility is "left out," it is ordered to knowledge of the real,
concrete world, to "physics," as Thomas calls this knowledge.

The second level of abstraction is from the "sensible . . .
common matter; not from intelligible common matter, but only
from individual matter."[7] Here, too, we prescind from the individual "this" (from the individual matter) and apprehend a universal. But this universal prescinds also from the qualitative
determinations which are given through sensibility (from sensible
matter). Thus it remains a universal which first of all retains an
intrinsic ordination to some "this" in which it can be realized
(not from common matter) and, secondly, is itself quantitative
(intelligible matter), a "substance" (in the broadest sense: a
"something"), "insofar as quantity inheres in it."[8] Thus, this
second level of abstraction is related to the quantitative many of
the same as such, to "being as the principle of number"; it sup-
plies the objects of the mathematical sciences.

The third degree of abstraction forms the "abstraction from
intelligible matter also": "for there are certain things which can
also be abstracted from intelligible common matter, such as
being, one, potency, and act, and other things of the same sort,
which can also exist without any matter as is clear in immaterial
substances."[9] Accordingly, on this level we abstract from everything material, quantitative. How is this possible? The object
from which these transcendentals are supposed to be abstracted
is a material thing, that is, a something in which a quiddity
(form) is concretized in an empty, indeterminate "this" in itself
(matter). If one wanted to take the description of this third
abstraction as the text seems to require at first sight, in the
consideration of this material thing we would prescind from its
matter. Then the "prescinding" consideration would be directed

---

[7] S.T. I, q. 85, a. 1, ad 2.
[8] Ibid.
[9] Ibid.

to the form, to the quiddity in itself. From the series of determinations which together make up this form, it could ultimately select only a few definite ones to which to direct its attention. But then it is simply impossible to see how in such a conception of abstraction it could be shown to be possible that this prescinding consideration, without becoming positively false, could prescind from the essential ordination to matter which belongs necessarily to the form and thus to all its determinations. As such, everything quidditative given in sensibility is given of matter, is related to a "this" which is always distinct from it and to which this quiddity applies. Even assuming that an intrinsic and necessary relation to matter does not belong to some determinations of form (their transcendental notes), still, the conception of the third abstraction just indicated, as a mere detaching and leaving out of notes, does not in the least make it intelligible how such an abstraction could know that the relation of these transcendental notes to matter, which they *de facto* have in the sensibly given thing, is *merely de facto,* and does not belong to them of their essence. A comparison with non-sensible (non-material) things in which such transcendentals perhaps are found without this reference to matter (which always makes things finite in space and time) is impossible, because in principle such objects in their own selves cannot be given to us on that basis on which alone, according to Thomas, objects are to be met with originally, on the basis of the imagination. That this consideration is Thomistic will be shown in a moment. If it is correct, then it follows necessarily: the abstraction of the third degree cannot consist in a mere dissociation of the sensibly intuited given; in other words, it cannot be at all an accomplishment which could be ascribed to thought as the *representation* (*Vorstellung*) of a quiddity. For thought as the mere representation of a quiddity can ultimately conceive only the sensibly given, in whatever combinations and separations that might take place. But something sensibly given and merely represented essentially retains its relation to matter, hence to space and time.

191

2. The Third Level of Abstraction as a Moment in the Judgment: Agent Intellect as the Exclusive Power of Forming Metaphysical Concepts

Now, as a matter of fact, neither does Thomas consider the third abstraction as a process of selection performed by a thought which merely represents. According to Thomas, the third abstraction is essentially a moment in the judgment and only in it. That this is the case can be shown from two lines of thought in Thomas: first, he relates the third abstraction, in contrast to the other two, explicitly to the judgment; secondly, he emphasizes that, in principle, the *modus significandi*, hence the mode of the merely representative (*vorstellenden*) apprehension of a quiddity, never reaches a transcendental essence.

The third abstraction is a moment in the judgment and only in it. This follows first of all from *In Boethii de Trinitate* q. 5, a. 3. The Article asks: Whether a mathematical consideration is without matter and motion.[10] It is not possible here to interpret in

[10] In all the editions which were available to me (Parma [1864] XVII, 386a; edit. Antverpiae [1612] XVII, fol. 130r, col. 2B; edit. Venetiis [1747] VIII, 379; edit. de Maria [Tiferni Tiberini, 1886] opusc. III, 361; edit. Mandonnet [Paris, 1927] opusc. omnia III, 113), the text is somewhat corrupt at the end, but in such a way that for anyone who has read the whole corpus attentively, the difficulty can easily be removed. Without any doubt the text at the end must read: *Sic igitur in operatione intellectus triplex distinctio invenitur. Una secundum operationem intellectus componentis et dividentis* (judgment), *quae* (to be taken with *una* [*distinctio*], not with *operatio*) *separatio dicitur proprie*. *Alia secundum operationem quae format quidditates rerum* (that is, the *simplex apprehensio indivisibilium*, of the *quod quid est*), *quae* (this second *quae* of the sentence, unlike the first, does not refer to *operatio*, but to *alia* [*distinctio*]) *est abstractio a materia sensibili* (that is, from matter as determined by sensible [first] qualities, by *qualitates sensibiles a quibus dicitur materia sensibilis*). *Et haec competit mathematicae* (not: *metaphysicae*, as the editions have it, for according to the whole corpus of the article it is mathematics which abstracts from sensible matter; cf. *loc. cit.* ad 4: *mathematica non abstrahit a qualibet materia, sed solum a materia sensibili*). *Tertia* (*distinctio*, which according to the corpus in any case takes place *secundum operationem quae format quidditates rerum*) *secundum compositionem* (Antwerp and Mandonnet read: *oppositionem;* Venice and de Maria: *compositionem;* actually, however, in accordance with the corpus perhaps it should read

192

detail the unusually long corpus of the article. We will select only what is important for our question. In answer to its question Thomas develops the three levels of abstraction as the foundation of his three-fold division of the sciences (physics, mathematics, metaphysics). Thomas is working from the notion, not explicitly mentioned, that abstraction is to be understood first of all as *"distinctio,"* as the apprehension of a "what" while prescinding from another "what" in such a way that the first can be thought without the second.[11] With this presupposition the corpus of the article begins by distinguishing the two-fold operation of the intellect: the simple apprehension of a known, a quiddity (*intelligentia indivisibilium,* of the *quid est*) and the

"abstractionem," for *compositionem* and *oppositionem a particulari* do not make any sense, or at least are not usual) *universalis a particulari.* This: *secundum . . . to particulari* corresponds to the *second quae* sentence in the second level of abstraction and is the specification within the *distinctio secundum operationem quae format quidditates rerum,* to which *operatio* the second *and* third levels of abstraction belong. *Et haec competit etiam* (this *etiam* should be struck out) *physicae et est communis omnibus scientiis* (that is, as the lowest level of abstraction it is of course presupposed for mathematics and physics), *quia in omni scientia praetermittitur quod est per accidens* (that is, the concrete "this" as such) *et accipitur quod est per se* (the quiddities, which can be known only of the former).

In the editions there is a mistake which affects the sense in the first half of the corpus too; it must read: *Si vero unum ab altero non dependeat secundum id quod constituit rationem naturae, tunc unum* (the *"non"* which follows at this point in the editions should be struck out) *potest ab altero abstrahi per intellectum.* The corrections suggested here (with the exception of the omission of *"etiam"*) are confirmed by the new critical text based on the autograph by B. Decker (in: *Studien und Texte zur Geistesgeschichte des Mittelalters* IV, Leiden, 1955). The text in question reads in this edition: *Sic ergo in operatione intellectus triplex distinctio invenitur. Una secundum operationem intellectus componentis et dividentis, quae separatio dicitur proprie; et haec competit scientiae divinae sive metaphysicae. Alia secundum operationem, qua formantur quidditates rerum, quae est abstractio formae a materia sensibili; et haec competit mathematicae. Tertia secundum eandem operationem (quae est abstractio) universalis a particulari; et haec competit etiam physicae et est communis omnibus scientiis, quia in scientia praetermittitur quod per accidens est et accipitur quod per se est."*

[11] Wherefore at the end of the corpus he can then summarize the three kinds of abstraction as a *triplex distinctio.*

193

judgment (*enuntiatio*).[12] Now Thomas ascribes metaphyiscal abstraction to the judgment, physical and mathematical abstraction to the *intelligentia indivisibilium*. The two-fold division of the operation of thought at the beginning of the Article is not meant merely as an arbitrary starting point. For it is taken up again at the end of the corpus: "Thus, therefore, a three-fold 'distinction' is found in the operation of the intellect. One according to the operation of the intellect as composing and dividing, which is properly called separation. And this belongs to the divine science, or metaphysics . . ." Thus Thomas assigns the abstraction of metaphysical objects unambiguously to the judgment, while the other two levels have a relation to the simple apprehension of a quiddity.

This statement is important for us. Just by itself it shows that in the preceding section we were moving in the direction of Thomistic thought when we meant to find the *excessus* to the metaphysical realm in a pre-apprehension of *esse* which takes place only in the judgment. In the preceding Article, Thomas gives no evident reason why he assigns metaphysical abstraction precisely to the judgment. He only says that metaphysical objects are really separated (some partially) from what is material. That is correct, but obviously it cannot be meant as the ultimate reason for the distribution of the three levels of abstraction to the judgment and to the simple apprehension which we just mentioned. For it is too self-evident to have been able to be overlooked by Thomas that what is objectively separated can also be represented separate from each other in a simple apprehension, presupposing however that this latter, as it is in man, can be an apprehension of metaphysical objects at all. If this presupposition does not prove true, then to assign metaphysical objects only to the judgment as he did makes sense all right, but then we

[12] It was said earlier that these two operations of the intellect should not be understood as two modes of the intellect's activity, each one existing by itself, but as moments of the one thought which mutually condition each other, and moreover this is also confirmed by the text treated here itself, since the third abstraction, which is the foundation of the other two, takes place in the judgment, so that the other two as the process of the *intelligentia indivisibilium* are founded upon the judgment.

must ask further for a deeper grounding of this incapacity of the simple apprehension. It must lie in its essence itself, and not only in the fact of the real separateness of these objects from what is material.

The same result is to be had from an exact interpretation of *In Boethii de Trinitate* q. 6, a 2. The question is: Whether in the realm of the divine the imagination is left altogether? Thomas goes on to say that the "principle" of all knowledge is in sensibility (sense and imagination). From it there arises first of all the apprehension of the senses, then the apprehension of the imagination, and finally intellectual apprehension. Judgment always stands at the end. Yet according to Thomas the term of knowledge in physics is again the senses ("the knowledge ought to terminate in the senses, be brought back to the senses"), in mathematics it is again the imagination ("terminate in the imagination, be brought back to the imagination"). Now, one could presume that Thomas will establish for metaphysical knowledge also a "terminating," a "being brought back" to something upon which the judgment rests as upon its objectively possessed object, and he has prepared this term insofar as at the beginning he placed intellectual apprehension alongside of apprehension of the senses and apprehension of the imagination, so that the content of this intellectual apprehension would be that upon which the metaphysical judgment rests as upon its foundation. But, as a matter of fact, Thomas says nothing of the kind. He only says, negatively: "And so, in the realm of the divine, we should be brought back neither to the senses nor to the imagination." Is that only accidental, and due to a little carelessness in working out the train of thought? In the light of the third Article of the preceding Question 5, one can answer in the negative without hesitation. The intellectual apprehension as such cannot be the "term" of a metaphysical judgment. Such a judgment also tends away from the intellectual apprehension, which is not to say that it does not need or does not presuppose it as something permanent just as much as the phantasms.[13] In-

[13] See ad 5.

tellectual apprehension as such cannot give a metaphysical object representatively, "since the phantasms are to the intellective soul as objects";[14] "they are compared to the intellect as objects."[15] For further confirmation of this interpretation, we refer to *De Malo,* q. 16, a. 12, corp. There, the species is the ground of the simple apprehension, the "intelligible light" is the ground of the judgment. It will be shown later that the intelligible light is nothing other than the dynamic pre-apprehension of being in its totality given with the essence of spirit. Hence, just as the pre-apprehension is the possibility of judgment in the *De Malo,* so here in *In de Trinitate* it is in judgment alone that being and its transcendentals reveal themselves.

From the two articles of *In Boethii de Trinitate* which refer metaphysical knowledge to the judgment alone, excluding simple apprehension, the question arises why the simple intellectual representation of a quiddity cannot represent a really transcendental quiddity. We find the answer in what Thomas says about the *modus significandi* in which we apprehend metaphysical objects. *Significare* means designate (*bezeichnen*). Hence it is a question of the words with which we denote metaphysical objects. But words, as opposed to sentences, are the verbal expression of the simple apprehension. Hence when Thomas says that the *modus significandi,* as opposed to the judgment, is always and essentially inadequate and unsuitable with respect to metaphysical objects, he is maintaining there that the simple apprehension as such is not able to represent a metaphysical object. That must be explained briefly.

The inevitable way we speak is the consequence and expression of the inevitable way we think.[16] The individual word (*nomen*) is the expression of an individual concept, hence an indication of the *intelligentia indivisibilium* (simple apprehen-

---

[14] *Ibid.,* corp.
[15] *Ibid.,* ad 5.
[16] *S.T.* I, q. 45, a. 2, ad 2: *modus significandi sequitur modum intelligendi.* See q. 13, a. 1, corp., etc.; q. 18, a. 2, corp.: *sic nominamus aliquid, sicut cognoscimus illud.*

sion); the *oratio* (*enuntiabile*) is an indication of the judgment.[17] Thus if we establish whether a word of human speech by itself alone is able to express what is specific to a transcendental object, that is, an object fundamentally transcending the spatio-temporal, we have also established thereby whether a simple apprehension as such is able to represent a metaphysical object. Thomas finds in human speech two kinds of "names," abstract and concrete.[18] These two kinds of names are essentially connected: we cannot think a concrete except as a something of a definite kind (and so in this kind have already thought an abstract), nor an abstract except as the way in which something is (and so in the something we have simultaneously thought a concrete).[19] But from this it follows that a name alone, and hence an intellectual apprehension as such, is never able to represent a metaphysical object. The concrete word, just as the abstract as such by itself, retains an intrinsic ordination to matter, to the plurality of the same, to quantity,

[17] *Periherm.* lib. 1, lect. 4 (Parma 8b): *unum nomen ponitur ad significandum unum simplicem intellectum . . . sed oratio significat ipsam conceptionem compositam. S.T.* I, q. 85, a. 2, ad 3: *ratio quam significat nomen est definitio; et enuntiatio significat compositionem et divisionem intellectus.*

[18] See *S.T.* I, q. 3, a. 3, ad 1; q. 13, a. 1, ad 2; q. 32, a. 2, corp.; *S.C.G.* I, 30 etc.

[19] In other words, we can conceive a *concretum* (an existent real in itself) only as a *compositum* of a *quod est* and a *quo est. S.T.* I, q. 3, a. 3, ad 1: *apud nos non subsistunt nisi composita.* Q. 13, a. 1, ad 2: *omnia nomina a nobis imposita ad significandum aliquid completum subsistens significant in concretione prout competit compositis.* Q. 3, a. 5, corp.: *animal sumitur a natura sensitiva per modum concretionis; hoc enim dicitur animal, quod naturam sensitivam habet.* Similarly, q. 85, a. 5, ad 3. And vice versa: we cannot conceptually represent an *abstractum* except as something through which something possesses its determinateness, only as a *quo aliquid est. S.C.G.* I, 30: *intellectus noster . . . quod vero ut simplex* (that is, as not composed of a something and its mode of being) *significat,* (*significat*) *non ut quod est, sed ut quo est,* Briefly: *abstracta* (designate indeed something simple, but) *non significat ens per se subsistens, et concreta* (designate indeed an *ens per se subsistens,* but) *significant ens compositum: 1 Sent.* dist. 4, q. 1, a. 2, corp. See also dist. 33, q. 1, a. 2, corp.

197

to space and time. For the something which is simultaneously thought in the concrete name as different from its kind and to which the content of the abstract name is referred is matter. The reason for this phenomenon in all our human words is intelligible after the chapter on sensibility: in this phenomenon is revealed the origin of our knowledge from sensibility as its abiding foundation. Whence it comes that "with regard to its mode of signifying, every word (which is to be applied to metaphysical objects) is deficient."[20]

This consideration confirms that Thomas does not think that the act of knowing in which a metaphysical object is reached is the intellectual representation (*Vorstellung*) as such. The third level of abstraction, then, is of an intrinsically and essentially different nature than the first two. It cannot be thought of as separating and leaving out individual determinations from the totality of the essential determinations represented by reason of the first abstraction, and this in such a way that then, without anything further, only transcendental determinations are left. For then these transcendental determinations would have to be represented (*vorgestellt*) as such. Certainly these are really represented in their content. Thomas says that explicitly,[21] and otherwise, of course, it would be impossible to see how anything could be known of them at all. But precisely what the metaphysical abstraction must make explicable is how it is to be known that what is represented is really possible not only in the way in which it is represented and expressed, how it is to be known that what is signified (*significatum*) and the mode of signifying (*modus significandi*) (which is something in the *significatum*) can be separated without the *significatum* losing all objective meaning thereby. The intellectual representation as such, which always represents in this *modus significandi*, cannot accomplish that because what precisely is to be sur-

---

[20] *S.C.G.* I, 30.

[21] Cf. the texts quoted about the *modus significandi*, where this situation is always presupposed. The *nomina* are as a matter of fact affirmed of the metaphysical object.

mounted in this abstraction is what clings essentially to the representation, the relation of what is represented to matter, and this manifests itself inevitably in the *modus significandi*.

One could now point to the fact that, according to Thomas, the inapplicability of what is intellectually represented to metaphysical objects, which inapplicability is given with its *modus significandi,* is removed by a negation. That is correct. Thomas does think that transcendental concepts (being, one, true, and so on) are acquired by negating and exluding the relatedness of the content of our representation to matter.[22] But there still remain two questions: first, what the abstraction, understood as a negation in the way just indicated, really is. The "no" as the fundamental act of such an abstraction is not a represented content alongside of others, and besides, the relation to matter in what is represented is not negated in such a way that it would no longer be represented simultaneously. For such an understanding is rejected precisely by the proposition that in principle the *modus significandi* in a simple apprehension is never suitable for a metaphysical object. Then what is the "no" to this *modus significandi?*

From this follows the second question: a "no" to the *modus significandi* has the possibility of opening up knowledge of a metaphysical object and of letting the *significatum,* separated from the *modus* by the "no," be known as really possible only if this real possibility, intrinsically independent of a concretion in matter, is grasped somehow or other antecedent to this "no," the possibility, namely, of the remainder which is left in the content of the intellectual representation after the "no"; and is grasped in such a way of course that this remaining possibility does not appear in what is represented as represented, for otherwise the negation in the represented content would no longer have any essential meaning, since the metaphysical ob-

---

[22] *In III De Anima* lect. 11, n. 758: *omnia quae transcendunt haec sensibilia nota nobis, non cognoscuntur a nobis nisi per negationem.* See *S.T.* I, q. 84, a. 7, ad 3: q. 88, a. 2, ad 2; *I Sent.* dist. 8, q. 2, a. 1, ad 1; *In Boeth. de Trin.* q. 6, a. 3, corp., second half.

ject could be apprehended even without negation, which is precisely what Thomas denies. Thomas is perfectly clear about the necessity of apprehending the real possibility of the remainder of the intellectual representation that is left after the negation, and of apprehending this antecedent to the negation.[23]

So it follows from the problematic of the *modus significandi* in the simple apprehension that abstraction as the apprehension of what is metaphysically universal must be an act that pre-apprehends metaphysical being without representing it objectively. Then, on the one hand, the represented content can correctly be liberated from its relation to matter by a negation (insofar, of course, as it does not necessarily imply such a relation of itself), without itself being eliminated as really possible, or at least becoming unknowable; and, on the other hand, since the metaphysical object is not already represented objectively in itself in the simple apprehension as such, this negating representation of the content of the intellectual representation, which content in itself is related to matter, is indispensable for knowing a metaphysical object thematically at all. Thus this problematic points in the same direction in which we have already been led by the consideration of the two articles from *In Boethii de Trinitate:* the decisive abstraction of metaphysical determinations takes place in the judgment.

If, therefore, we established from Thomistic presuppositions in the preceding Sections that the judgment attains to an *esse* that is absolutely unlimited in itself and thus transcends limitation by matter, now we can say vice versa that in the judgment as such a knowledge of *esse* opens up, *esse* is "abstracted," and this knowledge goes beyond what is able to be represented positively in the intellectual apprehension. Consequently, if according to earlier considerations *esse* reveals itself in the pre-

---

[23] *De Pot.* q. 7, a. 5, corp.: *intellectus negationis semper fundatur in aliqua affirmatione . . . unde, nisi intellectus humanus aliquid de Deo* (and thus of all metaphysical objects) *affirmative cognosceret, nihil de Deo* (that is, of the positive content in the light of which we apprehend God) *posset negare.*

apprehension which is the condition of the possibility of judgment, and if according to our present considerations *esse* is abstracted in the judgment, and the power of such abstraction is called in Thomas the agent intellect: then the agent intellect is to be defined as the power which pre-apprehends *esse* absolutely. This perhaps at first surprising definition is to be further verified as Thomistic in the next Section. From that it must then follow that the agent intellect so defined grounds the possibility of the other two levels of abstraction, and this explains the relationship of the three levels of abstraction which up to now were simply juxtaposed.

But before that, we will try again briefly to throw some light on our thesis from another point of view, the thesis that *esse* is reached and disclosed not in the intellectual apprehension, in the abstractive concept—insofar as it is different from the judgment—, but only in the judgment itself. It cannot be objected against our interpretation that Thomas also knows a formal abstraction that is accomplished by conceptual apprehension "by which the form and so also the 'form of forms,' being, is liberated from matter."[24] First of all "formal abstraction" and "judgment" in Thomas cannot simply be played off against each other; the third level of *abstraction,* as was explained above, is necessarily and exclusively a moment in the *judgment.* But a purely conceptual, formal abstraction (in the apprehension precisely as such), as distinguished from the judgment as such, cannot reach precisely that "form" which is being in itself. For transcendental *esse* taken strictly has no quidditative form different from itself which would adequately preserve what is "formal" in being.[25] Being can never be "liberated" (*abgelöst*) in the abstractive concept in a (quidditative-universal) differentiation from itself, but can only be *re-realized* (*nachvollzogen*) in that synthesis of the universal and the singular, of form and subject, of possibility and actuality which it itself is "in itself" (*an sich*) but that means in the affirmative

24 Cf. J. de Vries, *op. cit.,* p. 408.
25 See above, Section VI, 3, note 30.

synthesis of the judgment. Precisely what *esse* is not is a universal concept such as the apprehension (as such) forms; as was said above, its "formal element" is *sui generis*. "Universal" being also contains in itself all specific differences, it is not merely a pure genus. It "is" in itself the "relation" (*Beziehung*) between the universal and the singular, between form and matter, and only within its horizon, already disclosed, does that "distinction" (*Unterscheidung*) and that "liberation" (*Ablösung*) become possible which the so-called (total and) formal abstraction of the intellectual apprehension (as such) accomplishes. This conception of being in the metaphysics of knowledge says in its ontological formulation that transcendental being shows itself to be *analogous in itself*, and not only subsequently (through a "comparison").

IX. THE AGENT INTELLECT AS THE POWER OF THE *EXCESSUS* TO *ESSE*

The agent intellect is characterized by Thomas as the power of forming the first principles of transcendental validity. On the other hand, all these principles are related to and grounded upon *esse*. Consequently, the agent intellect is defined essentially for Thomas by the fact that it apprehends *esse* absolutely. For the reasons already explained, this apprehension cannot be understood as representation (*Vorstellung*). Hence there remains as the only possible mode of this apprehension an *excessus* beyond the sensibly concretized being to *esse* absolutely, and this *excessus* results in the judgment. The agent intellect is fundamentally and decisively characterized by this pre-apprehension because, by the apprehension of *esse* and the first principles included in it, what is sensibly given becomes actually intelligible. But up to now the agent intellect was defined in a formal way, precisely as the power to make something actually intelligible. These connections are now to be shown in detail in Thomas.

1. The Fundamental Characterization of the Agent Intellect by the Abstraction of the First Principles

Thomas establishes an essential connection between the first principles and the agent intellect. By these first principles are meant the most basic principles of being and of thought, for there is question of the "universal principles of all the sciences,"[1] hence not merely the principles of the science which is concerned with thought as such, but also those sciences which are related to being as such. The agent intellect is the ground of the first principles.[2] "From the natural light itself of the agent intellect the first principles become known."[3] Similar expressions are found again and again.[4] Now it could be thought at first that there exists between the agent intellect and the first principles the same relationship that exists in general between the agent intellect and abstract essences: it is the power of abstracting them, and accordingly, insofar as it is the ground of the most universal concepts, it also produces the most universal principles which are based upon the most universal concepts. That is indeed correct, but it does not completely describe the relationship between the principles and the agent intellect as Thomas sees it.

For Thomas the first principles are not just any product of the intellect, but the fundamental product. And they are fundamental not perhaps merely because these principles are precisely the most universal, and so are implicitly contained in all other specific propositions and concepts, but because they are the expression of the scope of the agent intellect, and because the agent intellect accomplishes the abstraction, the "making things intelligible," through them as its "instruments." The first prin-

[1] S.T. I, q. 117, a. 1, corp. Further texts in Hufnagel, *Intuition und Erkenntnis* . . . , pp. 200ff.
[2] *De Anima* a. 5, corp.
[3] *In IV Metaph.* lect. 6. n. 599.
[4] See *II Sent.* dist. 28, q. 1, a. 5, corp.; *III Sent.* dist. 23, q. 1, a. 1, corp.; *De Ver.* q. 9, a. 1, ad 2; q. 10, a. 13, corp.; q. 11, a. 3, corp.; *De Anima* a. 4, ad 6; a. 5, corp.; *Quodl.* 10, a. 7, ad 2; *S.T.* I, q. 79, a. 5, ad 3; q. 117, a. 1, corp.; I-II, q. 53, a. 1, corp.; *S.C.G.* II, 78; III, 46; *In VI Ethic.* lect. 5, n. 1179.

ciples, as they occur in specifically human knowledge, are the index of the scope, and thus of the nature, of the agent intellect: "The first . . . principles . . . are in us as instruments, as it were, of the agent intellect by whose light the natural reason lives in us. Wherefore, our natural reason can attain to the knowledge of nothing to which [a somewhat fluid, imprecise relation to "nothing"] the first principles do not extend."[5] The scope of the first principles is the index of the strength of the illuminating power of the intellect. The first principles contain in themselves a participation in the "light" of the agent intellect.[6] The agent intellect uses these principles as "instruments" to accomplish its abstractive function: "The principles themselves are related to the agent intellect as certain instruments, because through them it makes things actually intelligible."[7] But making things actually intelligible is the formal metaphysical expression for the essential and only function of the agent intellect.[8] Thus the first principles as the instrumental principle for abstraction stand on the side of the agent intellect.

But this seems to bring Thomas into a contradiction. For the first principles are simultaneously for him a result of the abstractive activity of the agent intellect also.[9] If this contradiction is to be avoided, then we must understand the first principles as the first and proper result of the agent intellect, and all further abstraction of other essences as a mere consequence of this fundamental and decisive abstraction. This justifies our going backwards and defining the intrinsic nature of the agent intellect precisely from the first principles as its decisive result.

[5] *De Ver.* q. 10, a. 13, corp.; similarly, *II Sent.* dist. 28, q. 1, a. 5, corp.

[6] *De Ver.* q. 9, a. 1, ad 2.

[7] *De Anima* a. 5, corp. Similarly, a. 4, ad 6: in the *reductio intellectus possibilis in actum* the *principia demonstrationis* are the *instrumenta* of the agent intellect as the *artifex*.

[8] See *S.C.G.* II, 76; 96; *De Spir. Creat.* a. 9, corp.; a. 10, corp.; *S.T.* I, q. 54, a. 4, corp.; q. 79, a. 3, corp.; *De Anima* a. 4, ad 4, etc.

[9] *In IV Metaph.* lect. 6, n. 599; n. 605; *In III De Anima* lect. 10, n. 729; *II Sent.* dist. 17, q. 2, a. 1, corp. towards the end.

2. Making Possible the Abstraction of Principles by the Pre-Apprehension of Being in Its Esse

The first principles are based on the first "*conceptiones*,"[10] so that Thomas characterizes the relationship between the agent intellect and the first conceptions in the same phrases with which he describes the relationship between the agent intellect and the first principles.[11] The first and most basic concept that is apprehended and upon which the most basic principles are founded is "being" (*ens*).[12] So the knowledge of the first principles, which characterizes the agent intellect fundamentally, is based upon the abstractive knowledge of being. Accordingly, if the nature of the agent intellect is to be clarified, we must ask what this being is which the agent intellect grasps. From the fact that it is to ground the metaphysical principles, it follows that it cannot coincide with the being which is the highest concept of material things: "something of the kind which is able to be repeated in many of the same." Hence, Thomas always

[10] *In IV Metaph.* lect. 6, n. 605. For the concept of the *conceptiones: Quodl.* 8, a. 4, corp.

[11] *De Ver.* q. 11, a. 3, corp.

[12] *De Ver.* q. 1, a. 1, corp.: *Quod primo intellectus concipit quasi notissimum et in quo omnes conceptiones resolvit, est ens . . . unde oportet, quod omnes aliae conceptiones intellectus accipiantur ex additione ad ens.* See *S.T.* I, q. 5, a. 2, corp.; q. 11, a. 2, ad 4; I-II, q. 94, a. 2, corp. etc. The principle of contradiction as the first metaphysical principle is based on this *conceptio prima: S.T.* I-II, q. 94, a. 2, corp.; *In IV Metaph.* lect. 6, n. 605, wherein it is to be noted that there is an order among the principles (*S.T.* II-II, q. 1, a. 7, corp.) as among the first *conceptiones* (*S.T.* I-II, q. 94, a. 2, corp.; I, q. 16, a. 4, ad 2; *De Pot.* q. 9, a. 7, ad 6 and *ad ea quae in oppositum objiciuntur*). For the principles being founded on *ens*, see also *S.C.G.* II, 83.

Perhaps it is useful to point out that when Thomas explains *ens* as what is first apprehended, that is not meant in the sense that the first human act apprehends *ens* in its metaphysical purity by itself. The same holds of the first principles. It only means that in every objectively apprehended object, *ens* (and the first principles) is simultaneously apprehended as the metaphysical ground of the possibility of the former. What the temporally first apprehended object is concretely in any given case does not enter into the consideration at all, and is a question of no philosophical interest.

distinguished carefully between being as the principle of number and metaphysical being[13] which he calls being without qualification, or "universal being, being which is derived from *esse* itself," as opposed to being as the principle of number, which is a "special genus of being in the genus of discrete quantity."[14]

But how is this metaphysical being reached by the agent intellect? Every intellectual content known representatively from sensibility is essentially related to matter, hence has intrinsically and necessarily in itself a ground of possible multiplication, and thus does not reach beyond being as the principle of number.[15] In fact it seems as though we have gone off in a false direction in our considerations so far, because at first sight it is highly improbable that the abstraction of being could ground the possibility of the abstraction of the other universal essences. For the greater or lesser degree of empty universality does not seem to offer any basis for making the one abstraction the possibility of the others, unless by the term "being" as applied to what is grasped in abstraction something would have to be understood which does not simply stand beside the other universal concepts to be abstracted as still more universal and more empty.

That this assumption really proves correct for Thomas is shown from how he understands being. If we were afraid that being stood alongside the other universal concepts as only more universal and more empty, and, apprehended as "something of such and such a kind" just like any other concretized universal

13 *In III Metaph.* lect. 12, n. 501; *In V Metaph.* lect. 10, n. 901; *In IV Metaph.* lect. 2, n. 559; *In X Metaph.* lect. 3, n. 1981; lect. 8, n. 2093.

14 *In IV Metaph.* lect. 2, n. 559. Therefore Thomas frequently emphasizes that metaphysical *ens* and its unity, under which God and other immaterial things are apprehended, should not be confused with the *ens* as the *unum quod est principium numeri*. The first *ens unum secundum esse* is not dependent on matter. See *S.T.* I, q. 11, a. 3, ad 2; a. 30, a. 3, ad 2; *I Sent.* dist. 24, q. 1, a. 1, ad 1; *De Pot.* q. 9, a. 7, corp.

15 See *In VII Metaph.* lect. 9, n. 1477: *Materia sine qua non potest concipi intellectu forma, oportet quod ponatur in definitione formae.*

206

in its synthesis of a something and a form, it betrayed its inevitable relation to matter, that would be to see being precisely from the aspect which is *not* essential to it in the Thomistic concept of being as distinguished from "thing" (*res*). "Being is derived from the act of existing, but the word 'thing' expresses the quiddity or essence of a being."[16] "The word 'being' is derived from the existence of a thing."[17] "Thing is derived only from the quiddity . . . but being is derived from the act of existing."[18] The quiddity spoken of in these texts is precisely the represented object of the simple apprehension as such. As such a quiddity, actually only a "what" in a "something" can be intellectually represented, and so the relation to matter cannot be eliminated. But in his description of the concept of being, Thomas bids us understand being not as thing, not according to its quiddity, but according to its *esse*. Now, earlier explanations of Thomistic texts have shown that *esse* is the object of the judgment. Hence, if being, insofar as it expresses *esse,* is what is first grasped by abstraction, is the fundamental abstraction, then abstraction must abstract being insofar as it is grasped in the judgment as *esse*. When Thomas says that being is what is first abstracted, he is saying that *esse* as universal in the sense already explained is the first thing that is abstracted. Consequently, if the function of the agent intellect was defined as the apprehension of the first principles by the abstraction of the concept of being, this means that the agent intellect attains to *esse*.

This result will appear less unusual if the following is noted: the knowledge of the principles is dependent on sense knowledge.[19] Hence when the one human knowledge made up of sensibility and intellect comes upon the sensible, real object, the apprehension of being as *esse* and of the first principles has to ensue. But in this one encounter between the one human knowledge and the real object, the first actually accomplished act is a judg-

16 *De Ver.* q. 1, a. 1, corp. and ad 3 (second series). See *I Sent.* dist. 8, q. 1, a. 1, corp.

17 *I Sent.* dist. 25, q. 1, a. 4, corp.

18 *In IV Metaph.* lect. 2, n. 553.

19 *S.C.G.* II, 83; *De Anima* a. 4, ad 6; *S.T.* I-II, q. 51, a. 1, corp.

207

ment: a quiddity is apprehended as belonging to the object really given in sensibility. But this reference to the real object is a judgment, and in fact one necessarily given simultaneously with the abstraction of the quiddity from the real object, since the quiddity is liberated as belonging to this real thing. The awareness of the origin of the quiddity from the real thing is nothing other than the reference of the quiddity to the real thing and thus a judgment.[20] Hence if being is abstracted in the encounter with the real, sensible existent, it takes place in a judgment.

If it has thus been confirmed anew from the viewpoint of the first principles as the first characteristic products of the agent intellect that the essence of the agent intellect is an apprehension of *esse*,[21] the question still remains why this pre-apprehension of *esse* is the condition of the possibility of the abstraction of any universal essence (form, quiddity) at all. Not until this question is clarified can it be said that the pre-apprehension of absolute *esse* constitutes the nature of the agent intellect. Not until then will we be able to reach a philosophical understanding of the many images and analogies with which Thomas tries to describe the essence of the agent intellect and which up to now had to remain out of consideration here.

We begin once again with the concept of being which the agent intellect apprehends. "The word 'being' is derived from the existence of a thing." We know already what *esse* means in Thomas: the one full ground of all possible objects of knowledge as the index of the absolutely unlimited scope of the

---

20 See *S.C.G.* I, 59: *intellectus tamen incomplexus* (that is, the simple apprehension) *intelligendo quod quid est* (the quiddity) *apprehendit quidditatem in quadem comparatione ad rem; quia apprehendit eam ut huius rei quidditatem.* But the *comparatio ad rem* is already familiar to us as an essential characteristic of the judgment. Therefore the first acquisition of a quiddity (abstraction) takes place as a judgment. The simple apprehension can in no way be understood as an independent function alongside of judgment. It is *essentially a part of the judgment,* so much so that as such it cannot occur in real human thought at all by itself alone. One always thinks a quiddity as the quiddity of a thing, and thus has judged. Or, one thinks something (hence again a quiddity) about a quiddity, and again has judged.

21 Why this grasp can only be thought of as a pre-apprehension has already been discussed in our earlier considerations.

pre-apprehension. Hence if every intellectually apprehended object (every concrete being) is apprehended as a limited *esse,* then it is apprehended in the pre-apprehension of the unlimited scope of all the possible objects of thought altogether. But this says that thought is with the individual object to be apprehended at the moment by the fact that it already finds itself somehow or other (that is, in the pre-apprehension) with the totality of its possible objects (whereby "totality" is not meant as the quantitative accumulation of the individual objects, since *esse* is this totality in the sense already established, as the one original ground of all determinations of the possible objects). But this enables knowing to experience the form of the object which is given to it at first sensibly—even if this form might be at first only the sum of the sensibly apprehended qualities of the thing—as a limitation of this *esse.* In the pre-apprehension of *esse,* thought apprehends the form as a limiting potency of being, because in this pre-apprehension it has already and always transcended the concrete given with its determinations.

To this extent the *excessus* to *esse* is already and always the negation of the apprehended individual being. The metaphysical possibility of a "negation" and "removal" as an essential function of knowledge is grounded in this *excessus.* The *excessus* makes intelligible why the negation and removal are not merely a suppression of a part of the content of knowledge (which suppression is of no importance for the knowledge), but really reveals new and real objectivity. The explicit negation is grounded in the *excessus* as the already accomplished "negation" of the individual object in its *esse* limited by its form. It relates itself to something in the conceptually given object and thus opens up the way, as it were, for the thematic apprehension of that which the intellect has already and always pre-apprehension even before the explicit negation in order to apprehend the individual object. Since, vice versa, this "whither" of the pre-apprehension is always given only as that of a *pre*-apprehension, since, in other words, the apprehension of an individual object is the condition of the possibility of the awareness of the pre-apprehension, this latter can be apprehended thematically only in a reflection that

209

includes a negation. Thus explicit metaphysics appears as an essentially reflexive science which operates by negation. But we will have to go into that in more detail later.

But even this has not yet made clear how the form is apprehended as universal by the pre-apprehension of *esse*. So far it only follows that the form is able to reveal itself as limitation, as a potency for *esse,* through the pre-apprehension, but not how it can manifest itself in the pre-apprehension as act in relation to matter as its potency. We said in an earlier consideration that any theory that has the acquisition of a universal essence come about by a comparison is inadequate. The reason why the comparison itself forces us into the question about the condition of its own possibility lies in the fact that a comparison already presupposes as antecedent to itself the apprehension of an essence as such which is able to be common to what is to be compared; it requires that the dissociation of the form from its "this" be already accomplished, since concrete things as such cannot be compared with each other. Of course to be able to be compared, they must as a matter of fact be similar in themselves. But the question is precisely how that wherein they are similar can be seen by itself, although it is not something in addition to that by which the concrete things are two and different from each other. This is utterly inconceivable except by the fact that they are both related to a unity which, itself incomposed, already lies prior to the constitution of the unity of what is common in the two things.

The Thomistic principle is valid in this case, too: "Unity must be found *before* multiplicity. . . . Whatever is of itself many does not come together into one unless it is united by something composing it.[22] For if different things are united in something, there must be some cause of this union, for different thing are not united of themselves."[23] It is to be noted here that what "composes" as "cause" of the unity must be one in the respect in which the unification takes place. But now we

---

[22] *S.C.G.* I, 18.
[23] *S.T.* I, q. 65, a. 1, corp.; see q. 11, a. 3, corp., *tertio.*

have reached a unity antecedent to the merely factual similarity of two forms possessed sensibly which makes it possible to apprehend this similarity. The forms are apprehended as potencies of the one *esse* to which the *excessus* attains, and so it is possible to know them as similar or the same. Hence the formation of universal concepts becomes possible through the *excessus*. But then the *excessus* to *esse* has shown itself to be the condition of any abstraction at all, and thereby of the first and second levels of abstraction as well. The third level of abstraction is the possibility of the first two, although it does not become explicit until the end.

Thus the *excessus* to absolute *esse* has turned out to be the essential and only metaphysical expression of the intrinsic nature of the agent intellect. Hence we are now in a position to explain correctly the variegated array of images and concepts with the help of which Thomas tries to describe the essence of the agent intellect, without running the risk because of them of understanding them in the light of their historical origin in a way that would give us an un-Thomistic notion of the agent intellect. We will carry this investigation further because the correctness of our results so far will be confirmed if we readily succeed thereby in acquiring a really philosophical sense for the images and concepts with which Thomas tries to grasp the essence of the agent intellect.

3. The Ontological Interpretation of the Light-Image (The Light as That Which Is Simultaneously "Seen" in the Object and Makes Possible A Priori the "Visibility" of the Object)

One of the images most used to describe the function of the agent intellect[24] is the notion that the phantasms are illuminated

---

[24] For the fact that there is question of an image: *S.T.* I, q. 67, a. 1, corp.: *metaphorice in spiritualibus dicitur . . . ; De Anima* a. 4, ad 4: *comparatio luminis ad intellectum; In Lib. de Causis* lect. 6 (Parma XXI, 729b): *per similitudinem dici potest lumen.*

211

by the agent intellect as a "light."[25] What does Thomas want to say in this image? If we just take the image itself, it says first of all that there is question of making the phantasm visible through the agent intellect. In general, that is the function of a light with respect to its illuminated object. Being visible is of course in our case being conscious.[26] In the case of abstraction it is not a question of any consciousness of the phantasm at all, because this latter is already known by the one human knowing through sensibility, and therefore what is so known as such does not have to be known again in another (intellectual) way.

In this connection, the misunderstanding must again be avoided that in abstraction in Thomas there is question of transferring a content of knowledge from one cognitive faculty to another. It is the one man who knows the contents of his cognitive faculties, and it is therefore senseless to have him know something twice in two cognitive faculties. It is not the powers that know, but man: "It is said *more* properly that man knows through the soul"[27]; "for, properly speaking, it is not the senses or intellect which know, but man through them both."[28] Hence, when there is question of abstraction, the unity of consciousness is already given from the outset for Thomas. What is given in sensibility, to the extent that it is given there, is by that very fact also given for the intellect, since properly speaking nothing at all is given for the faculties, but for the knower through them. What must still be given in the intellect, therefore, beyond what is given sensibly in sensibility is in the strictest sense and exclusively that which cannot be given in sensibility because of its material essence.

Thomas develops in detail and in principle the relationship of

---

[25] Cf. M. Honecker, "Der Lichtbegriff in der Abstraktionslehre des Thomas von Aquin": *Phil. Jahrb.* 48 (1935), pp. 268–88. The Thomistic texts are also to be found there.

[26] *S.T.* I, q. 67, a. 1, corp.: *postmodum autem extensum est (nomen lucis) ad significandum omne illud quod facit manifestationem secundum quamcumque cognitionem.*

[27] *S.T.* I, q. 75, a. 2, corp. and ad 2.

[28] *De Ver.* q. 2, a. 6, ad 3; see *De Spir. Creat.* a. 10, ad 15; *S.T.* I, q. 76, a. 1, corp.

two faculties in the one man in the same sense with regard to the question of the relationship between will and intellect.[29] A corresponding application of these thoughts, bringing in the idea of the order of the procession of the potencies from the substance of the soul,[30] would further confirm the correctness of our understanding. Abstraction is not supposed to explain how the intellect knows what sensibility apprehends, but how it knows it as *universal*. When Thomas says that the intellect knows "only" the universal,[31] he does not contradict our explanation. This statement is not supposed to express a regrettable defect in our intellect, but this Thomistic thesis is only the self-evident expression of the fact that, on the one hand, it follows necessarily from the unity of human knowing that in this one knowing the one function as such neither must nor can accomplish what the other has already essentially accomplished, and that, on the other hand, the ontological intensity of the intellect as such finds expression precisely in the fact that it knows the sensibly given within being in its totality, and therefore as universal. Moreover, sensibility is the sensibility of the spirit because the intellect produces sensibility as its potency and thus retains in itself sensibility's accomplishment as its own.[32] That spirit at the human level of being must produce from itself sensibility as its own potency but different from itself is, of course, the index of its ontological weakness (*Seinsschwäche*).

In this connection, let us note the following: the chapter on sensibility has shown that a receptive, non-creative knowledge of an object essentially requires sensibility,[33] that there can be intuition only through sentient reception.[34] When Thomas de-

[29] See *S.T.* I, q. 82, a. 4, ad 1; q. 87, a. 4; I–II, q. 17, a. 1, corp.; a. 3, ad 3; *III Sent.* dist. 23, q. 1, a. 2, ad 3; *De Ver.* q. 22, a. 12, corp.
[30] *S.T.* I, q. 77, a. 6; a. 7, and the parallels.
[31] *S.T.* I, q. 14, a. 11, ad 1; q. 86, a. 1, etc.
[32] See *S.T.* I, q. 77, a. 7, corp.
[33] See, for example, *De Anima* a. 20, ad 6.
[34] Therefore, in order to explain a knowledge of the material individual as possible for the pure intellects, Thomas also tries to construct a knowledge of this material individual from the creative knowledge of

nies that the intellect has knowledge of the singular insofar
(and only insofar) as the intellect is distinct from sensibility
and is only *one* moment of the one consciousness of the one
man, then, given its presuppositions, that is self-evident, but it
must not be misunderstood in the way indicated. If, then, Thomas
grants to the intellect an apprehension of the material individual,
not indeed directly, but "through a certain reflection, through a
conversion to the phantasm,"[35] he is just expanding the narrow
concept of intellect once again into that of the one consciousness.

Thus, what is made visible by the light of the agent intellect
is only that the quiddity which is had sensibly is universal, that
it can be the form in many "this's": "to know that which exists
in individual matter [hence, the qualitative content remains in
the individual matter, that is, in the phantasm known sensibly],
not as it exists in such matter, is to abstract the form from the
individual matter which the phantasms represent."[36] The knowledge of the "not as" is all that abstraction as such accomplishes.

Now, to what extent does the "light" of the agent intellect
make possible such an understanding of what is sensibly given?
The very actuality of a thing is in a certain way its light."[37] The
level of being of an existent is its "lightsomeness" (*Lichthaftig-
keit*). Although in the context of the text this is said first of all
of the thing to be known, it also holds of the agent intellect. For
in the first place, for Thomas the capacity to know and to be
known are always parallel and correspond to the level of being.
And secondly, the sentence preceding our text reads: "That by
which something is known can be called, by analogy, a light."
But the agent intellect is that by which the content of the phantasm is made knowable as universal, hence it is "that by which
something is known." Hence we can say that its light is its

God. See *S.T.* I, q. 57, a. 2; *S.C.G.* II, 100; *De Ver.* q. 8, a. 11, corp.;
IV Sent. dist. 50, q. 1, a. 3, corp.; *De Anima* a. 20, corp. and ad 8;
Quodl. 7, a. 3, corp.
[35] *S.T.* I, q. 86, a. 1, corp. etc. For the whole last section, see Rousselot, *op. cit.*, pp. 110–13; Maréchal, *op. cit.*, pp. 156ff.
[36] *S.T.* I, q. 85, a. 1, corp.
[37] *In Lib. de Causis* lect. 6 (Parma XXI, 729b); see *De Anima* a. 15
corp.: *lumen intellectuale sive intellectualis natura.*

ABSTRACTION

specific intensity of being (*Seinsmächtigkeit*), its actuality. This must already belong to it in itself, independently of the phantasm, for it is supposed to be the ground of a definite way of understanding what is sensibly known, hence it cannot itself as such be grounded in sensibility or be caused by it. Therefore, the agent intellect is already and always in itself at this level of being, always in act.[38] "The agent intellect is only agent, and in no way patient."[39] Hence, if the light of the intellect is to be understood, it is important to understand this actuality better.

It can be said first of all, in general, that this actuality must be an ontological actuality which somewhow or other already belongs in the realm of knowing and knowability, of being as being-present-to-self. For otherwise it would be impossible to see how this actuality could be a "light" which makes something knowable. One could be tempted to object against this consideration that according to Thomas abstraction is an unconscious process. But in the text which suggests this understanding, Thomas only wants to say that knowing as such, that is, as consciousness, is an affair of the possible intellect, or better, of man through the possible intellect.[40] But Thomas does not want to say that the light of the agent intellect is not somehow known itself. The contrary assumption goes against the basic conception of the Thomistic metaphysics of knowledge just by the fact that according to this conception the knownness of a thing is directly proportioned to the level of its being (*Seinshöhe*), but the agent intellect is so very much the expression of the ontological level of man[41] that its function consists precisely in bestowing its form upon what is sensibly material, thereby making it actually intelligible.[42] Now Thomas

[38] See *S.T.* I, q. 54, a. 1, ad 1; *III Sent.* dist. 14, q. 1, a. 1, sol. 2, ad 2; *De Ver.* q. 16, a. 1, ad 13; q. 20, a. 2, ad 5; *De Virtut.* q. 1, a. 1, corp.; a. 9, ad 10; *S.C.G.* II, 76; *In III de Anima* lect. 10, n. 732–733.
[39] *S.T.* I–II, q. 50, a. 5, ad 2.
[40] See *De Spir. Creat.* a. 10, ad 15.
[41] *II Sent.* dist. 20, q. 2, a. 2, ad 2 (the *intellectus agens altior quam intellectus possibilis*); *De Anima* a. 5, ad 10.
[42] *II Sent.* dist. 20, q.2, a. 2, ad 2; *De Ver.* q. 10, a. 6, corp.; q. 20, a. 2, ad 5; *S.T.* I, q. 87, a. 1, corp. (*lumen intellectus agentis . . . actus ipsorum intelligibilium*); *III Sent.* dist. 14, q. 1, a. 1, sol. 2, ad 2.

215

also says explicitly that the light of the agent intellect is apprehended, and his effort to understand the mode of this apprehension correctly should not keep us from seeing his fundamental conception clearly in the first place.

According to Thomas, the light of the agent intellect is the *medium sub quo* of the knowledge of the object.[43] It can be said of such a medium that "it is related to our possible intellect as the light of the sun to the eye"[44]; it is the general making possible of intellectual seeing without supplying a definite object from itself[45]; it is that "by which something becomes actually visible."[46] Now, this light is seen as such a *medium sub quo*, although not as an object. This follows precisely from the relationship of light to that which is made knowable by it: "For since everything which is known is known by the power of the light of the intellect, the known itself as such includes in itself the light of the intellect as participated."[47] Thus the light of the agent intellect is contained in the known object as such as a constitutive element. But if it belongs to it as known ("as such"), it is known simultaneously (*miterkannt*). The same thing follows even more clearly from the way Thomas defines in general the relationship of an illuminating *medium sub quo* to what is illuminated. Since he himself draws the parallel between the illumination of the object by natural light and the illumination of the sensible object by the light of the agent intellect under the general concept of the *medium sub quo*, we have the right to apply general principles about the knowledge of light itself to the agent intellect, so long as Thomas does not

---

[43] *De Ver.* q. 18, a. 1, ad 1; *Quodl.* 7, a. 1, corp.; *IV Sent.* dist. 49, q. 2, a. 1, ad 15.

[44] *Quodl.* 7, a. 1, corp. The comparison is to be handled cautiously of course: see *De Anima* a. 16, corp., from which it follows that the emphasis is on *lumen*, not on *sol*.

[45] *IV Sent.* dist. 49, q. 2, a. 1, ad 15: *hoc est quod perficit visum ad videndum in generali, non determinans visum ad aliquod speciale objectum.*

[46] *De Ver.* q. 18, a. 1, ad 1.

[47] *De Ver.* q. 9, a. 1, ad 2, See *ibid.: lumen contentum in cognito percepto.*

explicitly deny them. One text in which the parallel itself is developed by Thomas will not be taken into consideration yet because of its obscurity, but it is to occupy us shortly. The same holds for a text from the *Commentary on the Sentences,* which taken by itself could perhaps arouse the suspicion that it did not yet contain the unambiguous Aristotelianism of the older Thomas.

"In one way light is the object of sight; in another way it is not. For, insofar as light is not perceived by our sight except by the fact that it is united with some limited body by reflection or in some other way, it is said not to be the object of sight of itself; rather, color is the object, which is always in a limited body. But, insofar as nothing can be seen except through light, light itself is said to be visible."[48] We have the right to apply this general principle to our case since Thomas also has the intellectual object united with the light of the agent intellect,[49] and since in the text cited he applies this principle to the light of faith, which he often places parallel to the light of natural knowledge.[50] Thus we can say: the light of the agent intellect is itself apprehended by thought, not indeed insofar as it is itself the object upon which knowledge gazes, but insofar as it is known simultaneously as the ground of the visibility of the object. When, therefore, Thomas says that the agent intellect is related to the possible intellect "not as object, but as making the object actually such,"[51] this does not exclude its

---

[48] *De Ver.* q. 14, a. 8, ad 4. Of course it is irrelevant for our considerations whether or not Thomas describes the actual relationship of *natural* light and its knowability correctly, and even whether or not he always maintains this description. See *De Ver.* q. 8, a. 3, ad 17; *S.T.* I, q. 56, a. 3, corp. etc. It is sufficient that in the way described above he sees at least *one* possible mode of knowing light (it is irrelevant here whether he knows still another way), and that we have the right to apply this one to our case.

[49] *De Ver.* q. 9, a. 1, ad 2; see *S.T.* I, q. 87, a. 1, corp.: *lumen intellectus agentis . . . actus ipsorum intelligibilium.*

[50] *S.T.* I, q. 12, a. 2, corp.; I–II, q. 109, a. 1, corp.; II–II, q. 8, a. 1; corp.; q. 15, a. 1, corp.

[51] *S.T.* I, q. 79, a. 4, ad 3.

217

light from being known, but only means that it is only *seen simultaneously* (*mitgesehen*) as the ground of the intellectually apprehended object.

We are now in a position to read correctly a text in which what we have so far tried to reach through combinations of texts is treated explicitly: "Corporeal light is of its essence not seen except insofar as it becomes the reason of the visibility of what is visible and the form, as it were, which makes them to be actually visible; for the very light which is in the sun is not seen by us except through its likeness existing in our sight. . . . And likewise, the light of the agent intellect is known by us through itself insofar as it is the reason for the intelligibility of the species, making them actually intelligible."[52] This text has been left out until now because of its obscurity. At first sight, it seems to be contradictory. First of all, a parallel is obviously supposed to be drawn ("And likewise . . . ") between seeing natural light and seeing spiritual light. But at the same time the opposite seems to be the case (corporeal light is *not* seen—the light of the intellect is known). Now, of course, it must be said that the contrast in the formulation is supposed to be brought to an actual parallel through the "except" and the "insofar as." But the question arises: does this double limitation in the subordinate clauses (except . . . insofar as) eliminate the affirmation of the main clause (is not seen . . . is known of itself), or does it let it stand with this precision? If the parallel is not to be destroyed, only the latter can be the case.

But then it is true that the light of the intellect is really apprehended in itself, although of course only in and at the apprehension of the intelligible universal with its content originating in sensibility. This understanding of the text also satisfies the context of the whole article. Thomas only wants to maintain that the actual knowledge of the essence of one's own soul is possible only with the help of the object originating in sensibility. The further explanation in the text, to what extent the light of the sun is in the eye, is irrelevant to the parallel, and there-

---

[52] *De Ver.* q. 10, a. 8, ad 10; similarly, q. 9, a. 1, ad 2: *cognitum inquantum huiusmodi includit in se intellectuale lumen ut participatum.*

fore does not need to occupy us here. Thomas only gives it in order to maintain the complete parallel as it was drawn in objection ten, but in itself this would not be necessary. Thus this text also confirms the results already reached independently of it.

Now neither should the clearest and least ambiguous text in Thomas arouse suspicion anymore that it speaks more the word of Augustinian apriorism than that of an Aristotelian empiricism because it is from the *Commentary on the Sentences*. "Everything that is known is not known unless it is illuminated by the light of the agent intellect and received in the possible intellect. Wherefore, just as corporeal light is seen in every color, so too the light of the agent intellect is seen in everything intelligible, not however as object, but as the medium of the knowledge."[53] That it says: "as the medium of the knowledge" can offer no difficulty. As the whole direction of the article shows, we must only avoid the understanding that the light of the agent intellect taken *by itself* is always already present in the spirit as the *object* of knowing. This is not the case; the spiritual light is only seen "because everything which is known is not known unless it is illuminated by the light of the agent intellect."[54] The "as the medium of knowledge" we can render as "not as though the light of the agent intellect were an object of knowledge taken by itself, but to the extent that, as a constitutive element in the object of knowledge [the actually intelligible], it enters into this object." That this is all that is implied is shown from the fact that, according to Thomas, the phantasm, too, enters into the object of knowledge only as a medium of the knowledge, not as a knowable object already spiritually apprehended by itself,[55] without it being able to be denied thereby that its content is really known. Elsewhere, also, the concept "medium of knowledge" is used in such a way that it becomes clear that it, too, is itself known in the knowledge of that object whose medium of knowledge it is, and thus it is not disclosed subsequently to it as perhaps merely

[53] *I Sent.* dist. 3, a. 5, corp.
[54] *Ibid.*
[55] *De Ver.* q. 2, a. 6, corp.

a presupposition of knowledge.[56] Hence, the light of the agent intellect is known simultaneously in the object.

In the light of our considerations thus far it now becomes clear how Thomas understands his Aristotelian aposteriorism: for him there are no innate ideas.[57] But in the intellectually known, an *a priori* element which spirit brings with it from itself is known simultaneously (the light of the agent intellect is seen), and this is the condition of every objective knowledge (it is not known unless it is illuminated by light). This *a priori* element of all knowledge is therefore not an innate idea, since it is only known simultaneously as the condition of the possibility of the intellectual apprehension of what is given sensibly— namely then, when it exercises a "formal" function in respect to the material of sensibility. Therefore, Thomas can also designate the light of the agent intellect as form in respect to the sensibly given,[58] and the sensibly given as the "material element" of knowledge.[59] Therefore, *spirit* and *sensibly given* are related in the constitution of the intelligible as act and potency.[60]

This way of speaking should not be rendered harmless by finding in it only the statement that the agent intellect is the act of the phantasm only insofar as it produces something intelligible as an efficient cause which is absolutely distinct from what it produces. Its light is rather contained intrinsically and constitutively in what is actually intelligible and thus is really known simultaneously. Thomas teaches an apriorism not in the harmless sense of an efficient cause antecedent to the effect, but in the sense of *an a priori element inherent in the known as such.* Corresponding to this, this sentence in Thomas is also to be taken seriously: "It cannot be said that sense knowledge is the whole and perfect cause of intellectual knowledge; rather, it is in a certain way its material cause."[61] This sentence is not only intended to say

[56] *De Ver.* q. 2, a. 9, corp.
[57] *S.T.* I, q. 84, a. 3.
[58] *III Sent.* dist. 14, q. 1, a. 1, sol. 2, ad 2.
[59] *S.T.* I, q. 84, a. 6, corp.: *materia causae.*
[60] *De Ver.* q. 10, a. 6, corp.; *De Spir. Creat.* a. 10, ad 4; *Compend. Theol.* c. 88.
[61] *S.T. I*, q. 84, a. 6, corp.

that the phantasm of itself cannot exercise any influence on the intellect. Rather it is not in itself actually intelligible (which it could be even if it could not exercise any influence on the intellect) and becomes actually intelligible only when the light of the intellect as *a priori,* formal element is joined with it as material cause, and the former is therefore known simultaneously in the actually intelligible.

It does not need to be gone into at length how the formal-material union between the light of the agent intellect and the phantasm cannot be thought of in the strict sense, after the manner of the union of a material form and matter in natural things. For otherwise this form of the light would itself be limited by the matter of the phantasm, and a spiritual, immaterial knowledge, which is supposed to be made possible precisely by the light, would not come about in principle.[62] Insofar as this *a priori* element is known only as the "form" of the phantasm, it is of course in this respect also *a posteriori* to the knowledge of the phantasm, and to that extent we can speak of an "abstraction" from the phantasm. The relationship of reciprocal priority which Thomas often stresses in the relationship of form and matter is valid here also.[63]

Consequently, we must say: in abstraction the light of the agent intellect is known simultaneously (*miterkannt*) in the universal object, and this light is the actuality of the knower himself, from which it follows again that this actuality is such that of itself it has its knownness (*Erkanntheit*) in itself when it becomes the form of the sensible content.[64] But how is it possible that the actuality of the knower is the actuality of the known? This question, which the consideration of the speculation about light in the Thomistic doctrine on abstraction forces upon us, recalls first of all the Thomistic proposition: "the in-

[62] Cf. Maréchal, *op. cit.,* pp. 134f.
[63] For example, *De Ver,* q. 9, a. 3, ad 6; q. 28, a. 7, corp.; *In V Metaph.* lect. 2, n. 775, etc.
[64] For this expression see, for example, *III Sent.* dist. 14, q. 1, a. 1, sol. 2, ad 2, where the *una natura luminis* (*animae intellectivae*) appears as the form (hence as *actualitas*) of what is to become actually intelligible through an *assimilatio.*

tellect and the actually intelligible are the same,"[65] and should serve to assure us that the developement has not departed from the thought of Thomas. From what was said it follows further that the actuality of the agent intellect is the actuality of the intelligible insofar as the sensibly apprehended content is distinct from what is intellectually apprehended. For it was for the sake of this content that an "illumination" of the phantasm was required. Now in what does the actuality of the agent intellect consist, and to what extent does it confer universality upon this sensibly given content when it becomes its actuality? If this question is answered, then the metaphysical content of the figurative description of abstraction as an illumination of the phantasm by the light of the agent intellect will be understood.

First, however, there is a further difficulty against our results so far which has to be mentioned. We have come to an understanding of the illumination of the phantasm which identifies this illumination with the actual process of abstraction. The response to objection four in the seventh Article of Question 85 in Part I of the *Summa* seems to contradict this. There "illuminate" is clearly distinguished from "abstract." Now Thomas does not make this distinction anywhere else. His formulations elsewhere at least do not allow us to presume anything of such a distinction, in fact seem to exclude it. Thus, for example, ". . . intellectual light whose part it is to make things actually intelligible"[66]; or "the very fact that the light of the agent intellect is not the act of any corporeal organ . . . suffices to explain the fact that [the light] can separate the intelligible species from the phantasms."[67] In *De Anima* a. 4, ad 4, we read that the agent intellect is necessary "to make what is potentially intelligible actually intelligible," and that it is called "light" precisely for this reason. "The light of the agent intellect . . . is the reason for the intelligibility of the species, making them actually intelligible."[68]

[65] *S.T.* I, q. 14, a. 2, corp.; q. 55, a. 1, ad 2; q. 85, a. 2, ad 1, etc.
[66] *III Sent.* dist. 14, q. 1, a. 1, sol. 3, corp.
[67] *De Spir. Creat.* a. 10, ad 6.
[68] *De Ver*, q. 10, a. 8, ad 10.

Thus, the light always appears as that which produces what is actually intelligible. But if an actually intelligible is present, the abstraction is already accomplished. An operation of light on the phantasm which precedes abstraction is improbable because it is difficult to imagine what it would consist in, since it either removes the organic mode of being of the phantasm which, correctly understood, already means abstraction itself, but literally understood is denied by Thomas[69]; or, if the illumination leaves the phantasm as a material, organic structure, it is impossible to see what it could contribute to the abstraction. Hence, if one does not want to assume that in the problematic text, Thomas himself was misled by the plurality of possible formulations of the one thing into overlooking, in this one instance, the fact that his two images ("illuminate" and "abstract") do not mean two different things, then the only possibility that remains is that in this text, Thomas uses the word "illuminate" for something which he expresses otherwise elsewhere: for the information of the sensible by spirit, which spirit lets sensibility emanate from itself as its own power and thus retains it in itself. These things will be spoken of later when we must treat the conversion to the phantasm itself, the origin of sensibility from the intellect, and the cogitative sense. The context of the problematic text points clearly in this direction.

It can already be made clear to some extent at this point that an illumination in the second sense indicated is very closely connected with the illumination we spoke of first. Insofar as abstraction is conceived as taking place by the fact that the sensibly known content is informed by the light of the agent intellect, there is already included in this concept a conversion of the intellect to the phantasm as a turning of the light to what is sensibly known. With that, the abstraction as well as the conversion is already accomplished, and at one time the abstraction as such, that is, the knowledge of the *a priori* form which can be known only as united with the sensible content, and at another time the conversion to the phantasm, that is, the union of

[69] *S.T.* I, q. 85, a. 1, ad 3.

the *a priori* form with the sensible content, whereby it is by that very fact conscious, can each be correctly designated illumination. In the second case, the illumination can be correctly distinguished from the abstraction as following formally from its essence (and only thus!). Even Thomas himself distinguishes between the action according to which the agent intellect makes the species actually intelligible, and the knowing itself as the (formal) effect of this action.[70] We shall have to speak further of all this below.

We return to the question: In what does the actuality of the agent intellect consist, and to what extent does it confer universality upon the sensibly given content when it becomes its actuality? Thomas defines the agent intellect as the *"quo est omnia facere."*[71] Thus the agent intellect, insofar as it is able to make (*facere*) the totality (*omnia*) of possible objects into actually knowable objects by the power of its pure spontaneity (*semper actu*)—although not all at once—contains this totality in itself in a certain way. Therein consists its actuality as actuality in the dimension of knowing. But, on the other hand, it does not already have of itself the totality of possible determinations with itself, for otherwise it would have to be able to present this to the possible intellect by itself alone, without the help of sensibility and its *a posteriori* material.[72] These two affirmations about the actuality of the agent intellect can be harmonized only by the fact that it is the spontaneity of the human spirit, which spontaneity is dynamically ordered to the totality of possible objects[73] and as such already anticipates (*vorwegnimmt*) in its dynamic orientation the totality of all objects according to their most universal metaphysical structure

[70] *De Ver.* q. 8, a. 6, corp.

[71] *S.T.* I, q. 88, a. 1, corp.

[72] *In III de Anima* lect. 10, n. 739; *De Spir. Creat.* a. 10, ad 4; *De Anima* a. 5, ad 6 and ad 9; *S.T.* I, q. 88, a. 1, corp.: *ad ea* (to the *omnia fieri*) *active se extendens.*

[73] The intellect could be called Thomistically *potentia ad actum respectu totius entis universalis,* and in fact *active se extendens,* formulations which appear in *S.T.* I, q. 79, a. 2, corp., and q. 88, a. 1, corp.

(*sub ratione entis*),[74] and yet still needs the determinations of sensibility in order to present an object to the possible intellect at all, and in it these metaphysical structures of the object.

Thus the agent intellect apprehends the individual determination of sensibility (phantasm) in its dynamic ordination to the totality of all possible objects, to *esse,* as we can say on the basis of earlier considerations, and hence it apprehends this determination as being. Insofar as it apprehends this material of sensibility within its anticipatory (*vorwegnehmenden*) dynamism to *esse,* it "illuminates" this material, gives it those metaphysical structures of being which were expressed in the first principles; its actuality becomes that of the actually intelligible, and thus lets the universal be known in the sensible. Thomas meant nothing else when he said that the first thing apprehended through the activity of the agent intellect is being, in which the first principles become illuminated in the light of the agent intellect, whereby something actually intelligible comes to be in which the sensibly given participates in the light of the agent intellect.

Thus from an examination of some individual formulations[75] of the essence and operation of the agent intellect our earlier results are confirmed: the agent intellect is the spontaneous pre-apprehension (*Vorgriff*) of *esse* absolutely, and thereby it is the faculty which apprehends the universal.

Attention is called only incidentally to a line of thought in Thomas whose meaning follows from what has been said so far. If the agent intellect is the highest faculty of man, and if it must be understood as the faculty of the *excessus* to *esse* absolutely, and if in it absolute *esse* is simultaneously affirmed, then as a matter of fact the agent intellect is the metaphysical point at which the finite spirit comes upon his openness to, and his

[74] See *De Ver.* q. 22, a. 12, corp.: *ratio autem agendi est forma agentis per quam agit, unde oportet quod insit agenti ad hoc quod agit,* etc.

[75] If we were striving for completeness, we would have to examine further what Thomas means when he considers the agent intellect as the first cause along with the phantasm as intrumental cause. But such an examination would lead to the same result.

dependence upon, God. And that is true not merely in the general way in which every finite being points to Absolute Being, but in such a way that absolute *esse* is implicitly and simultaneously affirmed (*implicite mitbejaht*) in every act of the agent intellect, in every judgment. For this reason, Thomas can understand the agent intellect in a special way as a participation in the light of Absolute Spirit,[76] not merely because, being dependent on this, it is as a matter of fact similar to it, but because finite spirit is spirit only through the pre-apprehension of absolute *esse* in which Absolute Being is already and always apprehended. "All knowledge is derived from the uncreated light."[77] "All knowing beings know God implicitly in everything they know."[78]

X. ABSTRACTION AS COMPLETE RETURN

In order to see what direction the final consideration of this chapter must take, we must go back briefly in our discussion. Man always finds himself with the world as objectively apprehended. We asked about the conditions of the possibility of such knowledge. The receptive intuition (*hinnehmende Anschauung*) of the other of the world was shown to be possible only in sensibility as an act of matter. Such sensibility, as the being-given of form (of being) to what is other than itself, can indeed then receptively accept the other because it *is* the other, but it cannot make possible an *objective* knowledge because it cannot differentiate itself ontologically from the other. The capacity of the subject to differentiate itself over against the other which is had in sensibility we called thought (*Denken*). This differentiation in thought takes place in an abstraction of the knowledge from the sensibly possessed object, and in a reference of the ab-

[76] Texts in M. Grabmann, *Der göttliche Grund menschlicher Wahrheitserkenntnis nach Augustinus und Thomas von Aquin* (Münster, 1924), pp. 53ff.; Maréchal, *op. cit.*, pp. 322–325.
[77] *De Pot.* q. 5, a. 1, ad 18.
[78] *De Ver.* q. 22, a. 2, ad 1.

stracted knowledge to the other, as the two inseparable moments of the one objective knowledge of the world, and only in this is man present to himself. We called this differentiation in thought of the knowing subject from the known object the "complete return."[1] We said that the complete return takes place in the abstraction. Now, after the conditions of the possibility of abstraction have been shown in the preceding sections, it still remains to examine whether these conditions make the complete return intrinsically intelligible. Once this has been done, so far as it can be done at this point, and thus the essence of the return itself has been understood, then it will be possible to take up the conversion to the phantasm directly, since it is nothing other than the subject, which became free of the world in the complete return, turning to the world.

We will try to clarify the question as to whether in abstraction we have grasped the complete return in its possibility, by asking first of all how Thomas himself understood this return.

1. The Formal Essence of the Complete Return to Self (A Form Subsisting in Itself)

Thomas speaks quite often of a "reflection" of the potencies "upon their act, upon their knowing," of a "return to one's essence through a certain reflecton," of a "reflection" of the potencies "upon themselves," of a "complete return." We will leave out of consideration for the moment whether these expressions intend to say essentially the same thing, or whether they mean essentially different spiritual occurrences. We begin tentatively with a still vague understanding of these expressions: the intellect, of which all these expressions are affirmed, is somehow or other present to itself through this return, it knows its act as distinct from its object, it grasps itself as acting and thus itself as distinct from its known object. We will leave out of consideration for the moment whether such an occurrence is

[1] The expression follows *In Lib. de Causis* lect. 15 (Parma XXI, 742–743) (this is the source for Thomas); *De Ver.* q. 1, a. 9, corp.; q. 10, a. 9, corp.

227

meant as a characteristic of every spiritual act, or only of an explicitly reflexive act.

Thomas traces the possibility of such reflection back to the immateriality of the reflexive principle.[2] It is important first of all to understand this statement. Why does materiality prevent reflection? In connection with this statement, Thomas calls be-ing-material a "being given over to another," a "being depen-dent on matter,"[3] a "being poured out over matter."[4] Thus this is put forward as the ground of the not-being-present-to-self (of the "not-knowing-itself," of the "not-returning-to-self," etc.). Just from these formulations alone it can be seen that the ground of the impossibility of a reflexive presence-to-self is only the ontological expression of what is grounded: something is not present to itself in knowledge because ontologically it is with the "other" ("given over to the other"). Thus the reason offered is not the better known, the self-evident, but that which first discloses itself in what is to be explained. Prime matter in the strict metaphysical sense—that is what is in question here, not the common concept of "matter" in the sense of physics—is that "other" in which being (form), which in itself expresses presence-to-self, can lose itself ("be poured out") to such an extent that the form is present to itself only as with the other (sensibility), or exists at all only as the form of the other, mere "matter." A being which is ontologically present to itself is by that very fact present to itself in knowledge, so that it is deter-mined precisely from this what being is, and the intrinsic variation of being is shown in the intrinsic variation of being-present-to-self: "To return to one's essence [in knowledge] is nothing else than for a thing to subsist in itself. . . . The form, insofar as it has *esse* in itself, returns to itself."[5] Thus we have

[2] *S.C.G.* IV, 11; *S.T.* I, q. 14, a. 2, ad 1; q. 87, a. 3, ad 3; *I Sent.* dist. 17, q. 1, a. 5, ad 3; *De Ver.* q. 22, a. 12, corp.

[3] *I Sent.* dist. 17, q. 1, a. 5, ad 3; *II Sent.* dist. 19, q. 1, a. 1, corp.: *essentia fixa stans non super aliud delata.*

[4] *S.T.* I, q. 14, a. 2, ad 1. See q. 76, a. 1, corp. ("*immergi*" of the form in matter); *S.C.G.* II, 68.

[5] *S.T.* I, q. 14, a. 2, ad 1.

come again to the first metaphysical presupposition with which the first chapter of our second part began.

If in general it is also intelligible now what Thomas means by the statement that a material being does not come to itself, and that an immaterial being is essentially present to itself, nevertheless, we have not yet grasped the specific mode of man's complete return. For Thomas, human knowledge means a complete return, but essentially in such a way that this coming-to-oneself (*Zu-sich-selbst-kommen*) is a coming-from-another (*Von-einem-andern-herkommen*), to which mode of being-present-to-self the image of a return (*reditio*) is most suitable: "The intellect reflects upon itself and is able to know itself [this statement refers to immaterial being in general]. But there are different degrees of intellectual life, for the human intellect, although it can know itself [although the complete return of spiritual being belongs to it essentially], nevertheless, it takes the first beginnings of its knowledge from without [its being-present-to-self is a coming-from-another], because it cannot know without a phantasm [because its being-present-to-self is essentially based upon sensibility as being-with-the-other]"[6]; in other words, since it is a "proceeding from without," not a "*per se cognoscere seipsum*" ["self-apprehension-through-itself"].[7] Hence, man's being-present-to-himself comes from sensibility, is possible only in and through the fact that he knows the other. But how is it possible at all then? Receptive being-with-the-other means sensibility, and it is essentially impossible for sensibility to differentiate itself from this other. Even if we assume a "faculty" of self-possession different from sensibility (thought [*Denken*], spirit [*Geist*]) even if we assume (and this will be taken up later) that these two faculties are understood in the unity of their origin and cooperation, the possibility of a return to oneself from sensibility as the permanent "whence" of this coming-to-self is still not yet clarified.

For a complete return to be grasped as possible in its univer-

[6] *S.C.G.* IV, 11.
[7] *Ibid.*

sal, formal essence, which still prescinds from the specifically human form of the return, the being that is present to itself must be immaterial, it must subsist in itself. This is also true, correspondingly, of the human return to self. "The soul . . . a form subsisting in itself."[8]

2. The Complete Return Specific to Man
(The Return in a Conversion to the Phantasm)

But that still does not yet grasp the specifically human return metaphysically; on the contrary, to ascribe an *esse* subsisting in itself to the soul seems to eliminate such a return: to be present to self in knowledge should mean ontologically subsisting in itself, but then such an ontological being-present-to-self seems by strict conceptual necessity no longer able to be with the other, even if it would have been ontologically the form of the other, if a "being given over to another," a "being poured out over matter" would have belonged to it, and thus if it would have been with the other through sense knowledge. Thus the return to oneself seems conceivable only in a separative withdrawal from matter, only in a flight which perhaps originates from sensibility, but does not remain in it permanently, but rather leaves it, so that sensibility would not remain the sustaining ground of the possibility of the return, even if we presuppose them to be simultaneously possible in the same subject. The complete return would not be in itself a permanent "proceeding from without." Assuming that in its return the subject brings its knowledge from the other along with it, "abstracts" it, as it were, from sensibility which is posited as necessary in order to receive this knowledge originally, assuming further that this bringing-along is the condition of the possibility of the return, then is the specifically human mode of being-present-to-oneself made intelligible as a permanent coming from sensibility? Obviously it is, under two conditions.

    1. It must be intelligible how such a knowledge can be ab-

[8] *S.T.* I, q. 51, a. 1, corp.; q. 75, a. 2, corp.; a. 6, corp. etc.

stracted. This bringing-along knowledge in the return of the subject to itself is the first presupposition of the fact that the being-present-to-self is a "proceeding from something external." For otherwise the subject would fall back into unconsciousness, or it would apprehend itself and determinations in itself independently of its sense knowledge. There would be question of a being-present-to-oneself which would not be being-present-to-self over against another, would not be a *return*. Therefore the subject must experience itself as knowing something of another. But that means: it must "abstract," or more exactly: it must be something immaterial subsisting in itself and come to consciousness of its essence (that is, to being-present-to-self) in that it knows a universal ("something") of something material (of another). What is fundamental for the possibility of abstraction as such has already been discussed. If this is presupposed as taking place in something subsisting in itself (in which alone it can take place), then the first condition is fulfilled under which a being-present-to-oneself can be conceived as a permanent returning from sensibility.

2. It must become intelligible how this "abstracted" knowledge of the other brought along, as it were, in the return reveals itself as "form," as determination of the other, and thus discloses its origin in sensibility. That is the presupposition of the fact that the subject can experience himself as knowing something of *another*. This is a condition which was already contained somehow in the first. But there the emphasis and hence the proof of the possibility was upon the "something" which is known of another. Here it is a question of knowing the known something as precisely the "what" of *another*. It cannot be said that this question is already settled by the fact that the other as such is had concretely in sensibility. For sensibility does not know itself *as* different from the other. Spirit knows itself, and as human spirit it knows itself as knowing another. Hence spirit itself as such must know the other. How that is possible is a question which is made difficult precisely by understanding being as being-present-to-self.

For even assuming that the human spirit is "determined" by sensibility, that is, is brought to that level of the intensity of being to which a being-present-to-self necessarily belongs of itself, then perhaps it would be intelligible how the ontologically elevating determination (form) received passively from sensibility would be conscious, but not how the other as such is revealed in its own self through it, for this form would be conscious as what it is, as a determination of the conscious subject itself present to itself. Thomas is aware of this problematic: knowing and known are the same. The determination by which something becomes a knower is ontologically a determination of the knower. But this determination is supposed to manifest itself as a determination of the known insofar as the known is differentiated from the knower. This problem of the transcendence of knowing is not a problem of sensibility. Things can manifest themselves to sensibility of themselves, and it can be said here without hesitation that "the sensible in act is the sense in act."[9] With the ontological level of sensibility (sense in act), the apprehension of the sensible (sensible in act) is given necessarily. For this level of being is always a "being given over to another," an ontic being-with-the-other. It is otherwise with spirit: spirit subsists in itself. How can it still hold here that "the intelligible in act is the intellect in act,"[10] when this intelligible is not supposed to be the knower himself, but the other distinct from him? Still, we must settle this question if we are to understand the complete return in its specifically human mode.

Thomas says at one point: "Non-knowing beings have nothing except their own form; but a knowing being is such that it also has the form of another. For the species of the known is in the knower."[11] The first sentence is clear. But the "For" of the second sentence is problematic. Why does the species ground the possibility of apprehending the form of the other *as* that of the other? For, Thomistically, the species is not the known as such, but the ontological determination of the knower himself which is

[9] *S.T.* I, q. 14, a. 2, corp.
[10] *Ibid.*
[11] *S.T.* I, q. 14, a. 1, corp.

232

antecedent to the knowledge as its ground.[12] Hence if the species makes the one who is to know really a knower, then it seems to be able to be known only as the ontological determination of the knower himself. Thomas himself draws this conclusion: "The species . . . of the known thing in act is the species of the intellect itself [it is the ontological and conscious determination of the intellect itself] and so, through it, it is able to know itself."[13] In contrast to the "For" mentioned, this "and so" is perfectly clear, given its Thomistic presuppositions.[14] But why, then, does not the following statement hold here as well: "For, what appears within will prevent the knowledge of something external, and it will obstruct, that is, impede the intellect, and in a certain way it will veil it and prevent it from seeing others."[15] As ontological actuality of the intellect itself, the species brings it about that the intellect has "a certain determined nature," as it were, so that "that nature, connatural to itself, prevents it from knowing other natures."[16] The fact that the species depends causally, at least mediately and partially, on an external influence explains nothing. For nothing justifies our explaining that the object, which, precisely as "phenomenal," is already and always ap-

[12] See *De Ver.* q. 1, a. 1, corp.: the ontological *assimilatio* (through the species) to the object is the foundation of knowledge. Likewise, *S.T.* I, q. 54, a. 1, ad 3. For the fact that the *assimilatio* comes about through the "species": *I Sent.* dist. 3, q. 1, a. 1, obj. 3 and ad 3. Cf. Maréchal, *op. cit.*, pp. 63–65; 254f. For the species, see further: *S.T.* I, q. 14, a. 2, corp.; q. 56, a. 1, corp.; q. 88, a. 1, ad 2: the *similitudo rei cognitae* must be *quasi quaedam forma ipsius cognoscentis.*

[13] *In III de Anima* lect. 9, n. 724.

[14] *De Spir. Creat.* a. 8, ad 14: *intellectus in actu est intellectum in actu inquantum informatur per speciem intelligibilem. Ibid.: in his quae sunt sine materia* (what the soul is insofar as it knows intellectually) *idem est intellectus et quod intelligitur.* And on the other side: *S.C.G.* II, 98: *Intellectus igitur possibilis noster non cognoscit seipsum nisi per speciem intelligibilem qua fit actu in esse intelligibili.* It is clear: one and the same ontological actuality (species) is supposed to cause the presence of the spirit to itself and to reveal the object standing over against the spirit.

[15] *In III de Anima* lect. 7, n. 680.

[16] Notice that even in the example introduced by Thomas there is question only of an accidental change in the subject, and this makes knowledge of the other impossible.

prehended as other, is disclosed as other by a causal inference. The species is conscious as an ontological actuality of the subject and thus manifests nothing of its causal dependence on the external thing,[17] prescinding completely from the fact that the species of the intellect as such, as opposed to sensibility, is a product of the agent intellect alone.

On the basis of this problematic one thing can be said first of all: if the ontological actuality of the species (as a spiritual, ontological actuality in the strictest sense) is to be the presence-to-self of the spirit and the manifest determination of the object set over against the spirit, that is conceivable from the outset only insofar as the species contains and manifests determinations which can belong to the spirit and the object in common. Determinations of something material as such (of a qualitative and quantitative kind), which can belong ontologically only to a material being, cannot as such enter into the intelligible species strictly as such. Otherwise they would also have to be able to become determinations of the spirit ontologically. They are sensibly known by the one sentient-spiritual knowing as such. Thus we have come again to the conception of the intelligible species which we have already come upon quite often.

Of course it does not follow from this that a purely spiritual knowing cannot know something material. But it does follow that a material being is only knowable either by the fact that through its own form it is known receptively as first-known through *sensibility,* or, where no sensibility is possible, by being apprehended by a creative knowledge in and at its creative ground itself. When Thomas speaks of an intelligible species which is produced by the agent intellect, that is usually a term which also includes what is given and simultaneously understood in sensibility, precisely insofar as it is apprehended under the light of the agent intellect. This takes care of explaining some Thomistic texts in which a too narrow interpretation could see a difficulty against our explanation of what a determination of the

---

[17] *Illud quod intelligitur, non est ut passum sed ut principium actionis* holds here also. See *De Ver.* q. 8, a. 6, ad 8 and corp.; a. 7 ad 2 (second series); ad 2 (first series).

234

intellect as such is in the strictest sense, that is, what the intelligible species is in the narrowest sense. This inclusion of the content given only sensibly within the properly ontological determination of the intellect (which therefore taken strictly can also be known "intelligibly" by itself) in the one complex concept "intelligible species" in a somewhat broader sense is therefore completely justified and appropriate, since the "intelligible" in the narrowest sense is only conscious in the apprehension of what is sensibly given.

With this distinction between the intelligible in the strictest sense and the sensible content remaining in sensibility, the problem only seems to become still more complicated: we have the sensibly known content in sensibility on the one hand, and the (presupposed for the moment) conscious ontological actuality of the spirit on the other. This ontological actuality of the spirit (intelligible species in the narrowest sense) should allow nothing to be intellectually conscious except what can reveal the structure of the knower and the known object at once. With this presupposition, the intelligible species *can* reveal the structure of the object insofar as subject and object ontically correspond in it. But to what extent does the intelligible species of the spirit, which is its ontological determination, *actually* manifest itself as the structure of the sensibly given? In the Thomistic formulation: wherein lies the possibility that the light of the agent intellect, which is the spirit itself, is seen only insofar as it is as a matter of fact participated in by the sensibly known quiddity, and indeed in such a way that this quiddity itself remains in its sensible givenness?

Let us presuppose for a moment that this question is answered. Is the return then grasped in its possibility? Certainly. The soul is apprehended as subsisting in itself. As such it is present to itself, supposing only that it is with anything at all. Insofar as it is with something only as a sentient knower, it is present to self only over against another, only thus does it accomplish a return to itself in the proper sense. The only thing presupposed is that it comes to itself from sensibility in such a way that its sense knowledge is the permanent condition of its being-present-to-itself. But this can only take place in such a way that it knows the sensibly given intellectually. Insofar as its knowing is its being, the question remains, how its known ontological determination can and must appear as that of what is sensibly known. We have come again to the question which we just faced.

But actually this question is none other than the question about the conversion to the phantasm. The statement, something is known only in a turning to the sensibly given, says (if a double, identical knowledge is not to be set up in sensibility and understanding, which would make the proposition meaningless from the outset): what is in the proper and strict sense intellectually known is known only insofar as it is apprehended in the sensibly known and as true of it. But how that is to be grasped in its possibility was precisely the question into which the consideration of the possibility of a human complete return forced us. Thus the problem of abstraction becomes necessarily the problem of the conversion to the phantasm, and thus, vice versa, abstraction shows itself to be a necessary, intrinsic moment in the conversion to the phantasm. Hence it is clear that the investigation of the third chapter is an integral component of *the* question which is now to be taken up under its own name, and which therefore always presupposes the results of the third chapter, the question about the conversion to the phantasm.

CHAPTER FOUR

CONVERSION TO
THE PHANTASM

I. DEFINING THE QUESTION

THERE is question first of all of reviewing our considerations so far in order to establish unambiguously what we are asking about when we speak of the conversion to the phantasm. The phantasm cannot be considered a "thing." It is the keyword designating sense knowledge as such. When, therefore, it is asserted in the proposition about the conversion to the phantasm that human intellectual knowledge takes place essentially in a turning to the phantasm, this says that intellectual knowledge is possible only with a simultaneous realization of sense knowledge. But from this simple consideration it follows: the proposition about the conversion becomes senseless from the outset if it is understood as the assertion of a necessary union of two knowledges identical in content on different levels. Not only—and this is clear of itself from earlier considerations —must intellectual knowledge as such accomplish something which is essentially impossible to sense knowledge as such, but also the matter cannot be imagined as though, in the intellectual knowledge as such, the whole content of the sense knowledge is repeated on another level with the addition of that content which is inaccessible to sense knowledge. For if the content of the sense knowledge itself were repeated on the level of thought, it would be impossible to see what meaning a conversion to the sense knowledge could still have for this intellectual knowledge as such, nor why and how knowledge identical in content would be given twice in the same consciousness.

Hence conversion to the phantasm does not mean intellectual knowledge "accompanied by phantasms" (which after all are not things, but a content of the one human consciousness to which thought also belongs), but is the term designating the fact that sense intuition and intellectual thought are united in the *one* human knowledge. It is for this reason that in the preceding sections the conversion did not show itself to be a process following the complete return (and hence the abstraction), but an essential moment in it. Being-present-to-oneself and abstraction are intrinsically and essentially a knowing-something-of-another, and therefore are already themselves a conversion to the phantasm.

Therefore, it is not surprising that actually we were already speaking of the conversion to the phantasm quite frequently in the course of the chapter on abstraction: we spoke of the concretion, of the knowledge of the known intelligibility as a "what" in a something, of the return from sensibility, of the illumination of the phantasm, of seeing the light of the agent intellect in the species (in the broader sense), of the *modus significandi:* all just so many concepts which already include the conversion to the phantasm in themselves.

Just from this it follows that in this chapter our task cannot be that of proving that the conversion to the phantasm is a factual characteristic of human knowledge. It has already been affirmed as such in the initial decision about the place from which Thomas asks at all about the essence of human knowledge; it has already been simultaneously affirmed in all the considerations of the preceding chapter. Rather what we must do is grasp it in its *possibility*. In this respect what has gone before has left a place for this question, and it is from what has gone before that we must discover what still remains to be asked.

The last two chapters proceeded in such a way that the ontological constitution of man was disclosed in certain characteristics of human knowledge. From the question, What are the conditions of a receptive, intuitive knowledge?, we arrived at the essence of sensibility, and thereby, at the essence of man as a sentient knower: act of matter, form of a body. From the insight into the possibility of a judgmental, universal knowledge attaining to the in-itself (*Ansich*) of the object differentiated from the subject, we arrived at the essence of thought, and thereby, at the essence of man as spirit: *excessus* to *esse* absolutely; a form subsisting in itself.

But this shows the ontological constitution of man, which manifests itself in his knowledge as the possibility of this knowledge, in a peculiar duality which almost seems contradictory: man is at once "subsisting in himself" and "actuality of the other [of matter]." Thus the question follows necessarily: How is this duality of determinations in the ontological constitution of man to be grasped from a more original unity without the duality being eliminated? Conversion to the phantasm is the expression designating the essential unity of the one human knowledge, and therefore, it requires that the unity of this knowing be grasped from the unity of the ontological constitution of man as its origin, for only then can it be grasped itself.

This original unity of man's being as the ground of his one knowledge cannot be meant, as is obvious, as that which is self-evident, as that which is already known in itself, independently of its unifying function. It must manifest itself in the very thing which is to be unified, not as a subsequent bond, but as the one essence unified in itself which, in order to come to itself, lets what is distinct from itself come forth from itself, and which therefore also holds together in unity that which is distinct as the fulfillment of its own essence: the essence of man unifying itself into its own unity (*sich zu seiner Einheit selbst einigendes Wesen*).

239

From the fact that the pre-apprehension of absolute *esse,* which takes place in the judgment, has already and always surmounted the horizon of space and time, although only in a pre-apprehension (*Vorgriff*), it follows that "spirit" (*Geist*) in man, however much it would be blind without the intuition of sensibility, is the more original element in man, and that the one unifying knowledge and the one unifying being of man are more originally defined by what we call "thought" (*Denken*) in the one human knowledge. Therefore, it will be our task to grasp the plurality and unity of man's cognitive powers in the light of the original essence of precisely human intellectuality. If in the preceding chapter, agent intellect was the Thomistic term under which we had to look for that which enables us to grasp human knowledge as spiritual, so too, *possible intellect* will be the key word which enables us to grasp this spirit as *human,* and to do this precisely in such a way that the nature of human knowledge as a whole follows from it. Beginning in this way with the possible intellect, sensibility will have to be shown to be *its* power, through which, as its own and as different from itself, the human spirit is what it has to be. But this will mean that we shall have also grasped the possibility and the necessity of the conversion to the phantasm.

If, then, sensibility must be able to be experienced as the faculty of specifically human spirituality, this fact must manifest itself in sensibility itself. The human spirit releases sensibility from itself in such a way that it has already and always gathered it in again also, and this in such a way that sensibility accomplishes its own work as that of the spirit. Insofar as the spirit releases sensibility from itself as a faculty for itself, the spirit appears alongside sensibility, as it were, as a power different from and coordinate with it, and having its own function which, subsequently, so to speak, converges with the function of sensibility in the one human knowledge. This unified center of spirit and sensibility as coordinate powers which, insofar as this center as such also belongs to sensibility, is an indication of the origin of sensibility from the spirit, since it is an indication of the original unity, is treated by Thomas under the heading of the cogitative sense. If the possibility and necessity of the conversion to the phantasm must follow from the nature of the possible intellect, then the cogitative sense as the unified center of thought and sensibility is nothing other than the realization [*Vollzug*] of the conversion. This indicates in a preliminary way the two key words ("possible intellect" and "cogitative sense") under which the theme of this chapter is to be found in Thomas.

II. THE POSSIBLE INTELLECT

A dual series of statements about the possible intellect follows just from the term itself. It is *intellect:* it has already been determined in two respects what intellect is intended to express in Thomas. And each of these respects discloses, in a fundamental dimension of human *knowing,* an essential characteristic of human *being,* and both characteristics are mutually the condition of their respective possibility, and so ultimately constitute only one determination of human being and knowing. Human knowing is realized (*vollzieht sich*) in a complete return, and so is the act of a form subsisting in itself. Human knowing is the judgmental affirmation of a universal about something, and thus shows itself to be sustained and made possible by the pre-apprehension of *esse* absolutely, wherein we found the decisive characteristic of the agent intellect in its ontological constitution. Now a brief consideration of the relationship between the agent and possible intellect in Thomas shows that in this Thomistic characterization of human knowing, the essence of the possible intellect as intellect is grasped simultaneously. For however much Thomas maintains the real distinction between the agent and possible intellect,[1] just as

[1] In *S.T.* I, q. 79, a. 4, ad 4; a. 7, corp.; *S.C.G.* II, 77; *In III de Anima* lect. 10, n. 732; *De Spir. Creat.* a. 9, corp., at the beginning; a. 10 ad 4; *De Anima* a. 3, ad 18; a. 4, ad 8, etc., the objective distinction is always clearly presupposed. It is expressed explicitly in: *S.T.* I, q. 79, a. 10, corp.; *II Sent.* dist. 17, q. 2, a. 1, corp.; *Compend. Theol.* c. 83;

241

much do they form for him, as essentially complementary moments of the one knowing, a unity of such a kind that in the
characteristics of the one the ontological structure of the other
is revealed. The one knowing follows from both functions.[2]
Hence they are essentially complementary faculties which in
their essence, prescinding from spontaneity and receptivity respectively, are of the same kind. If, then, the agent intellect is the
spontaneous, dynamic ordination of the human spirit to *esse*
absolutely, the "*quo est omnia facere*," then the possible intellect
as intellect is the potentiality of the human spirit to comprehend
esse absolutely in receptive (*hinnehmender*) knowledge, the "*quo
est omnia fieri*."[3] The receptive (*empfangende*) breadth of the
possible intellect is the same as the apprehensive (*zugreifende*)
breadth of the agent intellect.[4] The metaphysical essence of the
possible intellect is also grasped simultaneously in what was
said about the agent intellect: the breadth of its receptivity is
not what is intrinsically spatio-temporal, being as the principle
of number, but *esse* absolutely, the *esse* which is negatively and
in every direction unlimited in itself. "The intellect considers its
object according to the common notion of being because the
possible intellect is that by which it is to become all things."[5]

The possible intellect is *possible*. It is not until this statement
is made that spirituality is apprehended for the first time precisely in its human peculiarity. The "potentiality" of the spirit in
man says not merely that the spirit can be understood, like
every finite cognitive faculty, as ontologically antecedent to
the actual realization of knowledge. That this is not the full
sense of the Thomistic statement follows just from the fact that

88. For the real distinction between an active and passive principle, see,
for example, *In IX Metaph.* lect. 1, n. 1781ff.

[2] *De Anima* a. 4, ad 8; *De Spir. Creat.* a. 10, ad 15.

[3] *S.T.* I, q. 88, a. 1, corp.; *In VI Ethic.* lect. 1, n. 1119; *In III de
Anima* lect. 10, n. 728.

[4] *S.T.* I, q. 88, a. 1, corp.: *intellectus agens . . . ad eadem se active
extendens ad quae se extendit intellectus possibilis receptive.*

[5] *S.T.* I, q. 79, a. 7, corp.; see also I, q. 5, a. 2, corp.; q. 79, a. 9, ad
3; q. 82, a. 4, ad 1, etc.

Thomas does not allow such a potentiality to be given in a finite, intuitive intelligence (an angel). An "angel" has no possible intellect.[6] Finite, intellectual, intuitive knowledge cannot be called possible intellect because such a being is of itself present to itself, and does not first come to itself through the reception of another manifesting itself. "The intellect . . . of an angel, because it has an essence which is as act in the genus of intelligibles, an essence present to itself, is able to know that which is intelligible in it, namely, its own essence, not through some likeness, but through itself."[7]

In this text, Thomas gives this metaphysics of a finite, intuitive intelligence as contrasted precisely with the possible intellect. It contains in brief everything that Thomas has to say on this limit-idea (*Grenzidee*) of our human spirit. An intuitive intellectuality is ontologically "being only as present to itself [an essence . . . present to itself]," for it is absolutely without the *other* of matter.[8] But on the basis of his conception of the relationship between being and knowing, it necessarily follows for Thomas that such a being is present to itself in knowledge simply because it is ontologically present to itself. Therefore, in contrast to human knowledge, the first object of the knowledge of an angel is its own essence, and through this it knows everything else.[9] Consequently, such intuitive intellectuality is not receptive, for its "object" is its own being, hence this latter does not "encounter" it, it does not have to manifest itself to the intellect from itself, it has no possibility of hiding itself from it.

In the light of this it becomes intelligible what possible intellect *qua* possible means. It is being, that is to say, being-present-to-oneself, complete return, but it is not of itself already and

[6] *S.T.* I, q. 54, a. 4; *S.C.G.* II, 96. These go beyond the conception of the question in *II Sent.* dist. 3, q. 3, a. 4, ad 4.

[7] *De Ver.* q. 8, a. 6, corp.

[8] See *S.T.* I, q. 50, a. 2; *II Sent.* dist. 3, q. 1, a. 1, corp.; *S.C.G.* II, 50; 51; 91.

[9] *S.T.* I, q. 12, a. 4, corp.; q. 84, a. 7, corp.; q. 85, a. 1, corp.; q. 87, a. 1, corp.; *De Ver.* q. 8, a. 3, corp.; *De Malo* q. 16, a. 12, ad 4.

always present to itself. By itself it cannot give itself immediately to itself; it comes to itself only insofar as it receptively allows another to encounter it, and without this receptive letting-self-be-encountered by another it is itself not present to itself. "An angel knows itself through its own essence . . . but the human intellect is in the genus of intelligible things only as a being in potency . . . wherefore, it is called possible. Therefore, considered in its essence it is potentially able to know. Wherefore, of itself it has the power to know [to experience something receptively], but not to be known [to be present to itself], except through that by which it becomes actual [except by the fact that it comes from the sensible with which it has become one in sensibility]."[10] The "only potentially intelligible" must be understood correctly. It is not the potential intelligibility of the sensible. For the sensible by itself never has in itself the possibility of a complete return. Here, the potential intelligibility is supposed to distinguish the human spirit only from intuitive, intellectual knowledge, not from sensibility. Its differentiation from the latter is already in the word intellect. It is already implied in this word that there is no question of a being and a knowing that arises by the fact that a being (form) loses itself completely in the other of matter and thus as such never comes to itself in principle.

So the possible intellect as possible comes to exist at the mid-point between a separated form and a form whose ontological actuality exhausts itself in the determination of matter, and this mid-point is ontologically definable only by being distinguished from these two extremes. Indeed the essence of the possible intellect can be defined relatively simply from the way that it knows: it is that being which is present to itself in the knowledge of another. But as soon as this definition is to be "translated" into ontological terms, it can be discovered only as the mid-point between two different definitions: in its being-present-to-itself the possible intellect is a form subsisting in itself[11]; in

[10] S.T. I, q. 87, a. 1, corp.
[11] S.T. I, q. 75, a. 2, corp.; a. 6, corp., etc. Thomas even calls the soul *separata: S.T.* I, q. 76, a. 1, ad 1.

its drive (*Zwang*) to let itself be encountered by another it is sensibility: form of matter, form of a body.[12] Only in this duality, in which both definitions mutually and intrinsically modify each other, is the possible intellect grasped ontologically.[13] Insofar as the drive to let itself be encountered by another, in order to be present to itself, is derived from the fact that the intellect indeed really is intellect, that is, the intellect is able to be present to itself, but it is not present to itself through its mere existence (*Dasein*)—which is precisely what is said by the term possible intellect—, *possible intellect is the most adequate and most simple conception for human knowledge and for human being altogether.*

This also enables us to understand the sense of other formulations by which Thomas tries to grasp the specific nature of human being and knowing: "the soul is the lowest in the genus of beings which know and are known."[14] The soul is essentially the lowest conceivable possibility of intellectual being, since it is understood as a being that is really able to come to itself, but of itself alone it is not present to itself. To that extent, and only to that extent, Thomas compares it with prime matter[15] and calls it a "clean slate."[16] Not as though, like prime matter, it were completely indeterminate in itself and received every determination only from another and absolutely passively. It really apprehends itself in every act of knowing, and what is really intelligible is its own light which it imparts to its objects actively and spontaneously, so that all of this is not given to it from

[12] *S.T.* I, q. 76, a. 1, corp., etc.
[13] For this, see *ST.* I, q. 76, a. 3; *De Ver.* q. 16, a. 1, ad 13: *et per essentiam suam (anima) spiritus est et per essentiam suam forma corporis est et non per aliquid superadditum.* See also *De Spir. Creat.* a. 2, corp., where it becomes clear that Thomas was aware of the problematic of this dual statement (*difficultas quaestionis*): *praedicta (formasubstantia spiritualis) coniungantur.*
[14] *S.T.* I, q. 51, a. 1, corp.; q. 75, a. 7, ad 3; q. 77, a. 2, corp.; q. 79, a. 2, corp.; q. 89, a. 1, corp.
[15] *De Anima* a. 8, corp.
[16] *Ibid.*

245

without. But nevertheless it apprehends all of this only insofar as a sensible object of itself manifests itself to it, and must manifest itself, for the intellect of itself is only in potency to apprehend itself: it is possible intellect.

III. THE (POSSIBLE) INTELLECT AS THE ORIGIN OF SENSIBILITY

For a correct understanding of what follows a preliminary remark is necessary. Lest our further considerations be burdened with questions which do not belong here with absolute necessity, in its presentation the following section consciously simplifies the Thomistic train of thought. Thomas distinguishes the substantial, essential ground of human knowing from the cognitive faculty in the proper sense, from the (possible) intellect in the strictest sense.[1] From that there follows for Thomas the necessity of clarifying the relationship of the essence of the soul to its potencies.[2] With a reference to Siewerth, these questions can be left aside here. Therefore, when we speak of the possible intellect in what follows, it is meant as a totality in which the substantial ground lets the intellect (possible and agent) flow from itself as its potency—"it flows from the essence of the soul as from a principle"—, and keeps it with itself as its perfection—"it is received as in a subject."[3] We are only asking about the relationship of the (possible) intellect, understood in this broader sense, to sensibility. Thomas himself refers to such a conception of the (possible) intellect: according to him, the intellect can be considered not only "as a certain potency," but also "insofar as this potency is rooted in the essence of the soul."[4]

[1] *S.T.* I, q. 79, a. 1, and parallels. Likewise, q. 77, a. 1, and the parallels posing the question more generally.
[2] *S.T.* I, q. 77, a. 6, and parallels. Cf. Siewerth, *op. cit.*, pp. 22–31.
[3] The terms are in *S.T.* I, q. 77, a. 6, corp.
[4] III Sent. dist. 15, q. 2, a. 3, sol. 2, ad 2.

1. The Fundamental Structure of the Sensibilization (Versinnlichung) of the Possible Intellect

The (possible) intellect is a spirit which of itself exists in potency to be actually present to itself. In virtue of its being, it must of itself place itself in the possibility by which it is enabled to come to itself. Insofar as this essentially does not happen by the fact that it is already of itself always present to itself, this coming-to-itself (*Zu-sich-selber-Kommen*) is possible only by the fact that it comes to itself in the receptive letting-itself-be-encountered (*hinnehmenden Sichbegegnenlassen*) by another as what is immediately and first apprehended. Therefore, in virtue of its being, the (possible) intellect must of itself create the possibility that another can encounter it objectively as its first-known.

Now the first section of the second chapter has shown that a knowledge which receptively accepts what is other than itself as its first and immediately (hence intuitively) apprehended object is essentially sensibility, is conceivable only as the act of matter.

Consequently, it follows from this that the possible intellect can establish itself in the real possibility of being spirit only by becoming sensibility. Since, on the other hand, the possibility of a complete return, wherein lies the essence of being-spirit, essentially requires that the intellect as returning to itself be not sensible, but free from matter, subsisting in itself, this becoming-sentient (*Sinnlichwerden*) of the (possible) intellect can only be understood in such a way that it lets sensibility emanate (*Entspringen*) from itself as its power, without losing itself completely in it; hence in such wise that it keeps with itself the sensibility emanating from itself, as indeed its own power, but subordinate to itself, while it itself appears as a non-sentient power alongside of sensibility and acts as such. Thus the (possible) intellect appears as the origin of sensibility in such a way that it is a power in its own right alongside of it, but sensibility, since it emanates from the possible intellect and thus is its actuality, is the already realized (*schon vollzogene*) turning of the intellect itself to the other, is conversion to the phantasm.

247

2. The Necessity of the Sensibilization
in Accordance with the Specific Nature of Human Spirit
(The Problematic of the Body-Soul Relationship)

We must show that this line of thought is Thomistic.
Nothing more is to be said here about sensibility as a single
potency for an intuitive, receptive knowledge of another. We
will only refer to a short text as something of a random sample
which shows precisely in its incidental nature how self-evident
this conception was for Thomas. *De Anima* a. 20, ad 6, deals
with the solution of a difficulty against the thesis that an angel
or an incorporeal soul can know the material individual. The
presupposition of the difficulty and of the answer is that we are
dealing with an intellectuality which does not possess sensibility.
The difficulty urges that an intellectual determination of a pure
intellect (a species) cannot let an individual, material "this" as
such be known. The solution of the difficulty does not concern
us very much here.[5] What is important in this connection is
what Thomas concedes to the objection: a knowledge of a
purely intellectual kind would be essentially unable to apprehend the individual if it were to receive this latter from without
and would have to let itself be determined by it: "if the species
were received from things, they would not be able to be the
proper intelligibility of the individuals from which they are
abstracted."

Now it is clear that a receptive knowledge necessarily knows
an individual, since everything exists as concrete. Consequently,
there is no receptive knowledge for Thomas ("receiving species
from things") which does not essentially include sensibility.
Corresponding to this, it also says: "The intelligible species is
not received from the thing except through the mediation of
the phantasm"[6]—in other words, receptive knowledge is essentially sentient. The sentence just cited is perhaps the briefest
expression of the metaphysical concept of sensibility in Thomas.

[5] It tries to solve the difficulty through an immediate participation in
the creative knowledge of God.
[6] *II Sent.* dist. 3, q. 3, a. 1, ad 2.

For him, "not to receive knowledge from things" and "to know without the investigation of reason and without any admixture of *sense*" are the same.[7] When a knowledge is not receptive because there is no sensibility, the knowledge must be creative, or must participate in a creative knowledge as such. For this reason it is said of angels that "they do not acquire knowledge from things, but have a quasi active knowledge, and so do not need a sensitive soul."[8] Therefore, an intellect which is not already of itself present to itself must necessarily let a sensibility emanate from itself in order to possess it as its own power.[9] Thomas treats this origin of sensibility from intellect explicitly under two headings, first in the question of the relationship between body and soul (and this again in a dual framework: whether the intellective principle is united to the body as a form,[10] and whether the intellective soul is appropriately united to such a body[11]), and then in the question of the origin of one potency from another.[12] We will bring in what is important in our context from both of these questions, which of course overlap.

Although Thomas usually approaches the substantial unity of body and soul, the spiritual soul as the form of matter, from the fact that the one man meets us as the subject of spiritual and sensible activity, even in this question the line of thought which concerns us here is not missing. In this question, Thomas already understands sensibility to be required by the specifically human mode of the spiritual. "But because our human soul's knowing [of the specific kind we have already described] needs powers which operate through certain corporeal organs, namely, the imagination and the senses, this very fact means that it is naturally united with the body for man to be complete."[13] It is

---

[7] *II Sent.* dist. 3, q. 3, a. 4, ad 1.
[8] *II Sent.* dist. 14, q. 1, a. 3, ad 3.
[9] A similar development as in *De Anima* a. 20,, ad 6, could be carried out with *Quodl.* 7, a. 3, corp., where it is treated in more detail.
[10] For example, *S.T.* I, q. 76, a. 1, and parallels.
[11] For example, *S.T.* I, q. 76, a. 5, and parallels.
[12] *S.T.* I, q. 77, a. 7, and parallels.
[13] *S.C.G.* II, 68 at the end. See the development in II, 83.

clear, then, that the necessity (and hence, the origin) of sensibility is grasped from the specific nature of human intellectuality, and sensibility, for its part, can only come to be by the fact that the spirit of man becomes the actuality of matter,—the form of a body.

Similarly, Thomas says at another time, "From the operation of the human soul [according to the context, this is meant as spiritual], its mode of being can be known. For, insofar as it has an operation transcending what is material, its *esse* is elevated above the body and does not depend on it; but insofar as it acquires immaterial knowledge from material knowledge, it is clear that it cannot be complete in its kind without a union with the body."[14] Admittedly, it is not expressed clearly in these texts what is the specific nature of the intellect as such which of itself requires sensibility.

This connection becomes clearer where Thomas treats the question: whether the intellective soul is appropriately united with such a body.[15] The metaphysical presuppositions which Thomas reveals in answering this question, whose actual purpose does not interest us here, are always presented identically in the texts mentioned: the ontological constitution of the principle which confers actuality (the form) determines in its specific nature whether and how this principle requires of itself another real principle of empty, indeterminate potentiality in order to realize its essence in it: "Since form is not for the sake of matter, but rather matter is for the sake of form, it is from form that we must learn the reason why matter is such,[16] and not vice versa."[17] Then the specific nature of the human spirit is examined, from which its necessary relation to matter is supposed to follow. Thomas states first of all: "It holds the low-

---

[14] *De Anima* a. 1, corp. Similarly, a. 2, corp., towards the end.

[15] See *S.T.* I, q. 76, a. 5; *De Malo* q. 5, a. 5, corp.; *De Spir. Creat.* a. 7, corp.; *De Anima* a. 8, corp.

[16] The formulation of the fundamental principle is always aimed at the special question of the article in question. But it obviously also holds for the question whether and why a form has an intrinsic ordination to prime matter in general.

[17] *S.T.* I, q. 76, a. 5, corp.; similarly, *De Malo* q. 5, a. 5, corp.

est rank among intellectual substances."[18] Through this comparison the human spirit already appears placed over against the limit-idea of the intuitive intellectuality of angels. This lowest conceivable spirituality is defined more precisely: "It is not naturally endowed with the knowledge of truth as are angels[19]; it is not . . . naturally endowed with intelligible species . . . as are superior intellectual substances[20]; the human soul . . . is potentially intellective."[21] These characteristics coincide with what was said about the nature of the possible intellect.

Lest the possibility of understanding the Thomistic conclusion from these characteristics be precluded from the outset, it is to be noted that the "being naturally endowed with the knowledge of truth," the "being naturally endowed with intelligible species" cannot simply be understood in some ordinary conception of having innate ideas of something. A species is for Thomas first of all an ontological determination of the spirit which precedes knowledge as such as its formal cause.[22] As such an ontological determination of the spirit, if it belongs to it "naturally," hence if it is to be essentially an expression of its ontological intensity produced by the soul itself with the possibility of being a formal principle of knowledge, a species is dependent on the ontological intensity of the spirit itself. Hence, if according to our presupposition it can produce knowledge of something by way of formal causality, then logically it is necessary that the spirit has already apprehended itself in advance. Expressed in other words: what is supposed to be of itself alone the ontological ground of something actually intelligible is itself necessarily already actually intelligible in itself, is already and always present to itself like an "angel"; wherefore the reference to the superior intellectual substances in this text is not accidental.

Hence if it is denied that any intelligible species (hence those also by which a knower can apprehend himself, that is, an

[18] *S.T.* I, q. 76, a. 5, corp.; similarly, *De Anima* a. 8.
[19] *S.T.* I, q. 76, a. 5, corp.
[20] *De Anima* a. 8, corp.
[21] *De Malo* q. 5, a. 5, corp.
[22] See, for example, *De Ver.* q. 1, a. 1, corp.

251

essence that is already in itself "act in the genus of intelligibles")[23] is already given in itself to a knower through its
essence (*naturaliter*), then neither is this knower in itself already present to itself, but is rather "potentially intellective."
This is the definition of the human level of being. Now, from
this definition, Thomas concludes necessarily: "It must
gather [the knowledge of truth] . . . via the senses[24]; it
must receive intelligible species from external things through
the mediation of sense powers[25] . . . through the senses it
receives the intelligible species through which it becomes an
actual known."[26] If the spirit of itself alone has not already and
always consciously possessed itself or another, then it is immediately evident that it must receive its knowledge "from external things."

But Thomas immediately arrives at the necessity of a *sentient*
reception of the other. Therefore it is logically necessary for
Thomas that receptive acceptance as such be sentient, if this
conclusion is not to be too hasty and unjustified. We do not
have to go into this logical necessity in more detail here; it has
already been shown earlier. But this brief conclusion shows
how self-evident it was for Thomas. From the necessity of a
sentient reception of an object different from the knower,
Thomas then concludes further to a substantial unity between
the spiritual principle and the material sensibility.[27] Hence if
spirit as specifically human requires sensibility, then it must
produce this of itself by way of formal causality, since as itself,
that is, as capable of knowledge, it is and can be thought of
only with sensibility, but "nature does not lack anything that is
necessary to it," as Thomas says in this context.[28] Thomas then
treats this formal production of sensibility explicitly also as the
intellect's own realization of its essence.

[23] See, for example, *S.T.* I, q. 87, a. 1, corp.
[24] *S.T.* I, q. 76, a. 5, corp.
[25] *De Anima* a. 8, corp.
[26] *De Malo* q. 5, a. 5, corp.
[27] See the texts in notes 3, 4, 5 on p. 291.
[28] *S.T.* I, q. 76, a. 5, corp.

In the Thomistic texts used so far, which came from the question about the relationship of body and soul, it has become clear that Thomas derives the necessity of sensibility from the specific nature of the human spirit. On the other hand, it was not said in these texts how the intellect is related to the sensibility that is necessary to it. This question is treated explicitly in the texts on the origin of one power from another. There it is said explicitly that sensibility emanates (*entspringt*) from the intellect. On the other hand, it is only in a very general and formal way that these texts treat the problem, why the intellect lets sensibility emanate from itself. So it is only together with the series of texts just treated that these texts offer the whole of Thomas's thought on the question with which we are occupied in this section.

3. The Formal Structure of the Relationship of Origin Between the Powers to Each Other and to Their Substantial Ground (Natural Emanation)

To understand correctly what follows it is to be noted at the outset that in the question of the origin of one power from another and from the substantial ground of the spirit, we are not at all dealing with the relationship between a finished, complete existent as an efficient cause and an effect produced by it, but remaining extrinsic to it. Rather we are dealing with the intrinsic metaphysical constitution of an individual essence in itself as a single being in the plurality of its powers. Therefore, this unity can neither be conceived simply as the connection of an effect with its productive cause, nor as the subsequent union of powers already constituted in themselves. The former Thomas denies explicitly here,[29] and the latter goes completely against the Thomistic notion of the priority of the unity of an essence with respect to the plurality of its determinations: "what is multiple is not united of itself."

Therefore, the plurality of powers which intrinsically constitute an existent, if they are not to be disputed away monisti-

[29] See *S.T.* I, q. 77, a. 6, ad 3; a. 7, ad 1, q. 77, a. 1, ad 5.

cally, can be conceived as those of a single existent only if the plurality to be unified is conceived as arising out of a single origin in which the plurality, antecedent to itself, is already and always one. Thomas calls this emanating: *origo, fluere, resultatio, emanatio.*[30] This emanating is situated at the mid-point, hardly able to be further defined, between an efficient causality, in which what is produced is indeed different from the origin, but it really does not have to determine the origin itself permanently[31]; a simple essential determination, which is identical with the essence as origin and so does not ground any plurality of powers[32]; and finally an accidental determination of an existent produced accidentally from without,[33] which indeed formally determines this existent as really different from itself, but does not form any essential unity with it, as is the case in the relationship of the soul and its cognitive powers, and the latter among themselves.[34] Consequently, we are dealing with the unfolding, which is essentially given simultaneously with a unified existent, of its essence from its innermost core into the plurality of its powers in which it is first itself.

For the sake of later considerations we must insert a brief reflection here which can be added appropriately to what was just said. It is indeed correct that Thomas maintains that an immanent action properly speaking, in the sense of an efficient causality, is possible only where there is a plurality of parts in the existent which influence each other in such a way that the produced determination is never that of the producer, but that of another part.[35] In the case of the emanation of a power, however, the productive and the receptive principle are

---

[30] *S.T.* I, q. 77, a. 6; a. 7.

[31] Otherwise it would be an active and passive potency in the same respect, which Thomas rejects for immanent action also insofar as this is thought of as efficient causality in the strict sense.

[32] Thomas explicitly makes this distinction precisely in our question: *De Anima* a. 12, ad 7; ad 8.

[33] *S.T.* I, q. 77, a. 1, ad 5; a. 6, corp.

[34] *Ibid.; De Anima* a. 12, ad 7; *I Sent.* dist. 3, a. 4, a. 2, corp.; *sunt de integritate animae.*

[35] See *S.T.* I–II, q. 9, a. 3, corp. and ad 1; II–II q. 59, a. 3, corp. at the beginning; *De Malo* q. 2, a. 11, ad 8; q. 6, a. 1, ad 20, etc.

strictly identical. Hence when in texts like *S.T.* III, q. 32, a. 4, corp. and ad 3; *II Sent.* dist. 18, q. 1, a. 2, corp.; *III Sent.* dist. 3, q. 2, a. 1, corp· and ad 6; *In VII Metaph.* lect. 8, n. 1442, a-h, etc., Thomas denies that the productive and the determined principle can be strictly identical, such a statement cannot be played off against the concept of an emanation (*resultatio*), and holds only for the production of a determination in the sense of a transient efficiency as such in the proper sense, which Thomas, for reasons which we will not go into any further here, also sees at work in the usual immanent action of a living being. If, therefore, it turns out later that an emanation from the patient itself of what is produced always belongs intrinsically and necessarily to transient action (to efficient causality in general), although in this case, what emanates does *not necessarily* emanate from the patient, then texts like those just cited cannot constitute an instance against this conception. The "passivity" of the "patient" does not exclude that "what is suffered" emanates from the patient itself.

It is true, however, that the relationship between action (*actio*) in the sense of efficient causality, usually the only one Thomas treats, and emanation (*resultatio*) is not clarified in Thomas to any great extent. Almost always, Thomas begins with the causally efficient influence of one thing on another, and from that he defines the concept of emanation, subsequently and almost exclusively negatively, so that it is not surprising that the point of origin of an emanation often appears merely as a passive principle, without it being able to be concluded from this that by this definition he intended to deny to this passive principle an *actio* in the sense of emanation. The more original and genuine metaphysical view, which understands transient action as a deficient mode of the self-realization (*Selbstvollzug*) of an existent in an emanation, comes to expression only rarely, and then rather vaguely.[36] Nevertheless, it would be completely wrong to want to draw from texts like *S.T.* III, q. 32, a. 4, corp., etc., conclusions which would destroy the undoubtedly Thomistic concept of emanation (*resultatio*). The concept of

[36] As, for example, *S.C.G.* IV, 11.

255

emanation, which is to be described more exactly in a moment, shows that Thomas knows a receptive principle (*principium susceptivum*—thus, a passive principle) which *as such* is an active principle (*principium fontale activum*). If, therefore, Thomas explains something as a merely *passive* principle, then (prescinding from the obvious "exception" of prime matter) it is still far from being settled that an active production of its determination in the sense of an emanation is also to be exluded from this "passive" principle. Active causality is excluded from such a passive principle only in the sense of a causality in which concept and word are oriented towards the efficient, transient causality of physics.

After this digression we must further clarify the concept of emanation itself. According to Thomas the powers emanate from the substantial ground. From this conception there follows the relationship, conceivable only dialectically, between the essential core of an existent and the powers emanating from it. This substantial center (essence, *principia speciei*) is the origin which lets them emanate (*entspringenlassender*) and the receptive (*empfangender*) origin at once. It is the origin which lets them emanate: Thomas calls the essence the "principle" of the powers.[37] He explains the word principle as the "whence" of a process,[38] and emphasizes that the reference to an "origin" is the essential element in its meaning[39]; he knows the term "principle and fountain,"[40] which can also be used in this context[41]. This origin is an origin that lets them emanate: an "active principle,"[42] a root,[43] an origin from which the powers

[37] *S.T.* I, q. 77, a. 6, corp.; *De Malo* q. 4, a. 4, ad 6, etc.

[38] *S.T.* I, 33, a. 1, corp. Correspondingly, the origin of a power is a "*procedere*": *IV Sent.* dist. 18, q. 1, a. 2, sol. 1, ad 2.

[39] *S.T.* I, q. 33, a. 1, ad 3. Corrspondingly, the soul is the origin of the potencies: *IV Sent.* dist. 44, q. 3, a. 3, sol. 1, corp.

[40] *S.T.* II–II, q. 26, a. 3, corp.; *S.C.G.* I, 68.

[41] See above, chapter one, III, 3. Correspondingly, *potentiae derivantur ab eius essentia:* III, q. 7, a. 2, corp.

[42] *S.T.* I, q. 77, a. 7, corp.; a. 6, ad 2.

[43] *De Ver.* q. 14, a. 5, corp.; *De Virtut.* q. 1, a. 4, ad 3; *Compend. Theol.* c. 89 (*radicantur*); *S.T.* I–II, q. 37, a. 1, corp.; q. 77, a. 1, corp.; III, q. 46, a. 7, corp. at the end; *De Ver.* q. 26, a. 3, corp.; a. 9, corp.;

"flow,"[44] which it actively produces as cause,[45] as "productive."[46] What lets something emanate must somehow already have in itself what emanates[47]: it is origin "insofar as it is in act,"[48] as such it is "more perfect" than what emanates,[49] and thus is it explained that what has emanated (*originatum*)[50] can bear in itself the characteristics of its origin (although possibly in a diminished form).[51] Further, the origin is the end (*finis*)[52] of what emanates, the origin intends itself in letting it emanate, it lets itself flow out into its powers in order to be itself, for there is question not of producing a separate other, which producing already presupposes the producer as complete, but of the origin itself coming-to-its-end (*Zu-ende-Kommen*), of its unfolding out into its own essence (*ad completionem subjecti*).[53] Thus the origin which lets emanate reveals itself as a receptive origin: *susceptivum principium*.[54] The origin as receptive receives in itself what emanates as its fulfillment; it would be less perfect without the emanation which it retains in itself; it is related to it as being in potency for it[55]; it grows to its fulfillment only through less perfect stages.

Now it is not merely the form as the substantial ground of an essence in relation to the powers in general that is related as an

---

De Malo q. 3, a. 9, corp.; De Anima a. 4, ad 1; a. 11 corp. at the end; Quodl. 11, a. 5, corp.

[44] De Ver. q. 14, a. 5, corp.; q. 25, a. 3, ad 2; a. 6, ad 1; De Spir. Creat. a. 2, ad 5; De Anima a. 11, ad 17; S.T. I, q. 77, ad 1; I–II, q. 110, a. 4, ad 1; III, q. 62, a. 2, corp.; q. 89, a. 1, corp.; III Sent. dist. 27, q. 2, a. 4, sol. 3, ad 2; IV Sent. dist. 1, q. 1, a. 4, sol. 5, corp.; IV Sent. dist. 17, q. 1, a. 1, sol. 1, ad 3.

[45] S.T. I, q. 77, a .6, ad 2 and corp.; a. 1, ad 5: ex principiis essentialibus speciei causatur.

[46] S.T. I, q. 77, a. 6, corp.

[47] IV Sent. dist. 44, q. 3, a. 3, sol. 1, corp.: Ut in radice per modum . . . quo principiata sunt in principiis suis.

[48] S.T. I, q. 77, a. 6, corp.

[49] S.T. I, q. 77, a. 7, corp., and ad 3.

[50] I Sent. dist. 3, q. 4, a. 2, corp.

[51] II Sent. dist. 24, q. 1, a. 2, corp.

[52] S.T. I, q. 77, a. 6, ad 2; a. 7, corp.; De Anima a. 13, ad 7.

[53] S.T. I, q. 77, a. 6, corp.

[54] S.T. I, q. 77, a. 6, corp and ad 2; a. 7, corp.

[55] S.T. I, q. 77, a. 6, corp.; see a. 7, corp.

257

origin that lets emanate and receives at once. Where a plurality of powers flows from an essential ground, this unfolding of an essence from its central point into the plurality of its powers takes place in a definite "order." "The process from one to many takes place in a certain . . . order."[56] Just as the innermost origin of a single existent is *one,* so too it is *one* in its fulfillment, in its end. Therefore, letting the powers emanate takes place in an ordination to this one goal which is anticipated in the one origin and in which the origin reaches its end. A plurality of powers emanating from the origin is therefore conceivable only as a plurality of partial moments in the one movement towards the goal, and this goal assigns its definite place in this movement to everything which emanates.[57]

Now with regard to the order of these partial movements, its formal scheme is the following according to Thomas: seen from the origin which lets emanate, the series of origins begins with the emanation of the more perfect emanation and ends with the less perfect. Seen from the receptive origin, the series is reversed: the origin receives the less perfect in itself first, and then the more perfect.[58] Thus it is self-evident that in its unity with its origin (and hence in the same respect in which the one origin can be considered, that is, as origin which lets emanate or as receptive origin), what has emanated first is the origin of what emanates second, and so on. Thus one power flows from the other. The relationship between the origin and what emanates obtains also between the powers themselves in the way just indicated.[59]

This relationship, especially what concerns the peculiar reversal in the sequence of origins, is still further clarified if we go back to the metaphysical relationships in a *motus* as Thomas

[56] *S.T.* I, q. 77, a. 4, corp.

[57] Since the origin can be considered as an active power (Thomas himself calls it *principium productivum, activa causa*), it holds here also: *unius potentiae non possunt simul esse* (we have here the *simul* of the metaphysical constitution of an essence) *plures actus, nisi sint subordinati.* See *S.T.* I, q. 58, a. 7, ad 2; q. 62, a. 7, ad 3, etc.

[58] *S.T.* I, q. 77, q. 7, corp.

[59] *Ibid.*

258

sees them according to our earlier investigations. Although there is no question now of a motion in the strict sense (that is, of the time-forming motion of the material as such), nevertheless the concept of motion in the broader sense can be applied anywhere where there is question, as in our case, of a principle and an end, of an agent and a patient, of things objectively different.[60] In our consideration of the Thomistic concept of motion it was shown that the motion takes place in each of its partial movements by the fact that the self-mover reaches out (*vorgreift*) to the farthest goal of the movement, and thus already has it in itself in this reaching out. So it becomes intelligible how according to Thomas the origin which lets emanate lets its most perfect power emanate first insofar as it produces the emanations as a whole by the fact that it is striving towards its fulfillment, and in this movement towards the most perfect power it produces the emanation of the lower powers. In this sense the higher power can be what has emanated first and be itself the origin of the lower powers, without this statement contradicting the other, according to which the same origin as receptive receives the lower power first and only then the higher in the lower.

In similar cases in which two things are mutually the origin of their respective being, Thomas often distinguishes between efficient cause and final cause.[61] But insofar as the end and goal, in order to be able to be origin, must already be given in the productive origin[62]—"for the act is in the potency itself in a certain way,"[63]—the explanation of the relationship of origin

---

[60] Thus change of quantity (which stands in a similar relationship to the corporeal substance as the powers to the spiritual) is a *motus: I Sent.* dist. 17, q. 2, a. 1, ad 3. Thomas knows a *motus secundum quodcumque adhaerens essentiae: De Virtut.* a. 11, ad 3.

[61] *S.T.* I–II, q. 33, a. 4, ad 2; *II Sent.* dist. 36, q. 1, a. 3, ad 2; *IV Sent.* dist. 17, q. 1, a. 4, sol. 1, corp.; *De Ver.* q. 28, a. 7, corp.; *De Virtut.* q. 1, a. 12, ad 5; *In V Metaph.* lect. 2, n. 775.

[62] *S.T.* I–II, q. 1, a. 1, ad 1; *De Pot.* q. 5, a. 1, corp. An "intentional" pre-possession of the end presupposes its ontological one, an ontological ordination of the power to its end, and this is the condition of the possibility of anticipating the end in knowledge.

[63] *S.T.* I–II, q. 27, a. 3, corp.

among the powers on the basis of the relationship between efficient and final cause would come to the same result as we have just developed it from the concept of motion.

It is self-evident that this whole relationship of origin among the powers cannot be thought of as a process that happens once and for all, that ran its course perhaps at the temporal beginning of a human existence and then ceased. Rather the powers are held permanently in this relationship of emanation from the substantial ground and from one another. That is shown just from the fact that Thomas always speaks of the origin in the present, in the fact that, as all his considerations show, in speaking of the natural emanation he wants to make intelligible the permanent, "present" constitution of the spirit, and not a definite historical moment in its existence. In this natural emanation Thomas sees further the condition of the possibility of the fact that one power can keep another under its influence permanently ("move other powers")[64] which would not make any sense if the origin of the power meant a unique, transitory event. The human spirit exists permanently in letting its powers emanate and only in this way. The same thing would follow from a consideration of the function of the substance with respect to quantity, which is kept in being permanently through the substance.[65] For this function is placed parallel to the origin of the powers by Thomas himself.[66]

4. The Specific Relationship of Origin Between Intellect and Sensibility

What was said up to now in a general and formal way about the metaphysical constitution of an essence through the origin of its powers from its substantial ground and from one another can now be applied to the relationship of the intellect and sensibility.

First it can be said briefly: The intellect is the origin which

[64] De Ver. q. 14, a. 5, corp.
[65] See S.C.G. IV, 65; S.T. III, q. 77, a. 1, corp., etc.
[66] S.T. I, q. 77, a. 7, ad 2.

lets sensibility emanate; sensibility is the receptive origin of the intellect. "According to their natural origin, the senses . . . come from the intellect in a certain way; insofar as the soul has a sensitive power, it is considered as subject and in a sense the material element with respect to the intellect."[67] In the article just cited, Thomas grounds the application of the relationship of origin of the powers which was just described to the relationship of thought and sensibility only by the formal propositions: sensibility exists for the sake of thought, and compared with it, is the less perfect. Although this foundation is quite general and formal, it shows clearly enough how according to Thomas the origin of sensibility and thought from each other is to be conceived.

First of all, it is clear from what has already been said that the emanation of the powers from the substantial ground can only be conceived as *one,* so that the emanation of several powers (that is, in our case the intellect and sensibility) can only be understood as partial movements of the one movement of the metaphysical self-realization of the one human spirit. Wherefore, this one movement is directed towards the fulfillment of the human spirit. Thus it proceeds towards the final goal of its constitution, hence to that which is most perfect in it. For Thomas this is the intellect. In the intellect the one human knowing reaches its full constitution.

Why is the intellect more perfect in relation to sensibility for Thomas? The answer to this question decides whether the order of powers in Thomas becomes intelligible. In connection with the question about the relationship of origin of the powers, Thomas does not go any further into this presupposition.[68] Hence we must clarify this question from other considerations in Thomas. It almost seems at first as though our earlier con-

---

[67] *S.T.* I, q. 77, a. 7, corp. In *I Sent.* dist. 3, q. 4, a. 3, the relationship of sensibility and spirit is seen only from the receptive origin, so that only the relative priority of origin of sensibility is brought out there. In *De Anima* a. 13, ad 7, the relationship is seen from the origin that lets emanate, and so the priority of the spirit in the emanation of the powers is made explicit.

[68] *S.T.* I, q. 77, a. 4, corp.; a. 7, corp.

siderations point in another direction. Knowing is primarily intuition. But sensibility is the only human power of intuition for Thomas. Therefore, is thought not rather the auxiliary power to sensibility, and therefore, as the less perfect, since "blind" in itself, does it not emanate out of sensibility? But this consideration does not decide the question. For the intellect is not "blind in itself" in the proper sense if it can let sensibility emanate from itself as its intuition.

But for Thomas, certain other considerations are decisive to establish the greater intensity of being (*Seinsmächtigkeit*) of thought in relation to sensibility. Thus, for him, knowing is essentially a having-the-known-with-oneself through identity with it: "Knowledge is had of things insofar as they are in the knower."[69] The perfection of a cognitive power is measured, therefore, according to the measure of its potentiality (its scope) for such a having-with-oneself: "And so, the nobility of the operation of the intellect is measured by the nobility of the intellect."[70] Now, it has already been shown that, according to Thomas, the scope of the intellect (at least insofar as it gives rise to the preapprehension) surpasses the field of imagination which is limited to being as the principle of number within the horizon of space and time. Therefore, the intellect is "more perfect" for Thomas than sensibility. It is only a variation of the same thought when the same conclusion is drawn from the immateriality of the spirit and the materiality of sensibility. For the materiality of a cognitive faculty ultimately expresses a lower degree of ontological intensity because it confines knowing, which is being, to the realm of the imagination; it consigns the knowing being to the other of matter, and thus does not let it come to itself; wherefore the possibility of the complete return and the measure of it also become the metaphysical measure of the ontological intensity of an essence and its powers.[71]

Presupposing this, the general principles about the relation-

[69] See *S.T.* I, q. 19, a. 3, ad 6. Similarly, q. 19, a. 6, ad 2; q. 82, a. 3, corp., etc.
[70] *S.T.* II–II, q. 23, a. 6, ad 1.
[71] See *S.C.G.* IV, 11, etc.

ship of two powers can now be applied to spirit and sensibility in man. The substantial ground of all those determinations and powers which constitute human knowing is subsisting in itself, and therefore disposed for being-present-to-itself. It is thus an origin which lets emanate a single emanation (a single procession towards its complete self-constitution) which strives towards its end and goal, the complete potentiality for being-present-to-itself. Because this complete potentiality for being-present-to-itself is called intellect (possible and agent as a unity), the intellect is the first emanation from the origin which lets emanate insofar as, being the end and goal of the one emanation, it gives orientation and consistency to the whole emanation. Insofar as this presence-to-self has its origin in its mere potentiality (possible intellect), it can constitute itself as complete potentiality only in that, in striving towards the intellect, the substantial ground produces originally a power for the receptive intuition of another, a sensibility. Since intuition is the first presuppostion, the first essential dimension of any knowledge at all, sensibility is therefore the first to be received in the receptive origin.

Its formation is realized in a dual process. The subsisting ground unites itself with the other of matter into one existent: "the soul is the form of the body"; in this substantial unity of spirit and matter it forms sensibility as a power in the narrower sense. Since in *S.T.* I, q. 77, a. 7, Thomas poses a more limited question related only to the relationship of the powers as such, the first phase of the formation of a receptive intuition, the substantial unity of spirit and matter, is not treated explicitly there. But it has already been shown to be required in Thomas by the essence of intellectual knowing, and is also affirmed implicitly and simultaneously in this Article insofar as a sense power is essentially a material power according to Thomas. If in its projection out towards intellectual knowing as its complete being-able-to-be-present-to-itself, the origin has thus let sensibility emanate and has received it into itself (insofar as the origin communicates itself and its being to matter substantially, and receives sensibility as a power into the whole of this substantial unity),

263

then the intellect as a power along with sensibility can itself be received into the origin as receptive. Thus it is the second which the origin as already become sentient receives into itself, since it is the origin's own fulfillment.

IV. THE ORIGIN OF SENSIBILITY
AS CONVERSION TO THE PHANTASM

In the light of the result we have reached, the origin of sensibility from the intellect can be understood as the decisive conversion to the phantasm, and thus our earlier results can be further developed themselves. But first a few further elaborations must be added to the last section.

In the course of its own self-constitution, the substantial, spiritual ground forms its own sensibility for itself, and in this process of becoming spirit it receives it into itself as the first of its faculties. In the chapter on sensibility, it has already been shown that sensibility is "passive" with respect to the individual, external object only in a definite, limited sense, that it is already of itself possession of world because it exists in the other. If this sensibility appears now as emanating from the spirit, if it is shown to be produced by the spirit as its active principle, then this means at the same time that the spirit already and always has in itself its possession-of-the-world as produced by itself. The spirit itself actively opens for itself its access to the world in letting sensibility emanate; it forms of itself the horizon within which the individual, sensible object can encounter it as already and always open. Thomas himself speaks of a "motion which goes from the soul to the thing; it begins from the mind and proceeds into the sensitive part insofar as the mind rules the inferior powers, and thus mingles with individuals."[1] Lest we let ourselves be misled by the "insofar as . . . it rules" into watering down the text, it must be noted that, for Thomas, the ruling (moving) is grounded in the continual emanation of what

[1] *De Ver.* q. 10, a. 5, corp.

is ruled from what rules.[2] Thus, sensibility is the power of intuition of the spirit itself in its specifically human form.

Since sensibility emanates from a spiritual ground, and in fact, insofar as this ground unfolds out towards it own end and goal ("The sensible is ordered to the intelligible" which is the "principal end" of the human soul[3]), for this reason human sensibility bears the mark of the spiritual in itself because of its origin and its end, between which it is permanently held. "The power of one potency which precedes is left in the one which follows."[4] "But that which has its origin in another brings its form and species from the other."[5] Therefore, human sensibility is "a certain deficient participation in the intellect,"[6] that is, consequently, first of all a real participation, not in the sense of a subsequent analogy between sensibility and spirit which is of no consequence for sensibility itself, and which somehow brings both of them under a single formula, but in the sense that sensibility stands essentially and necessarily under the law of its origin, which is the spirit. That sensibility is merely a *deficient* participation is basically only an indication of the specific nature of the human spirit itself, which comes to itself from the other and hence from matter, and for that reason must give itself over to sensibility which does not transcend the finiteness of time and space. The spirituality of sensibility is still to be discussed under the heading of the cogitative sense. It has been referred to here because in *S.T.* I, q. 77, a. 7, corp., Thomas himself connects this fact with the origin of sensibility from the spirit.

This origin of sensibility from the intellect must now be further understood explicitly as the real conversion to the phantasm. To do this we must pose the question again that was raised earlier. What does conversion to the phantasm mean? The term says that the intelligible universal, the intelligible species in the strict sense, is known only in and at the sensibly known and so in a turning to it. It has already been shown that

[2] *De Ver.* q. 14, a. 5, corp.
[3] *De Anima* a. 13, ad 7.
[4] *II Sent.* dist. 24, q. 1, a. 2, corp.
[5] *II Sent.* dist. 26, q. 1, a. 4, ad 5.
[6] *S.T.* I, q. 77, a. 7, corp.

the "intelligible" in the strict sense is the light of the agent intellect, the *a priori* structure of the spirit itself, and this becomes conscious as the "form" of what is sensibly known. Thus the conversion to the phantasm is nothing other than the illumination of the phantasm by the light of the agent intellect, through which illumination the abstraction is already accomplished. *Conversion to the phantasm and abstraction are moments of a single process and are inseparably related to each other in a relationship of reciprocal priority.* Insofar as abstraction is conceivable only in a "penetration" of the light of the agent intellect "into" the phantasm, the conversion is logically prior to the abstraction; insofar as the conversion as a *conscious,* spiritual process already presupposes a spiritual knowing, hence an abstraction, the abstraction is prior to the conversion. So it was not surprising that the problematic of abstraction and of the abstractive complete return became the question about the conversion to the phantasm. Both require an understanding of the relationship of spirit and sensibility. This has been defined up to now as consisting in an emanation of sensibility from spirit as its own power retained within it. Have we already grasped there in principle the possibility of the conversion to the phantasm also, which as an illumination of the phantasm by the light of the agent intellect also accomplishes the abstraction and the complete return?

1. The Intrinsic Information (Durchformung) of Sensibility As Conversion to the Phantasm

Before we answer this question we must first show more explicitly and directly than heretofore that for Thomas the conversion to the phantasm is objectively the same process as the abstractive illumination of the phantasm by the light of the agent intellect. We begin with the fact that the conversion to the phantasm is the condition of the possibility of spiritual apprehension as such, and therefore is logically prior to the latter. "The soul cannot know without a phantasm."[7] That holds not merely for

---

[7] *In III de Anima* lect. 12, n. 772.

the first acquisition of knowledge, but also for every actual, conscious awareness of already acquired knowledge.[8] Thus the conversion to the phantasm belongs right in the essential definition of human intellectual knowing.[9] So it is self-evident that the conversion cannot be something subsequent to intellection, that is, to the apprehension of the universal, to abstraction, but is an intrinsic moment in it and belongs to its definition. Insofar as the "conversion" to the object can be distinguished from "seeing" the object, the conversion is prior to the apprehension of the universal. Thus Thomas likes to designate the unified process of apprehending the universal through a conversion to the phantasm as a unified process as "seeing the intelligible species (the universal) *in* the phantasms."[10] In any case, it is clear that the knowledge of the universal as such and the conversion coincide objectively.

But it can be shown further that the conversion coincides objectively with the abstraction as such, insofar as the abstraction, as an act of the one abstracting, can be conceived in a certain way as prior to the knowledge of the abstracted universal. Abstraction in this sense has already been shown to be a kind of "information" (*Information*) of the phantasm by the light of the agent intellect, so that in the phantasm this light becomes visible to the possible intellect, and so in this light the possible intellect can apprehend the sensible content as universal, since, as actuality of the spirit, this light is nothing other than its ordination to the absolute *esse* which is apprehended in the pre-apprehension, and through this *esse* it experiences every individual, sensibly-given existent as limited. Now Thomas himself calls this abstraction a "conversion of the agent intellect over (*super*) the phantasm,"[11] from which arises the knowledge of the universal. In so doing Thomas himself calls the process of abstraction a conversion to the phantasm. It is not perhaps only a question

[8] *De Anima* a. 15, corp.
[9] *I Sent.* dist. 3, q. 4, a. 3, corp.
[10] *S.T.* I, q. 86, a. 1, corp.; I–II, q. 113, a. 7, ad 5; II–II, q. 180, a. 5, ad 2; III, q. 11, a. 2, ad 1; *S.C.G.* II, 73; *In Boeth. de Trin.* q. 6, a. 2, ad 5, etc.
[11] *S.T.* I, q. 85, a. 1, ad 3.

of a similarity of words which in reality designate two different conversions. For since both (that is, the conversion to the phantasm and the conversion of the agent intellect over [*super*] the phantasm) are prior to the apprehension of the universal as the condition of its possibility, it is simply impossible to see how and why they are still to be distinguished. They are both the same, and the formal effect of this one and the same conversion is the knowledge of the universal as a *conscious* possession of the universal, which as such can, of course, also be called abstraction.

2. The Act of the Cogitative Sense as Conversion to the Phantasm

The same result can be reached in another, rather more roundabout approach. Since this approach prepares the way for answering the real question of this and the following section, this second proof is not superfluous.

We begin with a text which seems to contradict our earlier interpretation of abstraction as a process which is identical with the illumination of the phantasm by the light of the agent intellect. In this text the illumination is distinguished from the "abstraction": "and they are illuminated . . . and again . . . are abstracted."[12] The dual statement that makes the distinction is explained by Thomas in the next two sentences: "they are illuminated . . . ; but it abstracts . . ." Hence, the second sentence must tell us how Thomas understands this "abstraction" which he distinguishes from the illumination. This abstraction takes place "insofar as through the power of the agent intellect we are able to receive for our consideration the natures of species without individual conditions . . . " It is clear that the illumination distinguished from abstraction is only a "considering" of the universal, taking the universal into consideration, in other words, the conscious possession of the universal as such. Consequently, the process by which such a universal is given for consideration by its being constituted such is already

[12] *S.T.* I, q. 85, a. 1, ad 4.

268

presupposed, and hence must already have taken place itself in the illumination. Therefore, insofar as the abstraction in the sense used here is only the self-evident, formal consequence of the illumination, it is not surprising if Thomas elsewhere designates the whole process of abstraction, including the knowledge of the universal, as illumination.

Now according to this text, in what does the illumination, in which we have to see the actual process of abstraction, consist? Thomas tells us in a way not yet familiar to us from our earlier considerations: "They are illuminated indeed (the phantasms) because, just as the sensitive part is made more powerful (*virtuosior*) by its union with the intellect, so too by the power of the agent intellect the phantasms are rendered more suitable (*habilia*) for the intelligible 'intentions' to be abstracted from them (whereby this 'to be abstracted' is to be taken in the sense just indicated, that is, as 'to be able to be received for our consideration,' as consciousness of the constituted universal as such)." This explanation of the illumination first sets up a parallel: "just as . . . so too . . ." As can be seen at first sight, it is a question of the parallel between the relationship of powers among themselves and that of their acts: sensitive part—intellect on the one hand, and phantasm—power of the agent intellect on the other. In each instance there arises from this relationship a "spiritualization" of the sensible (more powerful—more suitable). In the framework of Thomistic metaphysics it is self-evident[13] that the relationship of the acts is only a consequence of the relationship of the powers to each other.

We are now in a position to understand to some extent the "union" of the powers through which sensibility becomes more powerful. Sensibility is united with the intellect because it emanates from it, and is permanently retained in it as its power. Therefore, it is true of sensibility: "the power of one potency which precedes is left in the one which follows," and therefore it is from the outset, intrinsically and "originally," informed by spirit; it is more powerful (*virtuosior*). It is already evident here that the possibility of an abstraction is grounded in the emanation

[13] On this, see *S.T.* I, q. 77, sed contra.

of sensibility from the spirit. But we will have to speak further about that later. Now corresponding to this relationship of the powers, the acts of sensibility, the phantasms, are "more suitable" (*habilia*), and this for the purpose of seeing the universal in them. And the actual abstractive process of the illumination consists in this suitability of the phantasms.

We will now explore what this suitability is, not as yet from the intrinsic meaning of what the origin of sensibility from the spirit signifies, but by simply making first of all two statements: 1. this suitability follows from the origin of sensibility from the spirit; 2. it is of such a kind that the universal can be seen in the phantasm without anything further, since, in order to complete the abstraction, only a "consideration" as such follows this suitability as produced by an illumination.

In order to prove that the illumination thus understood coincides objectively with the conversion to the phantasm, we must anticipate briefly here the concept of the cogitative sense. Let one sentence suffice at this point as a vague description of what it is: the cogitative sense is the center in which spirit and sensibility, which emanated from spirit, merge together in the one human knowing. The proof which concerns us here is carried out in two steps: the illumination in both of the features which we just mentioned takes place in the cogitative sense (as act); at the same time the act of the cogitative sense is objectively identical with the conversion to the phantasm. This shows that the abstractive illumination itself takes place in the conversion to the phantasm.

It is true of the cogitative sense (1) what Thomas says in the text we are considering about that part of sensibility upon which the illumination touches: from its union with the intellect it is made more powerful. The cogitative sense has its proper function not simply from sensibility as such "(not through that which is proper to the sensitive part), but through a certain affinity and proximity to the universal reason through a certain overflow,"[14] and indeed from the fact that it is joined to the

[14] *S.T.* I, q. 78, a. 4, ad 5.

270

reason (*iungi*).[15] The cogitative sense (the particular reason) is produced by a kind of "continuation" of the spirit into sensibility ("the mind . . . is continued in the sense powers").[16] Thus, as emanating from the spirit and therefore especially "informed"[17] by it, the cogitative sense offers (2) the universal to view. "The cogitative sense apprehends the individual *as* existing in the *common* nature, which it can do insofar as it is united with the intellect in the same subject."[18] This apprehension of the individual in the common nature is impossible to mere sensibility as such.[19] At this point, the universal as such is not yet known by itself, but nevertheless the abstraction in its decisive point has already been accomplished. For the only thing that remains to be done is to focus upon the one "part" of the already accomplished differentiation between the individual as such and the common nature. Just as this differentiation took place in sensibility through the spirit, so the spirit (and only it) beholds in sensibility ("in the phantasm") the common nature already differentiated in it. Hence, the phantasms are really "more suitable" in the cogitative sense for the universal to be seen in them.

Consequently, the cogitative sense offers an already differentiated unity of the individual as such and the universal: "the individual in the common nature." But this proves that its act takes place by a conversion to the phantasm, that its act is objectively identical with it. This finishes the second step of the

[15] *S.T.* I–II, q. 74, a. 3, ad 1. See *III Sent.* dist. 26, q. 1, a. 2, corp.; *In II de Anima* lect. 13, n. 398.

[16] *De Ver.* q. 10, a. 5, corp.; see *ibid.*, ad 2 and ad 4. See also *De Ver.* q. 2, a. 6, corp., where the broader concept *imaginatio* appears for the cogitative sense. Likewise, *IV Sent.* dist. 50, q. 1, a. 3, ad 2, in contr.

[17] For this expression, see the general principle: *actus* (of a lower power) . . . *recipit formam et speciem a superiori potentia vel habitu, secundum quod ordinatur inferius a superiori:* S.T. I–II, q. 13, a. 1, corp.; see q. 17, a. 4, corp.

[18] *In II de Anima* lect. 13, n. 398. See also *Post. Anal.* lib. II, lect. 20 (Parma 225a), where probably the same thing is meant objectively, although in vaguer terms: . . . *sensus est quodammodo et ipsius universalis . . . apprehendit universale in particulari.*

[19] *In II de Anima* lect. 13, n. 398.

proof that the abstractive illumination of the phantasm coincides
objectively with the conversion to the phantasm. The differentiated unity of individual and universal is in the cogitative sense.[20]
Insofar as the cogitative sense is the unified center of spirit and
sensibility[21]—"it pertains to the sensitive part,"[22] in such a way,
however, that the "affinity and proximity to the universal reason"
is essential to it, so that it does not exist in animals[23]—, it can
be looked at from the viewpoint of sensibility as such and of
intellect as such. As sentient "power" it is of itself the "particular
reason,"[24] that is, the power which apprehends individual "intentions."[25] On the other hand, together with that it is the point
where spirit breaks through into sensibility, or better said, the
first emanation from spirit to sensibility. Therefore, insofar as
the spirit knows the individual, this takes place in that the spirit
continues on precisely in the cogitative sense. Just as sensibility
apprehends the common nature in the cogitative sense as its
power, because the cogitative sense is spiritualized (of course it
apprehends the common nature in the *individual,* since the cogitative sense is sentient), so the spirit apprehends the individual in
the cogitative sense as *its* power, because the cogitative sense is
sensibilized (of course we mean the individual in the *common
nature,* since the cogitative sense is spiritualized). Both sentences
describe one and the same center between spirit and sensibility.

In Thomistic language these two sentences read: "the cogitative sense [as the highest power of sensibility] apprehends the
individual as existing in the common nature . . . insofar as [the

20 See *De Principiis Individuationis* (opsc. 29): *quidditas rei materialis in ipsa sua particularitate est objectum rationis particularis.*
21 *III Sent.* dist. 23, q. 2, a. 2, sol. 1, ad 3: *est in confinio sensitivae
et intellectivae partis.* See *De Ver.* q. 10, a. 5, corp., where the cogitative sense is called *"potentia media"* (see also the previous *loc. cit.,*
corp.; ad 2 and ad 4).
22 *S.T.* I–II, q. 30, a. 3, ad 3.
23 *S.T.* I–II, q. 74, a. 3, ad 1 (*prae aliis animalibus*); I, q. 78, a. 4,
corp.; *II Sent.* dist. 25, q. 1, a. 1, ad 7; *III Sent.* dist. 23, q. 2, a. 2, sol.
1, ad 3 (*in solis hominibus*), etc.
24 *S.T.* I–II, q. 51, a. 3, corp.; I, q. 79, a. 2, ad 2; q. 78, a. 4, corp.;
q. 81, a. 3, corp., etc.
25 *S.T.* I, q. 78, a. 4, corp.; *In VI Ethic,* lect. 1, n. 1123: *collectiva
intentionum particularium; In I Metaph.* lect. 1, n. 15.

cogitative sense] is united with the intellect,"[26] and likewise "the mind . . . mingles with individuals through the mediation of the particular reason . . . which is also known as the cogitative sense."[27] The second of these two sentences is important in our context and we must show briefly that it is Thomistic. Once this is done, then it has been shown that the concrete in its already differentiated unity of common nature and individual is present in the cogitative sense, and thus the interpretation of what the cogitative sense accomplishes, based at first only on *In II de Anima*, lect. 13, will be confirmed.

Thomas denies that the intellect strictly as such can know the material individual.[28] If now in its turning to the cogitative sense it were to know the individual in its *undifferentiated* individuality as does pure sensibility, this denial would make no sense. Yet for all that, the intellect in its "continuation" is supposed to know the individual, accordingly the intellect *itself*,[29] not perhaps merely the sensibility of the cogitative sense considered as a power *different* from the intellect. Consequently, if the intellect itself were to know the individual in absolutely the same way as sensibility does, its distinctive feature as spirit (by which it knows the universal) would be completely eliminated; in this act it would simply be sensibility. Hence, when Thomas says that the intellect knows the individual with the help of the cogitative sense, that can only be meant in the sense that in the cogitative sense the individuality and the common nature are given in a differentiated unity for the intellect, which keeps the cogitative sense with itself as *its* power and just by that fact always knows what is given in it. Otherwise one would have to arrive at the Thomistically untenable notion that the intellect sometimes cannot exercise its abstractive activity, although a phantasm is given to it. This notion is Thomistically

[26] *In II de Anima* lect. 13, n. 398.

[27] *De Ver.* q. 10, a. 5, corp.

[28] *S.T.* I, q. 14, a. 11, ad 1; q. 50, a. 2, corp.; q. 56, a. 1, ad 2; *S.C.G.* I, 63; *De Ver.* q. 2, a. 5, ad 1; *De Malo* q. 16, a. 7, ad 5; *De Anima* a. 20, corp.; *In II de Anima* lect. 12, n. 377; *I Sent.* dist. 36, q. 1, a. 1, ad 1.

[29] See *In III de Anima* lect. 8, n. 712; *IV Sent.* dist. 50, q. 1, a. 3, corp.; *etiam per intellectum . . . cognoscit singularia.*

untenable because the spontaneous activity of the agent intellect is necessarily constant ("the agent intellect . . . always in act") and because an immaterial knowledge is just by that fact already universal. Now as a matter of fact Thomas also says again and again that the intellect knows the individual with the help of the cogitative sense.[30]

According to what was said about the cogitative sense as the boundary of sensibility with spirit, we can also understand of the cogitative sense those texts which speak in more general terms of sensibility as such ("sensitive part," "imagination") as the auxiliary of the intellect in apprehending the individual.[31] Hence the intellect apprehends the individual "in the common nature" in the cogitative sense. Since in the cogitative sense the common nature is already differentiated from the individuality, the cogitative sense (as act) offers the possibility of apprehending the universal in it. Thus there has followed for the cogitative sense too the two characteristics of the abstractive illumination which were pointed out above: its foundation in an emanation of sensibility from the intellect, and the suitability of the individual given in sensibility for the universal to be seen in it.

3. The Essence of the Reflection in the Act of the Cogitative Sense

Now the act of the cogitative sense coincides with what Thomas calls the conversion to the phantasm. Thomas often calls the apprehension of the individual by the intellect a reflection,[32] whereby of course the notion is to be avoided that there is question of a subsequent "reflection" that is of no consequence for the apprehension of the universal itself. "In knowing its object,

[30] De Ver. q. 10, a. 5, corp.; ad 2 and ad 4; q. 2, a. 6, ad 2; De Anima a. 20, ad 1, in contr.; In VI Ethic. lect. 1, n. 1123; IV Sent. dist. 50, q. 1, a. 3, ad 3, in contr.

[31] De Ver. q. 2, a. 6, corp.; q. 10, a. 5, corp.; S.T. I, q. 86, a. 1, ad 2, etc.

[32] See besides the texts to be mentioned here, e.g., S.T. I, q. 86, a. 4, corp.; II–II, q. 47, a. 3, ad 1 (II Sent. dist. 23, q. 2, a. 1, corp.: the reflection on act and potency).

which is some universal nature, it returns . . . to the phantasm from which the species was abstracted."[33] In other words, by the fact that it knows the universal, the intellect has already and always gone back to sensibility. One would therefore misunderstand Thomas if one wanted to understand his presentation of the individual moments in a human act of knowledge in their logical sequence as a series of individual acts. The "reflection" upon the act, upon the content of the act (species), and upon the latter's sensibly conscious foundation (phantasm)[34] are moments which constitute the *one* act of knowledge which attains to the object itself, the intelligible. For the act itself also belongs to the "objects" of this reflection, and yet Thomas says explicitly: "by the same act it knows itself and knows that it knows."[35] Therefore, the same holds also for the other moments upon which the reflection is directed. Of course this is not to say that the individual moments which constitute the one human act of knowledge in its spiritual-sensible unity cannot also be made by themselves the objects of a *subsequent*, explicit reflection.

In the first, "natural" act of knowledge, which attains to the things of the world disclosed in sensibility, all the moments in it, prescinding from the material object, are only "implicitly given," known "in the background" as it were. It would be otherwise in an intellectual-intuitive knowledge: here the essence of the knower is present to itself as its proper object, and therefore its fulfillment also, the act of knowledge itself, is not merely implicitly apprehended, but is the first thing apprehended "objectively." Thus it is clear that if the human act as such is itself to become an object of knowledge explicitly, this can only take place, in contrast to God and the angels, in a second act which is grounded in an act focused naturally upon the wide world. Articles such as *S.T.* I, q. 28, a. 4, ad 2; q. 87, a. 3, corp. and ad 2 mean this and only this.

[33] *De Ver.* q. 10, a. 5, corp.

[34] *IV Sent.* dist. 50, q. 1, a. corp.; *De Ver.* q. 2, a. 6, corp.; q. 10, a. 5, corp.; *De Anima* a. 20, ad 1, in contr.

[35] *I Sent.* dist. 10, q. 1, a. 5, ad 2; dist. 1, q. 2, a. 1, ad 2: *eadem operatione intelligo intelligibile et intelligo me intelligere.*

It is to be noted from the outset that these articles are dealing with the knowledge of one's own act as an explicit, thematic object. This is in accordance with the development of Questions 86–88, where the individual areas of cognitive objects are treated; wherefore only an explicit knowledge of these objects can be meant. Thus *S.T.* I, q. 87, a. 3 is also dealing with an explicit knowledge of the human act, a knowledge which makes this act its actual object; it is dealing with a "perfect knowledge."[36] It goes too much against the conception which, in principle, Thomas has of the essence of an immaterial act[37] for us to be able to assume that in his later writings he has overlooked or denied that a complete return, an apprehension of oneself, is given necessarily with an immaterial act. And yet, we read in the *Summa* that "to return to its own essence is nothing else than for a thing to subsist in itself"[38]; hence, so long as Thomas ascribes a self-subsistence to the soul,[39] he cannot have wanted to deny of it a complete return given immediately with self-subsistence.

What Thomas is insisting on in texts like *S.T.* I, q. 87, a. 3, and *In II de Anima*, lect. 6 (n. 308) is only that what is immediately and objectively apprehended are things of the world, and nothing else. An implicit apprehension of the act in the act itself is not hereby excluded, all the less since Thomas already says in the *Commentary on the Sentences:* " . . . the acts by which it knows a horse and by which it knows its act as act are numerically different,"[40] and yet in the very same text ("the same act is loved through the act which it itself is"), Thomas knows a reflection identical with the first act itself. Nor is there any cogent reason to assume that Thomas has essentially changed his conception of this reflexive apprehension of the individual because in his later writings he no longer brings out individually and explicitly the whole series of moments which

36 See *S.T.* I, q. 94, a. 2, corp.
37 See *III Sent.* dist. 23, q. 1, a. 2, ad 3.
38 *S.T.* I, q. 14, a. 2, ad 1.
39 *S.T.* I, q. 75, a. 2.
40 *I Sent.* dist. 17, q. 1, a. 5, ad 4.

are simultaneously known in an act. The same shorter formulation as in the later writings[41] is already found in its content in the *Commentary on the Sentences*.[42]

As soon as it becomes clear that the reflection in which the individual is known is not a series of acts, but belongs essentially to every human act of knowledge,[43] and that the decisive element in the apprehension of the individual is the "continuation" of the spirit into sensibility, while the apprehension ("reflection") of the other moments of the act as such (of the act and the species), as much as they too are immediately apprehended simultaneously with the apprehended object in the same act, contributes nothing essential to this apprehension, then it can no longer appear strange that in his later wrtings Thomas has the apprehension of the individual, which he still calls reflection even there, take place simply by a turning of the spirit to sensibility. This is all the more true insofar as he already does this in his earlier writings, as was said, and describes the same reflection in earlier and later writings as taking place with the help of the cogitative sense.[44]

Now this reflexive apprehension of the individual, in which the universal is already given in its differentiated unity with the particular, is realized in the conversion to the phantasm. That is an explicit thesis in Thomas: "But [the intellect] can know the singular indirectly and as though through a certain reflection." How does Thomas explain this reflection? He continues

---

[41] See, for example, *S.T.* I, q. 86, a. 1, corp.; *In III de Anima* lect. 8, n. 713: *per quandam reflexionem, inquantum redit super phantasmata, a quibus species intelligibiles abstrahuntur.*

[42] *II Sent.* dist. 3, q. 3, a. 3, ad 1: . . . *per reflexionem quandam intellectus ad imaginationem et sensum, dum scilicet intellectus speciem quam a singularibus abstraxit, applicat formae singulari in imaginatione servatae.*

[43] For that reason an interpretation of the reflection texts in question (*De Ver.* q. 10, a. 5, corp.; q. 2, a. 6, corp.; *De Anima* a. 20, ad 1, in contr.; *IV Sent.* dist. 50, q. 1, a. 3, corp.) in the sense that an "inference" would be made from the intelligible to the act, from there to the species, and finally from there to the phantasm and the singular, is impossible from the outset.

[44] *IV Sent.* dist. 50, q. 1, a. 3, ad 3, in contr. (ca. 1256–59); *In VI Ethic.* lect. 1, n. 1123 (ca. 1269–72).

immediately: "because, as was said above [q. 84, a. 7], even after it has abstracted the intelligible species, it cannot actually know through them except by turning to the phantasms in which it knows the species . . . So, therefore [notice that what follows is introduced as a consequence of the conversion] through the intelligible species it knows the universal itself directly, and indirectly the individuals whose phantasms they are. And in this way it forms this proposition: Socrates is a man."[45] Consequently, the reflection on the individual coincides with the conversion to the phantasm.

But this apprehension of the individual in the common nature which takes place in the cogitative sense has already been shown to be objectively identical with the decisive, abstractive illumination which introduces the differentiation (suitability) in the sensibly given, and this makes it possible to apprehend the universal in it spiritually. This shows that this abstractive illumination itself is identical with the conversion to the phantasm. The conversion to the phantasm is not merely a turning of the spirit to sensibility which is logically prior to the actual knowledge of the universal and makes it possible, but is precisely that movement of the spirit in which the sensible content is informed, as it were, by the *a priori* structure of the spirit, by its "light," that is, is seen within absolute being which the spirit pre-apprehends, and is known thereby in its universality. Abstraction and conversion are two sides of the one process. Abstraction comes about insofar as a conversion of the *a priori* structure of the spirit to sensibility takes place. When this conversion takes place, the sensible is known in its universality, is "abstracted." And insofar as this *a priori* structure of the spirit (the really universal intelligible species in the strict sense) can only be known in the sensible to which it is turned, every abstraction (that is, knowledge of the universal) is essentially a conversion to the phantasm.

Thus it is shown that Thomistically the possibility of abstraction and that of conversion must be grasped together. This one possibility of the one abstractive conversion to the phantasm

[45] *S.T.* I, q. 86, a. 1, corp.

must now be shown explicitly to be grounded in the emanation of sensibility from the spirit.

V. THE ORIGIN OF SENSIBILITY FROM SPIRIT

It has already followed from our investigations so far that Thomas himself saw a connection between the abstractive conversion to the phantasm and the origin of sensibility from spirit. The intrinsic information of sensibility by spirit, as the relation of the powers upon which the abstractive illumination as the activity of these related powers is based, resulted "from [sensibility's] union with the intellect." It cannot be doubted that this union itself is grounded in the emanation of sensibility from spirit, since Thomas explicitly teaches such an origin, as has been shown. Further, the cogitative sense, which was shown to be the place of the decisive abstraction, is joined with the spirit "according to a certain overflow (refluentiam)."[1] So the only task that still remains is to make this connection between the origin of sensibility and the abstractive conversion to the phantasm clearer in the light of what Thomas says of both taken by themselves. So what follows will be in its essentials a summary view of the theses already shown to be Thomistic.

The conversion to the phantasm means the relationship of an act of the spirit to one of sensibility. The relationship of acts is grounded fundamentally and essentially in the relationship of the powers. Therefore, a metaphysical understanding of the conversion to the phantasm will consist essentially in grasping the relationship of sensibility and spirit. Insofar as the conversion says that a spiritual knowing is possible for man only in an antecedent union of the intellectual act with the sentient act, the foundational relationship between sensibility and spirit must be defined as a union of the two, which union, since it belongs to the conditions of the possibility of human thought as such, cannot be something subsequent to its constitution, and there-

[1] In the good, Thomistic (at least in its spirit) *De Potentiis Animae* it says in chapter 4: *per quandam influentiam.*

fore must be understood as an original unity, as a unifying unity. This fundamental consideration forms the guideline for what follows.

This guideline itself would already have said everything that has to be said if the conversion to the phantasm had only to be grasped as the term itself must be understood at first and immediately. For if, as has already been shown, spirit constitutes itself in its own essence only insofar as it lets sensibility emanate continually from itself, and retains it permanently as its faculty, then it follows necessarily that the fulfillment of sensibility, its actuality in the actual sentient apprehension (in the possession of the phantasm) is an actualization of the spirit itself; and if spirit comes to its own fulfillment as a power only insofar as it permanently retains sensibility as a power (as the way to its end and goal, as it were), then its fulfillment in actual knowing is also possible only via the actualization of sensibility, it is essentially a conversion to the phantasm. Hence if the meaning and necessity of the emanation of sensibility from spirit is understood in the light of the specific nature of the human spirit, the conversion to the phantasm is also understood as possible and necessary in the very meaning of this term. But in the meantime this conversion to the phantasm has turned out to be objectively identical with abstraction itself. And so the further question is, whether in the emanation of sensibility from spirit the conversion is also grasped as abstraction. At least this much is clear, that the fundamental consideration just made can be for this new question no more than a general guideline for the direction of the following investigation. What is still to be clarified must be able to be reached in a confrontation of what was said up to now about the nature of abstraction and about the emanation of sensibility from spirit.

1. Spirit as Desire (Dynamic Openness) for Absolute Being

Abstraction as such has been understood so far in a peculiar dual statement about it whose intrinsic coherence still has to be more explicitly apprehended. Abstraction showed itself on the one hand to be grounded and accomplished in an *excessus* to absolute *esse,* and on the other hand as the becoming conscious of the *a priori* structure of the spirit itself in the sensibly given content which it informs. The definition of the essence of the possible intellect already given shows how these two definitions of the essence of abstraction are to be understood as one and the same. The essence of the spirit is the *"quo est omnia fieri"*: spirit is in potency for absolute being. It is "in a certain way (that is, in potency and in ordination towards) everything." Its becoming conscious of its *a priori* reality is therefore the pre-apprehension of absolute being, and vice versa.

As transcendent apprehension of absolute *esse,* this actuality of the spirit is a becoming, a dynamic orientation to the totality of its objects. Thomas also calls attention to this definition of the spirit frequently and forcefully. Since we are touching here upon the essential characteristic of the human spirit, under which the emanation of sensibility is to be grasped as its concrete application, we must go into this point in more detail.

The human spirit as such is desire (*Begierde*), striving (*Streben*), action (*Handlung*). For in itself it is *possible* intellect, that is, something which reaches its full actuality from its potentiality, and in fact by its own action, since by its own active power (agent intellect) of itself (always in act) it produces its object (the actually intelligible) from something only sensibly given. Desire as a characteristic of knowledge as such is brought out explicitly by Thomas. He knows not merely a mutual inclusion (*invicem se includere*)[2] of intellect and will as the acts of separate powers, so that knowledge acts and will acts have a reciprocal priority with respect to each other,[3] but the intellect also has a desire in itself as its own intrinsic drive. As such it is also a being (*res quaedam*)[4] with its own intrinsic structure (form, nature). But every being tends towards its own fulfill-

---

[2] *S.T.* I. q. 82, a. 4, ad 1.
[3] See *S.C.G.* I, 55; *S.T.* I, q. 16, a. 1; q. 82, a. 4, corp. and ad 1; I–II, q. 9, a. 1, corp.; q. 12, a. 1, corp.; II–II, q. 180, a. 1, corp., etc.
[4] For example, *S.T.* I, q. 82, a. 4, ad 1.

ment (*appetitus in bonum*)[5]: "whatever exists has some inclination and desire for something suitable for it."[6] As a being, therefore, the intellect as such also has its own intrinsic, natural desire for its own end.[7] Hence, being appetite in itself, the intellect is in movement towards its end and goal, towards its good, and this is truth, as can be said in general first of all.[8]

Now it can also be said of this goal: "a nature tends towards only one end,"[9] so that there is only a single end and goal,[10] however this is to be defined materially, or however man actually understands it in his decision. Therefore, every "movement" of the spirit, wherever it is directed, occurs (since otherwise there would be many independent goals) in virtue of the desire for the one end and goal.[11] Just as a single power cannot simultaneously be the potency of several acts, unless these are ordered to the one end and goal as its partial movements,[12] so too this principle holds absolutely for any act of a power at all. Every act of a power is caused by its final end: "the desire and the actions which are for the sake of the end proceed from the

[5] See *S.T.* I, q. 59, a. 1, corp.; q. 80, a. 1, corp.; I–II, q. 1, a. 5, corp.: *unumquodque appetit suam perfectionem . . . ut bonum perfectum et completivum sui ipsius.*

[6] *De Malo* q. 1, a. 1, corp.

[7] *S.T.* I, q. 80, a. 1, ad 3; q. 78, a. 1, ad 3 at the beginning; I–II, q. 30, a. 1, ad 3; *De Ver.* q. 22, a. 3, ad 5; q. 25, a. 2, ad 8; *De Virtut.* q. 1, a. 4, ad 10; *III Sent.* dist. 27, q. 1, a. 2, corp.

[8] *S.T.* I, q. 82, a. 3, ad 1; I–II, q. 9, a. 1, ad 3; q. 57, a. 2, ad 3; q. 64, a. 3, corp.; II–II, q. 180, a. 1, ad 1; *De Malo* q. 6, a. 1, corp.; *In IV Ethic*, lect. 4, n. 1239.

[9] *S.T.* I–II, q. 1, a. 5, corp.

[10] See *loc. cit.*, and a. 6, corp. Notice that objectively the reasons in Thomas (a. 5) go beyond the proof he intends in the first place, namely, "*quod impossibile est quod voluntas unius hominis simul se habet ad diversa sicut ad ultimos fines.*" The proof holds objectively for every appetite, not just for the will in the narrower sense, and the *simul* only leaves the possibility open that the free self-decision of man as such (*voluntas*) can variously determine the material content under which it understands its goal, and this does not come into consideration for the natural appetite.

[11] *S.T.* I–II, q. 1, a. 6, corp.; q. 12, a. 3, ad 2.

[12] *S.T.* I, q. 58, a. 7, ad 2; q. 62, a. 7, ad 3; I–II, q. 54, a. 1, ad 3.

end,"[13] whereby it is to be noted that besides the desire for the goal and the possession of the goal, every other act of a power must also be "for the sake of the end" if there are not to be several final goals. Therefore, every act of a power (not merely simultaneous acts) stands under the same law of the one desire for the one final end, and is caused in a pre-apprehension of this end. The final end of the one desire of the spirit, expressed formally first of all, is the "good of the intellect," truth as such. But this truth which is the good of the intellect is absolute being. For spirit is the potentiality for the reception of all being (*quo est omnia fieri; respectu totius entis universalis*)[14] and the active desire for it (*quo est omnia facere*).

But this also tells us what the end and goal of the spirit is. For the end of a power corresponds to the breadth of its scope, is nothing other than the material fullness of its formal object, and is therefore already implicitly designated by the formal object: "the perfection of any potency is determined according to its formal object."[15] "Anything is the perfection of a potency to the extent that the formality of the proper object of that potency pertains to it."[16] But it has already been shown that in its act the spirit apprehends every object in a pre-apprehension of absolute being, hence that this is its formal object. Thus in its pre-apprehension, the spirit already and always possesses in every act being in its totality, and seeks to fill up the formal emptiness of the being given in the pre-apprehension through the object of every individual act. Being as such in this material fullness, absolute being, is therefore the end and goal of the spirit as such. Every operation of the spirit, whatever it might be, can therefore be understood only as a moment in the movement towards absolute being as towards the one end and goal of the desire of the spirit.

[13] *S.C.G.* I, 76.

[14] See *S.T.* I, q. 79, a. 2, ad 3; a. 7, corp.; q. 54, a. 2, corp., etc. See also the earlier sections.

[15] *S.T.* I–II, q. 3, a. 8, corp.

[16] *S.T.* I–II, q. 3, a. 7, corp.

2. The Production of Sensibility
in the Desire of the Spirit for Absolute Being

From this it follows that the active producing, in which the spirit as the "active principle and end" lets sensibility emanate from itself, must be understood as a moment in its desire for absolute being. But from this it becomes evident that the emanation of sensibility from spirit is the possibility of the abstractive conversion to the phantasm. The origin of sensibility from spirit had been defined by the fact that, in producing the complete constitution of its own essence towards which it tends, spirit lets sensibility emanate from itself, bears it permanently in itself as its power, and informs it from the outset with the laws of its own essence, since it produces it in its striving towards its own fulfillment. But the desire of the spirit for its own fulfillment which produces sensibility has shown itself to be a desire for absolute being. But the desire for absolute being was shown earlier, under the heading of a pre-apprehension of being, to be the fundamental abstraction. Consequently, the spirit produces its sensibility in this desire for being which constantly pre-apprehends absolute being, and this is the abstraction.

It must produce sensibility, because in itself it is only desire (possible intellect). But insofar as it produces sensibility as a condition of its own fulfillment, it retains it from the outset (as power and hence also in its own actuality, in the phantasm) as its power under the law of a pre-apprehension of *esse*. The emanation of sensibility from the spirit is the decisive conversion to the phantasm, and insofar as this letting-emanate takes place in a pre-apprehending desire for being as such, this conversion to the phantasm is already and always essentially abstraction, the illumination of the phantasm by the light of the agent intellect. The individual sentient act and its object come to exist essentially in a power which itself is produced from the outset in the pre-apprehension of being as such, so that such an act, as the determination of such a power, participates precisely in the nature of the power producing it. Thus the act of sensibility is itself a moment in an act of the pre-apprehension of being, and so its object is always abstracted already.

What was said earlier about sensibility is to be noted here: it is already in itself complete possession of the world; in sensibility access to the world is already open in principle, and in fact opened by the spirit for itself, as we can add now. Since the determination of sensibility by the individual, sensible object does not first create its being-with-the-world, but is only the formal limitation and determination of an empty, but real, possession of world, this possession of world as a whole is that of a spirit, insofar as spirit contains a desire for being in its totality. As a merely formal limitation and determination of such a possession of world, an individual, external object which manifests itself to sensibility is then already and necessarily under the law of the spirit.

The spirit comes to its own essence, that is, to itself as the power which apprehends being as such, and hence to the actual apprehension of being, only insofar as it continually lets sensibility emanate from itself as the antecedent condition for this, and this in such a way that spirit and sensibility are reciprocally the receptive origin of each other in the way shown earlier. Insofar as the individual determination of sensibility by the external object as such adds nothing to the intensity of sensibility, being as already complete openness to world, the world is already had, in fact already produced in the actualization of prime matter, of the other, by the spirit in the formal activity of the spirit. And insofar as spirit already and always expresses the openness of being in its totality, the spirit-produced world as sensibly open already and always stands in the spiritual openness of being in its totality. But if sensibility itself is the receptive origin of spirit, then the conscious actuality of spirit is conscious as the actuality of sensibility. And since the actuality of the spirit can only be known if its receptive origin itself is complete actuality, in other words, if sensibility is actually knowing, then the actuality of spirit is known as that of the complete actuality of sensibility. The *a priori* actuality of the spirit becomes conscious as the form of the sensibly conscious given, of the phantasm. The origin of sensibility in the spirit, through which sensibility itself

285

is the receptive origin of spirit, appears as the ground of the possibility and of the necessity of the synthesis of the *a priori* form of the spirit with the *a posteriori* material of sensibility, insofar as this material is only the formal, limiting determination of an *a priori* possession of world produced by the spirit itself, of a pure intuition of space and time.

Insofar as the spirit is the origin that lets sensibility emanate, the sensibly known is always already *abstracted*, since it is apprehended within being as such towards which the spirit is tending in the production of sensibility. Insofar as sensibility is the receptive origin of the spirit, a conversion to the phantasm is always already accomplished, since being in its totality is only had in a sentient, intuitive possession of world. With that we have acquired a conception of the possibility of an abstractive conversion to the phantasm from the emanation of sensibility from spirit.

3. Proof of the Formal Structure of This Line of Thought in Thomas

Admittedly, in its final stages this proof had to rely more on the inner, driving dynamism of Thomistic thought than on explicit texts. Attention has already been called to the extent to which explicit indications of the connection between the abstractive illumination, taking place with the help of the cogitative sense, and the origin (union) of sensibility are available. Further, insofar as the common nature is apprehended in the cogitative sense, but the cogitative sense is always considered explicitly as a continuation of the spirit into sensibility, our explanation of abstraction is expressed explicitly by Thomas himself, although not under the name abstraction. Beyond that, an explicit and detailed synthesis of what Thomas treats separately under the two headings of abstraction and the emanation of sensibility from the spirit cannot be shown to be in Thomas directly.

Nevertheless, the formal structure even of the final stages of this line of thought can still be clearly shown to be Thomistic.

We will add that now as a kind of review and verification. The original unity of spirit and sensibility founds an "*ordo*," a metaphysical hierarchy of the powers.[17] Spirit and sensibility are thus "ordered" powers. In this ordered origin lies the foundation for the possibility of spirit "moving" sensibility.[18] But it necessarily follows from this that sensibility and its acts with their objects stand under the form of the spirit from the outset. "For whenever there are two moving or agent principles ordered to each other, that which is in the effect from the higher agent is as the formal element, and that which is from the lower agent is as the material element.[19] But since the higher are formal with respect to the lower, more perfect, as it were (and the relationship between sensibility and spirit is that of the less perfect to the more perfect),[20] whatever of the higher is participated in by the lower is the formal element."[21] Applied to the acts of such principles, the principle reads: "An act which is essentially from one potency or habit receives its form and species from the higher potency or habit insofar as the lower is ordered by the higher."[22] The same connection is expressed in other terms: "In all ordered active potencies, that potency which looks to the universal end moves the potencies which look to particular ends,"[23] whereby the possibility of the active moving of the lower powers is founded precisely upon this "ordination" as caused by a relationship or origin, since the less perfect (that is, "which look to particular ends") emanate from the more perfect.

But then it holds of this "movement" of the lower power by

---

[17] See *S.T.* I, q. 77, a. 4 and a. 7 in their objective connection.

[18] See *De Ver.* q. 14, a. 5, corp.: . . . *cum quaedam potentiae sint naturaliter aliis priores* (on the basis of their origin, as was said just before this) *et alias moveant* (wherein evidently the "*movere*" is ontologically the effect, and in knowledge the ground of the relationship of origin of the powers, which is what he is talking about in the text cited). . . .

[19] *De Ver.* q. 14, a. 5, corp.

[20] For example, *Quodl.* 11, a. 5, corp.

[21] *III Sent.* dist. 27, q. 2, a. 4, sol. 3, ad 2.

[22] *S.T.* I–II, q. 13, a. 1, corp. Similarly elsewhere also, for example, q. 17, a. 4, corp.

[23] *S.T.* I, q. 82, a. 4, corp.; I–II, q. 9, a. 1, corp.

287

the higher: the higher moves the lower power towards its own goal, or more properly, moves itself through it. "If there are many agents having an order among them, the actions and movement of all the agents must be ordered to the good of the first agent as to an ultimate end. For since the lower agents are moved by the higher, and since every mover moves towards its own end, the actions and movement of the lower agents must tend towards the end of the first agent."[24] Hence, if sensibility as the lower power through its origin from the spirit is ordered and moved by the spirit, then sensibility and its actuality are ordered from the outset in virtue of this original order to the end and goal of the spirit, to absolute being.

That the application of such metaphysical relations between two powers to the relationship of spirit and sensibility in order to clarify the abstractive illumination lies within the thought of the historical Thomas can be confirmed still further by showing that Thomas as a matter of fact goes back to the axiom mentioned in a quite parallel problematic. This occurs in the question, how a higher virtue (considered as an ontic power infused by grace) informs and moves another lower virtue which belongs to another psychic power.[25] This parallel[26] is all the more justified since Thomas himself in this question goes back to the emanation of the natural powers from the substantial ground and from each other.[27] But the development of this parallel would lead us too far afield into theological questions.

In the light of the results we have reached, certain ways in which Thomas speaks of abstraction, which had to remain outside our consideration so far, become more intelligible. In one text the phantasm is supposed to be the *instrumental cause* of

[24] *Compend. Theol.* c. 103, Similarly, *S.C.G.* III, 17.

[25] See, for example, *S.T.* II–II, q. 23, a. 8; II *Sent.* dist. 26, q. 1, a. 4, ad 5; *III Sent.* dist. 27, q. 2, a. 4, sol. 3, corp. and ad 2; *De Caritate* a. 3, corp.

[26] To see the parallels, cf., for example, *S.T.* I–II, q. 62, a. 4 with I, q. 77, a. 4 and a. 7.

[27] *S.T.* I–II, q. 110, a. 4, ad 1 and ad 4; III, q. 7, a. 2, corp.; q. 62, a. 2, corp.; q. 89, a. 1, corp.; *De Ver.* q. 25, a. 6, ad 1; *IV Sent.* dist. 1, q. 1, a. 4, sol. 5, corp.; dist. 17, q. 1, a. 1, sol. 1, ad 3.

the agent intellect in spiritual knowing.[28] In understanding this phrase the notion is to be avoided that the phantasm is a kind of writing instrument with the help of which the agent intellect produces a spiritual image in the possible intellect. The correct concept of the intelligible species in the narrower sense already forbids such an interpretation. This way of speaking can be understood correctly only if phantasm is understood in its true sense. If phantasm is understood as a formal determination of sensibility, which is a power of the spirit itself produced by the spirit, then it is self-evident that it is through its formal determination of such a sensibility, and not through a further influence on the spirit different from this, that the phantasm is the instrumental cause of the fact that the spirit comes to itself, that is, to being in its totality, and thus has already abstracted.

The spirit comes to its own fulfillment through its own spontaneous activity (agent intellect) when sensibility, which is the way to its fulfillment produced by itself, is itself actually completed by its formal determination, by the phantasm. The phantasm is an instrumental cause through its own being as completion of sensibility. There is no need of an influence of the phantasm on the spirit objectively different from that, especially since elsewhere Thomas explicitly rejects an instrumental causality of the phantasm beyond its being object.[29] An instrumental causality of the phantasm in the usual meaning does not make any sense just by the fact that something can be an instrument of another in the usual sense, without having had an influence on this other antecedently, only if it is itself known antecedently. That is the only kind of connection by which a spontaneous taking-hold of the instrument is conceivable. But this is as little conceivable precisely between the agent intellect and the phantasm as is an influence of the phantasm on the agent intellect which would be different from the formal determination of the imagination by the phantasm.

Further, abstraction is often depicted in Thomas as conditioned by a preparation (*praeparatio*) of the phantasms. Now

[28] *De Ver.* q. 10, a. 6, ad 7; *Quodl.* 8, a. 3, corp.
[29] *In I de Anima* lect. 2, n. 19; *III Sent.* dist. 31, q. 2, a. 4, corp.

this is at one time ascribed to the active influence of the spirit itself,[80] at another time to the sense faculties.[31] From the results obtained it is now evident that this apparently dual preparation is objectively *one*. By letting sensibility emanate, the spirit already and always exerts an active influence upon sensibility; from the outset it structures sensibility as a power in such a way that sensibility's formal determination, the phantasm, stands under its law. Insofar as sensibility communicates its spirituality to the phantasm as its determination, *it* prepares the phantasm on behalf of spirit for abstraction (this understood as the "insofar as we are able to receive the natures of species for our consideration . . ."). Insofar as this spirituality of sensibility is originally produced by the spirit itself, it is *the spirit itself* which effects this preparation of the phantasm, and for the same reason it then can also accomplish this in the *free* direction of sensibility, as soon as it is once present to itself. Then in this last instance also two preparations can be distinguished: that of sensibility (which is originally that of the spirit itself in its natural self-constitution) and that of the spirit as ruling freely over its sensibility, which second preparation again has its possibility in the first. Since the fundamental abstraction consists in letting sensibility emanate as a power of the spirit itself retained in the spirit which remains free (of whose freedom we will have to speak explicitly), Thomas can also say that the agent intellect does not work "directly" on the possible intellect, but on the phantasms.[82]

VI. THE FREEDOM OF SPIRIT

Although in the preceding section the emanation of sensibility from spirit as the possibility of the abstractive illumination was

---

[80] *S.T.* I, q. 85, a. 1, ad 4; q. 76, a. 2, corp.: *Oboediunt vires sensitivae intellectui et ei deserviunt;* II–II, q. 173, a. 2, corp.; *S.C.G.* II, 73 (*imperium rationis* over the phantasms); *In III de Anima* lect. 13, n. 791: *formare sibi aliquod phantasma; formare imaginativae virtutis phantasmata* through the *ratio: S.T.* I, q. 81, a. 3, ad 3.

[31] *S.T.* I–II q. 50, a. 4, ad 3; *S.C.G.* II, 73; II, 80. See also *S.C.G.* II, 60: the same as the opinion of Averroes.

[82] *De Anima* a. 18, ad 11.

understood in general outline, this explanation still needs an essential elaboration in one respect, in the sense of bringing something out which so far has been more a presupposition, or only hinted at. The emanation of sensibility from spirit was shown to be the possibility for the fact that the *a priori* actuality of the spirit becomes conscious as the form of what is sensibly given, and that thus the abstraction be accomplished. By way of parentheses, the emanation is understood here in a way which, on the one hand, does not belong simply to the essence of the emanation of a power or an ontological determination, and yet, on the other hand, is decisive for the fact that the spiritualization of sensibility really makes an abstraction possible.

1. Freedom as Transcending (Überspringen) Sensibility in Its Origin from Spirit

What was said above about the emanation of powers with respect to the emanation of spirit and sensibility holds in general, according to Thomas, for the constitution of the essence of an existent in the unfolding of its necessary determinations ("proper accidents"). The determinations of an existent which are necessary and yet different from the essential ground emanate from this ground; this ground unfolds into them.[1] Now just as the powers in the narrower sense also emanate from each other in a definite order, so too in general is the relationship between any of the determinations of an existent at all.[2] Hence according to Thomas, quantity is the first emanation in a material existent, and this receives in itself all the rest of the quali-

---

[1] *S.C.G.* V, 14: *accidentia sunt formae quaedam . . . a principiis substantiae causatae.* Similarly, *In IV Metaph.* lect. 2, n. 559; *De Malo* q. 4, a. 2, ad 9; *S.T.* I, q. 77, a. 1, ad 5; a. 6, corp. and ad 3 (*naturalis resultatio*), wherein it is to be noted that in this text Thomas is speaking quite generally about every *proprium et per se accidens. Principia subjecti sunt principia per se accidentis: De Virtut.* q. 1, a. 3, corp. See *De Spir. Creat.* q. 1, a. 11, corp.; *De Anima* a. 12, ad 7; *I Sent.* dist. 17, q. 1, a. 2, ad 2.

[2] *I Sent.* dist. 3, q. 4, a. 3, ad 2.

tative determinations of this existent as receptive origin.[3] But if the substantial ground of a material existent lets quantity emanate from itself as the first receptive origin of all the rest of its determinations, and retains it in itself, then it has become altogether quantitative, spatio-temporal itself; that which in itself would be simple and undifferentiated[4] has lost itself so much in the dispersion of matter, the ground of the quantitative, that no unity surmounting this dispersion remains to it any more through which it could be gathered to itself and present to itself.[5]

From this situation arises the question, why, in letting sensibility emanate, the spirit too does not so lose itself in the other, in matter, that it has its being only in the other, and so is no longer present to itself; why in this way precisely what is supposed to provide the possibility of the possible intellect (as possible) being-present-to-itself does not make a return to itself impossible. This question is simultaneously the question about the specific way in which the *a priori* structure of the spirit becomes the form of what is sensibly given. If this form (being as such) were to spiritualize the phantasm after the manner of a material existent, then it would be true of it too: "it does not exceed the proportions of matter," and it would be knowable only as such. The spirit itself would have become sensible in the conversion to the phantasm; the phantasm would no longer be known in the awareness of absolute being.

The presuppositions for answering this question are already

---

[3] IV *Sent.* dist. 12, q. 1, a. 1, sol. 3, corp.; dist. 16, q. 3, a. 1, sol. 1, ad 3; *S.T.* I–II q. 7, a. 1, ad 3; I, q. 77, a. 7, ad 2; I–II, q. 50, a. 2, ad 2; q. 56, a. 1,a d3; *In IV Metaph.* lect. 7, n. 635.

[4] *S.C.G.* V, 65: *remota quantitate substantia omnis indivisibilis est.* See also *S.T.* I, q. 50, a. 2, corp. It is dealing, of course, with an unreal supposition.

[5] Cf. expressions in Thomas such as: *forma non excedit materiae proportionem* (*S.T.* II–II, q. 24, a. 3, ad 2); *forma materialis non habens esse absolute in quo subsistere possit* (*II Sent.* dist. 1, q. 2, a. 4, ad 4); *forma quae non est per se subsistens, non habet alium modum a modo subjecti, quia non habet esse nisi inquantum est actus talis subjecti* (*IV Sent.* dist. 49, q. 2, a. 3, ad 6; see also *loc. cit.* a. 4, corp. at the beginning).

given to us: it is answered by establishing the end towards which the spirit is striving in letting sensibility emanate from itself. This end is not the other, matter, and therefore not sensibility either, but being as such, the spirit itself as non-sensible, since it produces sensibility in its desire for absolute being, which desire it itself is. Hence, insofar as it lets sensibility emanate, spirit has always already transcended the breadth of sensibility, the intellect as the origin letting sensibility emanate is what has first emanated from the substantial ground, and so is *prior* to every limitation of sensibility. Therefore, it cannot be the last thing received in sensibility as receptive origin in the sense that it becomes sensibility itself. Otherwise, of course, it would also be nothing over and beyond its receptive origin; the same thing twice would have both emanated from the origin and have been received in it. Thus spirit is before and after sensibility.

Therefore, it is true: "it is united with the other as conquering and holding sway over it . . . the essence of the soul is united with the body as its form, but not as a material form not having an absolute *esse* in which it could subsist."[6] ". . . in its power it exceeds corporeal matter . . . it holds sway over matter and is not immersed in it."[7] Thus the spirit remains nevertheless free in its letting-itself-emanate into sensibility. It is a form of matter which is subsistent in itself. And therefore its *a priori* structure is the form of the phantasm and yet a form which is present to itself; it is known as the structure of what is sensibly given, of the individual given in sensibility, but in such a way that it does not disappear in the individuality of the latter and conceal its own universality. That relationship of spirit as spirit and of spirit as the determination of matter, which is to be defined from both sides and to be grasped from the essence of the possible intellect as a more original unity, is also true of the relationship of the light of the agent intellect and the phantasm: "Therefore, the principle of the operation of intellectual knowing must formally (that is, as form) be in this

[6] *II Sent.* dist. 1, q. 2, a. 4, ad 4.
[7] *S.T.* I, q. 76, a. 1, corp. See *S.C.G.* II, 81; *De Spir. Creat.* a. 2, corp. and ad 2 and 4; *De Anima* a. 1, corp; a. 2, corp. towards the end.

man (as a material essence); but the principle of this operation is not a form whose *esse* is dependent on a body and bound to or immersed in matter . . . But if the things mentioned are united, it must be said that a certain *spiritual* substance (remaining such, that is, free of matter) is the *form* of the human body."[8] The things mentioned are united: the *a priori* structure of the spirit becomes the form of the sensibly given because sensibility is the receptive origin of the spirit, and yet it remains free, so that the spirit returns to itself and in sensibility knows the other, which it itself is in sensibility, *as* other, because the spirit itself is the origin letting sensibility emanate; not sensibility, but spirit itself is the end towards which its letting emanate tends.

We have already called attention briefly in the preceding section to a theological parallel to the relationship between the *a priori* structure of the spirit and the phantasm to prove that the problematic of that section cannot be unknown to Thomas. This parallel continues now in the problematic of this section too. Thus charity, for example, is the form, root and generative principle (*mater*) of the other virtues which produces the other virtues and directs and moves them towards its own goal,[9] and yet it does not disappear into them, it is in a certain sense outside them and remains in itself.[10] We cannot go further into this parallel here either.

Now this brings the problematic of the knowledge of the other as other and of the complete return to a relative conclusion. The other can be had in knowledge only insofar as the knower becomes the other: sensibility. The other can be apprehended as other only if the knower, together with the fact that it is the other, and through the fact that it is the other also "holds sway over it," is present to itself insofar as it produces this being-other in its striving-towards-itself, and thereby has always already surpassed the other. The *a priori* structure of spirit, the

---

[8] *De Spir. Creat.* a. 2, corp. See *loc. cit.* a. 9, ad 3: *forma transcendens corporis capacitatem;* and ad 4: *in definitione animae ponitur corpus.*

[9] *De Caritate* a. 3, corp. and ad 8.

[10] *Loc. cit.* ad 4 and ad 18.

knowledge of being as such, is therefore conscious not only as the structure of the sensibly given, but also as reaching beyond it, and hence the knower is present to himself as different from the other, he has returned to himself in knowing the sensibly given, and also knows the *a priori* form of the spirit as his own insofar as he elevates himself above the other.

This transcendence beyond the other of sensibility, which is the return of the spirit to itself, can be called Thomistically the freedom of spirit. The sensible is not free because it is an individual to the exclusion of something besides itself, and instead of its possible others. There is indeed a "freedom" of matter in itself ("free passive potency"),[11] but it is only the empty indifference of the absolutely indeterminate with respect to every determination, a freedom which is removed and so far as possible bound (*ligata*) by the determination of the form.[12] Through the determination of form matter as such becomes something definite, limited, something which has opposites, contraries alongside of it which contradict and oppose each other.[13] In spirit, the narrowness and constraint of the contraries is abolished. "Insofar as the formalities of contraries are apprehended, they are not contrary."[14] "According to this (spiritual) *esse,* the contraries are not contrary."[15] As intellectually known, all things belong to the same genus.[16] This freedom beyond the contraries (the "being disposed to opposites") is the distinctive mark putting rational potency above irrational potency.[17] Therefore, freedom in the usual sense is also derived for Thomas from the absolute breadth of the spirit (universality).[18] The spirit is free in contrast to sensibility, which always apprehends only the individual as here and now, and as such it excludes another from this

[11] *IV Sent.* dist. 44, q. 2, a. 1, sol. 1, ad 2.
[12] *Loc. cit.*
[13] *S.T.* I, q. 103, a. 3, obj. 2.
[14] *S.T.* I–II, q. 35, a. 5, corp. and ad 2; q. 64, a. 3, ad 3; *S.C.G.* I, 71.
[15] *III Sent.* dist. 26, q. 1, a. 3, ad 4.
[16] *S.C.G.* I, 55.
[17] *In IX Metaph.* lect. 2, n. 1789ff.; lect. 9, n. 1881, etc.
[18] *S.C.G.* II, 47 at the end; 48; *De Ver.* q. 22, a. 4, ad 2; q. 24, a. 1, corp.; a. 2, corp.

here and now. For spirit always apprehends the individual object insofar as it pre-apprehends being in its totality. But then it apprehends it in such a way that, as apprehended by the spirit, the individual object does not exclude any other besides itself from being known. For being in its totality has no contrary besides itself which would limit it over against itself and thus confine its scope.[19]

Therefore, if the freedom of spirit is only another name for the possibility of the pre-apprehension of being in its totality, and if, on the other hand, this pre-apprehension is only the consciousness of the essence of the spirit, by virtue of which it tends towards its own goal and in this tendency produces sensibility while surpassing it, and because it lets sensibility emanate in this way it does not become sensible itself, but remains "abstract" and returns to itself, then it can also be said that the possibility of abstraction and the complete return is grounded in the freedom of spirit. Spirit "holds sway over matter," it is its lord, although it binds itself to it, in fact (insofar as it comes to itself only in binding itself to it), *because* it binds itself to it: "it is united with the other . . . holding sway over it." In spite of and because of the conversion to the phantasm, spirit is present to itself, that is, free. "It is not subject to matter, so that it would be rendered matter."[20] "This (intellectual) light is not bound to the body."[21]

Because of its freedom, spirit appears as a power alongside of sensibility. Not indeed in the sense of a meeting of the two subsequent to their constitution, which gives rise to the problem of their collaboration, the problem of bridging the gap between the two. The spirit is indeed the origin letting sensibility emanate as the receptive origin of spirit. But insofar as spirit does not let sensibility emanate in such a way that it lets itself be completely dispersed in it, it retains the possibility of really coming to be according to its own essence, whose region lies ante-

---

[19] *S.T.* I–II, q. 64, a. 3, ad 3: *esse et non esse non sunt contraria, sed contradictorie opposita.*
[20] *De Ver.* q. 10, a. 8, ad 4.
[21] *De Ver.* q. 19, a. 1, corp.

cedent to sensibility and beyond it at once. And therefore the origin of sensibility, spirit, is not merely its deeper-lying ground, which could only manifest itself in it as merely sensible, but a power alongside of sensibility which possesses its own essence. But insofar as spirit possesses its own essence precisely insofar as it lets sensibility emanate, its non-sensible essence must manifest itself in sensibility itself; spirit must come to light as non-sensible in sensibility itself. Thomas calls sensibility as the manifestation of the non-sensible spirit the cogitative sense.

2. Negation as Measure of the Freedom of Spirit in Its Ordination to Sensibility (The Ontological Sense of "Nothing")

Let us add something by way of supplement to the considerations of this section which will settle one further problem explicitly which our earlier considerations came up against quite frequently: the question of the possibility of negation. "The first thing which the intellect comes upon is being (ens), and the second is the negation of being."[22] "Being itself, therefore, is known first, and then consequently non-being."[23] The whole Thomistic answer to the question is contained in these sentences. Being already and always expresses a synthesis of something quidditative (anything) with esse. Being as such, which is what is first apprehended (in the sense that it expresses the metaphysical structure of anything objectively apprehended in human knowledge at all), already and always expresses abstraction as the pre-apprehension of absolute esse and expresses the conversion to the phantasm, insofar as esse is known only in turning to a representative, and so ultimately sensibly given, quiddity (any quiddity). Thus fundamentally ens already expresses the origin of sensibility from spirit as the fundamental possibility of a synthesis of a sensible quiddity and universal being.

[22] De Pot. q. 9, a. 7, ad 15.
[23] In IV Metaph. lect. 3, n. 566; see S.T. I, q. 11, a. 2, ad 4; In VII Metaph. lect. 4, n. 1336: non ens is known "per posterius" to ens.

297

Insofar as spirit preserves its freedom in this synthesis, *esse* as such is already and always known simultaneously in the apprehension of being (*ens*); being as such is always already surpassed by the pre-apprehension of *esse* as such. Insofar as being, in order to be known objectively, is apprehended in this pre-apprehension, it is always already known as limited, "negated," and in fact according to what has been said, not perhaps by being seen against the "nothing" on which it borders and whose empty space it does not fill up, but through the knowledge of *esse* as such. This *esse* known in the freedom of spirit is apprehended as limited by the ultimately sensibly given quiddity, hence in the conversion to the phantasm in which the quiddity enters into a synthesis with *esse* which limits this *esse,* and this is the condition of the possibility of the consciousness of *esse,* although it does not deprive *esse* of its freedom, its universality. Thus the negation of the sensibly given belongs to the conditions of the possibility of any objective knowledge at all.

The negation (*remotio*), without which there is no metaphysics on the basis of the imagination,[24] is only the thematization of the pre-apprehension of *esse* which surpasses being, and only through this does the representatively given content become objective. Hence the negation is ultimately the thematization of an affirmation. The abstractive conversion to the phantasm is the ground of the necessity and of the possibility of such a negation. The negation is the measure of the freedom of spirit in its being bound to sensibility. Non-being is known, not insofar as being is held up against nothing, but insofar as *esse* as such is apprehended simultaneously. Otherwise there would have to be a grasp of nothing as such. Since this "nothing" has "nothing" to do with being, this grasp would not be borne (not "secondly," "consequently") by the knowledge of an existent. But for Thomas non-being is not an object which could manifest itself from itself,[25] the negation is not a specific mode of knowledge in

---

[24] *S.T.* I, q. 84, a. 7, ad 3.
[25] *S.T.* I, q. 16, a. 3, ad 2: *non habet in se unde cognoscatur.*

its own right.[26] Thus if every negation is founded upon an affirma-tion,[27] so too must the most radical negation, non-being. It is founded upon the transcendental affirmation (that is, necessarily affirmed simultaneously in any affirmation whatsoever) of *esse* as such, in fact this is of itself that negation without anything further. Absolute *esse* absolutely has no negation, no more non-being alongside of it. There is no realm of objects of knowledge which would be divided into real being and non-being as equal partners. That we might nevertheless always believe that in thought we can place non-being as such alongside of being as a coordinate object of our knowledge is only an illusion which stems from the fact that we know *esse* only in the mode of being, that there is no freedom of spirit for man except in being bound to sensibility, in the conversion to the phantasm.

VII. THE COGITATIVE SENSE

The cogitative sense has already been shown to be the mani-festation of the free spirit in sensibility itself, as the unified center of spirit and sensibility, as the place of the illuminative, abstractive conversion to the phantasm, as the measure of the fact that the spirit can move and inform sensibility and have it as the co-principle of its knowing because it actively lets it emanate from itself.

In the context of this work the doctrine of Thomas on the cogitative sense concerns us only from the viewpoint of under-standing the conversion to the phantasm. The decisive state-ments in Thomas about it from this point of view have already been treated. If we now elaborate these statements further, it will serve at the same time as a kind of review and verification

[26] *S.T.* I–II, q. 71, a. 6, ad 1: *affirmatio et negatio reducuntur ad idem genus;* q. 72, a. 6, ad 3: *negatio, etsi proprie non sit in specie, constituitur tamen in specie per reductionem ad aliquam affirmationem quam sequitur.*
[27] *De Malo* q. 2, a. 1, ad 9.

of the understanding of the conversion to the phantasm we have
already reached.

1. The Cogitative as the "Sentient" Power of the Conversion

First of all, cogitative sense and conversion say objectively the
same thing, or, if we want to take into consideration the fact
that the cogitative sense is intended first of all to designate a
power, and the conversion an actual realization of knowledge,
then we can also say: the cogitative sense is the power of conversion to the phantasm. If we take into account further that for
Thomas the cogitative sense is a sentient power (in a sense still to
be determined), then, taking into consideration what the conversion to the phantasm is fundamentally, our formula has to read:
the cogitative sense is the term designating the fact that sensibility is held permanently in the free origin which lets it emanate. That Thomas has the cogitative sense coincide objectively
with the conversion to the phantasm has already been shown in
Section 4.

This can also be verified in a somewhat different and simpler
way. Thomas explains explicitly that without the cogitative
sense (particular reason) man cannot know at all: "without
this (that is, without the particular reason which is called the
cogitative sense) the soul now (that is, in its earthly state) knows
nothing."[1] The reason for this, as follows from the context of
the response and of the whole article, is the necessity of turning to the phantasm and abstracting. The necessity of the cogitative sense and the conversion coincide, they themselves are
therefore objectively one. The same thing follows even more
clearly from a later work of Thomas: "but without this part of
the corporeal soul (that is, without the 'passive intellect') the
intellect does not know anything. For it does not know anything without a phantasm as will be said below."[2] Aristotle's

[1] *IV Sent.* dist. 50, q. 1, a. 1, ad 3.
[2] *In III de Anima* lect. 10, n. 745. *S.C.G.* II, 80 towards the end, also
has the conversion and the function of the cogitative sense coincide.

"soul knows nothing without a phantasm"[3] is only another expression for the conversion to the phantasm and therefore *S.T.* I, q. 84, a. 7, sed contra is the text of the Philosopher with which the conversion is proved. The proof given by Thomas ("as will be said below"[4]) of the necessity of the conversion is also of itself the proof of the necessity of the cogitative sense for Thomas. They are therefore objectively one.

2. The Cogitative Sense in Its Specific Sensibility

It has already been shown that the cogitative sense is the unified center of spirit and sensibility insofar as it is that power of sensibility proper only to man for which it is essential to stand under the guiding influence of the spirit as the continuation of spirit in sensibility. This result was confirmed by a consideration of the functions which Thomas ascribes to the cogitative sense. The cogitative sense is the potency for apprehending the individual object in a way which shows that the individual as such and the common nature must be given in it in an already differentiated unity.

The spiritualization of sensibility and of the cogitative sense is shown first of all purely extrinsically by the fact that practically all the names of the intellect's functions are transferred to it. Just as Thomas distinguishes in the intellect an intellect in the narrower sense and a *ratio*,[5] so too he distinguishes in the cogitative sense an intellectual and a rational side.[6] Just as the intellect divides and composes in the judgment, so too a *dividere et componere* is ascribed to the cogitative sense also.[7] Like the intellect, the cogitative sense "compares" (*confert*),[8] it is active in

---

[3] *De Anima* Γ, 7 437 a. 17.

[4] See *In III de Anima* lect. 12, n. 772; lect. 13, n. 791.

[5] For example, *S.T.* I. q. 79, a. 8, and the parallels.

[6] *In VI Ethic.* lect. 9, n. 1249; n. 1255.

[7] *S.C.G.* II, 73; *S.T.* I, q. 78, a. 4, obj. 5.

[8] *De Ver.* q. 15, a. 1, corp. at the end; see *In Metaph.* lect. 1, n. 15 (*collatio*).

inquirendo et conferendo,[9] it is designated as the power of apprehending relations (*collativa*) as is the intellect.[10] We can translate the word *collativa* as the power of apprehending relations, because what the cogitative sense accomplishes, namely, the apprehension of the sensibly given as useful, harmful, and so on, is distinguished explicitly from the instinct of animals,[11] which is able to accomplish the same thing as the cogitative sense, looking merely at the practical result. As such a power of apprehending relations, the cogitative sense is therefore also called the "particular reason," the "passive intellect."[12]

Now it is correct that Thomas ascribes these functions to the cogitative sense only with respect to the "individual intentions," the "particular intentions,"[13] that is, only with regard to individual objects, which for him is self-evident just by the fact that he holds that the cogitative is a sense power. But upon closer inspection it is evident immediately that this cannot be meant in the sense in which it belongs to any sense power at all to apprehend only the individual. The individual must be given in the cogitative sense in an already differentiated unity with the universal, the common nature.[14] We have already referred to texts which bring this out explicitly. But what was just said also confirms this explanation. An apprehension of relations which is explicitly distinguished from merely animal instinct, a comparison of many individuals among one another,[15] is incon-

9 *De Anima* a. 13, corp.

10 *In II de Anima* lect. 13, n. 396; *S.T.* I, q. 81, a. 3, corp.; q. 78, a. 4, corp.; etc.

11 *S.T.* I, q. 78, a. 4, corp.; *De Anima* a. 13, corp.; *III Sent.* dist. 26, q. 1, a. 1, ad 4: the instinct *"non confert."* Likewise, *S.T.* I, q. 83, a. 1, corp.; *II Sent.* dist. 24, q. 2, a. 2, corp.; dist. 25, q. 1, a. 1, ad. 7.

12 *De Anima* a. 13, corp.: . . . *collativa* . . . *unde et ratio particularis dicitur et intellectus passivus.*

13 *S.T.* I, q. 78, a. 4, corp., etc.

14 Notice: We are not speaking here about the relationship between nature and individual thing *in itself* (as C. Nink, *op. cit.,* p. 51, thinks), but about their mode of givenness in the cogitative sense. The same thing holds for Nink, *op. cit.,* p. 82, note 79: the point here is the specific mode of the individual thing's givenness in the universal concept.

15 *In I Metaph.* lect. 1, n. 15.

ceivable unless something common in the "individual intentions" is already set in relief, given, and apprehended, although it is not yet explicitly attended to as such. Therefore, the spirit must already be at work in the cogitative sense as the apprehension of the individual in this special sense. Hence Thomas traces this comparing of the cogitative sense, which is not proper to instinct, back to its "union with the rational soul,"[16] and therefore it need not be surprising either that in one text Thomas also traces the comparing, which distinguishes human practical behavior from the instinct of animals, back to the "lower reason" immediately, and identifies this with the "higher reason," the intellect,[17] just as in other places he also puts instinct immediately alongside the spiritual powers, without bringing in the human connecting link of the cogitative sense.[18]

This specific way in which the cogitative sense apprehends the individual follows even more clearly from the way in which the cogitative sense works together with the spirit in one particular instance. The inferential judgments of the practical intellect (intellectus practicus), in which a universal law of behavior (universalis sententia de operabilibus) is applied to a definite, individual case (particularis actus), are possible, according to Thomas, only with the help of the cogitative sense.[19] It presents the individual in such a way that the universal law of the practical intellect (opinio intellectus practici) can be applied to it. It is necessary for this because without it, as has already been shown, the individual as such cannot be reached at all.[20] But if the individual is to be given in the cogitative sense (and only in it) in such a way that the universal law can be applied to it, then the individual itself must be given in the cogitative sense as an instance of this law: the sensibly given cannot exist in the cogitative sense merely sensibly, that is, in its unrelated indi-

---

[16] III Sent. dist. 26, q. 1, a. 2, corp.

[17] II Sent. dist. 24, q. 2, a. 2, corp.

[18] S.T. I–II, q. 11, a. 2, corp.; q. 15, a. 2, corp.; q. 16, a. 2, ad 2; q. 17, a. 2, ad 3; q. 46, a. 4, ad 2; a. 7, ad 1.

[19] See S.T. I, q. 81, a. 3, corp.; q. 86, a. 1, ad 2; De Ver. q. 10, a. 5, corp., ad 2 and ad 4; IV Sent. dist. 50, q. 1, a. 3, ad 3, in contr.

[20] De Anima a. 20, a. 1, in contr.

viduality; the individual in the cogitative sense must of itself already contain a reference to the universal in itself, although this individuality and the common nature as the fundamental universal are not yet actually separated. The individual must be given "as existing in the common nature." What significance this insight into the essence of the cogitative sense has for the correct understanding of the abstractive conversion to the phantasm has already been shown in Section 4.

It was also shown there that the spirit as such is a constitutive element of this "sense" power insofar as the "affinity and proximity to the universal reason" is essential to the cogitative sense. From that it also followed that the cogitative sense is a sense power only insofar as it forms the unified center of spirit and sensibility. Hence there remains only the question why it is spoken of by Thomas so emphatically as a sense power. This question is clarified by a principle of appropriation which Thomas lays down in a similar question. Is freedom of choice a power different from intellect and will, since it has its root in the intellect and will in common, and if not, to which of the two powers does it belong? Thomas answers that the freedom of choice belongs to the will "but insofar as the power of reason and intellect remain in it." Hence if the freedom of choice is at least just as much an expression of the "power of the reason and intellect," why then is it nevertheless "principally an act of the will"? "For whenever something is the act of a potency insofar as the power of another potency remains in it, the act is always attributed to that potency by whose mediation it is produced."[21] Hence, the act proceeds originally from a potency, it bears the "power" of this potency in itself, since this power belongs intrinsically to the second potency also, but it unfolds in the medium (*qua mediante*) of this second potency, and only for that reason is it spoken of as the act of the second potency.

It is precisely this relationship that is present in our case. The differentiated unity of the common nature and the individual can unfold as a unity with an *individual* only in the medium of sensibility. For that reason, and only for that reason, the place

21 *II Sent.* dist. 24, q. 1, a. 3, corp.

of this unity, the power and its act, is called sensible. Consequently, this in no way denies that in this "sense" power (as in the free will) "there remains . . . the power of the reason and intellect," and that accordingly, as in the parallel case, here too it must always be added to this attribution of the cogitative sense to sensibility: "not, however, absolutely, but insofar as the power of the intellect or reason remain in it."[22] If the sensibility of the cogitative sense is understood correctly in this sense, then this characteristic does not offer any hindrance to understanding it as the place of the fundamental abstractive conversion to the phantasm, as the place of the freedom of spirit in its bond with sensibility. The cogitative sense is really the passive intellect: the center of the free spontaneity of spirit (intellect) and the reception of the encountering other in sensibility (passive).

3. The Cogitative Sense in Its Union with Imagination in the One, Original, Imaginative Power of the Spirit

In the chapter on sensibility the imagination was shown to be the foundation and root of all sensibility. If sensibility as a whole has spirit as its origin, and if the cogitative sense is the name for the point at which spirit lets itself emanate into sensibility and from which it permeates it, then it is to be expected from the outset that imagination and cogitative sense at least stand in the closest relationship, if they are not simply two names for the same reality. Now it is correct that Thomas distinguishes the imagination and the cogitative sense from each other as two powers,[23] and we do not have to investigate here

---

[22] Loc. cit.

[23] De Anima a. 13, corp.; S.T. I, q. 78, a. 4, corp. Thomas locates them physiologically in different places; see for both: IV Sent. dist. 7, q. 3, a. 3, sol. 2, obj. 1; for the imagination: II Sent. dist. 20, q. 2, a. 2, corp.; IV Sent. dist. 7, q. 3, a. 3, sol. 2, corp.; De Ver. q. 18, a. 8, corp.; for the cogitative sense: S.T. I, q. 78, a. 4, corp.; IV Sent. dist. 50, q. 1, a. 1, ad 3; S.C.G. II, 60; De Ver. q. 10, a. 5, corp.; q. 15, a. 1, corp. at the end. Yet the way in which the objective differences of the internal senses are introduced in De Mem. et Rem. lect. 2, n. 321 (sed Avicenna rationabiliter ostendit . . .) shows that Thomas had no decisive meta-

whether this distinction of the four internal senses, when meant objectively, is really demanded by the inner dynamism of the Thomistic metaphysics of knowledge, or is more a piece of tradition handed on uncritically. However the answer to this question would have to turn out, in any case one thing can be said: even an objective difference is an intrinsically variable concept. Two things are called objectively different when they are separated from each other and are absolutely different realities. Two powers can also be called objectively different in a certain respect when they belong to a single existent and form a single totality of meaning, in fact even when they belong to a common origin and owe their being almost to the same emanation.

Now imagination and cogitative sense are, at most, objectively different in this last sense. This is shown not only in the fact that, as sense powers, and in fact as sense powers which belong to the narrower region of the internal senses, both have the spirit as the origin which lets them emanate. In spite of their objective difference, again and again Thomas also has them emanate together. As the name itself says, the phantasm obviously belongs to the "phantasy or imagination which are the same thing";[24] the imagination is the power to form phantasms in itself freely[25] (wherein the spontaneity of the spirit itself manifests itself).[26]

physical interest in this thesis. "*Rationabiliter*" is often used in Thomas as opposed to "*demonstrative*." See *In de Caelo* lib. 1, lect. 12, and Rousselot, *op. cit.*, p. 149. Corresponding to this, quite frequently Thomas puts the responsibility for localizing the cogitative sense upon the "*medici*" or the "*Commentator*." Moreover, going by *S.T.* I, q. 79, a. 7, where the intellectual memory and the intellect are identified, it is not evident why the same reasons should not also hold for the sense memory, the imagination, and the common sense, why it does not hold here too: *ad rationem enim potentiae passivae pertinet conservare sicut et retinere.* It has already been observed frequently that in Thomas an "*oportet*" and a "*necessarium est*," as in *S.T.* I, q. 78, a. 4, corp., do not have to introduce a stringent conclusion. Cf. Rousselot, *op. cit.*, pp. 152ff.; pp. 161f.

24 *S.T.* I, q. 78, a. 4, corp.
25 *S.T.* I, q. 84, a. 7, ad 2; q. 85, a. 2, ad 3; *De Ver.* q. 8, a. 5, corp.; *Quodl.* 8, a. 3, corp.
26 *S.C.G.* II, 73: *secundum enim imperium intellectus formatur in imaginatione phantasma.*

On the other hand, it is precisely the cogitative sense which shows itself to be the locus of the conversion to the phantasm, so that the phantasm itself must be given in the cogitative sense. Moreover, the cogitative sense is the highest sense faculty, because, if we prescind from the *reminiscentia*, it alone is missing in animals; but on the other hand, the phantasm is the highest sense achievement, the intermediate link between matter and spirit,[27] hence it must belong to the cogitative as the highest sense faculty, and yet again it is precisely the imagination which also appears as the place of this intermediate link.[28] As powers to prepare the phantasm for the intellect, at one time the cogitative sense appears alone,[29] at another time along with the memorative sense,[30] at another time simply the "internal apprehensive powers,"[31] among which then the imagination too should be counted, and at another time the cogitative sense along with the imagination and memory.[32] Corresponding to this fluctuation, the cogitative sense with the memory and imagination as a whole is called once "particular reason, passive intellect,"[33] while elsewhere the cogitative sense alone appears under this name. In fact Thomas once designates the phantasy alone as passive intellect with an appeal to a text in Aristotle,[34] while elsewhere the same Aristotelian text is taken as a statement about the cogitative sense.[35]

Letting the definitions of the imagination and the cogitative sense merge in this way is not illogical inconsistency, but comes from the nature of the case, which, with all the perhaps necessary objective distinguishing of the two powers, again and again

[27] *S.C.G.* II, 96: *nihil autem est altius phantasmate in ordine objectorum cognoscibilium, nisi id quod est intelligibile actu.*
[28] *S.T.* I, q. 55, a. 2, ad 2; see *De Ver.* q. 19, a. 1, corp. at the end of the first section.
[29] *S.C.G.* II, 73.
[30] *S.C.G.* II, 80; 81.
[31] *S.T.* I–II, q. 50, a. 4, ad 3.
[32] *S.C.G.* II, 60. This report of Averroes' opinion is obviously Thomas's own opinion also (see the text just cited).
[33] *S.T.* I–II, q. 51, a. 3, corp.
[34] *In VII Metaph.* lect. 10, n. 1494.
[35] *IV Sent.* dist. 50, q. 1, a. 1, obj. 3 and ad 3.

forces one to see them as the unified totality of a single know-ing: as sensibility which emanates from spirit. Sensibility is there-fore originally and not subsequently the point, always already spiritualized and standing under the spontaneous formative power of the spirit, at which the spirit is able to receive passively, and yet in freedom, the formal limitation and determination of its *a priori* breadth. This description of sensibility touches at once the imagination and the cogitative sense. A further separation of the two is without any further fundamental significance for a metaphysics of knowledge.

The close, intimate connection between the imagination and the "common sense" as the one origin of the external senses has been shown earlier. So now the common sense, the imagination and the cogitative sense[36] in human sensibility merge together into an "internal sensibility." This emanates from spirit as a totality and is in turn the origin and root of the external senses, insofar as it emanates from spirit itself. It would be most ap-propriate to the nature of the case to designate this one internal sensibility from the viewpoint of the imagination as the imagina-tive power of the spirit. The spirit itself forms itself into the other of sensibility (form of the body and form of the sense powers), and in this letting-itself-emanate into matter it remains the free lord which forms matter in its imagination according to its own law. Edith Stein[37] translates *ratio particularis*, hence cogitative sense, as the "power of judgment" (*Urteilskraft*). Insofar as in the German philosophical tradition this word des-ignates the power to think of the particular as contained under the universal, this translation is correct, for the cogitative sense apprehends the individual in the common nature. Hence we can say: the power of judgment as the power to synthesize the

---

[36] The memorative sense as a merely preserving power does not have to be taken into account here, especially since according to *S.T.* I, q. 78, a. 4, corp., the imaginative sense already exercises this preservative function by itself, and the memorative sense is only an auxiliary func-tion for the cogitative (estimative) sense.

[37] In her translation of the *Q. disp. de veritate: Des heiligen Thomas von Aquino Untersuchungen über die Wahrheit* I (Breslau, 1931), for example, p. 274 (second edition: *Edith Steins Werke* III, Louvain and Freiburg i. Br., p. 1950ff.).

308

universal, *a priori* of the spirit with the *a posteriori*, sensibly given is formed by the imagination, by which spirit itself forms itself into sensibility.

VIII. INTELLIGIBLE SPECIES I

*Tracing the Problematic of the Intelligible Species
Back to the More General Problematic
of the External Determinability of an Existent*

From the whole of the Thomistic metaphysics of knowledge we have reached to some extent an understanding of what the conversion to the phantasm is intended to express in Thomas: *the unity of intutition and thought in the power of judgment (ratio particularis) as the expression of the original unity of the free spirit with the sensibility into which it forms itself.* Merely enumerating and interpreting the many texts as such[1] in which Thomas speaks explicitly of the conversion to the phantasm would not offer any further means of expanding or deepening this result. These texts confine themselves to repeating the thesis of the conversion. Therefore, it is only in an expanded and deepened treatment of the whole Thomistic metaphysics of knowledge that their interpretation could promise any advantage, and this cannot be accomplished within the scope of this work. Instead of that, we will select from the fundamental concepts of the Thomistic metaphysics of knowledge one which we have come to speak of quite often in the course of this work: the concept

[1] See (we are not striving for completeness): *S.T.* I, q. 12, a. 12, obj. 2; q. 75, a. 6, obj. 3; q. 84, a. 7; q. 85, a. 1, ad 5; q. 86, a. 1, corp.; q. 88, a. 1, corp.; q. 89, a. 1, corp.; a. 2, corp.; q. 118, a. 3, corp.; q. 111, a. 2, ad 3; I–II, q. 5, a. 1, ad 2; II–II, q. 174, a. 2, ad 4; q. 175, a. 4, corp.; q. 180, a. 5, ad 2; III, q. 11, a. 2; *S.C.G.* II, 59; 60; 73; 80; 81; 96; *De Ver.* q. 2, a. 6, corp.; q. 10, a. 2, ad 7; q. 19, a. 2, corp.; *De Malo* q. 16, q. 16, a. 8, ad 3; *De Anima* a. 15, corp.; a. 16, corp.; *In Boeth. de Trin.* q. 6, a. 2, ad 5; *In III de Anima* lect. 12, n. 771; lect. 13, n. 791; *De Mem. et Rem.* lect. 2, n. 311–17; *I Sent.* dist. 3, q. 1, a. 1, ad 5; *II Sent.* dist. 19, q. 1, a. 1, ad 6; *III Sent.* dist. 31, q. 2, a. 4, corp.; *IV Sent.* dist. 50, q. 1, a. 2, corp. and ad 6.

309

of the intelligible species. Insofar as we will try to expand and justify the meaning of this concept acquired so far, it will offer the opportunity to summarize and review what our investigations have shown to be the Thomistic doctrine of the conversion of the intellect to the phantasm. Consequently, there is question here too of explaining this concept only to the extent that it comes into consideration for an understanding of the conversion. All the rest of the problematic which is otherwise connected with this term is excluded here. Working out the problematic of the intelligible species will inevitably force us to take up again those questions which were left unsettled in the first section of the chapter on sensibility.

1. The Connection Between the Intelligible Species and the Conversion

First of all we have to present again the connection between the doctrine of the intelligible species and that of the conversion to the phantasm. Only then can it be determined in what respect we have to define the essence of the intelligible species. Conversion to the phantasm is the expression of the fact that sense intuition is the essential and abiding presupposition of all thought, and that it always lies at the basis of actual thought as something permanent. The ontological determination of the power of thought, which determines it in any given instance to the actual knowledge of a definite object, is called the intelligible species. That was the first, purely formal definition of its essence from which we set out. It must be expanded in such a way that the conversion to the phantasm follows from its essence as a necessary condition of actual knowing. Hence in the course of our investigation the intelligible species has been defined, first of all negatively, in such a way that, as the ontological determination of the intellect strictly as such, it cannot be taken as something existing in itself and filling intellectual knowledge with content. Then it was shown for the first time in a positive, although still formal, way to be what makes possible the actual pre-apprehension beyond the limitation of the sensibly

310

given, through which the sense content can be apprehended as universal. Then the species appeared as the conscious, ontological determination of the knower himself, which, along with being that, showed itself to be the ontological determination of the known, other object. These definitions of the intelligible species were come upon from the viewpoint of the conversion to the phantasm. There remains the question whether they can also be proven from what Thomas says explicitly of the intelligible species. If this succeeds, then our explanation of the conversion will be clarified and confirmed by going backwards from the concept of the species.

2. The Reduction of the Species-Concept to the More General Relationship of Intellect and Sensibility

Lest in explaining the meaning which the intelligible species has in Thomas we go astray from the start, it is necessary to note from the outset that such concepts are normally used in Thomas in extremely formal ways, and therefore that it is only with great caution that the content and meaning which the name would suggest can be ascribed to them. Certainly the intelligible species is again and again in Thomas something like an "intentional image" of the object to be known. That is so frequent and self-evident that we can spare ourselves a long list of texts to prove it. But on close inspection it is evident that to speak of the "image" of the object (*species, similitudo, imago, forma*) by which the intellect becomes aware of the object, because the object becomes interior to the spirit through its image, is itself an "image." To recognize that, it suffices to advert to divine knowing. The "species" by which God knows things is objectively His own real essence.[2] Hence we must always ask how and why something which is spoken of as species is an "intentional image" of an object. Its character as an image does not have to be the primary foundation of the species in its being, but can be a very secondary function of the "species." Every ontological determination of spirit which lets it know "something" can be the

[2] *S.T.* I, q. 14, a. 5; *S.C.G.* I, 46, etc.

species of this something, and in this formal expression, namely, the ontological determination is the species of this something, it remains completely open how the intrinsic nature of this ontological determination in itself is to be understood.

How cautiously we must proceed in defining the intrinsic nature of a human intelligible species can be seen from the following consideration: it is perfectly clear Thomistic teaching that the intellect presupposes sensibility as its receptive origin in its continual emanation. But then it can no longer be doubted in the framework of a Thomistic metaphysics that this relationship of the powers continues into that of their acts. Now the species is precisely the "actuality" of the intellect as "potency."[3] Therefore, it must necessarily bear in itself the peculiarity of its potency. Hence it is demanded by the nature of the case that the species be understood in a dual way: 1) as actuality of the intellect, insofar as the intellect includes sensibility as its receptive ground, and hence insofar as the species itself comprehends the phantasm; and 2) as actuality of the intellect, insofar as this latter remains free over against sensibility, and hence insofar as the species itself can be differentiated from the phantasm. Since Thomas usually speaks of the species in the purely formal way already indicated, he also does not have to keep these two meanings of species separate explicitly.

Only if one is clear about the first meaning of the species does it become intelligible how the phantasm can belong to the definition of intellectual knowing,[4] hence also to the definition of the ground of actual knowing, the species. Only then is the proposition, the intelligible species is seen "in" the phantasm, intrinsically intelligible at all.[5] Insofar as in this first sense of the intelligible species the conversion to the phantasm belongs intrinsically to its essence, and this conversion is the accomplishment of the agent intellect, it follows of itself that the activity of the agent intellect is required continually and in every case.[6]

[3] *S.C.G.* I, 46.
[4] *I Sent.* dist. 3, q. 3, a. 4, corp.
[5] See the eleventh and twelfth notes in chapter three, IV, 2.
[6] *I Sent.* dist. 3, q. 4, a. 5, corp.; *II Sent.* dist. 24, q. 2, a. 2, ad 1. The continual activity of the agent intellect is also affirmed simul-

And vice versa, this statement confirms our explanation of the intelligible species. If the species by itself, as a purely intellectual, ontological determination, provided an adequate "image" of the object, then a permanent activity of the agent intellect which turns to and illuminates the phantasm would simply be superfluous.

From such considerations the intelligible species, as a *purely* intellectual determination of the free intellect (second meaning), was understood in such a way that, taken by itself, it means nothing other than the *a priori* structure of the spirit itself as a power ordered to absolute being, which structure becomes the form of the sensibly given, without the material, sensible content being able to be thought of as passing over into the intellect. Now this explanation seems to contradict a thesis in Thomas. According to him, the species remains "preserved" (*conservari*) in the spirit even after actual thought, and in fact insofar as spirit is understood as differentiated from sensibility. In our explanation, on the other hand, it is just the *a priori* structure of the spirit itself which seems to remain after actual thought, but not the plurality of species. The clarification of this difficulty gives us the means of verifying our understanding of the conversion, this time from the Thomistic concept of species.

3. The Inclusion of the Phantasm in the Reality of the Species

According to Thomas the species remains in the possible intellect "habitually" after the formation of actual thought on the object given by the species.[7] What does that mean? If by species is understood an "intentional image," then by the species remaining

---

taneously by way of inference in the thesis about the permanent necessity of the conversion to the phantasm, since the latter coincides objectively with the former.

[7] *S.T.* I, q. 79, a. 6; q. 84, a. 4, corp.; a. 7, ad 1; I–II, q. 67, a. 2, corp.; *De Ver.* q. 10, a. 2; q. 19, a. 1, corp.; a. 2, corp.; *IV Sent.* dist. 50, q. 1, a. 2; *S.C.G.* II, 74; *Quodl.* 3, a. 21; 12, a. 12; *De Mem. et Rem.* lect. 2, n. 314ff.; *In III de Anima* lect. 8, n. 701–3.

habitually in the spirit as the platonic "place of the species,"[8] as the "treasury of intelligible species,"[9] it could be thought that the image of the object stands ready, as it were, in the spirit, permanently at its disposal, only without being considered at the moment, but capable at any time of again becoming the object of its attention. But even prescinding from the dubious problematic of taking the intentional image conceived as a thing as the starting point for an understanding of the Thomistic concept of species, this explanation would miss Thomas's meaning. For in this explanation the actual species would be distinguished from the habitual only by a consciousness which remains extrinsic to the species as such. That this is not meant by Thomas follows from the fact that he infers explicitly from the merely habitual presence of the species that it can become conscious again only by a new turning to the phantasm,[10] whereby this phantasm has the role of the object without which knowledge is inconceivable.[11] Just from that alone it becomes clear how little the "preserved" species can have the character of a representation portraying the object as its primary and fundamental characteristic.

But now what is the species that remains behind after actual thought? We will set out to answer this question from *De Mem. et Rem.* lect. 2, n. 316. Thomas wants to reject the opinion of Avicenna who is his adversary in this question about the perdurance of the species. If we prescind from Avicenna's conception of the agent intellect and of the way the species are acquired during actual thought, his opinion is that there remains nothing of an intelligible species in the spirit after actual thought, but in every new thought the intelligible species is acquired anew in a new conversion to the phantasm with the help of the sense memory. Consequently, only the general capacity for the formation of intellectual knowledge remains behind, and beyond that

---

8 So, for example, *De Ver.* q. 10, a. 2, obj. 1, in contr.
9 So, for example, *S.C.G.* II, 74.
10 *S.T.* I, q. 84, a. 7, ad 1.
11 *De Ver.* q. 10, a. 2, ad 7 (first series).

at most a general skill in forming the species anew (*habilitas
. . . aequaliter habilis*).[12]

Thomas states in opposition to this opinion: 1) the species
remains "in the possible intellect immutably, according to the
mode of (the intellect) itself." That means: the intellect as such
is not capable of undergoing passive change (*motus*) in the sense
that one ontological determination of the intellect means the exclusion of another (*pati cum abjectione et transmutatione*.)[13]
Therefore, a new determination of the intellect (for example,
another new act of knowledge) cannot exclude the previous
ontological determination of the intellect as such (that is, the
species determining it to its previous act of knowledge). The
species participates in the immobility (the "stable and immutable *esse*")[14] of the spirit; it remains "stably and immutably."
But from this characteristic and the reason for it, it follows nec-
assarily then that the species must remain absolutely the same,
that is, of the same degree of being, as it had been in the intellect as such during actual thought. For if it can come to be of
a lesser actuality at all, even only in degree, it can no longer be
seen why it could not completely disappear as in a "*pati*" in the
proper sense, and how the reasons for the opposite in Thomas
could still prove anything.

But the second characteristic of the species which Thomas
gives seems to contradict this: 2) what concerns the degree of
being (*gradus essendi*), the species remains only in a middle
mode between the pure potency of the spirit before thought, and
its pure act during actual thought;[15] the habitual being (*esse in*

12 *De Ver.* q. 10, a. 2, corp.; *S.C.G.* II, 74 (*potentia adaptata*).

13 *S.T.* I, q. 79, a. 2, corp.; I–II, q. 22, a. 1, corp., etc.

14 See *Quodl.* 3, a. 21, corp., etc. See also *S.T.* I, q. 89, a. 5, corp.
on the question why a form of the spirit can cease neither through its
opposite, nor through the destruction of its subject. Similarly, *S.C.G.*
II, 74; 76.

15 See also *De Ver.* q. 19, a. 1, corp. (*actus completus*); *De Anima*
a. 15, ad 17; a. 18, ad 5; *S.T.* I, q. 79, a. 6, ad 3; *De Ver.* q. 8, a. 14,
corp.; q. 10, a. 2, ad 4; *De Malo* q. 16, a. 11, ad 5; *Comp. Theol.* c. 83;
In III de Anima lect. 8, n. 703.

habitu) seems to be definable only as the boundary between not-yet-knowing and actual knowing, yet as an essentially lower degree of ontological actuality than that of the species during thought. With this definition of the species Thomas has explained indeed why of itself the species which perdures does not bring with itself an actual knowing as its formal effect. He must assume a lower degree of being for it, because the species as an ontological determination of the degree that it has in actual thought always and necessarily brings with itself actual knowing as its formal effect.[16] Therefore, if no actual knowing is given, the species must necessarily be of a lower degree of being than during the actual knowing.

These two statements about the species, which are in the same sentence in Thomas, can be understood as compatible only on the presupposition that, when the species becomes a determination of actual thought, the increase in the intensity of being which it experiences beyond its degree of being as habitual does not affect it at all insofar as it is a determination of the *intellect* as such, but only insofar as it is also in its essence the determination of a power which is fundamentally susceptible to such variations in the intensity of being, in other words, insofar as the species in its broader and complete concept includes the phantasm and hence sensibility. Then the species as a determination of the intellect as such can remain "immutable according to the mode of (the intellect) itself" even after actual thought, and yet, insofar as it includes in its essence the varying determinability of sensibility (as *pati cum abjectione*), it can revert to a lower level of being.

The third characteristic found in our text about the species shows that such a concept of the species with all its duality lies at the basis of these considerations: 3) the actual species are of such a kind, "that in a certain way (the intellect) sees them in the phantasms." This sentence is introduced as a conclusion

16 *S.C.G.* I, 46: *per speciem intelligibilem fit intellectus intelligens actu.* See also *S.C.G.* II, 74, where it becomes clear that this principle is presupposed by Thomas and for that reason he ascribes to the permanent species only a *medius modus inter potentiam et actum.*

("therefore") from the middle mode of the habitual species. The same connection is also shown elsewhere.[17] From earlier considerations we can already understand what "in a certain way" means in the sentence just cited: there is question only of a "certain" seeing of the intelligible in the phantasm, since what is seen in the phantasm is the *a priori* of the spirit itself in the freedom and differentiation of the spirit even in its information of the sensible material. But even if we leave open here what this "in a certain way" means, yet it follows from the third characteristic of the species that the phantasm belongs somehow to its complete essence, because only in the phantasm is it able to be had consciously. Now if this conversion to the phantasm, this "seeing the species in the phantasms," is introduced as necessary for bringing the species from its middle mode to act, then the conclusion suggests itself that the phantasm itself, and not an effect proceeding from it and remaining ultimately inexplicable, is that increment in the intensity of being which the species must still experience, and can experience because as a determination of the intellect as such it is immutable, and yet it includes the phantasm in its complete essence. This brings us, this time from the essence of the species itself, to the same understanding of the formal, instrumental causality of the phantasm as was developed earlier from a completely different viewpoint.

4. The Differentiation of the Phantasm (as Material Element) from the Actuality of the Species (as Formal Element)

If of itself this problematic of the essence of the intelligible species leads us back to the explanation already given of the conversion to the phantasm, yet even so it has not yet become clear what the species is in itself as a determination of the *spirit as such*. *S.T.* I–II, q. 67, a. 2, corp. brings us a step further in this question. The species that we are speaking of here is meant in the narrowest sense as a determination of the intellect as such,

[17] *S.T.* I, q. 84, a. 7, ad 1.

since the text is dealing with the question of the species remaining in the soul that is "separated" and free of the body. The species is related to the phantasm as the formal to the material element. For an understanding of this distinction Thomas only refers[18] to a similar relationship which obtains within a moral virtue.[19] To the complete concept of a moral virtue belongs the "sensitive part" with its "passion" and "operation" as the material element (which corresponds to the phantasm in our case), and as the formal element the "order of reason," that is, the intrinsic ordination of the material element to the total end of the spiritual person by the rational spirit, through which formal element sensibility receives an "habitual conformity . . . to the reason."[20]

So this reference at least lets us presume that in relation to the phantasm, the species is an *a priori* law of the spirit which informs the phantasm and makes it subordinate and subservient to the spirit's own cognitive goal. But we have already met the phantasm functioning as a material element earlier, and from there it can be determined more exactly what the species as its formal element is for Thomas. We can assume here without hesitation that there is question of the same relationship when, instead of material and formal elements, he speaks of matter, potency, and act. The phantasm appeared as material cause,[21] as potency,[22] with respect to the agent intellect and its light. The "one nature of light which (the intellective soul) has in act," that is, the agent intellect, is the form through which the spirit assimilates the sensible and thus makes it intelligible.[23] Hence if the species, insofar as it is a determination of the intellect alone, is the formal element with respect to the phantasm as the material element, then the species is essentially the light of the agent

<hr/>

[18] *S.T.* I–II, q. 67, a. 2, corp. and ad 3. For the intellect see also as a parallel to this text: I, q. 89, a. 5, corp.
[19] *S.T.* I–II, q. 67, a. 1, corp. is meant in the first place.
[20] *S.T.* I–II, q. 56, a. 4, corp.
[21] *S.T.* I, q. 84, a. 6, corp.
[22] *De Ver.* q. 10, a. 6, corp.; *De Spir. Creat.* a. 10, ad 4; *Comp. Theol.* c. 88.
[23] *III Sent.* dist. 14, q. 1, a. 1, sol. 2 ad 2.

intellect,[24] the *a priori* structure of the spirit, absolute *esse*.

This result does not have to cause surprise, for it is only the application of the general axiom in Thomas: "in every . . . action, that which is on the part of the agent is as a formal element; but that which is on the part of the patient or receiver is as a material element."[25] But in the one human knowing, the intellect is the spontaneous element, sensibility is the receptive element. The intellect must be related to sensibility as the formal to the material, especially since its act, as the higher of the acts of the two ordered powers, must by this very fact be formal with respect to the phantasm.[26] But the formal element of a purely spontaneous activity ("agent intellect in no way a patient") can only be the *a priori* essence of this power itself, but not a passively received determination. The determination of the intellect as such, which determination remains permanently only as the formal element of the one human act of knowledge, is thus the *a priori* determinateness of the spirit itself, which belongs to it necessarily and permanently in virtue of its own essence.

But that seems to throw us back to the position of Avicenna, which is precisely what Thomas wanted to refute: the species is the *a priori* structure of the spirit itself, which obviously remains even after the actual knowledge of a definite object given in sensibility. But Thomas maintains nevertheless that, because the species as such remains, the separated soul can again know at least the universal element in the objects it knew earlier,[27] whereby Thomas obviously understands by this universal element not only those ultimate, universal structures of an existent in general[28] which the separated soul can know in the apprehension

---

[24] *IV Sent.* dist. 46, q. 2, a. 2, sol. 3, corp.; *De Ver.* q. 20, a. 2, ad 5 (*formam suam eis [intelligibilibus] tribuit [intellectus agens]*).

[25] *IV Sent. loc. cit.* In *De Ver.* q. 9, a. 1, ad 12 it seems to be said explicitly that the illumination is what is formal in the spirit.

[26] See the texts in the nineteenth to twenty-third notes of chapter four, V, 3.

[27] *De Ver.* q. 19, a. 1, corp. (see a. 2, corp.); *De Anima* a. 15, corp. at the end, and ad 15; *S.T.* I, q. 89, a. 1, ad 3 (*non solum per species conservatas*), etc.

[28] See *S.T.* I, q. 89, a. 3, ad 4; a. 6, corp.; *S.C.G.* II, 81 at the end, etc.

of its own essence.[29] Now however the content of Thomas's opinion might be distinguished from that of Avicenna, the position of Avicenna (with the limitation and precision given above) is for us first of all at least a confirmation of the fact that our previous explanation of the Thomistic understanding of the species at least has not led us beyond the scope of what is a possible problematic in Thomas. In fact, we think that the statements in Thomas just mentioned can be understood in such a way that they are compatible with our previous explanation of the species, and only supplement it—*essentially*, to be sure—in such a way that what has been said heretofore about the species remains valid as the decisive element for the question posed in this work, although this supplement is important for the question about the knowledge of the separated soul, and therefore is more prominent in Thomas than in our context, which is concerned with the knowledge of man in this world.

If we consider the fact that in Thomas the "habit of science" is the sum of what has already been known and is still habitually known, and that for us up to now the intelligible species has included everything that is necessary for the habitual knowledge of one of these objects, then we can formulate this thesis with the words of Thomas as follows: "And so a habit of the intellective part is made up of the light (of the agent intellect) and the intelligible species of those things which are known through the species."[30] Hence the light of the agent intellect really belongs to the habit of science (and therefore to the individual intelligible species in the sense used so far, which is also the usual sense in Thomas). And that is all that we have explicitly proposed up to now. To show that still more can and must belong to the habit of science (namely, that which Thomas here calls intelligible species), and why and how this is so, is a new task. For this purpose the investigation must proceed somewhat further.

We just alluded to the fact that the determination of an ac-

29 *S.T.* I, q. 89, a. 2, corp.; *De Anima* a. 17, corp.
30 *III Sent.* dist. 14, q. 1, a. 1, sol. 2, corp.

tive, spontaneous activity as such can only be its own essence, and not a passively received determination. Now neither does the agent intellect suffer any determination in its activity;[31] it does not become other through a passive suffering from the side of sensibility when it communicates its *a priori* structure to the phantasms; the form of its activity is its own essence. Yet it seems as though the concept of the possible intellect as another power alongside of sensibility is introduced by Thomas, on the one hand, precisely in order to be able to understand the spirit as passively receiving and, on the other hand, lest the law of spontaneous activity just mentioned be violated, which is how thought must be understood. So the question is precisely, what does possible intellect mean? Is it the term designating the potency for a reception which is just as passive as that of sensibility, and yet is distinct from the reception of sensibility? The fact that it is commonly explained that way cannot justify an affirmative answer to this question. Or is possible intellect only the term designating the fact that the spirit *produces of itself,* and must produce and possess the power of reception which we call sensibility, so that it itself as producer is called agent intellect as having to produce, and as possessor is called possible intellect?

In the first explanation, sensibility (concretely, the phantasm) would ultimately be exercising of itself efficient causality on the spirit as passively receiving, which Thomas explicitly rejects. For, on the one hand, he explicitly denies that a determination which is actually intelligible can be produced in the spirit by the sensible-material object.[32] On the other hand, any other kind of antecedent determination of the spirit by the sensible object, which determination would not yet be actually intelligible, is also inconceivable. For as produced by something material, it would have to contain in itself the peculiarity of the

[31] *S.T.* I, q. 54, a. 1, ad 1; I–II, q. 50, a. 5, ad 2; q. 54, a. 1, corp.; *III Sent.* dist. 14, q. 1, a. 1, sol. 2, ad 2; *De Ver.* q. 10, a. 8, ad 11, in contr.; q. 20, a. 2, ad 5; *De Virtut.* q. 1, a. 1, corp.; a. 3, ad 5; a. 9, ad 10.

[32] *S.T.* I, q. 54, a. 4, corp.; q. 79, a. 3; *De Ver.* q. 8, a. 9, corp.; q. 10, a. 6, ad 1; *De Spir. Creat.* a. 9, corp.; a. 10, corp.; *De Anima* a. 4.

form of the material thing producing it[33]; therefore it would contain in itself the opposition of one material form to another, and thus the spirit's receptivity would be a *pati cum abjectione* (*per alterationem, per viam motus*): a becoming-determined in which one determination excludes and supplants the other. But Thomas does not know this kind of receptivity on the part of the spirit.[34] Even a subsequent determination of the efficient causality of the phantasm on the spirit after the manner of a merely instrumental cause would only be an evasion. For Thomas is clear about the fact that even such an instrumental influence presupposes a causality of the instrument in its own right which is proportioned to its own intrinsic nature,[35] and that that is inconceivable here in our case. It has already been shown that Thomas does not know of such an efficient causality even as merely instrumental (so far as this is to go beyond the determination of sensibility itself). But if it should be assumed that the agent intellect itself as efficient cause produces a species proportioned to the phantasm in the possible intellect, then it would have to be understood itself as determined by the phantasm antecedent to that, which of course contradicts its nature as pure spontaneity.

Hence there remains only the second possibility for explaining the possible intellect: the spirit is possible intellect, that is, receptive, insofar as it necessarily produces sensibility as its receptive intuition. And if the intelligible species as a determination

---

[33] *S.T.* I, q. 115, a. 1, corp. (and often elsewhere): *omne agens agit sibi simile. De Ver.* q. 8, a. 9, corp.: *oportet quod agens et patiens sint unius generis. De Pot.* q. 5, a. 1, ad 5: *cum agentia corporalia non agant nisi transmutando, nihil autem transmutetur nisi ratione materiae, causalitas agentium corporalium non potest se extendere nisi ad ea quae aliquo modo sunt in materia.*

[34] *De Ver.* q. 26, a. 1; *Quodl.* 2, a. 13; *De Spir. Creat.* a. 1, ad 20; *IV Sent.* dist. 44, q. 3, a. 3, sol. 3, corp. (*corpus in spiritum naturaliter agere non potest*); *S.C.G.* IV, 90 (*substantiae incorporeae . . . neque etiam formarum sensibilium susceptivae sunt nisi intelligibiliter*); *De Anima* a. 21, corp. In this text we can prescind from the intrinsic reasons given for this proposition.

[35] For this principle, see *S.T.* I, q. 45, a. 5, corp.; *De Ver.* q. 26, a. 1, corp. (*nisi exercendo aliquam [actionem] connaturalem*); *Quodl.* 3, a. 23, corp.; *S.C.G.* II, 21, etc.

of the free spirit as such is to be more than merely the general structure of the spirit, then this is conceivable only if the spirit actively produces sensibility not merely as a general, empty power, but in its concrete determinateness in each instance. Insofar as it actively produces sensibility in its varying, determined actualization, the spirit "suffers" a determination which goes beyond the producing of sensibility in general. In the spirit as a power which has actively produced this and that concrete act of knowledge in its sensible determinateness, a formal element can remain even after the cessation of the corresponding sensible determination which is more definitely determined than the law of the free spirit by which human sensibility in *general* is governed. Only because—and justifiably so in our question— we spoke of spirit and sensibility and their relationship in general could the impression arise that our explanation of the species coincides with the position of Avicenna in the point in question here. It is important now to clarify the solution just indicated and show it to be Thomistic.

5. The Concrete Actuality of the Material Element as Exclusive Production of the Formal Element (*The Soul, the Only Form of the Body*)

The problematic of the species-concept in which we became involved was this: the species appeared in Thomas, on the one hand, as a concrete determination of the spirit received passively from the external world, and, on the other hand, it was only the expression of the active, general operation of the spirit itself, its general, *a priori* law. But the apparent incompatibility of these statements about the species is only the particular instance of a more general problematic in Thomas. To make this more general problematic clear, we will begin with Thomas's proposition that in man the soul is the only form of matter.[36]

With this proposition the common conception of the soul is

[36] *S.T.* I, q. 76, a. 1; a. 3, and the parallels.

decisively abandoned, that conception, namely, which sees the soul as a kind of invisible spirit which carries on its activity in a body understood as a coordinate part of man, which body as material substance taken by itself has its own actuality in the first place. It is otherwise in Thomas: the "soul" is also the only actuality of the *body* itself as a material substance, it is not a spiritual essence in a chemical substance which has its own determinations from itself. The soul is visible because and insofar as the visible actuality of the body is its own actuality; it is invisible only insofar as the substantial ground of every visible, even merely material thing is invisible,[37] and above all, insofar as in the production of this visible actuality it keeps its own essence free in itself. Thomistically, man does not consist of "body" and "soul," but of soul and prime matter, which distinction is essentially "meta"-physical. Consequently, whatever actuality of a material kind belongs to man is completely the actuality of the soul which enters into the empty potency of prime matter, and it does not receive this actuality from the matter, although it can produce its own actuality only in matter and as the actuality of matter.

Nor are the accidental, non-essential determinations of human actuality excepted from that. Certainly they might depend on a cause extrinsic to the soul in their genesis ("*in fieri*"), and thus determine man in his actuality only "accidently;" in their being ("*in esse*"), however, they belong as such to the actuality of man, they are not only borne by the substance of man extrinsically as by an indifferent carrier, but they proceed from the substantial ground in a continual production. "The action of an accidental form depends on the action of a substantial form, just as the *esse* of an accident depends on a substantial *esse*."[38] The "depending" must be understood here as an emanation, since this text is dealing with quantity, and this metaphysical relationship of quantity to the substantial ground has

---

[37] *S.T.* I, q. 57, a. 1, ad 2; q. 67, a. 3, corp. (*nulla forma substantialis est per se sensibilis*); *I Sent.* dist. 19, q. 5, a. 1, ad 6; *In VII Metaph.* lect. 2, n. 1304.
[38] *S.T.* III, q. 77, a. 3, ad 2.

already been shown to be Thomistic.[89] Maybe this text is dealing in the first place with the "proper accidents" but the same thing holds for any accidents at all, since the non-proper accidents are borne by the proper accidents (for example, a definite shape by quantity), and for their permanent being as a determination of the substantial whole they too must have their permanent productive ground in this substantial whole. Hence, every determination of an existent, even accidental determinations, is a determination of the substance insofar as it emanates from the substantial, continually and actively producing ground, and is retained permanently in it.

It is important first of all to show still more thoroughly that this proposition is Thomistic: even the non-proper accidents owe their permanent being to their origin from the substantial ground. It was shown earlier that this proposition cannot be denied from the outset by an appeal to the passivity of the patient that Thomas often mentions.[40] Thus S.T. I, q. 104, a. 1, corp. says: "the *esse* of a house depends on the natures of those things (from which it is built)." The building materials are not merely "receptive," but also "conservative" of the accidental form of the house. "And in a like way must we see the situation in natural things." *De Ver.* q. 2, a. 3, ad 20 likewise presupposes that the essential principles are the ontological ground of an existent in all the dimensions in which it is determined and can be known. *De Ver.* q. 5, a. 8, ad 8 speaks of the "causes of being" as opposed to the "causes of becoming," whereby the cause of being is not merely God. According to *IV Sent.* dist. 12, q. 1, a. 1, sol. 1, ad 1, the substance is the "proximate cause of the *esse*" of the accidents. Corresponding to this, in *De Virtut.* q. 1, a. 3, corp., a triple function of the substance with respect to the accident is enumerated: it is its bearer, its potency, and its cause.

To be sure, in what concerns the production of the accidents by the substantial ground, Thomas distinguishes between the "proper accident" and the "extrinsic accident" (*accidens ex-*

---

[89] See the first note in chapter four, VI, 1.
[40] See chapter four, III, 3.

traneum): only the first is produced absolutely by the substantial ground; the substance is "only receptive" for the second.[41] But this is said first with regard to their becoming as such; and secondly, what precisely is in question is what must be understood objectively by the material cause (a *susceptivum*) of the permanent being of an extrinsic accident, especially since it is always a question of an accident which is a determination of a power or of quantity, which on their side are produced by the substantial ground. Obviously, therefore, the material cause is more than the indifferent carrier of such an accident, since it must produce the proper accident as determined by the extrinsic accident. Moreover, according to the sentence cited above, the extrinsic accident also needs a proximate cause of its *esse*. When, therefore, in *S.T.* I, q. 104, a. 1, corp. "conservation" as well as "reception" is posited for the extrinsic accidents also, that makes it clear enough how Thomas will have the concept of a material cause for the permanent being of such extrinsic accidents understood.

Thus *III Sent.* dist. 14, q. 1, a. 1, sol. 2, corp. distinguishes between the passive "transmutation" and a mode of being of this passive determination in which, from being a "passion," it has become a quality and a form, and as such it is "connatural to the passive thing itself," whereby the extrinsic accident is at least brought into the closest proximity to a proper accident. In *I Sent.* dist. 37, q. 1, a. 1, corp. the activity of the "conservative" element becomes clear: "When the builder is gone, the *esse* of the house is not removed; its cause is the weight of the stones which remains."[42] Corresponding to this, the "passion" is also a "going into act,"[43] an "operation."[44] In *De Anima* a. 12, ad 7 the "separable accidents" also appear as "caused by the principles of the individual." Such accidents as

[41] *S.T.* I, q. 77, a. 6, corp.; *De Spir. Creat.* a. 11, corp.; *I Sent.* dist. 17, q. 1, a. 2, ad 2; *De Ente et Essentia* c. 5.
[42] See also *De Pot.* q. 3, a. 11, ad 5: *retinere formam sibi traditam.*
[43] *III Sent.* dist. 14, q. 1, a. 1, sol. 2, corp.
[44] *S.C.G.* II, 57; III, 66.

are in question here must also be understood among these "separable accidents," since the classification of accidents given in this text obviously intends to be complete ("there are three kinds of accidents . . ."), and the extrinsic accidents do not fit under the two other genera. In agreement with this it says in *In. Boeth. de Trin.* q. 5, a. 4, ad 4: "The shape and all other accidents are consequent upon the substance as their cause; and so the subject is to the accidents not only as a passive potency, but also in a certain way as an active potency, and so some accidents are naturally perpetuated in their subjects."

It is clear here that the substance is actively productive with respect to all accidents, that an accident's permanent having-been-produced by its substance is the ground of its permanent being. This permanent producing depends on the specific nature of the substance in question. These connections will be important for understanding the species. The "stable and immutable *esse*" of the soul will have to be shown to be the ground of a permanent, productive retaining of the species. Since Thomas sees the permanence of the species grounded in the stable and immutable *esse* of the spirit, according to the text just cited the reason for this connection is to be sought in the fact that the intellect is related to the species as permanent "not only as a passive potency, but also in a certain sense as an active potency." In any case it follows clearly enough from the texts cited when taken all together that the non-proper accidents in their permanent being also depend on an active producing by the substance.

Hence the soul is not merely the only substantial actuality of man; it also produces by itself all accidental determinations insofar as it lets them emanate as different from itself, and receives them in itself as its own. It receives no actuality from a body which would have actuality of itself, but produces all the actuality of the body from itself, so that the actuality of the body is its own: "although the soul is perfected in the body (that is, in its own empty potency, in prime matter), however it is not perfected by the body. But . . . it perfects itself with the help of a compliant body (which "help" can only be the passive potency of prime matter, if the soul is not "perfected by the body," or an actuality of the body already produced by the soul itself, which works further as a means for further active producing by the soul)."[45] The only point we want to make in this whole consideration is this: to see that for Thomas the total actuality of man is a production of the soul.

But according to Thomas, every qualitative difference which would come to the soul (as form) from itself would be a specific difference,[46] and therefore the soul can have from itself no qualitative differences at all with respect to other souls. And yet it is precisely this soul that is supposed to be the unique, substantial, actively productive, ontological ground of the concrete actuality of the whole man. But in spite of the qualitatively completely identical ground of their essence, there exist considerable differences among men, as Thomas too could not have overlooked. If the form unites itself with completely indeterminate empty prime matter, then Thomas cannot simply trace such differences among men back to the "dispositions" of matter which, produced by external causes, would only be passively received by the soul and would continue to exist as caused from without, without being an effect of the soul itself.[47] Thus human sex, for example, depends on the disposition of matter,[48] and this disposition in turn on external circumstances and causes,[49] and yet such dispositions "in being" must depend on the form, must be "posterior" with respect to it.[50] The same

45 De Ver. q. 26, a. 2, ad 2.
46 See S.T. I, q. 47, a. 2, corp.; q. 50, a. 4; q. 62, a. 6, ad 3; q. 75, a. 7, corp.; q. 76, a. 2, ad 1; II Sent. dist. 17, q. 2, a. 2, corp.; De Pot. q. 3, a. 10, corp.
47 S.T. I, q. 76, a. 6; a. 7; II Sent. dist. 1, q. 2, a. 4, ad 3; dist. 2, q. 2, a. 3, ad 4; dist. 26, q. 1, ad 1, ad 5; S.C.G. II, 71, etc.
48 S.T. I, q. 115, a. 3, ad 4; De Ente et Essentia c. 7; De Ver. q. 5, a. 9, ad 9.
49 S.T. I, q. 92, a. 1, ad 1; q. 99, a. 2, ad 2, etc.
50 S.C.G. II, 71.

thing holds for human temperament,[51] and for human "individuality" in general.[52]

This brings us to a general problematic in which the question about the intelligible species is only a particular instance: the question about a concrete variable determination of an essence which must be actively produced by this essence in its concrete particularity, although the essence of itself is to be taken as completely the same qualitatively, and so the concrete determination is to be derived from an external cause. It is the question about something formal, that is, something stemming from the form as its active principle, which of itself already bears a particularity in itself beyond the identical universality of what is formal, which particularity appears first of all only as something passively received, as material. If we take into account that the concrete, accidental determination of an existent as such must come from an external cause, then the question proposed can also be formulated as follows: how can the determinateness of an existent from without (the material element) be actively produced by the receiver from within, and thus be the formal element?

That such is the case according to Thomas ought to have followed already from what has gone before. Formulated in this way, our question only places in question what Thomas formulates as a proposition: "with regard to their genesis the dispositions for form precede the form in matter, although they are posterior with regard to their being."[53] The dispositions depend ontologically on their formal production by the form (they are "posterior in being"), although on the other hand they themselves determine the form, since they are of course the "dispositions for form." This question about the identity of a determination received passively from without with one produced

---

[51] See *S.C.G.* II, 63; 65.

[52] *I Sent.* dist. 8, q. 5, a. 2, ad 6; *II Sent.* dist. 3, q. 1, a. 2, corp. and ad 1; a. 4, ad 1, texts wherein there is obviously question not merely of numerical multiplication, but also of an "individual" modification in the one form "man."

[53] *S.C.G.* II, 71.

in itself by the very existent so determined can be clarified only if the answer is in advance a clarification of what "being determined by an external cause" means metaphysically in Thomas. Thus the investigation also leads us back to the questions which in earlier investigations (chapter two, II) still had to remain unclarified.

IX. INTELLIGIBLE SPECIES II

Towards the Ontology of Inner-Worldy, Efficient Causality

1. The Question about the Species (as Permanent) as the Problem of Inner-Worldly, Efficient Causality

We must establish explicitly once again the point at which our investigation stands at the moment. The issue is the permanent preservation of the intelligible species (in the narrower sense) in the spirit as such. On the one hand, it was shown to be produced only by the active spontaneity of the spirit itself, and thus seems able to be nothing but the spirit's *a priori* structure itself; on the other hand, it appeared as the ontological determination of the spirit to the knowledge of a definite object, and thus seems able to be only a passively received determination, and so one proceeding from external influence. Hence the question arises how the species can be both at once: a creation of the spontaneous activity of the spirit which is of such a nature that as such it can manifest the external object as passively received. Further, this question was shown to be a particular instance of a more general problematic. This was shown by the fact that we began with the relationship between the soul as form and the body with its accidental determinations. Then in the process this problematic in its turn passed inevitably into one still more general, into the question about the relationship between the formal, essential ground of an existent in general and its accidental properties: accidental properties and determinations of an existent as such are always received passively as caused by

330

external causality, and yet must be produced by the intrinsic formal, ontological ground of the existent in question itself, so that this existent, insofar as it is itself as such the ground of these determinations, must have these determinations originally in itself, and would retain them in this original form in itself if the form could be thought of as distinct, as is actually the case with the spiritual soul on the basis of its existing-in-itself (*In-sich-selber-Stehens*), its freedom.

Consequently, the most general problematic just mentioned must be further clarified if any light is to be thrown on the question about the intelligible species as permanent. In this sense the problematic of the species in the metaphysics of knowledge is bound up with the clarification of this relationship in formal ontology. And yet on its side too, this and any consideration at all in formal ontology can really be developed *ontologically* only if it is transposed into a problem in the metaphysics of knowledge. Really ontological concepts can be acquired only in union with their corresponding concepts in the metaphysics of knowledge. An ontology of matter can only be constructed as the ontological application of a problematic in the metaphysics of knowledge. Now here the problematic in the metaphysics of knowledge is driven back to that most general problematic of the relationship between the essential ground of an existent and its accidental properties. Objectively that is the problematic of inner-worldly becoming, that is, the coming to be of new determinations in an existent through the influence of another existent, a becoming of such a nature that both existents are already presupposed in their being antecedent to and independent of the causal relationship.

That there is such an inner-worldly, efficient causality among material things is presupposed by Thomas; all that he tries to do is grasp its metaphysical possibility in that which it presupposes in the essence of the material thing.[1] Consequently, we must begin with the fact: one existent produces a new determination in another. We begin here at this point. In the whole of a

---

[1] See *S.T.* I, q. 115, a. 1; *S.C.G.* III, 69; *De Ver.* q. 5, a. 9, ad 4; *De Pot.* q. 3, a. 7, corp.

systematic, Thomistic metaphysics, which would have to start out with a metaphysics of human knowledge, the starting point would of course be different: it would be at sensibility, which immediately apprehends the property of another existent as such. This would be the genuine place for forming the concept of an influence of one existent on another.[2] But since in these concluding investigations the point is not to develop further the Thomistic explanation of human knowledge given so far, but to confirm it from the whole of Thomistic metaphysics as this is already available elsewhere, we begin here at the point mentioned.

2. The Apparent Dilemma of the Concepts "Action" and "Passion"

In such becoming (*motus*), Thomas distinguishes the active determining from the side of the agent, and the reception of the determination on the side of the patient: *actio* and *passio*. But already here an at least apparent obscurity in Thomas's conception sets in. On the one hand (first series of statements), action and passion appear as two different realities, as two different determinations, the one that of the agent, the other that of the patient. "Since action is in the agent and passion in the patient, the accidents which are in the agent and in the patient cannot be numerically the same, since one accident cannot be in different subjects.[3] It is one operation to make movement and another to receive it."[4] Corresponding to this, the action is "in the agent,"[5] it is a perfection of the agent

---

[2] See *De Pot.* q. 3, a. 7, corp.

[3] *II Sent.* dist. 40, q. 1, a. 4, ad 1. We can clarify later in what sense Thomas speaks here of *two* accidents.

[4] *S.C.G.* II, 57. As what follows shows, it is dealing with the difference which was expressed more clearly in the preceding citation. Likewise, *S.T.* I, q. 25, a. 1, ad 3 presupposes a distinction between *actio* and *passio*. *I Sent.* dist. 8, q. 4, a. 3, ad 3 also distinguishes the *actio . . . fluens ab agente* from its *opus* as a middle between the agent and its work. Similarly, *I Sent.* dist. 37, q. 3, a. 2, ad 3; *III Sent.* dist. 35, q. 1, a. 2, sol. 1, corp.

[5] *De Pot.* q. 8, a. 2, corp.; q. 7, a. 9, ad 7; *I Sent.* dist. 32, q. 1, a. 1, corp.; dist. 40, q. 1, ad 1; *S.C.G.* II, 9.

itself.[6] On the other hand (second series of statements), the movement indeed is supposed to be "from the mover," but only in the moved, and is not "of the mover as being in it."[7] "The act of the agent and mover takes place in the patient and not in the agent and mover[8]; movement is the act of the moveable"[9] And corresponding to this it says: "making . . . is not the perfection of the maker, but of the made,[10] action . . . is the perfection of what is made."[11]

Do these two series of statements simply contradict each other? In any case, to assume that Thomas's opinion changed, as is so popular with the "pure historians," does not work here because the supposed contradiction would be found in the same writings of Thomas.[12] Or is it a question of two series of statements which, when correctly understood and when it is shown that they must be so understood in Thomas, mutually include each other? A closer looks shows that the second assumption is the correct one.

3. Various Ways of an Influence Being-In the Patient (Received and Emanating Influence)

"No passive potency can go into act unless it is completed by the active form by which it is put into act . . . But the impressions of the agents can be in the patients in two ways: one way is that of a passion, namely, while the patient is in its transmutation; the other way is that of a quality and form when the impression of the agents has become connatural to the patient."[13] A consideration can be added to these sentences which

---

[6] De Pot. q. 7, a. 10, ad 1; III Sent. dist. 35, q. 1, a. 2, sol. 1, corp. (operatio . . . perfectio ipsius operantis).
[7] In XI Metaph. lect. 9, n. 2312; In III Phys. lect. 5 (Parma 301b).
[8] In III de Anima lect. 2, n. 592.
[9] S.T. I–II, q. 57, a. 5, ad 1.
[10] Loc. cit. See also q. 3, a. 2, ad 3; q. 31, a. 5, corp.
[11] S.C.G. II, 23. Likewise, I, 100; De Pot. q. 3, a. 15 corp.
[12] See S.C.G. II, 23 with II, 57; S.T. I, q. 25, a. 1, ad 3 with I–II, q. 57, a. 5, ad 1; I Sent. dist. 37, q. 3, a. 1, ad 3 (operatio agentis semper est perfectio patientis ut huiusmodi) with II Sent. dist. 35, q. 1, a. 2, sol. 1, corp.; De Pot. q. 3, a. 15, corp. with q. 7, a. 10, ad 1.
[13] III Sent. dist. 14, q. 1, a. 1, sol. 2, corp.

333

for its part can again throw light on the intrinsic compatibility of the series of statements just set over against each other. First of all, the sentences just cited say simply this: an influence can be in the patient in two ways. First (we are anticipating the second way), when the influence as such has ceased, when there is no more "transmutation." In this case the influence is received by the patient as a permanent quality (*qualitas*), as a permanent determination. Secondly, the influence can also be in the patient in such a way that the "impression" as a determination of the patient is present during and because of the still continuing influence of the agent on the patient. Depending on these two ways of the determination being-in the patient, it is called a "passion" (*passio*) or a "passible quality" (*qualitas passibilis*).

In itself this distinction offers no further difficulties to the understanding. It is also proposed by Thomas elsewhere,[14] although he does not always retain the distinction of "passion" and "passible quality" terminologically.[15] Yet there is hidden under this distinction a deeper problematic which was undoubtedly seen by Thomas, although not brought out explicitly enough. Each of these ways of an influence being-in (*Insein*) opens up two other ways of an influence being-in, although these are not simply identical with those brought out explicitly in the text.

The second way of an influence being-in the patient brought out explicitly by Thomas was of such a nature that the influence remained a permanent quality (of greater or less duration) of the patient even after the cessation of the external influence. But according to what was said earlier, a determination of an existent can be what it is for Thomas only if it is not merely "borne" and "had" by the patient extrinsically, but also produced continually out of the ontological ground of the patient itself. Only then does it become connatural. Consequently, in the duration of the passion after the transmutation an essential

[14] *De Ver.* q. 20, a. 2, corp.
[15] *S.T.* I–II, q. 110, a. 3, obj. 3; *In III Phys.* lect. 6 (Parma 305a); *In V Phys.* lect. 1 (Parma 380b), etc.

moment in the metaphysical structure of an external influence
manifests itself: the production of the influence by the patient
itself. We will call the determination of the patient produced by
external influence, insofar as it is produced by the patient itself,
the received (*übernommene*)determination (following the Thomistic usage: "to receive" [*recipere*] species, and so on), whereby
the receiving (*Übernehmen*) is to be understood in the sense of
an active production from the substantial ground of what is
receiving.

Now it is clear from the outset that the mere *passio,* as it is
distinguished by Thomas from the *qualitas,* is also a received
determination, since it is a property of the patient itself (there
is an exception to be mentioned in a moment).[16] The reception
of the determination, if it follows at all, cannot be placed in a
temporal sequence behind the actual influence of the agent, for
this influence is first itself by the fact that it produces a determination in the patient as a determination of the patient, which
determination, however, is that of the patient precisely and only
through the reception. Nevertheless, so long as the external
influence lasts, it conceals that causality which comes from the
ground of the patient itself as a cause of the determination, and
this causality first becomes evident when the transient action is
over and a quality has come to be from the passion. And vice
versa, the mere passion, although it already includes a reception

[16] That follows from the way in which Thomas (*III Sent.* dist. 14,
q. 1, a. 1, sol. 2, corp.) makes use of his distinction. For the actual
knowledge of the external senses the mere *passio* is characteristic, and yet
it is self-evident that the sensible species as received determination also
belongs to the patient in this process, since the *sentire* is an immanent
action of the sentient knower (*S.T.* I–II, q. 31, a. 5, corp.; *I Sent.* dist.
40, q. 1, a. 1, ad 1, etc.). But with the sentient knowing of an immanent action it is given that it presupposes a union of sensibility with
the sensible species (*S.T.* I, q. 12, a. 2, corp.). But in such a union the
sensible species must be a *received* determination of the sentient "patient." For this union is a "*recipere species sensibilis*" (*S.T.* I, q. 78, a.
4, corp.; *S.C.G.* II, 73; *I Sent.* dist. 22, q. 1, a. 2, corp.; *IV Sent.* dist.
44, q. 2, a. 1, sol. 3, corp.; q. 3, a. 1, sol. 3, corp.), an *immutari* (*S.T.*
I, q. 81, a. 3, ad 3; *IV Sent.* dist. 44, q. 2, a. 1, sol. 4, ad 1), the
species is a *principium formale* of the sentient act of knowing itself
(*S.T.* I, q. 56, a. 1, corp.).

(*Übernahme*), reveals the essence of the external influence of the agent on the patient. Precisely by the fact that it conceals the reception it manifests its own essence as such. Consequently, if we exclude the reception from the total phenomenon of the influence, the action of the agent in the patient as such must remain. Now the decisive thing is the insight that even this action still expands *in* the medium of the *patient*. For a transient action simply cannot be conceived without a certain inherence (*Insein*) of its being in the medium of the other (the patient). Hence if the transient action as such is to be conceived, then an inherence of the influence of the agent in the medium of the patient must be conceived which logically precedes the inherence of the determination through reception.

As follows from various indications, Thomas saw this situation, although it is not brought out explicitly enough in his writings. Thus Thomas says: "Every patient receives the action of the agent according to its own mode."[17] Just that implies in the reception on the side of the patient an intrinsic variability which differentiates the external influence as such (since it would always be the same taken by itself) from the influence as a whole, which includes the reception. Further, Thomas knows a variation in the reception, that is, in the way that the influence becomes a determination of the patient. He speaks of a reception which takes place only so far and so long as the influence of the external agent lasts, so that the received determination remains intrinsically and essentially dependent on the external influence.[18] In fact Thomas knows a case (the question whether it is actually given objectively is not relevant here of course) in which a reception does not enter in at all, although the influence actually expands in the medium of a patient.

According to Thomas, colors expand from the colored body in the medium of air. But the air suffers no "natural mutation," the colors are not in the air, in the translucent medium

---

17 *IV Sent.* dist. 44, q. 2, a. 1, sol. 3, ad 2.
18 *De Pot.* q. 5, a. 1, ad 6; q. 6, a. 4, corp.

"according to a natural *esse*,"[19] the color *non denominat aeram:* it is indeed in the air, but without being able to be predicated of it, that is, without becoming even only a transitory ontological determination of the air. But this denies the reception of the color by the permeable medium in the sense defined above. Nevertheless, even here Thomas maintains that there is an inherence of the influence of the colored body in the air. He also calls it a reception (*receptio*). According to what has been said, this reception is to be clearly distinguished from the inherence through reception. Hence according to Thomas, there is an inherence of the influence in the patient which is not already a reception of the determination through its being produced by the patient itself, through which production the influence first becomes a determination of the patient itself. According to what has already been said, we have the right to consider this kind of an inherence of the influence in the patient as belonging to every influence, and this inherence can always be considered as logically prior to the inherence through reception. We will call the influence in this kind of inherence the emanating (*ausfliessende*), not (yet) received influence.

[19] *IV Sent.* dist. 1, q. 1, a. 4, sol. 2, corp.; sol. 4, corp.; dist. 8, q. 2, a. 3, corp.; dist. 44, q. 2, a. 1, sol. 3, ad 2; sol. 4, ad 5; *S.T.* I, q. 67, a. 3, corp.; *De Ver.* q. 27, a. 4, ad 4; *De Pot.* q. 3, a. 7, ad 7; *Quodl.* 7, a. 2, ad 5. These statements about *colors* should not be confused with the question of the inherence of *light* in the medium of air. For light Thomas maintains a reception by the air (*habet esse naturale in aere: S.T.* I, q. 67, a. 3, corp.; *In II de Anima* lect. 14, n. 420; *II Sent.* dist. 13, q. 1, a. 3, corp.). Insofar, of course, as the light is received in the air during the actual influence of the illuminator (*S.T.* I–II, q. 171, a. 2, corp.; *De Ver.* q. 12, a. 1, corp., etc.), Thomas also applies terms which belong first of all to the mode of being of *colors* in the medium (*forma imperfecta, intenio: IV Sent.* dist. 1, q. 1, a. 4, sol. 2, corp. and ad 4) to the inherence of light in the translucent medium (*De Pot.* q. 5, a. 1, ad 6; q. 6, a. 4, corp.). More will have to be said about that below. Insofar as our only point here is to show that Thomas knows the concept of an inherence of the influence in the medium of the patient without a reception, it is irrelevant here whether or not the inherence ascribed to colors is compatible with other definitions of the essence of color in Thomas. For the nature of color according to Thomas, see *I Sent.* dist. 17, q. 1, a. 1, corp.; *De Malo* q. 2, a. 2, ad 5 and ad 11; *De Ver.* q. 2, a. 4, ad 4; q. 14, a. 8, ad 4, etc.

SPIRIT IN THE WORLD

As such it is called a non-received influence because, on the one hand, it must be considered as already produced in the medium of the patient, but, on the other hand, it must still be differentiated from the received influence, through which reception the influence first becomes a determination of the patient. Insofar as this non-received influence still must necessarily be a determination of an existent, it still belongs to the agent, it is produced by the agent as its own dermination, indeed in such a way that this determination belongs to the agent only insofar as the agent can produce it as its own only in the medium of the patient. As thus produced by the agent, it can be called emanating. This term has its Thomistic justification in the fact that Thomas himself conceives every influence as an emanation from the agent,[20] and designates the passion as "from the agent." Hence according to what has been said, the influence "as from the agent," that is, already prior to its inherence in the patient caused by a reception, has another way of inhering in the patient proper to itself as such.

This puts us in a position to understand, at least tentatively, the intrinsic compatibility of the series of statements about motion mentioned above. The first series of statements sees the action from the viewpoint of the non-received influence, which as such is still in the agent in a certain way. For as thus produced by the agent, it is its determination, its perfection, and in *this* sense still "in" the agent. The second series of statements speaks of the received influence. In the light of this concept these statements are self-evident. Essential for understanding the compatibility of these two series of statements is the insight that the action in the agent meant in the first series of statements expands in the medium of the patient, that an inherence in the patient already belongs intrinsically and essentially to the action as from the agent, and that this inherence is logically prior to the inherence through reception, and is not yet reception in the strict sense. It is reception in the strict sense that is intended in the second series of statements, and it is through this that the action becomes the perfection of the patient. Insofar as the concept of

[20] *S.C.G.* IV, 11.

the inherence of an influence in the patient without reception (or at least prescinding from it) shows the compatibility of the two series of statements, we have acquired a new proof for the fact that such an inherence belongs in principle to every influence, although Thomas understands it explicitly only where, according to him, there is no inherence through reception at all. Thomas calls this inherence without reception "intention" (*intentio*), "spiritual *esse*" (*esse spirituale*), "spiritual reception" (*receptio spiritualis*),[21] insofar as (a first basis for this terminology) for a merely phenomenological consideration of knowledge, which looks only to the intended, external object as existing independently of knowledge, the object of knowledge, when it is known, is also "in" the knower, without becoming the ontological (received) determination of the knower.

In the light of the concepts which have been established, we must now ask what exactly is the nature of the emanating (*ausfliessende*) influence, how it is related to the received (*übernommene*) influence, and how the medium of the patient, in which the emanating influence expands, is to be defined more exactly.

4. The Nature of the Emanating Influence

To begin with the first series of statements, it is first of all to be noted once again that the influence as coming from the agent is a determination of the agent itself, its perfection. Since what was said about the production of a determination by the determined itself is universally valid, the agent must let the influence which is its own determination emanate from its own substantial ground. By virtue of the spontaneous activity of its being, the agent produces its action as its own determination and perfection. The action, which for Thomas is the perfection of the agent, is thus necessarily conceived as a self-realization of the agent, as the being in which the agent comes finally to its own complete essence, to its perfection. It has already been said

[21] *De Pot.* q. 6, a. 4, corp.; *IV Sent.* dist. 44, q. 2, a. 1, sol. 3, ad 2; sol. 4, ad 5, etc.

in our general consideration of the self-unfolding of an existent through emanations that this kind of a production of one's own being can only with difficulty be comprehended within the usual categories commonly used in Thomas.

Nor do we have to go into the question any further here, why and how this self-production of the agent is possible only by the fact that the agent experiences as patient the influence of another, since what will be said about the patient holds also of the agent insofar as its being-agent itself presupposes an influence from without. This active production of its own being as agent is ordered according to the essence of the emanating ground, according to the mode of being of the form of the agent.[22] The less the form exists in itself, the less it is interior, present to itself, and the more it is itself given away from itself into the other of matter, then all the less does the activity produced by it belong to itself, all the more is it necessarily lost in the other and an emanation (*emanatio*) away from itself into the other.[23] It would lead us too far afield here if we wanted to try to show in detail in the light of this idea how the mode of being of the form of the purely material thing can be a complete production of its own essence just by the fact that it exercises influence on other existents, whereby it is already presupposed that activity beyond its mere existence necessarily belongs to every existent.

5. The Nature of the Medium of the Patient (The Concept of Matter, I)

We begin with the fact of such an influence on other existents. It has already been shown that Thomistically the first moment that is to be grasped in this process is the self-production of its being-agent (*Tätigseins*) by the agent itself. As has already been shown, this being-agent as such is realized essentially only in the medium of the patient, so that it itself, and not first the produced determination of the patient (the received influence), can be the determination of the agent only in the patient. Therefore we

[22] *S.C.G.* II, 20: *omne agens agit per formam qua actu est*, etc.
[23] *S.C.G.* IV, 11.

must determine more exactly how this medium of the patient, in which the agent is itself, is to be understood. The consideration which forced us to distinguish between the emanating, non-received influence and the received influence, that is, the influence produced by the patient itself, was based ultimately on the insight that something can be a determination of an existent only by the fact that it is produced by the substantial, ontological ground of the determined existent itself. But this says that this ground as such cannot be determined at all by an influence which is extrinsic and subsequent to its own potentiality and to its own self-constitution, by an influence which is an inner-worldly cause. This ground is called Thomistically (substantial) form. With regard to its form, an existent cannot in principle suffer (*erleiden*), in the sense of receiving an inner-worldly influence.

Consequently, if a being is to receive in this sense, then that is conceivable only under a two-fold presupposition: 1) The external influence strictly as such cannot already be a determination of the patient itself, otherwise it would already have been produced by the patient itself, hence it would not be coming from without in the strict sense. 2) Nevertheless this external influence must already be in the patient, otherwise it would have no relation to the patient at all. But these two presuppositions are conceivable only if a real principle of absolute indeterminateness belongs to the constitution of the patient. The ground (determinable only from itself) of the ontological determinations of an existent which unfolds into these determinations cannot simply coincide with the existent itself; the patient cannot be merely form. For otherwise the form as such would have to be the medium of the emanating influence as such. We have already concluded that it cannot be this medium in the sense that this influence is its own determination. But the influence cannot belong to it in another sense. For the form is essentially and exclusively to be conceived as the productive origin of the determinations of an existent. Therefore, what belongs to this origin as such becomes thereby essentially a partial origin of the determinations of an existent, and hence a determination of the existent itself.

If, then, the patient itself is not to be the ontologically determined bearer of the emanating influence, then it can be the medium of the emanating influence only if and insofar as an absolutely passive, and therefore of itself indeterminate, principle belongs to it which is a purely receptive, never itself productive bearer of a determination produced by a form, and in this principle this produced determination expands and is held. This passive, of itself indeterminate "wherein" (*Worin*) of an ontological determination is called Thomistically (prime) matter. An inner-worldly causality of one existent on another is therefore possible only when the patient is material. Its matter is the "wherein" in which the action actively produced by the form of the agent maintains itself as in its substrate. If the demonstration of the nature of the medium of the patient which we have indicated here only briefly, namely, that the medium is such that the emanating influence can exist in it without already being a determination of the patient itself, if the demonstration, I say, can be shown only with difficulty to be developed in detail and explicitly in Thomas, nevertheless the result itself is explicit Thomistic doctrine, and going backwards from this doctrine, the demonstration given could be shown to be Thomistic. We will indicate just briefly here that the result itself is Thomistic.

"Matter is related to an agent as receiving the action which comes from it; for the act which is of the agent as that from which it comes, is of the patient as that in which it is" (in this being-in [*receptio*], it is obviously a question of the inherence prior to the reception, for the action is explained immediately to be an actuality of the agent): "Therefore, matter is required by an agent to receive its action; for the action of the agent which is received in the patient is the act of the agent and (i.e.) of the form (of the agent)[24] . . . Every operation of a creature presupposes the potency of matter.[25] An active potency is such that it requires subject matter in which to act, insofar as it is imperfect and unable (to act) in the whole substance of the thing."[26] Our

[24] *S.C.G.* II, 16.
[25] *I Sent.* dist. 14, q. 3, corp.
[26] *I Sent.* dist. 42, q. 1, a. 1, ad 3.

342

thesis is formulated here with complete clarity: a cause which
does not bear absolutely the being of what is produced and the
being of the patient, hence which is only a cause for the determination of an existent which comes subsequently and in addition to the complete substance of the thing (and this is the way
we defined the concept of the inner-worldly cause), needs a
subject matter, whereby matter is to be taken in the strictly
metaphysical sense if the sentence is not to be an empty tautology.
"Created power presupposes matter in which it operates."[27]

Thomas is clear about the conclusions which follow from
this principle for the possibility of a reciprocal influence between those existents to which he ascribes no matter. Such
existents have no "window" through which direct intercourse
would be possible. The "speaking angel does nothing to the
angel to which it speaks,"[28] hearing what it says is brought
about through the "radiation (radiatio) of the divine light."[29]
The speech itself is only an "interior speaking,"[30] the knowledge
of this freely given speech of the speaker takes place in the
hearer through the same innate species (that is, through participation in the creative knowledge of God as such) through
which he knows the nature of the speaker.[31]

Thus it has been shown that matter, in the sense already defined earlier and manifesting itself anew in this situation, is the

[27] IV Sent. dist. 8, q. 2, a. 3, ad 2. Similarly, De Ver. q. 27, a. 3,
corp.
[28] De Ver. q. 9, a. 5, ad 2 and ad 5; q. 9, a. 6, ad 4.
[29] II Sent. dist. 11, q. 2, a. 3, ad 3.
[30] S.T. I, q. 107, a. 4, ad 1.
[31] De Ver. q. 9, a. 4, ad 11. This interpretation is also that of Cajetan,
Silvius, and others. It remains completely obscure in Thomas how he
thinks the illumination of the lower by the higher angel, which he
maintains is given and distinguishes from the locutio of angels, is accomplished more exactly. In any case, the locutio angelorum shows that
the illumination also cannot be thought of as a mutual, real influence
of the angels on one another. Therefore, the mere presence of an illumination in Thomas cannot be an argument against our interpretation
that in Thomas an inner-worldly influence is only possible on a material
patient.

necessary "wherein" of the reception of the determination of an existent by an inner-worldly cause, insofar as the emanating influence presupposed by this reception can expand and maintain itself only in matter.

An important conclusion from this insight can already be gained at this point with respect to the purpose for which this whole investigation was undertaken: it has been confirmed that for Thomas the receptive knowledge of an object is essentially sensibility. If knowledge in general is to be taken as an ontological process, and if receptive knowledge is possible only by the fact that the object of itself determines the knower to knowledge subsequently to the ontological constitution of the knower, then such a knower as so defined must be material, but that means it must know sentiently. Thus Thomas's insight is confirmed from the general Thomistic ontology of efficient causality, the insight that man has sense organs of a material kind because he can and must know receptively, and not vice versa: "the potencies are not for the sake of the organs, but the organs are for the sake of the potencies."[32]

6. The Connection Between the (Merely) Emanating and the Received Influence (The Concept of Matter, II)

We must now ask further about the connection between the merely emanating and the received influence. First of all, from the insight we have acquired it becomes intelligible how the emanating influence can and must expand in the matter of the patient. If we begin with the fact that as inner-worldly cause the agent itself is material, that is, therefore, that of itself the being of this existent itself lets its essence unfold in the other of matter, then it is intelligible that its emanating influence can maintain itself only in matter, since, as was shown, it can only be understood as the self-realization of the agent itself, and therefore it shares its mode of being.

But matter in itself is not this or that. As the ground of the

[32] S.T. I, q. 78, a. 3, corp.

plurality of the same[33] (it is only in this sense that Thomistically it is the ground of "individuality," but not of the "individuality" of a quidditative distinction of one thing from another)[33a] matter is esentially "one" and "many" at once. It must be one in such a way that it is not able to be repeated as the same, for otherwise a universal, specific concept of matter would have to be able to be formed, and the problematic of the repetition of the same, because of which matter is required, would begin all over again. But while remaining one, matter must at the same time be plural, for it is supposed to be precisely the ground, the empty "wherein," which can let the same (form) become many. Now this unity cannot be taken as that of a numerical one. For such a unity says precisely that such a one is quite able to be repeated as the same, and in fact indefinitely, and thus would make possible and require precisely the formation of a specific, universal concept of matter. If this says that matter is not something which is present in material things as multiplied itself, this negative statement does not contain the positive, namely, that material things would have their material principle in common as numerically one, that they would be different from each other

[33] According to Thomas, the problem of *individuation* has two aspects (*In Boeth. de Trin.* q. 4, a. 2; *S.T.* III, q. 77, a. 2, corp.; *III Sent.* dist. 1, q. 2, a. 5, ad 1; *IV Sent.* dist. 12, q. 1, a. 1, sol. 3, a. 3.): a) it must be asked how a known intelligibility, which is a universal quiddity (a form) which in itself can be related to many "whithers" and can be in many "whereins," becomes precisely this, that is, no longer able to be related to others (*incommunicabilis*), can no longer be "*in pluribus.*" In the earlier chapters of this work the concept of prime matter was acquired only from this problematic.

b) It must be asked how then these "whereins" of a form, which as such a last subject can no longer be "in" another, are distinguished from one another, and thus make the forms not merely *incommunicabilis*, but also *divisae* and *multiplicatae*. It is from this question that Thomas acquires the concept of *materia quantitate signata*. We will be dealing with this problematic in what follows. For the term *materia signata quantitate*, see *In Boeth. de Trin.* q. 4, a. 2, corp.: *materia efficitur haec et signata secundum quod est sub dimensionibus*, and ad 4: *materia signata* etc.

[33a] See, for example, *In Boeth. de Trin.* q. 4, a. 2, the first objections, where it becomes clear that individuation and diversity according to number (only) mean the same thing.

only in their formal half, as it were. Insofar as matter is supposed to be the principle of the repetition of the same, it must be one in such a way that what enters from it as principle into the plurality of the same is related to matter as a part to its whole, and in fact in such a way that the "part" is not "specifically" the same as the one whole of the one matter.

This essential characteristic of matter is, concretely expressed, absolute space.[84] Not as though absolute space constituted the essence of matter immediately. Because spatiality as such is visible, it cannot be for Thomas a substantial principle in itself.[85] But absolute space ("unlimited dimensions") belongs

---

[84] The spatiality (understood as *materia quantitate signata*) which is being spoken of here should not simply be made equivalent to locality, to a definite space. This latter is always relative to a network of relations that are extrinsic to the thing (a *denominatio ab eo quod est extra ipsum: S.C.G.* II, 16), while in contrast to this the intrinsic spatiality of quantity *inest per se et absolute* (*In V Metaph.* lect. 9, n. 892). Quantity is space as creating space, not as related to space given in advance and as only oriented within it. The *"receptibilitas"* of place and of matter are predicated only *"similitudinarie"* (of course on the basis of an intrinsic connection): *II Sent.* dist. 12, exposition of the text.

Time should really be mentioned here also, since quantity and spatiality in Thomas are not absolutely the same, and time belongs just as much to the modes of quantity as does spatiality (*De Pot.* q. 9, a. 7, corp.). Thus spatiality in Thomas is also rendered exactly as *quantitas dimensiva* or as *dimensio*, for example, in *S.T.* III, q. 77, a. 2, corp. But since as a matter of fact time in Thomas does not enter explicitly into the question about the *individuatio per materiam quantitate signatam*, but is always related only to *quantitas dimensiva*, the approach indicated, which is possible in itself, cannot be pursued any further here. But in any case Thomas saw the connection between matter and time, precisely because he does not want to ground extrinsic time exclusively in the unity of prime matter. (*S.T.* I, q. 10, a. 6, corp., where the *"nullo modo"* of *II Sent.* dist. 2, q. 1, a. 2, corp. is changed to a *"non sufficiens"*). Only once does time also appear briefly in connection with the question about individuation: *non enim individuatur per hoc quod recipiatur in materia nisi quatenus recipiatur in hac materia vel illa distincta et determinata ad hic et nunc: In Boeth. de Trin.* q. 4, a. 2, corp.

[85] *S.T.* III, q. 77, a. 2, corp.; *IV Sent.* dist. 12, q. 1, a. 1, sol. 3, corp.; *In V Metaph.* lect. 10, n. 901; lect. 15, n. 983. If quantity itself were a substantial principle, then the substantial form and the substance would have to be visible in their own selves, which Thomas denies: *In II de Anima* lect. 14, n. 420; *S.T.* I, q. 67, a. 3, corp., etc.

to matter in itself ("prior to the substantial form") and only thus can matter be the "wherein" of a plurality of the same.[36] Because it is of itself absolute space ("matter signed by quantity"), matter is "one" with parts, no one of which is the other, and all of which together do not form a specific concept (whose "logical" parts would repeat the whole in each instance, which is precisely *not* the case with the parts of matter as parts of the "unlimited dimensions"), but form precisely the one space. Thus the forms are in many "wherein's," as in the different parts of matter; they divide absolute space.[37] The plurality of matter is not that of a repetition of the same,[38] but is after the

[36] *IV Sent.* dist. 11, q. 1, a. 1, sol. 3, ad 4; dist. 12, q. 1, a. 2, sol. 4, corp.; a. 3, sol. 1, ad 3; dist. 44, q. 1, a. 1, sol. 1, ad 3; a. 2, sol. 5, ad 3; *De Ver.* q. 5, a. 9, ad 6. Compare further with each other:

S.T. I, q. 76, a. 4, ad 4:	*II Sent.* dist. 3, q. 1, a. 4, corp.:
1. *Diversae formae elementorum non possunt esse nisi in diversis partibus materiae.*	1. *Oportet . . . quod diversae formae . . . recipiantur in diversis partibus materiae.*
2. *Ad quartum (partium) diversitatem oportet intelligi dimensiones sine quibus materia divisibilis non est.*	2. *Sed impossibile est in materia intelligere diversas partes, nisi praeintelligatur in materia quantitas ad minus interminata, per quam dividatur, ut dicit Commentator . . .*

It follows from this comparison that Thomas still considers this view fundamental even in the *Summa*. The same thing follows from *S.T.* I, q. 50, a. 2, corp. (compare *Quodl.* 9, a. 6, corp.); q. 75, a. 7, corp.; III, q. 77, a. 2, corp.; *In Boeth. de Trin.* q. 4, a. 2, ad 3 and ad 5. If objectively, then, this Averroistic opinion is still taught even in the *Summa*, then we are freed from the task, which could not be accomplished within our framework anyway, of investigating here whether and to what extent Thomas is giving another opinion in *De Natura Materiae et Dimensionibus Interminatis*, cc. 4–7, than he gives elsewhere.

[37] *S.T.* I, q. 75, a. 7, corp.; q. 76, a. 4, ad 4; III, q. 77, a. 2, corp.; *II. Sent.* dist. 3, q. 1, a. 4, corp.; dist. 30, q. 2, a. 1, corp.; *IV Sent.* dist. 12, q. 1, a. 1, sol. 3, ad 3; *S.C.G.* II, 49; *De Malo* q. 16, a. 1, ad 18; *In Boeth. de Trin.* q. 4, a. 2, corp.

[38] Therefore, in the texts given Thomas always speaks of the "*partes materiae diversae*," of a "*divisio materiae*," etc. As far as I can see, he speaks of a "*multiplicari*" of matter only once (*I Sent.* dist. 2, q. 1, a. 1, ad 3), but for all that, in the same text matter is also called "*una numero.*" After what has been said, it should be clear that both expressions cannot represent Thomas's thought exactly.

manner of the division of space, which is one of itself, and as such extends into its parts. Therefore, as absolute space, matter is equally, and equally essentially, one and many in the way required. For neither is there anything in matter which would break up the unity of its unlimited extension by delimiting a part, and therefore it is one; nor is there anything in matter which, in the indifferent juxtaposition of the many parts, by precisely the same delimitation would force definite parts together into a unity which is more than the continuous infinity of matter in itself. This delimiting *division*, which as such establishes at the same time more genuine *unity* in what is delimited, is produced by the form. It is in this sense that we must understand Thomas when he calls matter "one through the removal of all distinguishing forms."[39]

But this essence of prime matter shows that a solidarity obtains among bodies as material things which does not come subsequent to their ontological constitution, but is their own ground. They are bodies related to one another because they are one in matter, and not vice versa. The "division" of matter as absolute space by form cannot be thought of as though it simply eliminated the original unity. Matter in its privatively unlimited potentiality is never actualized completely by the individual form.[40] The unlimited potentiality for ever different, definite dimensions ("limited dimensions") also belongs to this potentiality; the information of matter is at any given time a definite limitation of its absolute space. But as determined by a form, matter retains its potentiality for other forms, hence for another limited spatiality. Since this potentiality is privatively unlimited, the matter of a definite thing retains the potentiality for absolute space.[41] Consequently, if the matter of a definite body has a potentiality for absolute space,

[39] *S.T.* I, q. 16, a. 7, ad 2; *I Sent.* dist. 2, q. 1, ad 3; *De Ver.* q. 1, a. 5, ad 15.
[40] *S.T.* I, q. 66, a. 2, corp.; *II Sent.* dist. 12, q. 1, a. 1, corp., etc.
[41] Which, of course, precisely does *not* say that as remaining unlimited it could be actualized in a thing. Thomas explicitly denies that: *II Sent.* dist. 30, q. 2, a. 1, corp.; *S.C.G.* II, 16; *In III Phys.* lect. 10 (Parma 317b).

then this greater spatiality, of which the body has only a part so far, and for whose further parts it is still in potency, is not such that it would be different from the spatiality really present in others already. Otherwise, of course, potentialities for several absolute spaces would exist, which is essentially excluded precisely by the unity of matter as already defined. The potentiality for absolute space which belongs to the individual body as its own is thus essentially and seen from its own foundation, namely, matter, the real spatiality of the other body.

Now exercising influence on another was shown earlier to be first of all the self-realization (*Selbstvollzug*) of the agent from out of its formal ground. Now it has been shown that the self-realization of a merely material being can be realized only by expanding in the matter of the other. For the self-realization of a merely material being as such is the realization of the potentiality of matter, but this is always and essentially quantitative. Therefore, if there is to be a self-realization of a formal ground which goes beyond the expansion of its qualitative, substantial essence in the quantity corresponding to this,[42] it can be conceived only as an expansion via further spatiality. But this is the spatiality of the other. The emanating influence expands in the medium of the other, in the matter of the other, precisely because it is the self-realization of the agent, and this self-realization can be in the matter of the other because the real spatiality of the patient, because of the unity of matter, is already and always the greater potentiality of the agent. Since Thomas calls the non-received inherence of an influence in another a "spiritual *esse*," we can also formulate our result as follows: the self-realization of a material thing which goes beyond the constitution of its necessary, substantial essence (in which the proper accidents are included) is essentially (at least) a spiritual *esse*. Since the Thomistic concept of emanation means the same thing as self-realization, the following sentence in Thomas is now intelligible not merely as a statement of fact, but as expressing an

---

[42] What is meant by that will be shown more clearly in the question why the patient needs the emanating influence of the agent at all for its self-realization (in the reception of the determination).

essential necessity: "in which (inanimate bodies) emanations cannot take place otherwise than through an action of one of them on another."[43]

We are still occupied with the question of the connection between the emanating and the received influence. So far it has been shown at least in general outline why the emanating influence as the self-realization of the agent can and must expand in the medium of the patient, that is, in the matter of the other. If according to Thomas, as has already been shown, the reception of the determination by the patient is to be understood as the patient's own active production of the determination in an emanation (*resultatio*), then the next question is, why then does the patient need the emanating influence of the agent maintaining itself in its matter for such an emanation.

A substantial form as such has a certain negative infinity of itself. That is to be understood not merely in the sense brought out earlier, according to which the form in itself can subsist in many "whereins" of matter, can be related to many first subjects, but it is also to be understood in the sense that, within the limits of its own substantial content of meaning, the form can be the ontological, productive ground for many different, contrarily opposed determinations of itself. For, on the one hand, it has already been shown that according to Thomas the substantial, essential ground of a thing (which is productive because of the form) also lets its accidental determinations emanate from itself, and on the other hand, the accidental nature of such a determination already includes the possibility of another, contrary determination, likewise to be produced by the same essential ground. That is shown just in the fact that, where there is question of a "passible quality" as opposed to a "passion" in the narrowest sense, this quality, in its being which remains even after the influence from without, must be produced by the substantial ground of what is determined by it, and yet (as dependent on the external agent in its genesis) is only an accidental determination of an existent, which therefore must also be able to be determined by its contrary deter-

43 *S.C.G.* IV, 11.

mination. But it follows necessarily from this that this existent itself can just as well produce the contrary determination. So a certain positive, that is, active, indeterminateness belongs necessarily to the substantial form within the limits of its essence, insofar as the substantial ground of a thing determined by this form is the "receptive principle" of contrary determinations, and as such is also the origin that lets them emanate.

But that also gives us an insight into the fact that such a form is not an emanating (self-realizing) origin for the non-proper accidental determinations in absolutely the same way as it is for the accidents which emanate from it "*per se*" (for example, the powers of sensibility and of thought), and an insight into why it is not.[44] "An *esse* which is receptive of contraries belongs to a substance existing indifferently in potency, whether the substance is composed of matter and form or is simple."[45] But we know already that a reception is a letting-emanate, an active reception. Therefore in its formal, operative ground, the substance is originally inclined towards two contraries which it is able to let emanate in its otherness, in matter, as the unfolding of its essence. But the contraries are not able to be really actualized in matter together at the same time.[46] If, therefore, the substantial form seeks to realize the breadth of its possi-

---

[44] For this distinction of accidents, see *De Pot.* q. 5, a. 4, ad 3; *S.T.* I, q. 9, a. 2, corp.; q. 77, a. 1, ad 5; a. 6, corp., etc.

[45] *De Spir. Creat.* a. 1, ad 7. It is not in question here in what essentially different sense something immaterial can be *susceptivum contrariorum*.

[46] Whether and in what sense that is possible in something spiritual does not have to be investigated more thoroughly here: the immaterial form is always with being in its totality since, as subsisting in itself, it is always present to itself, but a *reditio completa* is only possible through the *excessus* to being absolutely. But in being as such the contraries are not contrary. From this it follows that in the knowledge of the contraries as well as in the free realization of its essence, the free form can actualize its whole essence at once in the decision for one side of the "contraries." So an "angel" decides essentially with the whole *virtus* of its essence, and in fact all at once (*S.T. I*, q. 62, a. 6, corp.; q. 63, a. 8, ad 3; q. 62, a. 5, ad 3, etc), and therefore irrevocably (*S.T. I*, q. 63, a. 6, ad 3; q. 64, a. 2, corp., etc.). All of this has as its background the thought that the self-realization of something immaterial as such takes place essentially all at once.

bilities, this happens on the one hand in an ordination towards the total breadth of its possibilities, and on the other hand, this realization is always possible only in determinations which in principle never realize the whole breadth of these possibilities at once.

But this says that at any given time the substantial ground, in its ordination to the total breadth of the possibilities of its unfolding, stands indifferently over against the individual, accidental determination which always makes the realization of the whole breadth of the possibilities *as such* impossible, and is of itself already inclined towards another possible determination. But this other determination, insofar as it too is a partial realization of the possibilities of the substantial ground and the limitation of these possibilities at once, also has no advantage over the first determination. Thus it follows from the breadth of the possibilities, which in material beings is always and in principle greater than any realization, that, on the one hand, the substantial, operative ground under each determination is already inclined to the other contrary, and thus is able to be determined to it, and that, on the other hand, it cannot have in itself the ground of this determination to one accidental determinateness rather than to another, and therefore must be determined from without. The reason for the preference of one accidental determination rather than another can be intrinsic to a producer, which stands open to a possibility beyond just this one determination, only when this producer, while preferring the one, still has and retains the other in a certain way, that is, when it remains with being in its totality, hence is spiritual and thus free.

It is to be noted in passing that it has also become clear now in what sense Thomas in *S.T.* I, q. 77, a. 1, ad 5; a. 6, corp., etc. lets the substantial ground be *only* the receptive principle for the accidental determinations, as opposed to the accidents which emanate from the essential principles of the thing. These accidents are unambiguously determined by the substantial ground in their definite being-thus (*Sosein*) also, and so belong in their being-thus to the essence of the thing. The accidental determinations indeed also emanate from this ground (since that is already implied by receptive principle), but their being-thus depends on external causality. It is only in this sense that the substantial ground is *merely* "passive" with respect to these accidents.

But this gives us an approach from a different viewpoint to a sharper understanding of what the inner-worldly agent has to accomplish with respect to the patient. It is not the ground of the ontological unfolding of the patient as such; it does not provide the determination of the patient in its being and from its ground, but only determines in which of the ways possible to the patient in itself, the patient realizes its own being, and is also, therefore, only the ground of the "becoming" of the determination and not of its being. Thus Thomas teaches explicitly first of all that the inner-worldly cause is only the ground of the becoming of the determination produced, not the permanent, productive ground of its being.[47] The sense of this statement is not self-evident at first sight. For if the becoming is considered the first moment, as it were, of the being of the determination,[48] then it would have to follow that the ground of the becoming could be and would have to be the sustaining ground of the being of the determination. If this is not the case, then "to be the ground of the becoming" cannot mean that this ground of itself places the determination in being (lets it come to be) even only initially, but only that it is the ground of the being-thus of what comes to be, as a cause, of course, not merely as a passive condition. This agrees with the fact that Thomas ascribes to the inner-worldly cause only the "determination," the "specification" of what comes to be, but not the production of its being.[49] Of course this statement cannot be understood as though the quiddity of the determination coming to be were pro-

---

[47] *De Pot.* q. 5, a. 1, ad 4 and ad 5; *I Sent.* dist. 37, q. 1, a. 1, corp.

[48] Thus, for example, Thomas understands the *"producere in esse"* (as the fundamental being of the *fieri*) as the first moment of a *"semper dare esse"* as the *conservari* (hence of the fundamental being of the permanent being): *S.T.* I, q. 9, a. 2, corp.; *II Sent.* dist. 15, q. 3, a. 1, ad 4 and ad 5.

[49] *De Pot.* q. 3, a. 1, corp.; a. 7, corp.; *S.C.G.* II, 21; *II Sent.* dist. 1, q. 1, a. 4, corp.; see also *S.T.* I, q. 104, a. 1, corp.

duced by the inner-worldly cause, and its *esse* by the patient itself under the influence of absolute being, whose continual operation in the patient belongs intrinsically to its constitution. A determination cannot be pieced together from its quiddity and its being in this way. So there remains only one possibility for a correct understanding of this statement: the external agent is the reason why the patient as such, to whose constitution belongs a continual self-realization and which stands continually under the intrinsic influence of God, unfolds precisely in this way rather than in another in its accidental determinations.

This brings us to the decisive point in the consideration of the general relationship between an emanating and received influence. How can an emanating influence, which is the self-realization of the agent in the medium of the patient, determine the active production of the determination by the patient itself in its being-thus in such a way that this determination of the being-thus does not however appear again as a determination received purely passively by the operative ground of the patient, and changing this ground as such ontologically?

The presuppositions for answering this question are already given to us. We must first of all look to the general relationship between matter and form. The material cause does not "produce" an effect "in" the form, that is, it does not bestow on it a determination which would be different from itself or the form.[50] Such a notion would destroy the concept of material-formal causality. The matter does not give the form a determination, but bestows itself upon it. Or, vice versa and better expressed: the form enters into the otherness of its material cause, gives itself away to it. In this act of information, which the form itself is, the form does not produce something different from itself, but the form itself taken as itself is the actuality of matter, and as such an actuality producing itself as the actuality of matter, the form is determined by the matter, and not by an efficient process from the side of matter.

"Through itself the form makes a thing to be in act since

---

[50] *De Spir. Creat.* a. 3, ad 21: *materia non subest formae mediante alia potentia.*

through its essence it is act (i.e. of matter), nor does it give being through some medium (i.e., through a determination or connection lying 'between' matter and form) . . . in its own self it is united with matter as its act."[51] But this also says vice versa: the "giving-itself-from-out-of-itself-into-matter" of the form (the *communicare* in the Thomistic expression) *is* already essentially its being-determined by the matter, since the form of itself is nothing but the act of matter. But if the form were taken to be determined by the matter through an efficient process antecedent to its information, then it would already be posited in its essence antecedent to this process and to its information; it would not be "essentially" the act of matter, and thus would be destroyed in its essence. Hence the passive essence of matter as such is already essentially the determination of the form for its actualization of the potentialities of matter. Thus the form "suffers" in the strictest sense only by the fact that it actively informs, since it is itself nothing more than the act of matter.[52]

In this process the information ought not to be thought of as a momentary event at the beginning of the existence of a thing; it is rather a continually renewed process, remaining fluid, as it were, because the existent arises out of the creative ground of God continually anew. From this it follows necessarily that there is no question here of a static relationship between form and matter that is fixed once and for all. The form is always the act of matter within the potentialities of its essence according to their various modes.

7. Reduction of Efficient Causality to Intrinsic Causality

Now it has already been shown that the influence of the external, efficient cause strictly as such must be understood as an emanat-

---

[51] *S.T.* I, q. 76, a. 7, corp.

[52] We do not have to go into the question here, what further metaphysical presuppositions lie at the basis of such a concept of matter and form and their reciprocal causality. Here, where there can be no question of expounding the whole of Thomistic metaphysics, the insight suffices that matter determines the form in its realization not by causing something, but by being there and being given to the form.

ing influence, that is, as self-realization of the agent in the medium of the matter of the other. If the self-realization of the agent thus expands and maintains itself in this matter, then the matter is thereby actualized in its potentiality in a definite respect, which in itself neither means that the other thing has already received a determination, nor can it be understood as though the determination, which the matter as such receives through the self-realization of the agent in it, is something different from this self-realization, since this determination must also be understood in the sense of a formal causality. But this limits the potentiality of matter in the privatively unlimited breadth it had in itself. For it is not possible that the same matter (the same "part" of matter) be the sustaining "wherein" of contrary actualities at once. Hence the potency, into which the form of the patient actualizes itself as the actuality of this matter, is limited and determined in a definite way.

"Considered in itself, matter holds itself indifferently to all forms, but it is determined to special forms through the power of a mover."[53] A corporeal principle is necessary for the being of a form "insofar as the form does not begin to exist except in matter; for matter which is disposed in any way cannot receive a form, because the proper act must be in its proper matter . . . wherefore, there must be something which changes the matter. And this is some corporeal agent to which it belongs to act by moving."[54] The active self-realization of the patient as such "suffers" the matter determined to be such and such by the agent, in other words the patient actualizes itself from out of its formal ground as the actuality of precisely *this* matter. Thus the patient itself actively produces its "suffering," its determination by the external agent. If we add further what will be said in a moment about the objective identity of the emanating and the received influence, then we have also clarified the sentence in Thomas cited earlier according to which the dispositions in their genesis are prior to the form, but in their being are after it: as emanating influence the disposition is prior to the form and be-

[53] *De Spir. Creat.* a. 3, ad 20.
[54] *De Pot.* q. 5, a. 1, corp.

longs to its material cause, as received influence it is produced by
the form itself in formal causality as the form's own being.

Now for Thomas the efficient causality of an agent causing
from without is only a tripartite mode of *intrinsic* causality.
For, on the one hand, this efficient causality presents itself as
a peculiar mode of a formal causality[55]: the action as self-
realization of the agent itself (the action is the perfection of
the agent). On the other hand, it forms at the same time the
specific mode of a material causality: the determinable matter
of the patient as the "wherein" of the self-realization of the
agent. And finally, it contains once again the aspect of a formal
causality: the active self-realization of the patient as the actualization of precisely this matter. As a consequence of such a
reduction of efficient causality to a tripartite mode of intrinsic
causality, it is no contradiction for Thomas that the determination of the patient from without is strictly identical with its own
act from within (as a determination of the formal, self-producing substantial ground), and this act cannot be understood
merely as a subsequent reaction to a merely passively received,
ontological influence of the external agent. In a material being
the determination produced by itself strictly as such can be determined from without.

Two considerations show that this reduction of efficient causality to intrinsic causality, in which an essence is constituted in
itself, is Thomistic: first of all, Thomas considers the transient
causality of something purely material as the only kind of emanation which is possible to a material being on the basis of
its intrinsic deficiency in being, whereby emanation according
to its "whence" and its "wherein" is always in each instance
what is most interior in the thing to which it belongs, that is,
its self-realization. Because in something purely material there
really is no longer any interior because of the "total dispersion of the form over the matter," its ultimate self-realiza-

---

[55] We do not mean a formal causality in the strictest sense, but what
Thomas calls *resultatio* elsewhere, which can be understood under
formal causality because as such it is neither an influence from without
nor outwards (*causalitas efficiens*).

tion is an expansion of its own essence into the other of the other, is thus transient causality, which is only a deficient mode of emanation in the proper sense, which as self-realization takes place in the interior of an existent.[56] Secondly, Thomas regards the highest mode of producing another, the creative action of God, no longer as an "action which goes out from the agent into an external patient," but as an immanent action of God, hence as the free self-realization of God Himself, which remains completely in Himself.[57] Thus the highest causality directed outward also shows itself *a fortiori* to be a mode of self-realization, and thus transient causality shows itself to be a peculiar mode of formal causality.

8. The Quidditative Identity of Emanating and Received Influence

At the conclusion of this general consideration of transient causality in the Thomistic sense, the quidditative connection between emanating and received influence must be examined still more explicitly. Because of the importance of this question for sense knowledge we must still clarify how the emanating and received influence are related to each other with regard to their respective, intrinsic quiddity. According to what has been said so far, inner-worldly causality as presupposing matter cannot from the outset mean in Thomas the merely regular connection of two phenomena (the "cause" and the "effect") in such a way that merely a quantitatively determinable, functional connection exists between them, without their being able to be compared in their intrinsic, quidditative nature. To act on another is for Thomas a "bringing self as realizing self into the medium of the other"; what is "in" the patient is therefore the agent itself in its completed essence, the emanation of the agent's own interior, its self-realization in that interiority which alone is possible to an essence which is exterior to itself.

---

[56] *S.C.G.* IV, 11 should be brought in here, but we cannot go into the interpretation of this text.

[57] *De Pot.* q. 3, a. 15, corp.

On the other hand, this self-realization as the being of the agent itself is borne by the matter of the other, hence as the actuality of this matter it is possible only insofar as this matter was already in advance a *potency* for this actuality of the agent. But as such it has been produced in advance by the form of the patient, for matter is a *real* potency only from the form whose matter it is.[58] But that means that the patient of itself (from its ground as formal) has produced the potency for the self-realization of the agent, and retains it permanently. That in its turn is only possible insofar as the patient itself (as form) is already and always really tending towards the actuality of such a potency. For an absolutely static potency as such would not be a real potency. But if the patient of itself is actively ordered towards the actuality of the self-realization of the agent, because it holds out to it the real potency for it, and if during the actual self-realization of the agent in the matter of the patient the contrary potentialities of the patient cannot be actualized simultaneously, and if, moreover, an actualization of disparate potentialities by the patient does not come into question at all, since, of course, it would have to be determined from without to these too, or it would have already actualized them: then the patient can realize from out of itself only what coincides quidditatively with the self-realization of the agent. Therefore, the received and the emanating influence cannot be distinguished in their intrinsic quiddity, but only by the fact that the agent realizes this quiddity as its own in the matter of *another,* while the patient realizes the same quiddity as its own in its *own* potency borne by itself.

"To move" and "to be moved" are the same in their intrinsic being. They are distinguished only by the fact that the being of what we call "to move" maintains itself precisely in the moved as an actuality of the mover; it produces the "to be moved" with its same intrinsic quiddity from out of the moved (the moved "moves *itself*"), and thus expands in the moved itself as an actuality of the *self*-mover. Perhaps Thomas would

[58] *De Ver.* q. 9, a. 3, ad 6: *forma est quodammodo causa materiae inquantum dat ei esse actu.*

refute examples which apparently contradict this by alluding to the fact that in most cases the action strictly as such, that is, insofar as it really expands in the *patient* as an actuality of the agent, is not accessible to us in its intrinsic quiddity at all, and, therefore, in place of the identity of the emanating and received influence, we are usually limited to a merely functional connection of regularity between a cause and an effect which are defined in terms of criteria which do not grasp the quiddity of the agent and the patient strictly as such at all.

In saying this we have not merely drawn a conclusion from presuppositions which are given in Thomas. Thomas also expresses our conclusion itself explicitly. What concerns the relationship of the quiddity of the agent and the patient as such, Thomas knows only two kinds of causes: the univocal cause and the equivocal (analogous) cause, that is, a cause which in its intrinsic nature *as* cause corresponds absolutely to what it produces, and a cause with which this is not the case. This apparently purely formal distinction acquires a metaphysical meaning immediately when we take into consideration how Thomas defines the equivocal (analogous) cause more precisely.

The analogous cause is the metaphysical ground for a whole realm of being (forms as such), not merely for an existent as merely this individual determined to be such and such; it is a universal and essential cause, not a particular cause, and as such it is the ground of being, not merely of becoming.[59] As such, it must be immaterial, for from the outset an existent individuated by matter cannot be the metaphysical ground of a form as such, and so not of being itself either.[60] Vice versa, the univocal cause is only the ground of becoming, not of being; it is only the ground of the individual as such,[61] and it is essentially material.[62] With regard to its quiddity, the form to be pro-

---

[59] See *S.T.* I, q. 13, a. 5, ad 1; q. 104, a. 1, corp.; *De Pot.* q. 5, a. 1, corp.; *I Sent.* dist. 12, q. 1, a. 2, ad 2.

[60] *De Pot.* q. 5, a. 1, corp.

[61] See the next to the last note; *De Ver.* q. 10, a. 13, ad 3; *De Pot.* q. 7, a. 7, ad 7 (first series); *S.C.G.* III, 65.

[62] *II Sent.* dist. 18, q. 2, a. 1, corp.

duced is in the universal cause not merely virtually, but actually, that is, the univocal cause produces what it is as producer.[63] It would lead us too far afield to show the connection between each of the individual characteristics in these two kinds of causes. It suffices here, where we are only concerned with establishing Thomas's opinion, that he knows only these two kinds of causes. But this says that the characteristics of the individual kinds of causes which were given are essential, and a characteristic of the one kind cannot be found in a cause of the other kind.

But as *permanent* ground of the being of a thing beyond its mere becoming, the analogous cause is precisely the opposite of what we understood by an inner-worldly cause. For Thomas, therefore, an inner-worldly cause is a univocal cause, that is, it causes that which it itself is as cause.[64] There is no place among these two possible kinds of causes for a cause which, although it would not be the permanent ground of the caused being of an existent, and therefore necessarily could not be equivocal, that is, essential and universal (since otherwise it would be its own ground), yet, with regard to the quiddity of the agent and patient as such, would only stand in a *functional* connection with the patient, that is, which would only be an equivocal cause. A cause *necessarily* produces univocally what it is, or it *cannot* be univocal, and so not inner-worldly either, since it permanently sustains that realm of being as such in which what is produced stands.

So far we have always actually understood the emanating and the received influence as two different ontological actualities, without wanting to commit ourselves to this conception already, and have therefore shown their qualitative correspond-

[63] *De Pot.* q. 5, a. 1, corp.
[64] In fact Thomas enumerates the *motus caeli*, to which he ascribes an influence on sublunary events, among the equivocal causes (*S.T.* I, q. 104, a. 1, corp.; q. 115, a. 3, ad 3, etc.). But this conception of ancient physics is harmonized again with the view just developed by the fact that the heavens have this power only under the movement of spiritual substances (*II Sent.* dist. 15, q. 1, a. 2, corp.; *S.G.C.* III, 23; *De Spir. Creat.* a. 6, ad 12, first series; *S.T.* I, q. 70, a. 3, ad 3), and that *determinata agentia ad species determinatas* are also still necessary (*De Anima* a. 8, ad 17).

361

ence independently of the question whether basically they are not both the same ontological actuality numerically, and are distinguishable only in relation to the two substantial grounds from which they emanate as identical. We were completely justified in understanding the emanating and the received influence, at least, tentatively, as though they were numerically different, even where both are given simultaneously. For Thomas knows an emanating influence which is never received at all, and in many cases the received influence continues on as a possible quality in the patient after the emanating influence has already long ceased. Since we have not distinguished all of these cases up to now, we necessarily had to distinguish the two influences numerically. But what is the relationship of the two so long as the emanating influence lasts and so long as during this external influence the received influence emanates from the ground of the patient? This question concerns us because the whole investigation of efficient causality was undertaken principally with a view to external sensibility, in which there is question precisely of the reception of a determination during the external influence.

This question seems to lead us into a dilemma: we have two substantial, actively self-producing grounds in their respective self-realizations, and so the emanating and the received influence seem to have to be understood necessarily as two ontological actualities, although qualitatively the same. We have the one medium of the same matter, as whose actuality both of these self-realizations are supposed to take place simultaneously, so that it is impossible to see how one and the same potency could be the medium which bears two (qualitatively) completely identical actualities of precisely this one material potency. This seems to have thrown us back again into the same apparent contradiction of the two series of statements at the beginning of this section: action and passion are two different accidents, since they are the perfection of the agent and the patient respectively; action and passion are the same with the two relations of "from which" and "in which."

"Something is multiplied numerically because of that from

which it has subsistence"[65]: a quiddity is given as multiple when its "wherein" is multiple. A form, which of itself is always one in its intrinsic quiddity, is multiplied only by the fact that it is the being of matter. "Therefore, since the form does not subsist of itself in these inferiors, there must be some (other) in that to which it is communicated through which the form or nature receives subsistence, and this is matter which subsists under material forms and natures. Moreover, because a material nature or form is not its own *esse,* it receives *esse* by the fact that it is received into something; wherefore, insofar as it is in different things, it necessarily has different *esse's;* wherefore, humanity is not one in Socrates and Plato with regard to *esse,* although it is one with regard to its proper formality."[66] But precisely because of the nature of transient causality, the emanating influence is such that it maintains itself in the matter of the patient. Hence if the difference of matter is the only reason why a form is able to be repeated, then it must be concluded vice versa, that the emanating and the received influence are one and the same, since they subsist in the one matter of the patient. Consequently, one and the same actuality is the determination of two substantial existents.

To understand this sentence we must recall again that the matter in individual, numbered things is necessarily one, that, consequently, the difference and plurality which the individual, material things have from their first ground is not that of an unrelated indifference to one another, but that in the "one" matter, in which everything material subsists, every individual is already the other because of its ground. The "independence" ("*Selbstständigkeit*") of the individual material thing cannot be explained from the independent existence (*Selbststand*) of what is spiritual, which alone is originally accessible to us. On the other hand, presupposing the identity of the emanating and received

---

[65] *De Pot.* q. 9, a. 5, ad 13.

[66] *De Pot.* q. 2, a. 1, corp. The text is different in the Parma edition and the Paris edition of Fretté. We are citing the Parma edition, and suggest further the *omission of the aliud.* The differences in the text are not important for our question.

influence (during the duration of the influence), it is more difficult to understand how this identity can be reconciled with the
fact that there are supposed to be two productive, substantial
grounds (that of the agent and that of the patient) from which
this one actuality emanates. To understand this it is important
to see that the two productions of the one actuality in the one
potency of matter from the substantial, formal grounds have an
essentially different character, and thereby mutually condition
each other.

We must begin with the proposition: "form is in a certain
way the cause of matter, insofar as it makes it to be in act; in
a certain way matter is the cause of form, insofar as it sustains
it."[67] It is to be noted here that the "making it to be in act,"
the actualization of the potency of matter, is a fluid relationship
remaining constantly in flux insofar as the form actualizes in each
instance the concrete, definite potentiality of matter. Therefore,
the form of the patient actualizes the received influence in the
course of its "making matter to be in act," because only the form
of the patient is substantially united with this definite matter.
The form of the agent produces its self-realization precisely into
the matter of the patient only in the course of its seeking a
"wherein" to sustain this self-realization ("it sustains the form
itself"), because this agent, since it is not substantially united
with the matter of the patient, reaches out to this only for the
sake of its own self-realization. So the two productions, although
they meet in the one ontological actuality, nevertheless have an
essentially different finality.

Moreover, they are mutually "dependent" on each other.
Because the self-realization of the agent takes place in the matter of the other, it is dependent on the matter of the patient;
but this matter is dependent on the form of the patient "insofar
as it makes matter to be in act." So the self-realization of the
agent is dependent on the "making matter to be in act" of the
form of the patient, and this actualization of the potency of matter necessarily becomes a simultaneous actualization of the self-

[67] De Ver. q. 9, a. 3, ad 6; see q. 28, a. 7, corp., etc.

364

realization of the agent when the form of the patient gives actuality to its matter during the self-realization of the agent. And vice versa: the self-realization of the patient, of its form, is dependent on its matter, "insofar as the matter sustains the form itself"; but in its concrete potency this matter is determined by the self-realization of the agent in it, whereby this self-realization then determines in its turn the concrete actualization of the potency of the matter by the form of the patient itself.

But if the two productions as such (the emanation [resultatio], insofar as it can be distinguished from what emanates [resultans], have a different finality, and in the process mutually condition each other, then neither can there ultimately be any difficulty in maintaining that what emanates from the two substantial grounds is one and the same actuality in spite of the dual origin itself. Looked at from the duality of the origin (and only thus), then it can also be said that the action and passion are two accidents. If in the preceding development we at first distinguished the emanating and the received influence not merely in the dual direction of their origin, but apparently in their absolute existence, and did not simply begin by establishing their identity, that was necessary because it was only in this way that the insight really could be gained that the influence is also strictly identical with what *emanates* from the productive, substantial ground of the *patient* itself, however much this emanation is determined in its quiddity by the external agent.[68]

A conclusion can be added here immediately: when a sentient knower produces his determination under the influence of a

[68] If in Nink, *op. cit.*, p. 184f. (note 169) the action is not merely *in* the patient, but is itself the perfection of the patient, then it is impossible to see—in a critical departure from our position—what that perfection of the patient is still supposed to be, which, indeed, is a result of the action of the agent, but is *really different from it* and is also only *passio*. The thesis proposed here cannot be weakened (as Nink tries to do) by a reference to the production of the world by God. For scholasticism itself (and precisely in Thomism) frequently emphasizes that the creative causality of God can precisely *not* be understood as transient, efficient causality (which is the only thing at issue in our analysis of *inner*-worldly, efficient causality). For this point, see *De Pot.* q. 3, a. 15, corp.

sensible object, then he produces in strict identity the self-realization of the sensible object itself. Insofar as this self-realization as a determination of the object is produced by the sentient knower himself, and so as participating in the ontological intensity of the knower, it is reflected against itself, it is sensibly conscious in the sentient knower. Insofar as the sentient knower lets this self-realization emanate in the otherness of matter, the self-realization is conscious as other (and hence by that very fact *not* as "species"). Insofar as the sentient knower does not re-realize (*mitvollzieht*) the point of origin which belongs to this self-realization from the side of the emanation from the sensible object, it apprehends this other, ontological actuality of the sensible object not *as* produced by the sensible object, but only in its absolute quality as other than itself.

X. INTELLIGIBLE SPECIES III

The Ontology of Inner-Worldly, Efficient Causality in Its Application to the Essence of Sensibility and of the Agent Intellect

The results of the preceding section will be made use of in two ways: first, we are now in a position to clarify questions about the essence of sensibility which were left unclarified in the second chapter. Secondly, the question about the intelligible species which was raised in Section VIII will also be able to be answered.

1. *Passion* (Passio), *Intention* (Intentio), *Spiritual* Esse in Thomas

A further preparatory clarification is necessary for the first question. It has already been said that according to Thomas external sense perception is a "passion" as opposed to a "passible quality."[1] First of all, therefore, we must define more precisely the essence of this passion. It has already been shown

---

[1] *III Sent.* dist. 14, q. 1, a. 1, sol. 2, corp.

that the passion of external sensibility cannot be understood in the sense of a merely emanating influence. Hence a reception takes place, that is, the substantial ground of the sensibility produces of itself precisely the external determination which makes the sensibility actually knowing. We had shown (in the example of the colors in the air) that Thomas calls the merely emanating, non-received influence a "spiritual esse," a "spiritual intention" (*intentio*). Attention was already called at the time to the fact that Thomas also knows the concept of such a spiritual *esse* in another sense, which of course is connected objectively with the sense brought out earlier. We must now get a clearer understanding of this other sense, since by doing so the passion and so the essence of sensibility can be clarified.

In a text where there is obviously question of a received influence (because it refers to light in the air, which has a natural *esse* in the air, as has already been shown), the essence of such an intention is described as follows: "For intentions of this kind depend on the natural forms of bodies [i.e., of agents] *per se* and not accidentally; and so their *esse* does not remain after the action of the agents has ceased."[2] And, in another text: "The intentions do not remain . . . except through the presence of the principal agent . . ."[8] First of all, it is clear just from this in what respect such a received influence, like the merely emanating influence (for example, of the colors in the air), can also be called intention: both depend "*per se*" on the cause not only in their coming to be, but also in their permanent being. It is to be noted here that the determination, when it remains permanently and *per se* dependent on the external agent in its being, does not perhaps cease to determine the patient after the influence from without because the patient is perhaps brought subsequently to a new determination by a new external influence. Rather the determination as such, and not, as it were, first at a def-

[2] *De Pot.* q. 5, a. 1, ad 6. That there is question here of a received influence is shown first from the fact that Thomas considers light a real property of air (*S.T.* I, q. 67, a. 3, corp.) and yet secondly, in the same *Summa* (I, q. 67, a. 3, ad 1; q. 104, a. 1, corp.; II–II, q. 171, a. 2, corp.), the inherence of light in the air is described in objectively the same way as in *De Pot.* q. 5, a. 1, ad 6.
[8] *De Pot.* q. 6, a. 4, corp.

inite endpoint and seen from this, is already and always a mere passion. But this means that during the passion the patient is inclined towards the opposite determination not only because it is also actively directed to this contrary determination (to that extent every accidental determination would merely be a passion), but already prior to this, and for a reason which must be intrinsically independent of this active direction to the contrary determination.

So the question arises, how and why a received influence, which as such is produced by the patient itself, yet can remain intrinsically dependent on the further continuous operation of the agent. Since we raise this question with a view to the influence of the sensible upon sensibility, the answer which Thomas gives to this question with regard to light does not come into consideration here, and therefore we can pass over whether this answer is compatible with the general doctrine of efficient causality explained in the preceding section, that is, presupposing this answer, whether a reception of the passion can still occur at all. According to Thomas, light remains in the air only during the actual illumination because "what pertains to the nature of the higher genus in no way remains after the action of the agent, just as light does not remain in a diaphanous substance after the illumination ceases."[4] The air is unable to receive the light in such a way that it can be and remain of itself its productive bearer because light is a superior genus; or seen from the other side: because the subject and patient is essentially inferior ontologically, it cannot produce the form of the agent from itself alone. For the complete form (as the form is called which is dependent on the external agent only in becoming) is in the subject according to the condition of the subject.[5] An extrinsic criterion for judging the possibility of the reception of an influence as a complete form consisted for Thomas

<hr>

[4] S.C.G. III, 65.
[5] S.T. III, q. 63, a. 5, ad 1. This is said in connection with the question about the *virtus instrumentalis*, whose mode of being is very frequently made parallel by Thomas with that of light in the air, and is likewise understood as "intentional" being.

in establishing whether the subject could become substantially that which the accidental form in question would necessarily contain as a qualitative expression of this substance.[6] Because the air cannot become an illuminating body, neither is it able to receive this luminosity as a passible quality; it has it only in an intrinsic, continuous dependence on the external agent.

Now this reason why the influence is received only as an "intention" obviously does not come into consideration for the relationship between the sensible as external agent and sensibility. For the sensible is obviously not "a nature of a higher genus," but rather just the opposite. Hence it cannot be the case that sensibility could not produce of itself alone the influence of the sensible. That it does not do so, that is, that it receives the emanating influence only as a passion, can therefore be due only to the higher ontological level of sensibility with respect to the sensible.

Our general consideration of efficient causality showed that the reason why the substantial, formal ground of a material existent produces the emanating influence of the agent as its own determination lies in the fact that this formal ground is actively ordered to such a determination as to its own self-realization, and so for it to produce this determination there is need only of a delimitation of its greater potential breadth. But if it has produced it, then in spite of its constant inclination towards another contrary determination, it can have of itself no reason to produce another. The real potency for a contrary determination, in which the substantial ground of the patient always stands, cannot as such be the reason for it. For this other determination is just as much only a partial realization of this potency in its total breadth, and so cannot be a reason to produce it rather than the other, because in producing it the potentialities of the substantial ground would be delimited and the substantial ground would lose itself just as much in it as it did in the first determination which it has received through an influence from without. If, therefore, the patient nevertheless lets its determination fall away, as it were, as a mere passion (and indeed

[6] *S.T.* I, q. 67, a. 3, ad 1.

not because of the impotency of a perhaps conceivable deficiency in being), then that is conceivable only if its return into the "situation of indifference" between the possible determinations does not really mean the loss of an ontological perfection, but is the expression of a continual "holding-oneself-above-these-determinations."

Consequently, then, this letting the passion go is not an indication of the inclination of the substantial ground to a contrary determination as such, but the expression of its superiority over every individual determination, which superiority does not first come to appearance in the reception of another, second determination, but was in advance the condition for the fact that the first determination was received merely as a passion. Of course an existent can also produce a determination as its quality (for example a power) when it is not inclined to another determination on the basis of a further potentiality. In general, therefore, in the reception of each determination taken by itself, the *further* potentiality as such is not present *as* the *ante*cedent ground of this reception. Hence a passion is only given where the further potentiality of the patient as such comes to appearance itself, where as such it is already given itself during each individual determination taken by itself. But if as such it is given itself in the act of the production of this or that determination, then it is *given* precisely not only as a potentiality for this *or* that determination (as with the production of a determination in efficient causality in general), but as a potentiality for this *and* that determination (because it is operative [*wirkend*], asserting itself [*sich durchsetzend*], and manifesting itself [*sich zeigend*]), and therefore, since a potency gives itself only in the act, it is certainly *not merely* potency in relationship to the actuality of this or that determination as such, but is itself, as manifesting itself, already actuality in itself. Expressed in another way: a determination is had as a mere passion when it is produced by its substantial ground insofar as this ground is already beyond it as maintaining itself in its further potentiality, insofar as this further potentiality itself as such asserts itself and so is actuality of itself.

370

But seen from the basic structure of a Thomistic metaphysics, this mode of being of a patient, which because of its *higher level* of being suffers its accidental determination only as passion, as intention, is already by that very fact the mode of being of a sentient knower. The statement, sensibility receives its determinations "after the manner of an intention," as a "spiritual *esse*," is thus not merely an obscure description which is taken from a vague analogy with spiritual knowing; it does not deny that sense knowledge apprehends the reality of the sensible in its own self in an ontological process; it has nothing to do with an explanation of knowledge as the reception of an "image" of the sensible. This statement is rather the essential definition of sense knowledge itself. The only thing presupposed is that one understands what passion, intention, and spiritual *esse* mean in Thomas. It is important now to show that the statement given is the essential definition of sense knowledge. Thereby the explanation (of which we gave only an indication) of the essence of a patient, which because of its level of being receives a determination from without only as a passion, will be able to be further clarified.

2. *"To Receive after the Manner of an Intention"* as the Ontological, Essential Definition of Sensibility

The Thomistic proposition that knowing is the same thing as immateriality has already been explained in its general meaning in another context. It must now be shown that the being of a patient (although material), which because of its *intensity* of being has its determination as an intention, expresses a first and specific kind of immateriality, hence is a knower, and in fact as material is a sentient knower.

Knowing is the ontological being-present-to-itself of a being. Therefore, an existent is non-knowing when and insofar as its being is not present to itself, but is with the non-being other of matter. And vice versa: to whatever extent a being becomes "free," to the same extent is it knowing. The being-with-matter of being which prevents knowledge has its clearest characteristic in the fact that the being (the form) is given away to the "this" of matter as precisely this matter in each instance. To the extent that the form becomes free, that is, therefore, is not absolutely given away to each definite "this" of matter, to the same extent is it present to itself, conscious. Now an existent which has its determination (which as received is *its* actuality) as a passion is thereby free in a certain way (although ultimately this freedom is only negatively definable in contrast with spirit and a merely material form). For when the determination is merely a passion, then this says that the formal ground producing it, in that it produces it, produces its own actuality as already reaching beyond this determination. The produced actuality is thus already and always more than the determination as individual in each instance, although this individual determination must be produced so that the patient can produce this total, greater actuality. The formal ground not only actualizes the determination itself as its actuality, but also places itself in its potentiality for *many* determinations into actuality, although this latter actuality must be empty in a certain way, since otherwise, of course, there would no longer be place for the determination from without, and the many contrary determinations as being many and contrary would be actualized in the one matter of the patient at once.

This (although empty) further potentiality for many determinations, which is present itself as *actuality* in the production of an individual determination, shows itself to be free in the fact that, as actualized potency, it is not exhausted in the actuality of the individual determination as a "this" in each instance. On the one hand, the formal ground itself has entered into actuality in the production of the individual determination and only thus, and yet, on the other hand, it produces itself not merely as the actuality of precisely this determination, but as actual it is already and always superior to every individual determination. But this means that it is in a certain way free, and in fact in the double and yet fundamentally single sense, that it can let each individual determination fall away, that is, it receives it from

372

the outset only as a passion, and that it has the determination so received as sensibly conscious. For since it is superior to the individual determination as actuality and not as mere potentiality, as actuality it is already in a certain way beyond the individual "this," and thus it is in a certain respect free, immaterial. And for that reason what belongs to the constitution of this actuality as precisely of this ontological level must be conscious: the produced individual determination, the passion itself *and* the further potentiality in which, as being itself *actual* during the passion, the individual determination comes to be. In other words, the form of the external agent is conscious, as is also "something" which, on the one hand, is related to the external determination as its potency (since it becomes conscious only with and during it), and yet which, on the other hand, appears as its greater *actuality* (since it is only then that the external determination can be received as a mere *passio*). Insofar as this "something," understood formally from the concept of passion, is the *a priori* potentiality (which becomes conscious) to receive the external determination as passion and thus as sensibly conscious, we can speak of this conscious "something" as pure intuition, as conscious, empty anticipation of the possible determinations, and this anticipation as such must become actual if the individual determination is to be a mere passion, and must be conscious as actual, because as actual it is raised above the individual "this" of the individual determination, hence in a certain sense is free and immaterial.

Here in this context it needs merely to be stated that with the formal concept of pure intuition acquired from the notion of passion we have objectively a formal definition of space and time as the *a priori* of pure sensibility. It must only be noted that the potentiality for many determinations, which is conscious as empty actuality, is the potentiality for material forms, hence for determinations of quantitative matter which is the ontological root of all temporality and spatiality. From pure intuition as the condition of the possibility of having the determination of the external agent sensibly conscious we can acquire the concept of the imagination and of the common sense as the root of the external senses. But it would lead us too far afield to go into that here.

If the sentient knower produces his determination as a mere passion, then it also follows from this that the lower ontological level of the sensible does not prevent its determination from being sensibly known. On the contrary: if sensibility can only be itself if it is determined from without, if this determination can only be known if it is received as a mere passion, and if in its turn this is only possible in view of the higher level of being of sensibility in relation to the determination as such, then the somewhat lower level of being of the determination, and thus of the sensible as such all together, is even a necessary presupposition of the intuitive, receptive knowledge of another. In fact, if the intensity of being of the sensible as such, and so of its self-realization in the medium of the knower, were not inferior, it could not expand as a mere passion at all. From this it follows with metaphysical necessity that the sense act with its ontological, reflected determination cannot in principle be perceived intuitively in its own self by another knower. Hence when Thomas says that while seeing a red thing the pupil is not red, that is correct not because the redness does not really exist in the organ as such in an intentional *esse*, but because this higher being as such together with the organ as such cannot be intuited by another at all because of its greater intensity of being, and so only for that reason it is not red in the sense of a quality perceivable by another.

Further, equally important conclusions about the nature of sense knowledge follow necessarily from the preceding section, so that it suffices to mention them explicitly in the summary. Before that, let us make sure explicitly that what has been said so far has kept within the Thomistic problematic. According to Thomas, sense knowledge is a reception of the form of the other as an "intention,"[7] as a mere "passion,"[8] as an "intentional and spiritual *esse*."[9] But according to Thomas

7 *S.T.* I, q. 78, a. 3, corp. (*intentio formae*).
8 *III Sent.* dist. 14, q. 1, a. 1, sol. 2, corp.
9 *In II de Anima* lect. 24, n. 553; *S.T.* I, q. 78, a. 3, corp.

the concepts passion and intention (spiritual *esse*) mean the same thing.[10] Therefore, we had the right to interpret sensibility from the concepts of intention and mere passion as these concepts are given in their general *ontological* sense, which is more readily accessible to us where we are not already dealing with knowledge. For otherwise there is always the danger that the expressions "intention" and "spiritual *esse*" in sensibility are understood only as other *gnoseological* words for sense knowledge, instead of as terms of a general ontological meaning which also have a sense where there is no question of knowledge as such. But it is obviously Thomas's intention to grasp the essence of sensibility *ontologically* if he defines it as the reception of an intentional and spiritual *esse*. Admittedly, the sense of the two concepts is somewhat obscured insofar as Thomas also understands by the term "mere passion" a passion where the reception of the form follows only during the actual influence of the agent because of the ontological deficiency or the ontological opposition of the patient. But that is obviously not the case with a sentient knower, since it is "more noble" than the sensible.[11]

But if, presupposing this, the concept of intention as mere passion is further developed, then the concept leads to an insight into an ontological relationship between the patient in a mere passion and its determination, and this relationship expresses a certain immateriality and therefore, according to the general principles of the Thomistic metaphysics of knowledge, necessarily means knowledge. Insofar as we have acquired the concept of sensibility from the general concept of being-determined by an external agent (which being-determined always presupposes the materiality of the patient), from the outset we are not in danger of going counter to the proposition in Thomas: "The sense must receive corporeally and materially a

[10] For the same reason something (light in the air, *virtus agentis in instrumento*) appears at one time as *intentio* (*De Pot.* q. 5, a. 1, ad 6; q. 6, a. 4, corp.), and at another time as mere *passio* (*S.T.* II–II, q. 171, a. 2, corp.; *De Ver.* q. 12, a. 1, corp., etc.).

[11] *In III de Anima* lect. 3, n. 612.

likeness of the thing which is sensed,"[12] without therefore being put into a position where it is impossible to acquire an ontological and not merely a gnoseological, metaphorical sense for the spiritual and intentional *esse* which is supposed to belong to the sensibly apprehended. The "immateriality" itself, which we infer from the "receiving after the manner of an intention," is explicit Thomistic doctrine: "(the sense power) has a certain immateriality."[13] And if we found this to be indicated ultimately in the fact that the substantial, formal ground places itself into actuality as a potency for many determinations at once and as a totality (although in an empty way to be filled at least partially by the individual determinations from without), that too is given in Thomas, although it is not explicitly acquired from the concept of intention.

For according to Thomas sensibility is already of itself and before the determination from without an act which is "just as when someone has knowledge (through the intellect) after he has already learned."[14] Hence sensibility of itself as actuality (*actus*), not as mere potency, must have already anticipated the breadth of its potentialities for determination from without (whereby it is precisely in a position to produce the external determination in such a way that it remains free with respect to it, and so produces it only as a passion), for otherwise Thomas could not say that sensibility is already of itself just as actual as one who has already learned, who already possesses his object habitually, hence has already actualized his potentialities for knowing. That Thomas meant this "always-of-itself-already-possessing-the-object" (*je von sich her schon besitzen des Gegenstandes*) as an empty anticipation (*Vorwegnahme*) of the objects is shown in the fact that he adds immediately that sensibility still needs the external object for actual knowledge.[15] Objectively the same thing is said by Thomas when he emphasizes that the senses of themselves must be free (*denudari*) from the forms which they

---

[12] *In II de Anima* lect. 12, n. 377.
[13] *De Sensu et Sensatio* lect. 2, n. 20.
[14] *In II de Anima* lect. 12, n. 374.
[15] *Ibid.*, n. 375.

are to know receptively.[16] For this being-free must be understood as a *positive* characteristic, not as a defect, not as the dominance of matter and its passive indifference to every form, through which, of course, matter is of itself always free (*nuda*) from form.[17] Therefore, this positive freedom from the form to be received must be understood in such a way that of itself sensibility in its self-realization already and always surpasses the individual form when it produces it.

3. The Results of an Ontology of External Influence for the Essence of Sensibility

We will now summarize what follows from our general consideration of the ontology of external influence for the essence of sensibility:

1. Sense knowledge as receptive, that is, as knowledge to be determined ontologically from within the world, presupposes sensibility as material being.

2. The determination by the sensible which is productively received by sensibility as its actuality is identical with the self-realization of the sensible in the medium of the sentient. This self-realization of the sensible in the medium of sensibility is thus at the same time actively produced by sensibility itself, without a merely passively received determination of sensibility preceding it which would be different from the self-realization of the sensible as its perfection, and from the conscious, immanent action of sensibility.

3. The existent which (because of its higher being) produces a determination as a mere passion (intention) knows this determination, and indeed on the basis of a pure intuition (of space and time) in which this higher being manifests itself, and because of this the determination becomes a mere passion. "To receive after the manner of an intention" is thus the ontological,

---

[16] *In II de Anima* lect. 23, n. 547; 548; *II Sent.* dist. 17, q. 2, a. 1, ad 4; *De Ver.* q. 22, a. 1, ad 8; *S.T.* I, q. 91, a. 1, ad 3; *De Anima* a. 8, corp.

[17] *De Spir. Creat.* a. 3, ad 20.

essential definition of sensibility, and hence, since receptive knowledge is essentially sensible (material), of any receptive knowledge as such at all. If we apply what was said to the concept of the sensible species, then it can be said further:

4. In its first and fundamental meaning, the species is not an "intentional" (in the modern sense) double of the external object after the manner of an image, but, as the self-realization of the sensible in the material medium of sensibility, belongs to the being of the object itself, since every emanating influence is a perfection of the agent. Insofar as this self-realization of the sensible can expand and maintain itself only in the medium of the patient (concretely, the sentient), the species, although belonging to the being of the sensible, is nevertheless a new self-realization of the sensible, and so as such does not already belong to the sense object in itself, insofar as this in-itself can be conceived as *prior* to the actual perception. This is not to deny that the qualitatively identical self-realization of the sensible could also expand in a medium other than that of sensibility if occasion arises. In fact Thomas assumes that explicitly for colors in the air, for example; in fact he even seems to ascribe to every body from the outset a continual expansion (which is not a *motus*) of its qualities into a medium as the highest and essential mode of its action.[18] But be that as it may, seen from the concept of the self-realization of the agent in the medium of the patient, from the action as a perfection of the agent, in any case the question, whether the object in its own self is apprehended by sensibility, would be far from settled in the negative for Thomas by the assertion that colors, hardness, and so on are only things which could be real "in" the organs of sensibility. But this self-realization of the sensible in the medium of sensibility is not a species (that is, does not enter into knowledge) until it is received, that is, until the determination is in the knower as produced by himself also.[19] Perhaps this also answers those ques-

---

18 See *De Pot.* q. 5, a. 8, corp.
19 With this point we believe that we have formulated once again our position with regard to Siewerth's interpretation—agreeing with it and correcting it at the same time.

tions which were still unanswered in the chapter on sensibility. The findings of that chapter do not have to be repeated again here.

4. The Intelligible Species in Its Own Being Distinct from the A Priori Structure of Spirit as Such

Our question about the possibility of an intelligible species which is more than the *a priori* structure of the spirit as such can now be posed again and answered. It has been shown more clearly than it was earlier that the determination of sensibility, the phantasm in the broadest sense of the word, is not produced by the sensible as an external agent in the sense that it is borne merely passively by sensibility. This determination is the self-realization of the patient as such because the received determination is produced by the patient itself. But it has already been shown that for Thomas the spirit is the free origin of sensibility which lets it emanate and receives it, whereby both spirit and sensibility stand in a permanent relationship of origin which is the foundation not only of their momentary becoming, but also of the permanent being of both. If, therefore, sensibility reaches its end insofar as it itself actively produces its determination from without, then this production issues from sensibility's own, permanent origin. The phantasm is produced by the spirit itself which reaches its end insofar as it forms itself into matter and lets sensibility emanate from itself in its full actuality in each instance. And since the phantasm, the sensible species as produced by sensibility itself, does not *presuppose* any merely *passively* received determination from without which would be *different* from the phantasm and so from the self-realization of the sensible in the medium of sensibility, the spirit, which as agent intellect actively produces sensibility and its determination, does not need any at first merely passively received determination in order to produce the phantasm freely, and thus to have already accomplished the abstraction in the conversion to the phantasm. What it presupposes in the process is a determination from without, the

379

emanating influence, that is, the self-realization of the sensible in the materiality of sensibility, into which the spirit, while remaining free, has already and always entered.

But if, as freely maintaining itself in itself, the spirit produces sensibility and its individual determination as its own fulfillment, then that peculiar duality in the being of the free spirit, the soul subsisting in itself, necessarily enters into the production of the phantasm also: since the soul is the form of the body, it is the actuality of the body, it "is" body; and yet (as opposed to animals) as free, it is actuality in itself, and therefore "has" a body. And so what Thomas formulates more generally holds of the phantasm also: "A form which does not subsist in itself does not have any other mode than that of its subject because it does not have *esse* except insofar as it is the act of such a subject; . . . but a form which subsists in itself has one mode insofar as it is a subsistent thing, and a certain mode insofar as it is the act of such a subject."[20] It is to be noted here that these two modes of the form subsisting in itself do not simply exist alongside each other unmediated (it has already been said earlier why the soul as spirit [subsisting in itself] is the form of matter), but precisely in its mode as free spirit the soul also has the mode which it has as act of matter. It does not merely add this latter act as such (as having emanated) to its essence as being completed thereby, but also has it in itself already as that which is to emanate, and therefore it already "has" that mode, which it "is" as act of such a subject, it already has it as a mode which belongs to it in advance as a thing subsisting in itself, which of course does not mean to say that it could have the mode which is to emanate without it also having really emanated. Therefore, for example, the soul has its individuation from its being as the form of matter and only because it became the act of matter, and yet it retains it even when it is no longer the form of the body.[21]

20 *IV Sent.* dist. 49, q. 2, a. 3, ad 6.
21 *S.T.* I, q. 76, a. 2, ad 2; *I Sent.* dist. 8, q. 5, a. 2, ad 6; *II Sent.* dist. 3, q. 1, a. 4, ad 1; dist. 17, q. 2, a. 2, ad 4; *De Spir. Creat.* a. 9, ad 3; *De Anima* a. 1, ad 2; a. 3, corp.

Now the same thing holds of the production of the material determination by the free spirit. When it produces the phantasm, it determines itself not merely insofar as, as the act of matter, it receives this determination as its matter into itself, but as free it has already actively determined itself, and so as separated soul it can retain in itself this determination which we called earlier the intelligible species in the narrower sense. The spirit produces the phantasm and, as free, already and always keeps it abstracted in itself (the intelligible species in the broader sense); but by the fact that the spirit produces the phantasm, it is, as the origin which lets the phantasm emanate, already determined in itself from the side of its freedom, logically before it receives the phantasm, and can keep this determination (the intelligible species in the narrower sense) in itself (in the "treasury of the species" or as separated soul) even when the phantasm is no longer given as a sensible determination. Whether such an intelligible species suffices for the knowledge of a soul free of its body is a question which does not concern us here. In any case it is already evident also that in the free spirit as such an intelligible species is given which goes beyond the light of the intellect, beyond the *a priori* structure of the spirit, without the agent intellect as such becoming a patient. That was the only thing in question in the problematic of section VIII.

This conception of the intelligible species as the self-determination of the free spirit in itself in the production of the phantasm can also be shown explicitly in Thomas, although not always with the desired clarity in those contexts which seemed to place our explanation of the whole Thomistic doctrine of abstraction in question again in section VIII. Thus, according to Thomas, the separated souls still have a relation to the singular objects known earlier through a determination (*determinantur*) or "through preceding knowledge," or "through some affection,"[22] through a disposition which remains in the soul,[23] through a "vestige of a preceding knowledge or affec-

[22] *S.T.* I, q. 89, a. 4, corp.
[23] *Ibid.*, ad 2 and ad 3.

tion."[24] In this text we must understand this knowledge (affection) not so much as content (*cognitum*), but rather as act (which is also the first sense of the word), since according to Thomas the individual in its individuality as such was never given at all in the intellect strictly as such. According to Thomas, consequently, there remains in the spirit as such a relation to the individual known earlier because it once produced this knowledge as act.

But then, nothing else stands in the way of explaining the intelligible species in the narrower sense in general in this way. Reference was made to the parallel case of the individuation which the soul acquires in its active information of matter in such a way that it has this individuation not only as the act of matter, but also as free spirit. This parallel was brought out explicitly by Thomas himself[25]: "But this limited *esse,* although it is acquired by the soul in the body (*in corpore*), is not acquired from the body (*a corpore*), nor through dependence on the body": the soul itself actively produces its determined being, and does not simply receive it absolutely passively from the body (*a corpore*), although the "what" which it produces in this way is determined by matter and its determination by the external agent (in the body. For this reason, it is said a little before, in somewhat careless terminology, that "it is only individuated from the body"). Thomas continues: "Wherefore, when the bodies are removed there still remains to each soul its limited *esse* through affections or dispositions which it acquired insofar as it was the perfection of such a body." We can apply this general proposition to our problem as follows: the intelligible species remains in the soul ("the limited *esse* remains"), since, retaining its freedom[26] as the form of the body ("insofar as it was the perfection of such a body"), the soul itself actively produced ("in the body, not from it") the phantasm ("affection or disposition").

The parallel between the general relationship of the form to

---

[24] *S.T.* I, q. 89, a. 8, corp.
[25] *I Sent.* dist. 8, q. 5, a. 2, ad 6.
[26] Since it belongs to the forms, which *retinent esse per se,* as it says right afterwards in the same text.

its matter and the determinations which the form itself produces in the body, not from the body, and the particular relationship between the intelligible species and the phantasm is clearly maintained by Thomas: "although the soul is perfected in the body [and in fact, according to the text just cited, in such a way that it retains this perfection], however, it is not perfected by the body . . . but . . . it perfects itself with the help of a compliant body [how this 'help of the body,' and so the external agent, is to be understood so that the 'perfection of the soul' does not again become a 'being perfected by the body' was explained sufficiently in section IX] just as the possible intellect is perfected by the power of the agent intellect with the help of the phantasms which through it become actually intelligible."[27] Just as the soul actively completes itself in matter (that is how "body" is meant here) as its material cause, so that every influence from without takes place only "by reason of matter," and thereby even the accidental determinations (sex, and so on) in the emanating influence from without are earlier in their genesis than the self-realization of the soul, and yet (as received determinations) they are the results of its productive actuality ("posterior in being"), so is it also in the special case of spiritual knowing. In its desire to be itself, the spirit lets sensibility emanate from itself insofar as it forms itself into matter, and since it has remained free in this information, it has already abstracted to the extent that, being the free origin of sensibility, it retains sensibility in itself as its power, and through sensibility produces the phantasm as a received determination of sensibility. And yet, it has also already and always subjected itself to the conditions of matter, to the laws of space and time, since it reaches the goal of its freedom only when it forms itself into the *other* of matter in the conversion to the phantasm.

[27] *De Ver.* q. 26, a. 2, ad 2.

PART THREE

THE POSSIBILITY OF METAPHYSICS
ON THE BASIS OF THE IMAGINATION

I. THE PROBLEM

The Unique Opening to Metaphysics as the Constitution of the Objective Openness of the World

THE introductory interpretation of *S.T.* I, q. 84, a. 7, has already shown how Thomas himself saw that in asking about the conversion to the phantasm, we are simultaneously asking about the possibility of metaphysics for a mode of thought whose only intuition is sense intuition. He says of this intuition: "The imagination does not transcend time and the continuum." This statement has two implications for our investigation: first, we cannot simply pass over this question about the possibility of metaphysics in the investigation of the conversion to the phantasm; but neither can we presume to want to ask and solve this question in its full amplitude, since this can only be done where the whole of metaphysics, and not merely the conversion to the phantasm, is to be treated. In what follows, therefore, all we will try to do is summarize once again in thesis form and in its objective context those aspects of the question which were raised incidentally in our investigation of the conversion to the phantasm. But this also means that we are no longer concerned here with proving what is still to be said in its particulars and in historical detail from Thomas. What follows must already have shown itself to be Thomistic in what has gone before.

We are asking about the possibility of metaphysics on the presupposition that all human thought remains permanently dependent on sense intuition. When we ask about metaphysics, we understand the word in the sense of the tradition from which Thomas comes, without, however, being able to lose sight of the fact that the sense, method, and limits of metaphysics, and thus metaphysics itself, are defined anew by the basis upon which alone it is supposed to be possible. In its ultimate purpose, metaphysics was defined for Thomas by the tradition as the "divine science about the first being."[1] "The whole of first philosophy is ordered to the knowledge of God as to its ultimate end."[2] But with regard to its object, it is the science of being as such, so much so that as theology and ontology it is only a single science: "for the science of the first being and the science of common being are the same."[3] "The consideration of common being pertains to that science to which pertains the consideration of the first being."[4]

But the relationship of these two "objects" of metaphysics is defined in Thomas in such a way that the Absolute Being as such is really not its object (*subjectum*) at all.[5] God Himself indeed belongs to the essences "which are complete essences in themselves . . . thing in themselves." But in principle it is precisely in this way that He cannot be intended by metaphysics; He is thus only in the word of His revelation. Metaphysics reaches God only as the ground (*principium*) of its object, common being, and it is essentially impossible for it, then, to make the ground so reached another "object" in a discipline of its own, as, for example, the heavenly bodies or the elements are apprehended at first as the ground of the transitory and of compounds respectively, but then are also studied as complete natures by themselves in their own sciences. God is a principle for human metaphysics in such a way that, essentially, He is accessible to it only in a science "which treats what comes from the principle." Metaphysical "objects" —existents which cannot be experienced—are accessible only insofar as the "ob-

[1] *In Metaph. Prooem. (scientia divina sive theologia)*; *In Boeth. de Trin.* q. 5, a. 1, corp. (*theologia id est divina scientia* as the names of metaphysics); *In VI Metaph.* lect. 1, n. 1170 (*scientia primi entis*); *In I Metaph.* lect. 3, n. 64 (*scientia divina*).

[2] S.C.G. III, 25.

[3] *In VI Metaph.* lect. 1, n. 1170.

[4] *In IV Metaph.* lect. 5, n. 593.

[5] For what follows, see *In Boeth. de Trin.* q. 5, a. 4, corp., and *In Metaph. Prooem.*

ject" of metaphysics, common being (which in itself is not an object, not a thing in itself), already presupposes them as its ground, without this ground itself being an object which could be investigated by itself. In metaphysics, "divine things are considered not as the subject of the science, but as the principle of the subject."

For Thomas, therefore, there cannot be a "special metaphysics" in the sense that in it definite metaphysical objects would be given to it as already known, and then their essence would be investigated and more precisely defined by it in their essence. Rather, such objects manifest themselves for the first time only as the end to which the disclosure of the only object of metaphysics, common being, reaches. "There cannot be a particular science about them (separated things)."[6] Therefore, in this sense also, the knowledge of God is only the ultimate end" of metaphysics. Every natural theology (Thomas calls it philosophical theology[7]) as a special discipline is, therefore, a repetition of general ontology or a usurpation of what can be possible only in a theology of sacred Scripture.

But God as the ground of the object of metaphysics is not the end of metaphysics in such a way that one comes upon Him "at the end," after one has apprehended the intrinsic essence of what is grounded taken by itself and without its ground. The objects of metaphysics (and so also their grounds) are indeed "known later with regard to us,"[8] later than what can otherwise be known, but this in such a way that they are "known first according to their nature." But precisely what this does not mean is that we grasp them subsequently to another knowledge which is grounded in itself, so that the object we know "subsequently" would only be the ground of the *object* known first, but not the ground of the knowledge of what is known first, and so would only as a matter of fact be prior in itself to what is known first, and perhaps still would be known by someone (for example, by itself) before our first objects. For

[6] *De Natura Generis* c. 6.
[7] *In Boeth. de Trin.* q. 5, a. 4, corp.
[8] *In I Metaph.* lect. 2, n. 46; *In Boeth. de Trin.* q. 5, a. 1, ad 9.

389

Thomas, rather, what is prior in itself is also prior in human knowing, but not as a known object, as "that which is first known," but as a "principle of knowledge," while the first *object* which is apprehended is really the material quiddity.[9] This principle of knowledge simultaneously and implicitly apprehended in the apprehension of the sensible object is the light of the intellect; in this light the "eternal intelligibilities" are simultaneously apprehended as the "first intelligibles."[10] But this means that the "first known with regard to itself" of metaphysics is already apprehended simultaneously and implicitly in the light of the intellect as the sustaining ground of the knowledge of the first human objects, the "first known with regard to us," although they are not represented objectively themselves. As "objects" they remain "known later with regard to us."

Why, for Thomas, the totality of the objects able to be reached in metaphysics must already be given simultaneously and implicitly with the light of the intellect which is apprehended simultaneously, is evident from earlier considerations: the first principles are grounded in the light of the intellect, in which principles common being is elaborated. But a metaphysical object is able to be apprehended by man at all only in the knowledge of common being. Hence, metaphysics is only the reflexive elaboration of all human knowledge's own ground, which as such is already and always posited simultaneously in this knowledge from the outset. When, therefore, in the texts just cited Thomas

---

[9] *S.T.* I, q. 12, a. 11, ad 3; q. 85, a. 5, corp.; q. 88, a. 3, ad 1. Actually what is necessary for understanding this text has already been said earlier. The interpretation of this text (in Hertling, Grabmann, Geyser, etc.) in its alleged opposition to Augustine, which Thomas is also supposed to have concealed, does not work. The opposition between Augustine and Thomas does not lie between aposteriorism in Thomas (of an "empirical" abstraction), and the a priori vision of divine ideas in Augustine, but between an apriorism of the intellectual light as a formal *a priori* of the subject in Thomas, and the apriorism of an idea objectively existing in itself in Augustine. For it has already been shown earlier that the light of intellect is not indeed apprehended objectively as a thematic object, is not "known" (*gewusst*), but is apprehended simultaneously, is "conscious" (*bewusst*), an a priori form of all objective knowledge.

[10] See further *S.T.* I, q. 16, ad 1. Cf. for this chapter three, VI, 4.

understands the light of the intellect as a "participated likeness of uncreated light," that is not merely a metaphysical statement of which the operation of the light of the intellect as the principle of knowledge is independent, but a definition which characterizes this light *as* the principle of *all* knowledge, since all knowledge is possible only in the pre-apprehension of absolute *esse,* and hence the implicit affirmation of absolute being is the condition of the possibility of any knowledge.

This places us again in a position to see the real point of departure for the question about the possibility of metaphysics in Thomas. Metaphysics is possible, then, insofar as a metaphysical realm manifests itself through the light of the intellect. But it has already been shown that this light is neither an innate idea, nor does it somehow permit an immediate vision of a metaphysical object, whether this be understood as "eternal truth" or as absolute being meant objectively. Rather this light is to be met first and originally only as a condition of the possibility of having objectively that something which alone is the immediate object of human knowledge: the universal material quiddity. "All the knowledge by which the intellect knows that which is in the soul (hence its own light also) is founded upon the fact that it knows its object which has a phantasm corresponding to it."[11] To put it another way: the light of the intellect is given first of all only and exclusively as a condition of the possibility of physics, of the science which has to do with "mobile being,"[12] hence with the quiddities of material beings. But this means that the light of the intellect can be shown to be the opening up of the metaphysical realm only by showing that it is only as such a disclosure that it can be the condition of the possibility of physics. Consequently, there is metaphysics for man only insofar as he has already made use of it for his physics. A realm of the metaphysical is opened up to man only insofar as this is necessary for him to be able to be in the world.

But then this raises the question whether metaphysics in the

[11] *III Sent.* dist. 23, q. 1, a. 2, ad 5.
[12] *In I Metaph.* lect. 2, n. 47, etc.

Thomistic sense is still possible at all, for it seems then that the formal, *a priori* principles (the light of the intellect) would only have to reach as far as that for which they appear as its ground, as far as mobile being, as the imagination as pure intuition of space and time. They do not seem to be able to reach further because the light of the intellect is given to us only as a formal *a priori,* as the form of the intelligible species which already and always includes the sense intuition, the phantasm, since it comes to be and remains in existence only in the conversion to the phantasm. This light, as the place where all necessary knowledge (the first principles) is found, can be understood only as a formal principle in the service of sense intuition, because according to Thomas, the spirit is in pure potency of itself, and the receptive intuition of another, which must be the fundamental act of such a spirit, is as such already and necessarily sentient. So a reflection on the formal principles of human knowledge seems to be able to disclose only the conditions under which the objects of sense experience as such stand, and which therefore from the outset do not open up a vision beyond the objects of human intuition, that is, beyond sensibility. Ultimately, then, physics (insofar as it comprehends in itself the question about the conditions of its possibility) would become the first philosophy; those "ancients" would have been correct, whose plausible opinion ("and this not without reason") Thomas describes: "For some ancients did not think that there were any substances except the mobile corporeal substances which physics treats. And so it was believed that they alone [that is, as physicists] decided about the whole of nature, and consequently about being, and so also about the first principles which must be considered simultaneously with being."[13] The knowledge of "the world"[14] would be true, and the whole of metaphysics. It needs no further explanation that, in posing the

[13] *In IV Metaph.* lect. 5, n. 593.
[14] "*Mundus accipitur hic secundum quod est continentia visibilium tantum et ita inter creaturas mundi . . . non computatur angelus*" (that is, a separated substance which belongs to metaphysics as Thomas understands the latter): *I Sent.* dist. 3, exposition of the first part of the text.

question about the possibility of metaphysics in this way, we have also formulated the problematic which follows for the possibility of metaphysics from the concept of the conversion to the phantasm.

II. THE POSSIBILITY OF METAPHYSICS

The Fundamental Act of Man as an Opening to Being as Such (Excessus)

How and why is metaphysics nevertheless possible for Thomas in the sense in which he understands this concept, possible in spite of, in fact, because of, the conversion to the phantasm? We will begin to answer this question with an indication which Thomas himself gives in the article about the conversion to the phantasm: *S.T.* I, q. 84, a. 7, ad 3. In spite of the necessary conversion of thought to the imagination, which is bound to space and time, metaphysics is possible through *excessus*, negation, and comparison.

We are dealing here with the first presuppositions for the possibility of metaphysics. In this text Thomas enumerates as such presuppositions only the three acts mentioned. The "knowing God as *cause*" refers to the development of metaphysics, which development already presupposes the three acts enumerated in their proper essence, as also becomes clear in the wording of the sentence in Thomas: "We know God as cause both through *excessus* and through negation." The first "and" joins *excessus* not with cause, but with negation (both . . . and), and so distinguishes it from the "as cause" as the presupposition for the fact that God is able to be known as the ground of the existent. For to know God as the ground of the existent does not mean: to know that God (as already known beforehand) is the ground of the thing, but: to know that the ground, already and always opened simultaneously in knowing the existent as being, is the Absolute Being, that is, God, and thus to know God for the first time. This explanation of the sentence is only a paraphrase of the statement that God is accessible to metaphysics only as the "principle of its subject," not as the subject. But if this explanation of the "knowing God as cause" is the only correct one, then it is self-evident that the fundamental act of metaphysics is not some causal inference from an existent as such to its ground, which also would not have to be more than an existent, but the opening of the knower to being as such as the ground of the existent and its knowledge. But that is given precisely in the *excessus*.

We cannot go into any more detail here about how *excessus* —negation—comparison here in *S.T.* I, q. 84, a. 7, ad 3 are related to the familiar three ways of knowing God (the way of causality—excellence—negation). In any case they cannot simply be identified, especially since the second series is obviously not always understood by Thomas in the same sense, in fact is not always enumerated in the same sequence.[1] Since the way of causality already presupposes the knowledge that the *esse* of the existent is "received,"[2] which knowledge of limitedness already presupposes a concept of being as such as its condition, it is evident that the *excessus* in the sense which we give it is already a presupposition for the way of causality. Further, *excessus*—negation—comparison here (*S.T.* I, q. 84, a. 7, ad 3) cannot be made equivalent to the usual three ways also because then either the most important and usually first mentioned way (the way of causality) would be missing, or a group of four would arise if one wanted to add the way of causality as indicated in the "as cause." It is to be admitted, however, that in *In Boeth. de Trin.* q. 6, a. 2, corp. the *excessus* is one of the three ways instead of the usual way of excellence (eminence). That need not be a reason for rejecting our understanding of the essence of the *excessus*, because the *excessus* as the pre-apprehension of being as such is as a matter of fact a condition

---

[1] See *S.T.* I, q. 12, a. 12, corp.; q. 13, a. 1, corp.; q. 13, a. 8, ad 2 (here the *modus eminentiae* comes first); q. 13, a. 10, ad. 5; *I Sent.* dist. 3, division of the first part of the text; *I Sent.* dist. 3, q. 1, a. 3, corp.; dist. 35, q. 1, a. 1, corp. (*remotio* is the first of the three); *De Malo* q. 16, a. 8, ad 3 (*negatio* is first).

[2] *I Sent. dist.* 3, division of the first part of the text.

of the possibility of the way of eminence, and so the two concepts can easily be interchanged in one instance.

If, according to Thomas, the ground of metaphysics is disclosed only by the fact that it shows itself to be a condition of the possibility of the knowledge of world, and if this is accomplished precisely in the conversion of thought to the sense intuition, that is, in the conversion to the phantasm, then *excessus,* negation and comparison must be the ground of metaphysics in such a way that they are the condition of the possibility for the knowledge of world by that mode of thought which is essentially dependent on sense intuition.

It is evident first of all that for Thomas, although *excessus,* negation and comparison are all necessary, yet they are not simply coordinate acts of the spirit which make metaphysics possible with equal primacy. First of all, the comparison, as a comparison between the metaphysical and the sensibly intuited object, obviously already presupposes an openness of the metaphysical realm in some form or other. Further, the necessity of a comparison does not so much make possible the apprehension of a metaphysical object for the first time, but rather is an indication of the fact that human knowing (in its present state) is only possible from sensibility. Hence the comparison is more a limiting condition of metaphysical knowledge than a condition which makes it possible in the first place: "Everything which we know in our present state is known by us through a comparison to natural, sensible things."[3] What concerns the negation (*remotio, negatio*), it has already been shown that for Thomas it is not of equal primacy with the affirmation. Limits and ends are known only by reaching out to a being more comprehensive than that whose limits are known, and in the knowledge removed (*removeri*): "The knowledge of a negation is always founded in some affirmation."[4] So only the *excessus* remains as the first and primary act which, as a condition of the knowledge of world, is to make metaphysics possible. It is im-

[3] *S.T.* I, q. 84, a. 8, corp.
[4] *De Pot.* q. 7, a. 5, corp.

portant, therefore, to define its essence with respect to physics and metaphysics.

If first of all we presuppose hypothetically that metaphysics is possible, this *excessus* is defined from the viewpoint of metaphysics by the following characteristics: although it must open up the metaphysical realm, of itself alone it cannot immediately present any metaphysical objects in their own selves as objectively visible. For otherwise it would be the intuition of an object manifesting itself from itself and received by man as different. But such an intuition is essentially sensible, hence as such it gives no metaphysical object. Therefore, the *excessus* can only be the actuality of a formal principle on the side of the subject of the knowledge. As such this principle is necessarily a condition of the possibility of the objects of the knowledge, of the actually intelligible, and hence the ground of *a priori* and necessary knowledge. If as the ground of the possibility of metaphysics this formal principle of knowledge is, on the one hand, to be capable of opening up the realm of being as such, and, on the other hand, since there is no metaphysical intuition, at the same time it does not present the metaphysical object itself, and therefore must be a formal principle of the mode of thought which is related to sense intuition, then both characteristics of this principle can be understood as compatible only in such a way that a pre-apprehending disclosure of being as such takes place only in a conversion to the objectivity of the sense intuition (whereby being as such is not intuited objectively, but is had only in a pre-apprehension), and this sensible objectivity can be had only through the disclosure of being as such in a human way, that is, as universal and standing opposite.

This brings us to the question: What characteristics of human, that is, objective, sense intuition presuppose the *excessus,* the pre-apprehension of absolute *esse,* as a condition of their possibility?

Human knowledge is first of all receptive knowledge, and to that extent it is sentient. But it is sentient in such a way that a true judgment is made on the object which manifests itself from itself, that is, human knowledge is universal and objective. Universality and objectivity are necessarily connected. Receptive knowledge as such is sentient, but this means that the sentient knower becomes the other ontologically, and therefore *as* sentient, what it precisely does not do is differentiate itself from the known. Hence, where receptive knowledge is to become objective, it must, on the one hand (as essentially receptive), be sensibility, which itself becomes what is received, and it must, on the other hand, know a universal quiddity of the sensibly intuited in order to make a judgment on it as object, and therefore it must differentiate this quiddity from the sensible mode of its givenness, in which the knower is the other. Therefore, as placed over against the object, the subject must be present to itself in such a way that being-present-to-itself and being related to what is sensibly intuited mutually and inseparably condition each other: the knowledge of a quiddity of something which is received is always possible only by the knowing subject setting itself *over against* the something which manifests itself and is received; and vice versa: the being-present-to-itself of the receiving subject, whose proper object is the other, is only possible by knowing a quiddity of a something which is set opposite. Human knowledge is a return to oneself in knowing a universal quiddity of another. Only in this knowledge with all these moments is an object in the world given to man.

This possibility of placing over against oneself as object what is had in the sense intuition as identical with sensibility, and of so doing in a true judgment affirming a universal about it, is grounded in a pre-apprehension. Through this pre-apprehension the form of the sensible object which is had in the concretion of sensibility is known as limited by the concretion, is thereby abstracted, and so opens up for the first time the possibility of relating the form thus abstracted to the object given in its own self in sensibility in such a way that it appears as objective (*gegen-ständiger*), and thus the knowing subject as such differentiates itself from the object in its universal knowledge and thereby accomplishes the complete return.

This pre-apprehension attains to *esse*. The breadth of this pre-apprehension is not merely the totality of what is representatively imaginable in sensibility, mobile being as the being which is the principle of number, world, but absolute being in its negative (not privative) infinity. Insofar as the pre-apprehension affirms the condition of its own possibility, and insofar as the "whither" of the pre-apprehension belongs to this condition, it affirms absolute being as possible and real beyond the world. With that, a being beyond the realm of the imagination is affirmed, and this affirmation is the condition of the possibility of objective knowledge of world because it takes place in *that* pre-apprehension which first makes possible such an objective possession of world.

It has already been shown that according to Thomas the *excessus* essentially takes place only in the judgment, and so the judgment is only the expression of the dynamic desire of the spirit for being as such. This also explains how absolute being can be given without being conceived, without being represented, in which case the basis of the imagination as the sole intuition would be abandoned. It is not intuited, that is, it does not come before the gaze of an intellectual intuition in its own self, but is affirmed simultaneously as the condition of the possibility of the objective knowledge of *that* existent which alone is represented to the intuition, mobile being (*ens mobile*), as the proper object of the one human knowledge.

This also gives us Thomas's fundamental direction for man in his pursuit of metaphysics. It is neither "realistic" nor "inductive" in the usual sense, since the light of the agent intellect is decisive for its possibility; on the other hand, since this light is the *a priori* and merely formal condition of the objectivity of the world, metaphysics does not consist in the vision of a metaphysical object, perhaps of being as such, but in the *transcendental reflection* upon that which is affirmed implicitly and simultaneously in the knowledge of the world, in the affirmation of physics. If the proposition is true: "It is necessary first to know the mode of a science before proceeding in the science to consider the things the science treats,"[5] and yet metaphysics is supposed

---

[5] *In IV Metaph.* lect. 1, n. 529.

to be the first science, then according to Thomas the reflection on that which makes metaphysics possible is already itself metaphysics, and basically is already the totality of what is accessible to human metaphysics. When man takes as the "object" of his knowledge in metaphysics that which he affirms simultaneously in the pre-apprehension which makes possible his knowledge of world, then he necessarily makes it a represented object in the only way in which he can have such an object at all: he represents it as a thing, as the things of the world are, because he can have no represented object at all without a conversion to the phantasm. But insofar as he again makes this representation of the metaphysical "object" itself possible by a pre-apprehension, while the pre-apprehension already and always negates what is represented, man has already and always negated the limitation of *esse* to mobile being by this judgmental pre-apprehension. Therefore, in a judgment he can remove this limitation by a negation (*remotio*), and thus in a judgment think the metaphysical object through *excessus* and negation without the object as such being immediately represented. In such a negation more can be apprehended by the judgment than that which belongs in the sphere of the imagination as objectively represented because the pre-apprehension, which is to present the objects of the imagination, has already and always opened up for this purpose the further horizon of absolute *esse*. By the fact that the pre-apprehension already and always brings every mobile being, as a synthesis of the sensible givenness with *esse*, into the absolute breadth of *esse*, which is disclosed in the pre-apprehension, and holds it over against this *esse*, since the spirit remains free in the synthesis, the negation of the sensible existent and the comparison between absolute *esse* and the intuited existent are already and always basically accomplished.

Thus negation and comparison appear as inner moments within the *excessus* itself, through which the *excessus* is first completely itself. When metaphysics reflects upon the *excessus*, they too are made explicit as fundamental acts through which alone a metaphysical object can be thought. But they are always founded upon the *excessus* as the pre-apprehension, as

SPIRIT IN THE WORLD

the act which pre-apprehends absolute *esse* merely in the apprehension of mobile being, and thus they give the metaphysical not in its own self, but only as the "principle" of the real object of the one human knowledge, the world.

III. THE LIMITS OF METAPHYSICS

Esse *Disclosed in the Pre-Apprehension as Empty* "Common Being" *with the Transcendental Modes Intrinsic to It*

This has also shown us to some extent already the limit which is drawn for such a metaphysics from the outset. The sentence in Thomas: "The whole consideration of the speculative sciences cannot be extended further than the knowledge of sensible things is able to lead it,"[1] now receives its full weight. This does not mean a limit from the side of the factually accessible, empirical material, but a limit which from the outset is already given simultaneously with the intrinsic structure of human knowledge, because the intelligible light of the agent intellect, which has been shown to be the power of the pre-apprehension of absolute *esse*, is always given only in the intellectual knowledge of the "form . . . of a sensible thing . . . insofar as the intelligible light . . . participates in it (the form)."[2] The more precise limit and so the concrete scope of Thomistic metaphysics can only be defined, of course, in an investigation of what is meant by the absolute being which is always posited simultaneously in the pre-apprehension. Such an investigation goes completely beyond the scope of this work. Only this much can be seen from the results already acquired here:

If the possibility and the limit of metaphysics consist only in the reflection on the *excessus* to absolute *esse* which makes physics possible, then the only metaphysical statements of a fundamental kind which can be made about an object beyond

[1] *S.T.* I–II, q. 3, a. 6, corp.
[2] See *ibid.*

the realm of our objects, that is, beyond the realm of the imagination, are the intrinsic moments in the concept of being as such itself. Thomas calls them the transcendentals,[3] and the essential ones are being, true, and good.[4] It is not possible here to go into the sense and number of the transcendentals, their derivation and the principle of this derivation, and the intrinsic completeness of the transcendentals actually mentioned. But it is thus already shown that the problem of the categories, the sense of the individual categories, and their number and derivation cannot be a central problem of Thomistic metaphysics. That which alone basically defines the object of human metaphysics and from the outset has limited the scope of what we can know about this object are the transcendentals. Thomas was explicitly aware of this. He emphasizes again and again that we do not possess a knowledge of the quiddity of "separated things" (that is, of everything which is not a mobile being) which belongs to them as such.[5] We only know of their existence, so that of their essence we only know implicitly what is necessarily given implicitly in the knowledge of their existence, that is, the transcendental determinations in that intensity of being in which they necessarily belong to an existent or to absolute being as such without material limitation. But that defines the metaphysical object only from the empty concept of being. For although *esse* is in itself the full ground of every existent, nevertheless, this fullness is given to us only in the absolute, empty infinity of our pre-apprehension or, what is the same thing, in common being with the transcendental modes intrinsic to it. And so it remains true: the highest knowledge of God is the "darkness of ignorance."[6]

What concerns the categories specifically (especially that of

---

[3] See *De Ver.* q. 1, a. 1, corp.; q. 21, a. 1, corp.; a. 3, corp.; *De Pot.* q. 9, a. 7, ad 6 and *ad ea quae in contrarium; I Sent.* dist. 8, q. 1, a. 3; *De Natura Generis* c. 2; *S.T.* I, q. 30, a. 3, corp. and ad 1; q. 39, a. 3, ad 3.

[4] See along with the texts in the previous note: *S.T.* I, q. 16, a. 4, ad 2.

[5] Cf. A. D. Sertillanges, *Saint Thomas d'Aquin* I, II (Paris, 1912), pp. 178–182. The corresponding holds also for the knowledge of angels.
[6] *I Sent.* dist. 8, q. 1, a. 1, ad 4.

substance), Thomas emphasizes explicitly that there is no natural genus common to material things and the separated substances, so that the applicability of the categories to the objects beyond the material world and the imagination is not a presupposition of Thomistic metaphysics, but a task which can only be undertaken subsequently to its constitution as a metaphysics of being and its transcendental modes, and from this position. I only wanted to point out this Thomistic statement that the metaphysical and the material do not participate in a natural genus.[7] A more thorough investigation of this point would show that the analogy of being in Thomas is not merely a construction designed to help towards the conceptual, negative definition of the essence of God, but already has its starting point where the experience of world is transcended in a pre-apprehension through *excessus* and negation. In fact, the concept of being is not first of all univocal, in order then to be expanded analogously afterwards, but as the form of the pre-apprehension it is analogous and becomes univocal in the conversion to the phantasm as the being of material things. The analogous is the ground of the univocal, and not vice versa: "Everything univocal is reduced to a first one which is not univocal but analogous, and this is being."[8]

But the categories themselves are in the first place not metaphysical concepts, but concepts of physics (whereby, of course, this is to be understood as a philosophical discipline), modes of being of mobile being as such. That follows simply from the doctrine of the conversion to the phantasm. In any case, the fact that they have validity beyond the realm of the imagination, and in what sense and to what extent they do, would need a proof of a kind similar to what we at least tried to indicate for the concept of being. But such a proof would be objectively identical with answering in detail the contrary question, how in an abstractive conversion to the phantasm the *a priori* forms of sensibility are unified with those of the spirit, which are given

---

[7] See *S.T.* I, q. 88, a. 2, ad 4; q. 66, a. 2, ad 2; *In Boeth. de Trin.* q. 4, a. 2, corp.; *De Natura Generis* cc. 6–7, 9, 14.

[8] *S.T.* I, q. 13, a. 5, ad 1.

in the pre-apprehension, into the pure concepts of the one, human, objective experience. It is only by answering this question that the beginning which was made in Thomas with the doctrine of the conversion to the phantasm would really be carried through; only then would we really know what the conversion to the phantasm is. Thomas did not develop his starting point in this way. Indeed we find in him the knowledge that only two categories are not limited from the outset to definite regions of existents, namely, substance and relation, so that these can come into consideration for an analogous application to absolute being.[9] Thomas sees further perhaps that the peculiarity of our intellectual thought, the fact that it must proceed through judgment and inference and so on, is grounded in sensibility;[10] he calls attention in general to the fact that space and time, the *a priori* forms of sensibility, enter into intellectual concepts: "It knows with the continuum and with time through the phantasms in which it considers the intelligible species;[11] the continuum and time are in the soul's thoughts"[12]; according to Thomas the affirmative synthesis essentially contains a temporal moment because of the conversion to the phantasm.[13] But in Thomas it does not come as far as a systematic, detailed demonstration of how the *a priori* forms of sensibility have their validity in the categories as the highest concepts of our univocal apprehension of the world. So logically neither can a systematic critique of their transcendental use be expected from him.

This statement is important for us in still another respect. For it is clear, and more explicitly so than up to now, that beyond what has already been said we cannot expect in Thomas a development of what is meant by the conversion to the phantasm.

[9] *S.T.* I, q. 28, a. 2, corp.; *I Sent.* dist. 8, q. 4; a. 2; a. 3; dist. 22, q. 1, a. 3, ad 2, etc.
[10] *S.T.* I, q. 85, a. 5; *II Sent.* dist. 3, q. 1, a. 2, corp. etc.
[11] *S.T.* I–II, q. 113, a. 7, ad 5. See *I Sent.* dist. 38, q. 1, a. 3, ad 3.
[12] *De Instantibus* c. 1.
[13] *S.C.G.* II, 96, towards the end; *S.T.* I, q. 85, a. 5, ad 2; *I Sent.* dist. 8, q. 2, a. 3, corp.; *De Ver.* q. 8, a. 14, ad 12; *In X Metaph.* lect. 3, n. 1982.

Not as though Thomas had neglected to develop and make precise his doctrine of the conversion to the phantasm with the help of an experimental psychology, perhaps through an introspection which distinguishes between intuitive and non-intuitive elements of knowledge. He was not thereby guilty of any omission, since such a method can contribute nothing essential to his metaphysical question. For the question about the conversion, like that about abstraction, is not a question about the nature, peculiarity, and difference of finished, that is, already consciously given, human knowledge, but it is the question about the conditions of the possibility of its coming to be, so that the conversion is always already accomplished when a presumably "non-intuited content of thought" is given, and even the "most intuited" in man is given only because the abstraction has already taken place.

But it would have been possible, and lies altogether in the direction of the Thomistic problematic, to attempt a transcendental deduction of the categories. Thomas did not do that. His derivation of the Aristotelian list of categories[14] is nothing more than a subsequent arrangement of the categories already presupposed as given. It is only by such an original derivation of the categories that the question about the application of the categories within metaphysics could be solved fundamentally. Thomas is satisfied with a critique of the individual concepts in the particular instance of their application beyond physics. However, with this statement it ought not to be forgotten that the content and limits of human metaphysics are already designated in principle by *esse* and its transcendental modes which manifest themselves in the pre-apprehension.

Nevertheless, it is only such a transcendental clarification of physics that would be able to prove that metaphysics is not exhausted merely in its self-grounding (so that the transcendental reflection on the conditions of its possibility would already be the thematization of metaphysics itself as a whole), but beyond this, that it is able to be "categorical metaphysics"—that as an

14 *In V Metaph.* lect. 9, n. 889ff.

404

a priori investigation it does not merely consider physics, the "world," the *a posteriori,* as real negativity, to which it (as the metaphysics of the corporeal spirit) remains formally related, but that metaphysics itself, in its own *a priori,* first comes to itself in its *content* through the *a posteriori.* It is only in this way that the danger of a formal apriorism can be avoided unambiguously, which apriorism, moreover, misses the sense of the *a priori* itself. For every genuine, metaphysical *a priori* does not simply have the *a posteriori* "alongside of" or "after" itself, but holds it in itself, not of course as though once again the *a posteriori,* the "world" in its positive content were able to be resolved adequately into pure, transcendental apriority, but in such a way that the *a priori* is *of itself* referred to the *a posteriori,* that in order to be really itself, it cannot keep itself in its pure transcendentality, but must release itself into the categorical. Hence the openness of the *a priori* for the *a posteriori,* of the transcendental for the categorical, is not something secondary, perhaps merely a subsequent piecing together of two completely separable contents of reality and of knowledge, but it is the fundamental definition of the contents of the one metaphysics of man. And if the transcendental deduction of the categories as a mode of this self-definition of metaphysics (and not merely as physics) is left undone in Thomas—subsequent scholasticism has hardly developed this point beyond Thomas himself—, yet he constantly considered the categorical as the object of his metaphysical reflection.[15]

---

[15] See Urs von Balthasar in *Zeitschr. f. Kath. Theologie* 63 (1939). pp. 378f. The author has attempted a transcendental deduction according to Thomistic principles for certain categorical determinations of man (which as such are again to be specifically distinguished from sub-human categoreality, and precisely with respect to the possibility of their transcendental clarification). Thus for the *historicity* of man in *Hörer des Wortes,* pp. 138–211, especially pp. 162ff.; for the *racial unity* of the human race, for the origin of all men from a single couple, in "Theologisches zum Monogenismus" (*Schriften zur Theologie* I, [Einsiedeln, 1954]). pp. 253–322, especially pp. 311–322. For the fundamental question of the transcendental deduction of the categorical determinations of man, see the author's "Bemerkungen über das Naturgesetz und seine Erkennbarkeit": *Orientierung* 19 (1955), no. 22, pp. 239–243.

IV. MAN AS SPIRIT IN THE WORLD

However little it is expressed explicitly by Thomas, yet it has perhaps become clear in the course of this work how his whole metaphysical enquiry poses its questions from out of man's situation, and simultaneously places man in question. For although the basis upon which Thomas places all his philosophizing from the outset is the world, yet it is precisely the world into which the spirit of man—in turning to the phantasm—has already entered. For strictly speaking, the first-known, the first thing encountering man, is not the world in its "spiritless" existence, but the world—itself—as transformed by the light of the spirit,[1] the world in which man sees himself. The world as known is always the world of man, is essentially a concept complementary to man. And the last-known, God, shines forth only in the limitless breadth of the pre-apprehension, in the desire for being as such by which every act of man is borne, and which is at work not only in his ultimate knowledge and in his ultimate decisions, but also in the fact that the free spirit becomes, and must become, sensibility in order to be spirit, and thus exposes itself to the whole destiny of this earth. Thus man encounters himself when he finds himself in the world and when he asks about God; and when he asks about his essence, he always finds himself already in the world and on the way to God. He is both of these at once, and cannot be one without the other.[2]

But that means that man is essentially ambivalent. He is always exiled in the world and is always already beyond it. He is "in a certain way everything," and yet the object of knowledge essentially ordered to him is the essence of material things. His first and last science is metaphysics, the whole of which "is ordered to the knowledge of God as to its ultimate end," and yet

[1] See *S.T.* I–II, q. 3, a. 6, corp.

[2] For this (as for the whole section) see the author's: "Wissenschaft als 'Konfession'?" (*Schriften zur Theologie* III [Einsiedeln, 1956]), pp. 455–472; and: "Würde und Freiheit des Menschen" (*Schriften zur Theologie* II [Einsiedeln, 1955]), pp. 247–277, especially pp. 247–269.

406

it is said of him: "We know nothing but some of the lowest beings."[3] Each side of this ambivalence calls the other forth. If knowledge is primarily intuition, and if the only human intuition is sensibility, then all thought exists only for sense intuition. And if the meaning of sensibility as such is the necessity of action,[4] then all knowing seems only to serve man's vital self-assertion in the struggle, care, and pleasure of this world. Everything "metaphysical" seems to exist only to make possible this objective, sense intuition; we seem to know God, the "object" of metaphysics, only as the necessary horizon of the experience of world which is possible only in this way.

But because we know the world objectively, we are always already present to ourselves in a complete return; in turning out to the world we have turned back to ourselves. But then the horizon of the possible experience of world necessarily becomes a theme itself, metaphysics becomes necessary in man's existence. Insofar as we ask about the world known by man, the world and the man asking are already placed in question all the way back to their absolute ground, to a ground which always lies beyond the boundaries within man's grasp, beyond the world. Thus every venture into the world shows itself to be borne by the ultimate desire of the spirit for absolute being; every entrance into sensibility, into the world and its destiny, shows itself to be only the coming to be of a spirit which is striving towards the absolute. Thus man is the mid-point suspended between the world and God, between time and eternity, and this boundary line is the point of his definition and his destiny: "as a certain horizon and border between the corporeal and incorporeal."[5] Man: "existing as it were, at the horizon between time and eternity."[6] We would not be true to the ultimate purpose of

[3] S.C.G. III, 49.

[4] See S.T. I, q. 91, a. 3, ad 3; I–II, q. 31, a. 6, corp.; II–II q. 167, a. 2, corp.; In I Metaph. lect. 1, n. 14.

[5] S.C.G. II, 68.

[6] S.C.G. II, 81. Similarly, III, 61. In this phrase Thomas is quoting freely a sentence in the Liber de causis. Cf. O. Bardenhewer, Die pseudoaristotelische Schrift über das reine Gute, bekannt unter dem Namen Liber de causis (Freiburg, 1883), pp. 267ff.

this whole Thomistic metaphysics if we did not let its intrinsic movement reach that point towards which it is ultimately striving. Everything that we tried to grasp of Thomas's metaphysics of knowledge is situated by Thomas within the context of a theological endeavor. "It pertains to the theologians to consider the nature of man from the viewpoint of his soul."[7]

Man concerns Thomas the theologian at the point at which God manifests Himself in such a way that He is able to be heard in the word of His revelation: "from the viewpoint of his soul." In order to be able to hear whether God speaks, we must know that He is; lest His word come to one who already knows, He must be hidden from us; in order to speak to man, His word must encounter us where we already and always are, in an earthly place, at an earthly hour. Insofar as man enters into the world by turning to the phantasm, the revelation of being as such and in it the knowledge of God's existence has already been achieved, but even then this God who is beyond the world is always hidden from us. Abstraction is the revelation of being as such which places man before God; conversion is the entrance into the here and now of this finite world, and this makes God the distant Unknown. Abstraction and conversion are the same thing for Thomas: man. If man is understood in this way, he can listen to hear whether God has not perhaps spoken, because he knows that God is; God can speak, because He is the Unknown. And if Christianity is not the idea of an eternal, omnipresent spirit, but is Jesus of Nazareth, then Thomas's metaphysics of knowledge is Christian when it summons man back into the here and now of his finite world, because the Eternal has also entered into his world so that man might find Him, and in Him might find himself anew.[8]

[7] *S.T.* I, q. 75, Introduction.
[8] The author has attempted the concrete development of the Thomistic starting point of metaphysics with regard to man as a "Hearer of the Word" in his philosophy of religion: *Hörer des Wortes*, München, 1963 (ET *Hearers of the Word*, New York, 1968; reprint ed. 1994).

Breinigsville, PA USA
31 January 2010
231677BV00001B/60/A